FLY FISHING
CANADA

FROM COAST TO COAST TO COAST

Robert H. Jones, editor

JOHNSON GORMAN PUBLISHERS

Blue Ribbon Books are published by
Johnson Gorman Publishers
2003 – 35 Avenue S.W.
Calgary Alberta Canada T2T 2E2

Credits
Cover photograph courtesy of Tony Stone Images
Cover design by Boldface Technologies
Text design by Duncan Campbell
Printed and bound in Canada by Friesens for Johnson Gorman Publishers

Acknowledgments
Financial support provided by the Alberta Foundation for the Arts, a
beneficiary of the Lottery Fund of the Government of Alberta.

COMMITTED TO THE DEVELOPMENT OF CULTURE AND THE ARTS

National Library of Canada Cataloguing in Publication Data
Main entry under title:
Fly fishing Canada
Includes index.
ISBN 0-921835-56-6
1. Fly fishing—Canada. I. Jones, Robert H., 1935–
SH571.F59 2001   799.1'24'0971   C2001-910492-8

5 4 3 2 1

To those early members of the Outdoor Writers of Canada
who led the way in writing about Canada's marvelous fishing opportunities,
among them Gregory Clark, Mike Bolton, W.A. "Bill" Macdonald, Herb Smith,
Bob Turnbull, Kit Kitney, Pete McGillen, Grant Hopkins, Reg Fife, John Power,
Phil Kettle, Lee Straight, Jacques Boucher, Bob Rife, George Cooke,
Mike Crammond, Paul Provencher, Jack Herrity, Ralph Bice,
Francis McIlquham, King Whyte and Joe Masko.
Some are now gone, but their words will live forever.

CONTENTS

Editor's Acknowledgments

Obvious thanks to all of the contributors to this book, especially those who went beyond the original request for one chapter.

Special thanks to Dr. Martin Lamont and Vera Jones, who assisted with the editing and did all of the proofreading.

To Bob Rife, who, despite paralysis of his left side due to a then-recent stroke, provided three excellent chapters by pecking them out with one finger on his "wrong" hand.

To Jim Crawford for the valuable advice he offered based on his experience with compiling and publishing *The Gilly* in 1985, a very successful book (still in print) about fly fishing in British Columbia.

To George Will, George Gruenefeld and Bob Scammell, all of whom stepped in on short notice to fill a few voids, to Paul Marriner, who did so several times and to Wayne Phillips for providing some truly interesting recipes.

To Chris Marshall, who managed to come through at the same time that he was swamped with launching his new magazine, *The Canadian Fly Fisher*.

To Mark White, Drew Myers and Glen Hales for sharing some of their excellent photography.

To Kevin Fancy and Dr. Martin Lamont for helping to tie the flies required to fill gaping holes in the chapter on fly patterns. For various legitimate reasons (or so I was told at the time) some contributors were unable to provide flies for their chapters. As a result, we three tied 69 of the 150 patterns.

Finally, sincere thanks to Dennis Johnson, who, when he got wind of this project, had enough faith in what he read to publish it.

PREFACE

Robert H. Jones

THIS BOOK IS THE RESULT OF SHARING AN IDEA THAT caught on. With interest in fly fishing increasing at a phenomenal rate over the past decade or so, a book about fly fishing across Canada seemed like a winner. However, considering our country's size, radical diversification of geography, the hundreds of thousands of lakes and rivers involved, plus the active recreational fishery off the coast of British Columbia, it seemed logical that such a project should involve as many writers as possible in order to do it justice. With that thought in mind, on July 6, 1998, I drafted a letter and sent it to 21 fellow members of the Outdoor Writers of Canada (OWC). In it I proposed compiling such a book as a 100 percent volunteer project, with all profits shared equally between the OWC and Fly Fishing Canada. I felt that if a half-dozen members responded positively, the project might be worth pursuing. I received 19 replies—all of them offering variations of "Let's go for it!"

After a hectic period during which letters, faxes, e-mail and telephone calls flew back and forth from British Columbia to Nova Scotia and numerous points between, a format was discussed, ideas were exchanged and assignments handed out. We were under way by the end of August. As time passed there were a few dropouts and missed deadlines, but other contributors took up the slack, and as new members joined OWC, a few of them came on board. When we finally finished what was essentially a two-year project, 33 of Canada's best-known outdoor writers and photographers were involved, representing over 1,200 years of combined fishing experience.

At the outset contributors were told the only criteria were that their respective chapters must involve fishing with flies, either cast or trolled, and should give readers as much information as possible about where and when to go, how to get there, which tackle and patterns to take, and how best to use them. Other than that, there were no restrictions or formulas. I might be just a tad biased, but I think the result is a collection of informative and educational revelations concerning the diversity and abundance of fly-fishing opportunities available in Canada. Equally important, it makes for some highly entertaining reading. I hope you agree.

INTRODUCTION

Jack Davis

HERE I AM, SUPPOSEDLY RETIRED AS OF DECEMBER 1999, and those slave-drivers at the Outdoor Writers of Canada (OWC) and Fly Fishing Canada have me writing an introduction. I don't mind. I love writing, fly fishing and tying flies about equally. Unfortunately, my ability to wade babbling brooks and climb over beaver dams to reach promising trout waters has deteriorated with age, as have my eyes and digital dexterity. However, I can still see a computer screen and tap away at the keys, thereby deriving endless enjoyment.

During my 40-plus years as an OWC member, 14 as executive director, I have fished in every province except Newfoundland and Prince Edward Island (give me time—I'm retired now). During these piscatorial peregrinations, it has been my extreme pleasure to count as my companions some of Canada's finest and most famous outdoor writers, including Greg Clark, Pete McGillen, John Power, Mike Bolton, Kit Kitney, Reg Fife and W.A. "Bill" Macdonald. I can even recall fishing with two contributors to this book—Bob Rife and Burt Myers. Also, a few years ago as my fly-tying material was gathering dust, I gave it to an up-and-coming writer. He had joined OWC as an associate member, went on to become an active member, got involved as a director and is now one of our past presidents. And yes, Marty Roberts is also a contributor to this book.

An organization is only as good as its members make it, and OWC rates high on my list. During the 1950s, I taught fly-tying to young, handicapped adults. It was a very rewarding experience, and most of the material required was donated by many of those early OWCers.

A Tackle for Tykes program was another success, again thanks to the support of many early members. This program was created to supply less privileged youngsters with tackle and to take them fishing in the Toronto-area waters. Mike Bolton and the late George Cooke were regular guides and helpers on day-long fishing trips, and I know for a fact that we enjoyed those outings as much as did the kids.

Yes, it has been quite an enjoyable experience. I learned a lot from those "old timers" about fishing and writing and conservation, but it's just a matter of time before some of these "young pups" like Steve Galea, Gord Ellis, Kevin Fancy, Andrew Somerset, Bill Luscombe and Dave Smallwood are referred to as "old-timers." It's a label well worth wearing.

I am certain that the contents of this book will continue to revive my fly-fishing memories and add to my knowledge. After all, one never stops learning, and while it's true that I am reduced to trolling rather than casting flies, I still do so as often as possible. I am sure that those of you who read this book will also have some memories stirred, perhaps have the nucleus of some pleasant daydreams planted, and most certainly gain some knowledge about the fly-fishing opportunities available in this vast, marvelous land we call Canada. Enjoy!

CHAPTER I

THE OUTDOOR WRITERS OF CANADA

Robert H. Jones

FORMED IN 1957, THE OUTDOOR WRITERS OF CANADA (OWC) is a national organization of professional communicators who specialize in the outdoor field. Rigid qualifications for membership maintain this professional status and ensure accurate, unbiased representation to the public.

The range of membership categories includes newspaper and magazine writers, book authors, script writers, photographers, cinematographers, artists and illustrators, radio and television commentators, lecturers and public relations specialists for private industries or government ministries involved with the outdoors.

Objectives

To STIMULATE interest in and appreciation of the outdoors.

To stimulate high standards of craftsmanship among those concerned with the portrayal of outdoor life.

To cooperate with government agencies and others in support of the best possible use of Canada's natural resources.

Creed

WE BELIEVE THAT TRUTH, accuracy and fairness are fundamental in reporting the outdoors.

We believe the ethics of our craft demand a responsibility to search out facts and present them honestly and conscientiously.

We believe it to be a public trust never to permit personal gain to sway our judgment nor to stoop to plagiarism.

We believe that no member should solicit any goods and/or services for consideration, direct or indirect, whether promotional or otherwise, that would influence or appear to influence the truth, accuracy and fairness in his or her reporting about the outdoors.

CHAPTER 2

FLY FISHING CANADA

W. Jack Simpson, Executive Director

A FTER THE SECOND WORLD WAR, MATCH FISHING BECAME popular in many European and Commonwealth countries. As the number of competitions between countries increased, members of various organizing committees realized the benefits of amalgamating under a single governing body. At a 1952 meeting in Rome, Italy, a confederation was formed to organize and promote international fishing championships "on the basis of friendship and understanding as expressed through the Olympic ideal." The Confederation Internationale de la Peche Sportive (International Confederation of Sport Fishing) is comprised of four groups which represent freshwater fishing, saltwater fishing, fly fishing and competitive casting championships.

Fly-fishing competitions are governed by the Federation Internationale de la Peche Sportive en Mou (International Federation of Sport Fly Fishing). Each country may enter one team of up to eight persons: five anglers, one alternate, a team captain and a coach.

In 1987, Jack Simpson of Islington, Ontario, was contacted and asked to field a Canadian team for the World Fly Fishing Championship (WFFC) in England later that year. The challenge was accepted and the first Canadian team organized. Recognizing the potential these competitions had for promoting conservation, after the event Simpson enlisted the aid of several well-known fly fishers and outdoor writers in forming Fly Fishing Canada (FFC). This non-profit organization received its charter in 1988.

Since 1987, FFC has represented Canada every year at championships held throughout the world, including Kamloops, British Columbia, in 1993. The Kamloops event was significant as it was the first WFFC ever held in North America and the first to include a one-day conservation symposium, which has since become integral to all competitions.

In 1991, FFC led the effort which resulted in FIPS-Mouche reorganizing to provide a level playing field for all competitors and to rewrite the Competition Rules to introduce the "fish-friendly" catch-and-immediate-release procedures now in use.

FFC then developed a proposal to establish a Youth World Fly Fishing Championship and Conservation Symposium, and in 1998 the first event was held in Wales.

Although some anglers still balk at the concept of competitive fly fishing, these strictly catch-and-release events provide a focal point which brings fly fishers together from throughout the world, not only to exchange technical information about their sport, but also to address problems concerning conservation, water quality, habitat loss and other environmental problems. Through these exchanges many of the problems that plague fisheries in many countries may someday be beaten or at least controlled in a meaningful manner.

CHAPTER 3

IF I WERE A RICH MAN

Robert H. Jones

WHEN MY BROTHER-IN-LAW NICK WAS A MANITOBA GRAIN farmer, he used to wryly state that if he ever won big in the lottery, he would just keep farming until the money was all gone. That pretty well sums up my case in a like situation: I would keep writing, for it is a compulsion, a subconscious itch scratched only by putting words on paper. However, with the sudden disappearance of that annoying necessity called "earning a living," there would be an immediate reversal in the amount of time spent working versus fishing.

It is said that money can't buy happiness. Perhaps, but it certainly allows one to live extremely well while feeling miserable. I'm not ashamed to admit that I envy those who are rich, whether their money was earned through hard work, shrewd investments, an inheritance, or a lottery win. I simply consider the end result, then find myself wistfully humming snatches of "If I Were a Rich Man" from *Fiddler on the Roof.*

Should Dame Fortune ever reward my unwavering devotion to Lotto 6/49, many Canadians would benefit greatly from my windfall. This, because whenever a few dollars accumulates in my bank account, it is hastily converted into something useful—a new addition to my angling library, a fly line, a rod, waders to replace the patched-on-patches pair that causes terminal embarrass-

ROBERT H. JONES

Jack Simpson and Rory Glennie winter fly fishing, British Columbia

ment whenever I wear them. I would also fulfill a lifelong dream of fishing from one side of Canada to the other, thereby ensuring an even distribution of my wealth among deserving tackle-shop operators, airlines, guiding services and fishing lodges.

Dreams cost nothing but our time, so I invite you to join me on my journey of fancy. Some destinations I know personally, others are names planted during long-past conversations, or from magazines and books read when I was a youth yearning to follow in the footsteps of Lee Wulff, Joe Brooks, Ted Trueblood and A.J. McClane. Everything they wrote about fishing in far-off waters was committed to memory. While the passage of time had dimmed that intense flame of fanatical desire, this mythical infusion of ready cash has caused an instant conflagration of memories.

Canada is blessed with many species of worthy game fish, so hitting various regions at their peaks will require flitting back and forth like a blood-crazed mosquito at a nudist convention. This, however, should add greatly to the fun. Let's start with winter. . . .

Early evening fly fishing on Catface Bar in Clayoquot Sound, British Columbia

As a genuine, web-toed British Columbian, I prefer raincoats to quilted snowmobile suits, and ice is best contained in glasses for cooling drinks. We'll

Winter-run steelhead

devote January until early April to prowling around remote areas along the mainland coast of British Columbia, the western side of Vancouver Island and the Queen Charlotte Islands, where rivers with winter-run steelhead are plentiful. We fish close to the estuaries, so the steelhead are mint bright, with sea lice still clinging to them. In some areas we can deviate from flogging the rivers to explore nearby lakes for coastal cutthroat trout and Dolly Varden char, keeping an occasional fish for the frying pan.

On the Queen Charlottes, we cast flies for steelhead in the Yakoun and Tlell rivers, but when heavy rains color the water we might be

ROBERT H. JONES

Larry DesChene fly fishing steelhead on the Oyster River, British Columbia

MARK KRUPA

Black crappie, Ottawa, Ontario

tempted to switch to long casting rods and single-action Silex reels, then probe the heavy flows with simple yarn flies suspended beneath floats of cork or Styrofoam.

Around mid-April, we head to Ottawa, Ontario, for the spring rite of black crappie fishing in the Rideau River, upstream from the city. We cast tiny weighted streamers into the murky waters around bridges and canal locks, releasing all but the largest fish. The half-frozen crappie don't fight much, even on light-weight tackle, but their sweet white flesh provides a worthy feast to officially end winter.

Early May? Let's test the rainbow trout–filled lakes girdling Kamloops, British Columbia. We fly fish at Pass, Jacko, Peterhope, Stump and Roche, marveling when hooked trout jump higher and more often than any other freshwater fish we have ever encountered.

On the second Friday in May, we head back to Ottawa, arriving the evening before the season opening for pike and walleye. Northwest from the city, Fitzroy Harbour on the Ottawa River is in spring flood, and a series of waterfalls pour over the western wing

MARK KRUPA

What fly to choose?

of Chat Falls dam. Walleyes tuck in close to the foaming white water, and pike lurk in the calmer areas between. The walleye average 1–3 lb (900 g–1.4 kg), but the occasional bruiser goes better than 5 lb (2.3 kg).

A week later we check in at Clinton's Ash Rapids Resort on Lake of the Woods in southwestern Ontario. We throw Deer Hair Bugs and tiny poppers at smallmouth bass, which are abundant, pugnacious and eager to take whatever we offer. They charge our bugs repeatedly, exploding from the water time and again, until, at last, hooking themselves.

MARK KRUPA

Smallmouth bass

Walleye on the fly

Early June calls for a trip north of Baie-Comeau, Quebec, to the sprawling Reservoir Outard Quatre. There, we cast from shore for pike, using large Lefty's Deceivers. The fish are just beneath the surface, absorbing the sun's warming rays, and as our flies hit the water, three or four V-shaped wakes converge on them. Although the pike seldom exceed 10 lb (4.5 kg), it is wild, fast-paced fishing.

Next on our journey is southwestern Newfoundland for Atlantic salmon. At Burgeo we hire a guide to take us west onto the Cinq Cerf River, then east to the Grey. Neither are accessible by road, so fishing pressure is light and the daily catch ratio is respectable. We work our way in a clockwise direction around the province, stopping at well-known rivers like the Great Codroy, Highlands, Western Brook, Castor, Gander, Exploits and Salmonier. Too many rivers and too few days to do them all justice—but it's fun trying.

Grey River, Newfoundland

The rivers and lakes around Goose Bay, Labrador, harbor more Atlantic salmon, but we focus on trophy brook trout and ouananiche. Using the services of various outfitters throughout the area, we fly fish in lakes like Minipi, Igloo, Parke and Double-Mer, and rivers like the Eagle, Adlatok, Big and Hunt. The colorful brookies are strong, deep-fighting fish, while the slender ouananiche spend much of their time airborne, flashing silver in the sun as they try ridding themselves of the barbless fly and occasionally succeeding.

The Bonaventure River on the Gaspé

Now late July, we push farther north to Quebec's world-famous George and Koksoak rivers for Atlantic salmon. There is some serious hiking involved and it isn't easy fishing, but we discover why they keep attracting anglers year after year. Curiosity satisfied, we fly almost due north to Baffin Island for arctic char. The tent camps at Tongait, Kikertaluk and Koluctoo are spartan but comfortable, and we almost overdose on husky, bright-colored char before heading west to Tuktoyaktuk, where we search upstream along the Mackenzie watershed for

PAUL C. MARRINER

Arctic grayling, Northwest Territories

Casting flies on Kasba Lake, Northwest Territories

Brook trout, Goose Bay, Labrador

MARK KRUPA

DREW MYERS

DAVE SMALLWOOD

Robertson Falls, Churchill River, Saskatchewan

Canada's "mystery fish," the inconnu. Those who have fished for this largest member of the whitefish family, speak glowingly of their fighting abilities. Now on their home turf, we find them easily. The stories are true, for they fight with a ferocity similar to big muskies or chinook salmon.

As we work farther inland, arctic grayling rise eagerly to tiny, dark-patterned dry flies, and after each spirited tussle, we admire their sailfishlike dorsal fins and beautiful, iridescent colors before slipping the barbless hook free.

It's mid-August! We've missed the run of monster chinooks in British Columbia's Hakai Pass and Rivers Inlet, the trophy walleye on Manitoba's Red River, not to mention the trophy trout of southern Saskatchewan . . . so much to do, so little time. . . .

Eastward, this time to Nova Scotia for striped bass in estuaries along Northumberland Strait and the Bay of Fundy. Then, if weather and water levels cooperate, we'll drive to Normaway Lodge on the Margaree River to look for late-running Atlantic salmon.

Now, for a change of pace, let's head west of Fredericton, New Brunswick, to investigate whether or not Mactaquac Lake lives up to its reputation of offering some of the best, least-crowded, smallmouth bass fishing in North America. And it's impossible to be so close to the famed Miramichi River without paying our respects, so we'll drive north-east to Doaktown, stopping off at Old River Lodge. As anticipated, we find excellent salmon fishing at virtually all of the lodge's leased pools.

September already? Okay, let's head west to Calgary for a two-day float trip on the trout-laden Bow River. Rated by many anglers as the finest dry-fly trout water in the world, we see why after losing count of the deep-bodied rainbows and brown trout that rise to our offerings.

St. Mary's River, Nova Scotia

Back on Vancouver Island, we visit Tofino to cast streamer flies for coho in the waters of Clayoquot Sound. When hooked, they are supercharged with speed and strength. Speak not of the fighting prowess of any fish until weathering a few battles with 10-lb (4.5-kg) coho on fly-casting tackle.

As September draws to a close, we tear ourselves away from Tofino to head once more for Ottawa. There, we spend a full week prowling the Ottawa River within sight of the city skyline. Fishing with various Clouser Deep Minnow patterns, we catch walleye, smallmouth and largemouth bass, channel catfish, pike, and an occasional muskie. City fishing at its finest.

Landbreck Falls, Alberta

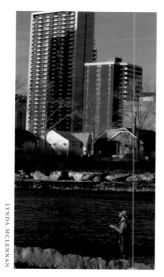

Bow River, Calgary

With early October leaves creating a brilliant kaleidoscope of color along the shorelines, the fish feed actively, instinctively preparing for winter months ahead. Time now to concentrate on muskies in the Ottawa and Rideau rivers. Relying on the stealth and quiet of a 16' aluminum canoe with a side-mounted electric motor, we use bass-weight tackle and work large Clousers along the drop-offs. It's a game of cat and mouse, slowly working those flies through the domain of these water wolves, and the gentlest of tugs jars our senses like an electric shock. It could be a 4" (10-cm) rock bass—or 4' (1.2 m) of sharp-toothed muscle and energy.

November? Back to British Columbia, where steelhead migrations are under way on many streams. We fish them in the world-famous Thompson River, marvelling at their average size and savage power. Then, over to Vancouver Island for steelhead in the Stamp, Gold, Cowichan and other rivers, which keep us happily occupied until New Year's Eve.

Miramichi River, New Brunswick

So here we sit with a noggin of Scotland's finest, reliving our past year and agreeing that it went much too quickly. Far too many places were missed or overlooked, but what the heck? Dreams are cheap, so let's do it again next year. We can start tomorrow morning. . . .

MARK WHITE

Silently searching for trout

CHAPTER 4

FLY FISHING CANADA:
A PHOTO JOURNEY

Gander River, Newfoundland

A silvery Newfoundland grilse

Fighting an Atlantic salmon

Fishing for Atlantic salmon on the Margaree Forks Pool, Nova Scotia

PAUL C. MARINER

MARK KRUPA

Fighting a Nova Scotia shad

A fine Atlantic salmon from Gaspé

ROBERT H. JONES

Fishing the Red Bank Pool on the Margaree River, Nova Scotia

Trophy brook trout

Feisty brook trout, Nova Scotia

Brook trout

Speckled quill (Callibaetis)

Golden stone fly on a wild rose

Fishing the Mosel River, Prince Edward Island

PAUL C. MARINER

Fishing for sea trout on a Prince Edward Island estuary

MARK KRUPA

Fishing for artic char, Northwest Territories

Arctic char

Flies for arctic char: Polar Shrimp (TOP), *Red and Silver* (BOTTOM)

Floatplanes arriving and departing, Northwest Territories

MARK KRUPA

A fine arctic char, Northwest Territories

MARTIN LAMONT

GEORGE GRENEFELD

A fine rainbow trout, northern British   *Brook trout*
Columbia

Lake trout weighing 24 ½ lbs caught on a Bead-Head Nymph

Releasing a trophy-sized lake trout, Kasba Lake, Northwest Territories

Helicopters are a popular means of travel to remote fishing locations

MARK KRUPA

MARK KRUPA

Walleye on the fly

Ouananiche offer fly fishers great sport

DAVE SMALLWOOD

Whitefish

Yellow perch

Arctic grayling

Black crappie

Early spring lake whitefish

Steelhead, Ontario

Trophy largemouth bass

Bluegill sunfish

Chub

Brown trout, Manitoba

Spawning steelhead on their redds

Float tube on Manitoba lake

Garpike with fly

GLEN HALES

Carp

GLEN HALES

Redhorse sucker

Smallmouth bass

Rainbow trout, Manitoba

Brook trout

The jewel-like beauty of the brook trout   *Brown trout, Vancouver Island*

Muskie

Rainbow trout, Crowsnest River, Alberta   *A typical Alberta foothills stream*

Cutthroat trout, Alberta

Arctic grayling, Northern Saskatchewan

Stunning scenery of the Rocky Mountains, Alberta

MARK KRUPA

DREW MYERS

Prime pike, Northwest Territories   *Pike feeding activity, Alberta*

JIM CRAWFORD

Elk River in the British Columbia Kootenays

Bull trout, Alberta

Average pike, Alberta

Prairie Creek, Rocky Mountain House, Alberta

Goldeye, Alberta

Skagit River, British Columbia

Rainbow trout, British Columbia

Steelhead, White River, British Columbia

Casting on Heffley Lake, British Columbia

Kokanee readily take flies

Late afternoon on Clayoquot Sound,
British Columbia

Heber River, British Columbia

Chinook salmon, Clayoquot Sound,
British Columbia

Float tube casting, British Columbia

Sea-run Dolly Varden, British Columbia

Pink salmon, Black Creek, British Columbia

Cutthroat trout, Puntledge River, British Columbia

Typical British Columbia interior lake setting

Smallmouth bass, Saltspring Island, British Columbia

Pink Salmon, Oyster Bay, British Columbia

Fighting a spirited chum salmon, Puntledge River, British Columbia

MARK KRUPA

ROBERT H. JONES

Cutthroat trout, British Columbia

Kelp greenling, Clayoquot Sound, British Columbia

ROBERT H. JONES

Angling on Clayoquot Sound, British Columbia

Barry Thornton's well-stocked saltwater fly box

Cutthroat trout

Fighting a spirited chum salmon in river estuary, British Columbia

Guide Lise Peters with a British Columbia coho

Pink salmon, Campbell River, British Columbia

Casting for pink salmon, Oyster Bay, British Columbia

Brown rockfish, Clayoquot Sound, British Columbia

Black rockfish, Clayoquot Sound, British Columbia

Pacific Mackerel put up a strong, fast-paced fight on fly-casting tackle

Lingcod, Clayoquot Sound, British Columbia

Yellowtail rockfish, British Columbia

Toothy lingcod are determined fighters

CHAPTER 5

SPRINGTIME IS TROUT TIME

Fred Wooding

A ROUND ABOUT THIS TIME OF YEAR APPROXIMATELY ONE-third of the Canadian population—mostly males—will succumb to one of the most communicable of all diseases. Known as "delirium piscatoria," this strange malaise is caused by what is generally referred to as "the opening of the trout season" and is commonplace throughout most of the northern hemisphere.

Depending on geography, symptoms of the disease show up with the first (however slight) indication that spring is on the way. In British Columbia it might be the return of the yellow warbler, in the Prairies the northward flight of the Canada goose, in Ontario and Quebec the running of the maple sap, and in the Maritimes and Newfoundland the simple melting of winter's snow.

But the symptoms are unmistakable: restlessness and irritability, a faraway look in the eyes, a fondness for outdoor magazines, resort folders and one-mile-to-the-inch maps of out-of-the-way places.

During such times the woman who can find her kitchen table clear of moth-eaten wet and dry artificial flies, lengths of leaders, landing nets, HDH double-tapered lines, sections of fly and spinning rods, and even a dried-up worm or two can count herself a fortunate creature indeed.

What causes this metamorphosis in normally rational, responsible men? A psychiatrist friend of mine began clinical studies on the problem and was making some headway until he, too, went trout fishing. Almost immediately his research stopped, and I've since been told that his wife has left him.

The men who go fishing during this season of the year are of two distinct types—those who are true trout fishermen and those who are not. In the latter group fall all who will take fish by any means permissible. They are amiable characters who, completely without qualms, will use worms, frogs or any other bait with any old kind of gear so long as they catch fish. The true fisherman, on the other hand, is usually an unregenerate snob who disdains everything but artificial flies. Even in this latter group, class distinction raises its ugly head. Often the relationship between the purist devoted to the dry fly and the man who stoops to wet flies and nymphs is cool and uncommunicative.

If there is a good deal of engaging nonsense about trout fishing, there is also a good deal of academic seriousness. And notwithstanding the breach in diplomatic relations between the "hardware" angler, the purist and the nonpurist, trouting inspires in men a friendly rapport unmarred by professional standing. I know of one tycoon whose bosom pal during May is an odd-jobber who hasn't owned a new suit in 20 years.

Fishing is not just an escape from the pressures of modern society. In reality, it is a return to the verities of life—a chance to get back to the serenity God intended for us. It sends men into deep forests or to placid streams, to places where once more—free from telephones and automobiles—they can hear the song of birds and enjoy the rich smell of a world coming to life.

If the truth be known, most anglers really care little whether they catch fish or not; what matters is the joy that is found in old clothes, the unbridled freedom from worry and the pursuit of an elusive quarry. When, by happy chance, he does connect with a trout and lands it, the angler for that moment is the happiest of men.

CHAPTER 6

ATLANTIC SALMON

Paul Marriner

Facts
Scientific Name: *Salmo salar*
Range: Throughout Atlantic Canada and Eastern Quebec
Average Size: 9 lb (4 kg)
Maximum Size: 80 lb (36 kg)

Introduction

HUNDREDS OF MILLIONS OF WORDS HAVE BEEN WRITTEN about Atlantic salmon, and I have contributed a few hundred thousand to the pile. Widely called "the king of game fish," this species has nonetheless suffered more at the hands of man than most. That it has survived at all is a testament to its tenacity and intricate survival strategy. Why is the Atlantic salmon so popular with anglers? Because it is a large fish that takes a fly on or near the surface, fights hard—often with many jumps—is available (depending on location) throughout the ice-free season, and is a gourmet's delight.

Atlantic salmon fishing is often considered a pastime of the wealthy. True, if you expect to land the most and the largest fish in privacy. Conversely, salmon anglers of modest means far outnumber their well-heeled brethren. Regardless, in Canada, access and regulations are a bureaucrat's dream, varying as they do between jurisdictions, regions and even individual rivers. One constant remains—one can only legally fish for Atlantic salmon with an artificial fly, unweighted in most jurisdictions.

To suggest that one could explore all the intricacies of salmon fishing and the attendant politics in a single chapter is ludicrous. Besides, if that were true I would have been out of a job many years ago. So, cliché or not, the following is merely a "once-over-lightly" treatment.

Life Cycle

ATLANTIC SALMON SPAWN in their natal rivers (or lakes in a few cases) in the late fall. The eggs hatch the following spring, and several months later the fry develop into parr. The rate at which parr grow is dependent on the water's fertility, but normally two to four years later they are ready to go to sea. Just before departure—another spring event—parr get a silvery coating and become known as smolts.

Once at sea they follow established migration routes. The progeny of some rivers travel great distances while others remain closer to home. Now one of nature's survival mechanisms asserts itself: Some salmon return to their birthplace having spent only one winter in the ocean. These are grilse. Others remain at sea for two or more seasons before returning and rate the title of salmon (to avoid needless repetition both salmon and grilse will be called salmon unless the distinction is necessary). Salmon size is directly related to the number of seasons spent in the ocean. Some rivers see only multi-sea-winter fish, others mostly grilse.

Virtually without exception they ascend the river they left to begin the process anew. The few that stray are available to increase genetic diversity and restock rivers struck by natural or man-made disasters. Both grilse and salmon are fertile, but the larger the female, the more eggs she carries.

When salmon enter a stream and how quickly they move to spawning areas depend on preprogramming and water levels. A lack of water often holds them in brackish regions near the river mouth until conditions improve. With spring and fall being the favored seasons because of consistent water levels, some rivers see salmon entering either early or late, while others get runs at both times. Some streams are blessed with fresh-run fish during the entire season. Variations in appearance and average size may be quite pronounced between runs in the same river, and often the fish are heading for different spawning areas.

Once in the river the salmon will move quickly if sufficient water is available, but slowly and intermittently otherwise. Salmon are, as already mentioned, very adaptable. While wanting to reach the same patch of gravel from which they hatched, should conditions preclude this, they will spawn over any satisfactory bottom. As additional protection, even male parr can fertilize eggs, though less effectively than a full-grown male.

After spawning, the salmon, now called kelts, may immediately drop back to salt water or overwinter in the river and return to the ocean just after ice-out in the spring. Some kelts regain their strength and return to spawn again—another survival tool. The number of multiple spawners returning to a specific river varies, but in recent years they are estimated to make up as much as 40 percent of the large salmon returns to the Miramichi River system.

Conventional wisdom is that during the journey to their redds, salmon do not feed. This has often been disputed by pointing out the fatal attraction of a worm (legal in certain parts of Great Britain) and instances where salmon rise like trout to a hatch of may flies. I have watched the latter event several times and caught fish by "matching the hatch." My favorite analysis was given by an eminent Scottish salmon biologist who is reported to have said with some pique, "Salmon do not feed, but fortunately for you anglers, they do take food." While at first glance this statement meets all the requirements of an extended oxymoron, a little reflection reveals its perfection.

Tackle

AN 8–9-WEIGHT ROD from 9–10' in length is the standard weapon. Two-handed rods are beginning to appear again on a few rivers, but cost will likely restrict their penetration. Nonetheless, I have found that a 15-footer has substantially improved my coverage of several difficult pools. Some anglers like to drop to a 7-weight when casting dry flies for extended periods. Lines are usually floating, but sink-tips may be needed in either high- or coldwater conditions. Rod-length leaders with 8–16-lb tippet strength are common, getting longer and finer under warm and clear conditions, and shorter when using sink-tips. Reels should be large enough to hold at least 150 yards (135 m) of backing.

Tactics

VIRTUALLY EVERY FLY-FISHING TACTIC not involving weight on the fly or leader has been used to tempt Atlantic salmon. Likely, the most common remains the classic wet-fly swing, in use for centuries and still just as effective under many conditions. Regardless, other methods like the Riffling Hitch, working the fly, Crosfield Pull, greased-line, Patent, upstream nymph, deep streamer, dry-fly presentations, harling, trolling, downwind drift and boat-drops all have their place. A brief description of each follows.

Classic Wet Fly

USED DURING ALL SEASONS, the classic wet-fly technique involves a down-and-across cast at an angle chosen to produce the most attractive fly speed (learned only through experience). Floating lines and rod-length leaders are summer standards, but colder or deeper water may demand sink-tip or even full-sinking lines to get your fly closer to the fish. Beyond its effectiveness, it is also one of the few techniques that permits orderly rotation of a group of anglers through a pool.

Crosfield Pull

THIS TACTIC WAS DEVELOPED by the late Ernest Crosfield to make his fly accelerate and swim properly. A wet fly is cast across-stream and stripped back quickly just under the surface. It will occasionally "wake up logy summer fish or induce a take from a salmon which has just rolled on the surface."

Riffling Hitch

PUTTING A COUPLE OF HALF-HITCHES with the leader behind the head of a wet fly will cause it to wake across the surface when cast downstream and across. The cast angle will determine the nature of the wake—too much and the fly throws spray, too little and it sinks. This method is popular in Newfoundland, but less accepted elsewhere.

Greased-Line

A TECHNIQUE SUBJECT to a variety of interpretations, but a working description for Atlantic salmon is as follows: A fly is cast across and slightly upstream. Mending the line permits a length of dead-drift float then additional mends and rod placement bring the fly across the stream much more slowly than if the swing speed was simply left to the current's devices.

Patent

VIRTUALLY ARCHAIC, but can still be pulled out of the bag when other presentations fail. A large streamer fly (historically No. 5/0 or larger) with plenty of mobile bits is cast either up- or downstream so it arrives in front of a visible salmon at its resting level. A downstream cast allows repetitive drifts with the goal of essentially teasing the salmon into taking by hanging an annoyance in its face.

Upstream Nymph

NYMPHING IS STILL A RARELY USED TECHNIQUE, but one with potential. Because weighted flies and/or weight on the leader are forbidden, it is mostly effective for a visible salmon in relatively shallow water (or over a lie known to be occupied). Indicators are legal, so anglers can easily detect the strike.

Deep Streamer

WINTER STEELHEAD TECHNIQUES have arrived on Atlantic salmon streams, particularly for late fall fish in very cold water. Hi-D sink-tips or full-sinking lines matched with ultrashort leaders are cast and mended to get the line to the bottom. Then the fly is swung directly in front of a salmon's nose. Such tactics have the potential to foul-hook fish, so ethical anglers do not strip line during the swing or set the hook until feeling the full weight of the salmon.

Working the Fly

MANY ATLANTIC SALMON RIVERS feature deep pools with too little current to swing a fly. Salmon often hold in such places, so stripping or using hand-twist retrieves are necessary to move the fly. Another situation where additional action may be desirable occurs when swinging flies that are tied with mobile materials like marabou. Here, small movements of the rod tip will activate the material. A minority of salmon anglers believe that all flies should be moved during the swing.

Dry-Fly Presentations

DRY FLIES ARE OFFERED DEAD-DRIFT, skated, or pulled across the surface. Often, particularly on public water where rotation rules apply, a dry is cast across the stream to a seam or known lie, with enough slack to yield a dead-drift. Mending extends the drift. Then, finally, if the fly is of the Bug or Bomber type, it is pulled under or skated and allowed to swing below the angler. Dry flies are primarily a summer technique and at times are much more effective than wet flies, particularly in the hearts and tails of pools.

Boat Techniques

TROLLING IS ILLEGAL IN MOST LOCATIONS, so be careful. The "how" is obvious; the "where" is usually lakes, extremely large rivers, or rivers in the midst of spring flood. Another technique, harling, uses boat control to move a fly back and forth across a large river (like "hot-shotting" with lures). Primarily a European technique, there are nonetheless several Canadian rivers where it is applicable. A lone angler can accomplish harling with the rod mounted in a holder, but more often it involves a professional boatman. Casting downwind from a free-drifting boat is also a technique with European origins and rarely applicable to North American conditions. "Fishing the drop" from a canoe is the usual boat technique in Canada. Simply put, a canoe is anchored at the head of a pool or run, the angler covers the water on both sides of the boat by casting, and then the boat slides downstream just far enough for the angler to begin again over unfished water.

Where and When

IF I GIVE YOU RECOMMENDATIONS ON THIS SCORE, I'm guaranteed to be either a hero or a bum with a 50/50 chance of being either. Nonetheless, I feel quite safe with the following: The largest salmon in North America swim up the Restigouche in New Brunswick, and the Grand Cascapedia and Moisie rivers in Quebec—where you can expect to empty your bank account. Rather limit out on catch-and-release every day? Then try the Gray River in Newfoundland or the Eagle River in Labrador, neither of which is inexpensive. Looking for the longest season in the country with the largest run of salmon in the world? Choose a visit to the Miramichi in New Brunswick. Regardless, there are scores of other rivers where, if your timing is right, you can catch either very large salmon or a catch-and-release limit every day for a week. For my part, I consider that Newfoundland has the widest selection of inexpensive, quality Atlantic salmon fishing on the continent.

Flies

SINCE THE FOURTEENTH CENTURY, tens of thousands of patterns have been presented to Atlantic salmon. Many of these appear in two fine books written by Joseph D. Bates Jr.: *Atlantic Salmon Flies & Fishing* and *Fishing Atlantic Salmon*. In my book, *Modern Atlantic Salmon Flies,* published in 1999, some 80 percent of the more than 300 patterns therein were previously unpublished. Frankly, if you hit it right, almost anything, including a bare hook, will take Atlantics. Nonetheless, each river or region has its favorites that have proven over the years to be consistent takers. I always recommend contacting a fly shop or lodge at your destination for the best advice (hopefully my book will also point you in the right direction).

Closure

I ADMIT IT—I'm an Atlantic salmon bum. Each season, for almost seven months, I follow the runs around, trying to fish the best available public water in four provinces. True, I often spend as much or more time talking about the sport as casting, but that is often the final stage in the evolution of a fly fisher. The lure and lore of Atlantic salmon fishing are irresistible.

PAUL MARRINER'S MUST-HAVE PATTERNS FOR ATLANTIC SALMON

- Spring: Polar Ice
- Summer: Fluorescent Green Cosseboom
- Fall: Canary

CHAPTER 7

A CLOSER LOOK AT QUEBEC'S
ATLANTIC SALMON

Paul Marriner

Q UEBEC BOASTS MANY OF NORTH AMERICA'S GREATEST Atlantic salmon rivers. For management purposes these are geographically divided into four zones: Gaspésie (Gaspé), Bas St-Laurant (Lower Saint Lawrence), Saguenay and Côte Nord (North Shore). There is a fifth zone, Quebec, but it's unimportant where salmon are concerned. Seasons and other regulations are generally determined by the zone.

Virtually all salmon rivers are managed by local groups known as ZECs (Zone Exploitation Controllée). While some private water still exists on certain rivers, most of the fishing is in the hands of the ZEC management. Anglers can fish the ZEC waters by participating in preseason and in-season draws or by purchasing day tickets. Usually, the best water is reserved for the draws (a limited number of anglers), but even the day-ticket sections (an unlimited number of anglers) occasionally produce excellent results. Note that several of the very best rivers have quite limited day-ticket access. Another recent development is the sale by the ZECs of blocks of time on the limited-access sectors to commercial guides or outfitters. Provincial regulations limit the scope of these sales, but for a last-minute Charlie searching for exclusive access, using the services of a guide or outfitter is an option well worth exploring.

Quebec rivers offer both wading and fishing from canoes. Guides are optional for wading, but some river sections can be fished only from boats, which, for visitors, obviously means hiring a guide.

My experience is limited to seven Quebec rivers, but I have little hesitation in roughly ranking them. The Grand Cascapedia (Gaspé) is the jewel in the crown: accessible, expensive, and the average fish size 20 lb (9 kg). The Moise (Côte Nord) has huge salmon, but is both expensive and difficult to access. I like the area around the town of Gaspé with its three rivers: York, Dartmouth and St. Jean. All three have useful, unlimited-access water, which offers the opportunity to move between rivers as conditions dictate. Another personal favorite is the Bonaventure (Gaspé), a beautiful river with a good run of salmon.

Patterns from local tiers for virtually all Quebec rivers can be found in my book *Modern Atlantic Salmon Flies,* and tackle recommendations are as outlined in the body of this chapter.

For more detailed information (such as catch data, types of water condition, and recommended fly patterns) on individual Atlantic salmon rivers in Quebec, check out the following web site: http://www.quebectel.com/saumonquebec/anglais/index.htm

ATLANTIC SALMON-STUFFED TOMATO CUPS

When you keep a big salmon, steak the front for grilling and use the tail portion for this dish. A great appetizer or fall picnic dish.
(Makes four servings)

¾ lb—Atlantic salmon, coarsely chopped—350 g
4—tomatoes
2—shallots, finely diced
1—garlic clove, finely diced
3 tbsp—dry bread crumbs, divided—45 mL
1 tsp—chopped fresh dill—5 mL
3 tbsp—olive oil, divided—45 mL
Salt and freshly ground black pepper

1. Split salmon tail, skin and remove any rib and pin bones.

2. Remove tops from tomatoes, scoop out seeds and pulp, turn upside down to drain. Before stuffing, dry with paper toweling and season with salt and pepper to taste.

3. In a bowl mix salmon with shallots, garlic, 2 tbsp (30 mL) bread crumbs, herbs and 2 tbsp olive oil. Spoon into tomato cups and mound the mixture so each contains a good serving. Sprinkle with remaining bread crumbs and drizzle with olive oil.

4. Bake in a 400°F (200°C) oven for 35 minutes or until salmon is cooked and lightly browned on top. Garnish with a sprinkle of dill. Serve at room temperature.

–Wayne Phillips

CHAPTER 8

AMERICAN SHAD

Paul Marriner

Facts

Scientific Name: *Alosa sapidissima*
Range: Primarily the Maritime provinces and St. Lawrence
tributaries as far as Montreal. Scattered populations in
southern Newfoundland and coastal British Columbia.
Average Size: 2 lb (900 g)
Maximum Size: Approximately 10 lb (4.5 kg)

Introduction

OFTEN CALLED "THE POOR MAN'S SALMON," SHAD ARE WIDELY overlooked as game fish in Canada. By swimming in the same waters as Atlantic salmon and sea trout (both much better table fare), shad have escaped attention. However, in rivers where salmon have disappeared and shad have survived, they offer sport to anglers of all ages and persuasions.

Most readers are probably familiar with some species of the herring family, either fresh or salt, so they can easily imagine a shad's appearance. Just picture a herring on steroids and you'll have it—silvery, forked tail, small head, coarse scales and a body somewhat narrow for its length and depth.

Shad are anadromous. Spawned in rivers, they migrate to the ocean to grow up before returning to the river and beginning the cycle again. Unlike some species which may spend up to three years in a river before heading to sea, young shad hang around for only four or five months. Most are five years old before spawning for the first time and may return several times during an average life of seven years. Run timing depends on latitude. In the Bay of Fundy, the first fish usually arrive in late April; in the Miramichi River, mid-May. By the end of the first week in July, most have reproduced and returned to the salt water (sooner in the early rivers).

Although fishable shad populations visit a score or more rivers in the Maritimes, only one river receives serious attention—the Annapolis River in Nova Scotia. Reasons for this anomaly will become clear shortly. To the best of my knowledge shad are not widely targeted in Quebec either, the exception being the Montreal area.

Tactics

THE TWO CONSTANTS of shad angling are small and deep. Young shad in a river feed on microscopic "bits and bites," and as adults in salt water, on plankton. When in the river to spawn, they don't feed, so anglers are trying to trigger an "aggression" response. To do this with any regularity, a fly must be presented close to where the fish are lying, i.e., on the bottom. Shad also have small mouths for their size, so large flies are less successful.

The basic presentation is unsophisticated. Cast across the stream, let the fly sink near the bottom, and then work it back with a twitchy retrieve. Shad are light takers, so set the hook at every bump, even if you are sure it's just the bottom. Don't give up if the first few casts reach the near bank without a hit— sometimes shad take a little while to warm up. Once they do, however, they often continue to take for a considerable period. In a packed pool, a persistent angler may take up to 50 in a few hours.

Depending on the size of the river, angling is from the bank or from boats. Trolling is practiced on some very large western rivers, but anchored boats are more common. A virtually untapped canoe fishery is available on New

Brunswick's Miramichi River. I'd guess that this famous Atlantic salmon river has one of the greatest unexploited shad runs on the continent.

Shad are most active in the evening. Later, toward dark, they may be seen swimming near the surface or splashing on top in a prespawn or spawning activity. Regardless, they will take at any time during the day. I favor the morning hours because even the best spots are usually vacant. Once school and the work day end, space beside these well-known holes is at a premium. On occasion shad will shut down, but these slack periods, often associated with visible swimming activity, are usually limited to a half hour or so.

So where are these "best" spots? While I have seen shad holding in shallow riffles, by far the largest schools are in slow-water pools. Nor are shad great leapers, so they will stack up in areas below an obstruction. And here, in addition to pollution, is a significant cause for the disappearance of shad from numerous rivers—for even a small weir defeats them.

The Fight

ALTHOUGH I HAVE READ about shad leaping like salmon, this is mostly in the imagination of the authors. True, shad will leap occasionally, particularly if given a helping hand by the angler, but this is uncommon behavior. Most fight deep, giving a battle equivalent to a brown trout of the same size.

Tackle

MY STANDARD SHAD ROD is a 9', 6-weight. Originally, I strung this rod with a 10', fast-sinking, sink-tip line. Now, however, I usually rely on sinking, braided leaders (from "fast" to "extra-super-fast") to get my fly in the target zone. Adjusting the length of the monofilament tippet fine-tunes the business end for small changes in depth. As well, after casting across-stream, an upstream mend will yield another foot of depth or more (depending on current speed) if required.

As expected, shad flies are not elaborate. Small Clouser Minnows, fly-rod jigs and simple Beadheads work well. One productive pattern mimics the most popular shad dart, a gold Beadhead and a white chenille body with a few winds of red chenille behind the bead. Another potent producer is one version of the Cubby Mini-Mite from Cortland. With its white soft-plastic body and pink ball jig-head, it's nothing more than a jig for the fly rod. Although not as effective as these weighted "flies," purists will succeed with a variety of small streamers in the popular shad dart colors.

Gustatory Quality

LIKE ALL MEMBERS of the herring family, shad are quite bony. This fact, or more likely the level of effort to produce boneless fillets (one source offers a 32-step process), eliminates them from my diet. I'm told they smoke quite well, but without personal experience I can't comment. The roe is prized by many, and there are numerous recipes for its preparation, two of which follow. Once again I lack experience, so you will just have to follow your nose. From the foregoing it should be obvious that I release all shad landed. Shad are commercially exploited—mostly in the Bay of Fundy to my knowledge—but I strongly suspect they are, after removing the roe, merely ground up as meal to be fed to aquaculture salmon or livestock. I have never seen it in stores or advertised by roadside fishmongers.

SAUTÉED ROE

1. Wash the roe carefully; don't break the membrane.

2. Sauté in butter over medium heat for 5 to 10 minutes, depending on size. Turn once.

3. To the butter in the pan, add lemon juice, salt and pepper. Use as a sauce and spread over the cooked roe.

OVEN-TOASTED ROE

(Makes four servings)

1 ½ lb—shad roe—700 g
1 tbsp—butter, melted—15 mL
1 tsp—prepared mustard—5 mL
3 tbsp—dry sherry wine—45 mL
1 tsp—anchovy paste—5 mL
3 drops—Angostura bitters
1 tbsp—Worcestershire sauce—15 mL
4 slices—hot buttered toast
Pinch—cayenne
Pinch—rosemary
4 sprigs—fresh mint
1 lemon, sliced

1. Place roe in saucepan over medium flame, cover with boiling water and simmer gently for 15 minutes.

2. While roe is simmering, blend all other ingredients except last two in mixing bowl.

3. When roe is done, drain, cut into 1" (2.5-cm) pieces and dip into mixture until well coated.

4. Arrange pieces on hot buttered toast and bake in preheated 400°F (200°C) oven for 5 minutes to allow mixture to permeate roe. Garnish with mint and lemon slices.

–Wayne Phillips

The Annapolis River

NOVA SCOTIA'S ANNAPOLIS RIVER and its tributaries comprise the shad habitat with which I am most familiar. Once a productive Atlantic salmon river, this lovely pastoral stream winds through Nova Scotia's most famous valley to the Bay of Fundy. Along the way it caresses the edges of verdant meadows and winds through stands of magnificent oak, maple and elm. Considering the devastation wrought on most of Nova Scotia's rivers by acid rain, rapacious logging practices, gross environmental mismanagement and ill-advised dams, it is amazing that the Annapolis still supports a substantial run of anything.

While floating some 20 miles of the river in 1998, I saw several thousand shad, some trophies among them. As the Annapolis stock comes from the Bay of Fundy, where shad are estimated to live longer than anywhere else, it is an excellent destination for anglers eager to see their names in the record books. At present, the resource appears very healthy. At this writing, Nova Scotia has no daily limit on the number of shad an angler can kill. I believe this is wrong, not because the resource is endangered, but because it sends the wrong message. It fosters a disrespect for this resource and, by extension, for others which are fragile.

Unquestionably, the center of Annapolis shad fishing is the town of Middleton. Just outside of town, a bridge crosses the river, and when the shad are running, it would be unusual to find fewer than a dozen vehicles parked in proximity. Anglers usually spread out for a half mile or so in either direction. To my knowledge, east of Quebec, Middleton is the only location of an annual shad tournament, which is usually held on the last weekend in May.

Depending on water temperature, shad begin appearing in the Annapolis as early as the second week of April. Regardless, the peak of the run is in the latter half of May. By mid-June the action has dwindled substantially. Because the Annapolis Valley is a major tourist center, accommodation of all types is plentiful. My only caution is that the area is also the home of deer ticks, so I advise anglers who decide to leave the beaten pathways to wear a hat, a jacket with tight cuffs and an undershirt with a tight collar. An additional precaution is to roll socks over pants.

Closure

UNLIKE SOME OTHER FISHERIES, shad are for everyone. I have fished with a five-year-old on one side and an octogenarian on the other. The necessary tackle is inexpensive, the techniques uncomplicated and the access easy. Certainly catching shad is a sport fishing experience worth having.

PAUL MARRINER'S MUST-HAVE PATTERNS FOR SHAD

- Bead Head
- Jig-Fly
- Simplified Clouser Deep Minnow

CHAPTER 9

DOWN-HOME SMALLMOUTHS

Paul Marriner

I SURVEYED THE FLOODED TIMBER AND WEED BEDS OF NOVA Scotia's Little River Lake for the first time. "It's largemouth heaven," I said to Perry Munro.

"Would be if we had them here," he replied. "But the smallmouth like it just as much."

So they do, for Little River Lake, located near Kentville in the Annapolis Valley, also offers the rocky shallows and reefs more often associated with smallmouth bass. This is also the case in scores of other artificial impoundments, lakes, ponds and rivers in Nova Scotia and New Brunswick.

Smallmouths arrived in New Brunswick at the end of the nineteenth century and were introduced into southern Nova Scotia a decade or so later. For more than a half century, existing as they did in trout and salmon country, the range of bass expanded slowly. Few anglers paid them much attention until a laundry list of influences altered everything: planned and unplanned introductions, dams, acid rain, global warming, abominable forestry practices, overfishing of trout, popularity of bass tournaments and more. For example, in 1949 there were about 10 bass lakes in Nova Scotia. By 1998 the number had escalated to nearly 100. New Brunswick presently claims some 45 bass lakes with about 11 considered quality fisheries.

Sadly, this superb game fish has become a Jekyll and Hyde—loved where it belongs, hated where it doesn't. The former is in waters too warm for trout and salmon, the latter where treasured coldwater species survive. Moreover, the blame for this disaster rests with neither the fish nor fisheries professionals, but with those infamous "bucket biologists." Bass anglers fish mostly from boats, and as many are equipped with live wells, it is easy for the ignorant to transport them to waters with access to Atlantic salmon rivers or to depleted but still viable trout lakes.

While smallmouth have enjoyed Maritime hospitality for a century, they find the larder limited. The primary forage includes nymphs (may fly, damsel fly, dragonfly), leeches, minnows, frogs, the fry of several nongame species and, most tragically in waters where they don't belong, salmon fry and parr and small trout.

Without crayfish to fill their bellies, the average East Coast bass is at least a ½ lb (225 g) lighter than those in Ontario. Expect to catch plenty 8–15" (20–40 cm) in length, but few much larger. Another explanation for the small average size is the lack of predation, hence, overpopulation. As these waters are absent of pike and muskie, bass dominate their habitat. Furthermore, Maritimers have yet to develop a taste for bass fillets, so they release most of their catch.

On a still May evening, boards and shutters still cover the eyes of cottages scattered along the shores of New Brunswick's Lake George. However, behind a watery mirror reflecting the sky's orange and pink veils, other eyes are wide open. In a month, dense reeds will pinpoint the shallow reefs, but now only the hardiest of last year's stalks penetrate the surface like the seemingly random pins of an unfinished string picture. Among these remnants the eyes cruise, sucking down the odd may fly that is too slow leaving the surface. When a white Deer Hair Slider plops down and quivers its distress, the tension mounts. Suddenly, the point of a V surges forward, slicing through the expanding rings. Then arrives a moment suspended, when otherwise hardened anglers dissolve into quivering humanitarians trying to save a creation of hair and feathers from annihilation. Slower wits are better off. Stunned into inaction by the spectacle, they fail to react until the victim disappears into a hole to the sound of a suction cup being pulled from a wall. Often the hook set would hang a tuna. Truly, for fly fishers, "eau de smallmouth" is bottled from surface water.

Surface-oriented smallmouth are aggressive and omnivorous. I have caught them on everything from No. 16 Comparaduns to 4/0 Dahlberg Divers, and a host of poppers, sliders and Atlantic salmon bugs in between. One enjoyable experience, which I have shared with Perry Munro and others, is to prowl among the lily pads on a sunny summer's day. Then, damsel flies flit over the surface, landing sporadically on the pads. While I have only rarely seen a natural one swallowed by a smallmouth, they are watching. Plunk almost anything beside an occupied pad and expect an explosion. True, a variety of excellent adult damsel fly imitations exist, but rarely, if ever, are smallmouth that fussy.

Unfortunately, smallmouth aren't always top-water terrors. Probing rocky shorelines or reefs with minnow, leech or nymph imitations and a floating line is a proven subsurface tactic. However, there are others. For example, consider an area where the bottom slopes gradually from shore and then drops suddenly into deeper water. A full-sinking line, with all of its irritating characteristics, presents a fly enticingly. Cast a Woolly Bugger, Zonker or Muddler up onto the shelf and begin the retrieve immediately. When the fly reaches the drop-off, slow your retrieve to allow the line's sinking belly to pull it down parallel to the slope. This technique once saved my day on Oromocto Lake in New Brunswick.

Here is another very specific but nonetheless useful bit of intelligence. When dams like the giant Mactaquac on New Brunswick's Saint John River create impoundments, the flooded valley sprouts a series of arms or back bays. Road builders cherish straight lines, so they frequently span these indentations with fill, through which is run a large culvert to allow water circulation, the direction of which depends on the flow through the dam. These culvert openings are often totally underwater, and bass find the reversing currents a prime source of suitable meals. Robert McNeil, a successful New Brunswick tournament angler, showed me such a spot, and if I wasn't certain I'm speaking to a different audience than his competitors, I'd zip my lip. We had gratifying success at his honey hole, and the concentration of bass was staggering. However, miss those underwater entrances by three or four feet and you go begging.

What are the smallmouth prospects for dedicated river fly fishers? Limited.

Unfortunately, one is the LaHave River in Nova Scotia, which still supports a reasonable run of salmon. Although some will disagree, a case can be made for killing every bass caught in the LaHave and contributing the carcass to the food-chain, if unwanted. Several smaller streams in the Halifax area also offer a pleasant wading experience. The top New Brunswick rivers are the St. Croix, Magaguadavic (lower section), Eel (downstream of the Ducks Unlimited impoundment at Benton) and Meduxnekeag (near Woodstock).

Prince Edward Island and Newfoundland have no smallmouth bass, but Nova Scotia and New Brunswick offer superb fly-fishing opportunities. Many venues are small and accessible, so can be easily fished from a canoe or float tube. Trophies are scarce, but anglers regularly land specimens up to 4 lb (2 kg). After a tour of several Yarmouth County (Nova Scotia) waters, a prominent American tournament angler called them the best bass habitat he had ever seen. High praise and likely deserved.

Where

NOVA SCOTIA'S SMALLMOUTH FISHERIES are concentrated to the south and southwest of Halifax. More than 20 bass lakes ring the city itself. *The Official Nova Scotia Fishing Map* pinpoints many of the province's bass lakes (send CDN $3.50 to Nova Scotia Fisheries, P.O. Box 700, Pictou, Nova Scotia, Canada B0K 1H0), and you can also request a free current listing.

The top professional smallmouth guide in Nova Scotia is Perry Munro of Munro's Mountain Maple Lodge (902-542-2658), near Wolfville. He is a well-known fly fisher, and his Carolina skiffs on Little River Lake (one of the province's best smallmouth fisheries) are stable and comfortable fly-fishing platforms.

New Brunswick's smallmouth fisheries are found in the southwest corner of the province and along the Saint John River valley. Perhaps the best choice for big bass is Harvey Lake, about 30 miles (48 km) southwest of Fredericton. River lovers might prefer the St. Croix River on the border between Maine and New Brunswick. For those wishing to use a guide, I highly recommend Mike Best (506-529-3609), who lives near St. Andrews, New Brunswick.

When

BOTH NOVA SCOTIA AND NEW BRUNSWICK have long seasons supported by very healthy smallmouth populations. The New Brunswick season is from
May 1 to October 15 (except in Maine-boundary waters, where the season is
April 15 to September 30). Nova Scotia welcomes bass anglers from April 15 to
October 31 (with a few minor exceptions). As elsewhere, best times come and
go. I prefer the early season, when the shallows have warmed enough to attract
feeding bass, but before the weeds have had a chance to get thick. Although it's
not likely to matter to most fly fishers, several months of the New Brunswick
season are catch-and-release only. Neither province requires a guide for smallmouth bass, and nonresident (nonsalmon) licenses are reasonably priced.

Tackle

MY RECOMMENDATIONS ARE SIMPLE: a 6-weight outfit with a floating
line and a spare spool with a moderately fast full-sinking line. For those rare
occasions when fishing the fly 1–2' (30–60 cm) deeper makes a difference, I
attach a sinking braided leader. I have never found bass to be particularly leader-
shy, so choose both the length and tippet strength to suit the size of the fly.
Although I have used a variety of flies for smallmouth over the years, lately I rely
on a variety of Woolly Buggers, Muddlers and Zonkers in No. 10–4 and a collection of deer hair and balsa or cork poppers and sliders.

PAUL MARRINER'S MUST-HAVE PATTERNS FOR EAST COAST SMALLMOUTH BASS

- Simplified Zonker
- Mohair Leech
- Deer Hair Bug

CHAPTER 10

ENTOMOLOGY AND OTHER LIFE-FORMS

Dr. Martin Lamont

A S A GROUP, INVERTEBRATES ARE TOUGH CRITTERS, successfully colonizing every habitat niche in the world. This includes harsh circumpolar regions locked in by frigid winter conditions for more than half the year, yet by spring thaw, dormant insects emerge to dominate the life-forms in sheer numbers. They develop, emerge, breed and replenish their cycle in a very brief time.

Being a major and essential factor in the food chain, insects are critical to all aquatic life-forms and provide the basic food of most freshwater fish species. It is not surprising, for example, to find that aquatic insects of the Arctic are similar to those of more southern latitudes and that all major groups are present. There are, however, fewer terrestrial species in the northern tundra and sparse marginal boreal areas.

The Ephemeroptera order—may fly is the generic term—is present wherever rivers flow. This raised-wing family has large transparent or opaque main wings, small rear wings and a segmented body with two or three long tails. There are considerable variations in coloration and size, even among flies of the same species. It is thought that the colder the air temperature, the darker the color. Spring hatches are slightly darker and larger than summer hatches.

By far the most widespread and most useful to fly fishers is the

Callibaetis/Baetidae family known as blue-winged olives. From an angler's perspective, correct identification is not critical. Merely observing the species and attempting to "match the hatch"—whether nymph, dun or spinner—will suffice.

Aquatic nymphal stages of may flies are important to fish and anglers. Fish intercept crawling nymphs as they forage on river bottoms and at the emergence stage as nymphs swim to the surface. The dun stage starts at the surface after a nymph crawls out of its redundant exoskeleton and floats on top of the water. With upright wings extended to dry prior to its first flight, it is vulnerable to feeding fish.

Following mating, a female may fly lays eggs in the water, and spent adults often fall onto the surface, where they are again available as food for the fish.

Fly fishers can match the nymphal stage by using various well-known patterns like the Gold-Ribbed Hare's Ear, Halfback, Pheasant Tail or March Brown, tied in No. 14–10, 2x, weighted or unweighted.

For adult stages try an Adams, Blue-Winged Olive, Royal Wulff, Light Hendrickson, Humpy or slim Tom Thumb tied with a yellow, green or red body, No. 14–10, 3x fine hooks.

A subspecies of Ephemeroptera is midges, smallest of the raised-wing flies, the hatches of which can be enormous. Use No. 18 and 16 midge-type, no-hackle dry flies in pale colors or black. When floated in the surface film, these can be useful for grayling and whitefish.

Another species inhabiting cold, fast-flowing waters is the stone fly of the Plecoptera order. These hard-winged flies have four long, narrow, shiny or horny wings. When a fly sits at rest, it appears somewhat caddislike with wings folded close beside the abdomen. They vary greatly in size—large specimens may have wing spans of nearly 2" (5 cm) while others are barely ¾" (2 cm).

Of several stone fly species in the Arctic, two predominate and are of interest to fly fishers: giant stone fly (Pteronarcyidae) and western yellow stone fly (Perlodidae).

Stone fly nymphs are creepers, actively crawling around rocky river-bed bottoms. They are robust creatures with antennae on the head, two tails and a wing case that becomes quite prominent. Some larger forms are carnivorous.

Fish often intercept migrating nymphs before they hatch. At maturity, nymphs crawl onto dry land during twilight nights. They seek shelter under rocks until their transformation is complete and then emerge as fully winged adults. Mating follows soon after. Then females return to the water, fluttering across the surface as they deposit their eggs. This disturbance attracts feeding fish like a dinner bell.

Fly fishers can represent smaller Perlodidae nymphs with yellow-tan or ginger-red stone fly patterns about No. 12, weighted or unweighted on heavy wire 2x hooks with straight eyes, also the large black Pteronarcyidae on No. 8–4 hooks. Straight hooks work well; however, special emergent-type hooks like Mustad 37160 are available. Tie the thorax as a flattened structure and emphasize the wing cases.

For adult stone fly patterns try a pale Elk Hair Caddis type tied with a yellow-olive body for the smaller yellow stone fly, and a large Deer Hair type with a dark body for the larger Pteronarcyidae.

The Trichoptera order is of great importance in all stages: larvae, nymph and adult. The larval phase is commonly seen crawling about on river bottoms or lake beds, where it creates a tubular-shaped, portable case from sand particles, gravel, wood chips and similar detritus. At full development it pupates within the closed case. When emergence occurs, while still in the pupal envelope, the insect swims to the surface using a pair of powerful paddlelike legs. It may simply sit there for a while, skitter across the surface in an effort to become airborne or crawl up the stem of a water plant where it hatches as an adult. Some species are nocturnal hatching, others diurnal.

Adults have no tails and four wings which are covered with tiny hairs. At rest they lie closely along the abdomen in an inverted V- or roof-shape. In flight an insect appears to be flying with its body vertical. Adults mate at rest, but egg-laying females return to the water where they are vulnerable to fish.

Northern fly fishers will be familiar with the Hydropsychidae group—the Net Spinning Caddis—a diurnal flying species. A net-spinner builds a web and tunnel of silk on or between stones on the riverbed, which funnels in minute organisms and vegetable matter flowing with the current. Turn over a few rocks to collect local caddis specimens for identification.

A good way to keep caddis identification uncomplicated is to group them as large (8–12" / 20–30 cm), medium (4–8" / 10–20 cm) and small (under 4" /

10 cm). You can further categorize them by colors and shades. Most are some shade of brown, ranging from pale yellow-fawn to dark red-brown, grey-brown to almost black. A general rule is to use larger sizes early in the season and smaller sizes later on. Caddis patterns can imitate cased larvae, pupae as they swim to the surface, winged adults trying to get airborne and egg-laying females.

Larva patterns can be tied in a basic "stick-fly" style, then colored green, olive brown, peacock herl, orange and yellow ribbed with pale yellow-green. Good sizes are No. 14 and 12 on long shank pupa hooks. Butt tags in fluorescent green or red are often incorporated as attractors. Fish these stick flies right on the bottom, very slowly.

For swimming pupae try a Gary LaFontaine–type of Emergent Sparkle Pupa or a sparsely tied, down-winged Swimming Caddis in No. 16, 14 and 12. Alternatively, patterns are the Careys and Halfbacks tied on middleweight wire hooks—2x or 2.5x long—and the soft partridge-hackled series: Partridge and Orange, Yellow, Brown, Green and Peacock in No. 18–12.

Emerging pupae in lakes swim upward with intermittent movements at a shallow angle. To copy this action, use a slow-sinking line and retrieve your fly approximately 4–6" (10–15 cm) then pause and repeat. For fishing in a river, use a floating line to make quartering downstream casts on a slightly slack line, presenting your fly on a dead-drift.

For adult imitations try the Elk Hair Caddis, Fluttering Caddis and Goddard's Caddis on No. 14–6, 2x or 3x hooks, in olive green, dark brown to light tan, or gray. This triangular- shaped pattern is very stable and can be skated upright without rolling over. Other patterns include Humpies and those ubiquitous Tom Thumbs.

A productive technique is to cast a dry fly ahead of cruising fish that are feeding on the surface and gently skate the fly to create a disturbance, which often triggers a strike.

Northern lakes are home to Gomphidae—club-tailed dragonflies—of which the nymphal stage is of interest to fly fishers. These large sedentary nymphs lie in wait to pounce on their prey, which can be any other invertebrate larvae or nymphs. The dragonfly nymph grows through instar, periodically molting its outer exoskeleton, and takes years to reach the adult stage. At emergence it crawls out of its aquatic environment onto the shore. There it splits out of the thorax and waits until the enlargement of its wings is complete before flying away as a dragonfly. The standard nymph pattern is a short-bodied deer-hair or seal-fur Gomphus in No. 8–4. Patterns representing adult dragonflies are of little use.

In the Amphipodae order is the very important freshwater lake shrimp or scud. Wherever present, fish feed on this species heavily. Amphipods are prolific breeders and available throughout the fish's active "eating season."

Scuds vary in size from less than ½–¾" (13–19 mm). They are olive green, or they may merge with the color of their surroundings. They are not open-water swimmers, but move along close to the bottom in short, hesitant, 3–6" (8–15-cm) spurts, so this is the way to fish it. The fly patterns are quite simple: No. 14–10, either 1x or 2x standard wet or special curved-back shrimp hooks. The basic tie is a seal fur body in olive, tan or gray, and a clear plastic shell back ribbed with gold or silver wire, or gray silk floss.

Hellgrammites occur in northern rivers and are particularly favored by grayling. Fly fishers have little from which to choose, the basic fly being a No. 6 or 4 straight-eyed streamer hook, weighted and tied black, with emphasis on the multiple legs. A substitute might be a black Woolly Bugger. Fish these deep, close to the river bottom.

If one insect family could be given a prize for colonizing coldwater lakes, it would be Chironomidae. This ubiquitous fly has thousands of forms; however, anglers should keep the diversity of the insect in focus by making patterns simple in size and color.

The insect develops through several stages. After an egg hatches into a larva, it takes on a blood-red, greenish or brown color. It is semi-mobile but spends most of its time in a tubular hole in the mud, where it feeds. At emergence into the pupal form, it leaves the tube and ascends straight up to the surface. Observant anglers will see the emergent form in the water surface. They may vary in size from ¼–¾" (6–18 mm) and in color from black (usually) to brown, olive-green, orange or red. They have distinct white breathing gills on top of the head–abdomen junction.

Upon reaching the surface, they wriggle to break through the surface film, after which the chironomid emerges from a splitting thorax as an adult flying form. Mating occurs almost immediately. Then a female drops her eggs into the water by skimming over the surface, dipping her abdomen into the water until the cycle is complete.

Fish feed most heavily on emerging pupae and occasionally on larvae and adults. Tie simple pupa imitations on No. 14–10, 2x hooks, using fine synthetic materials or peacock herl. The bodies can be black, gray, brown, green, olive or orange, and ribbed with gold, silver or copper wire, or gray silk. Adding a small herl head and prominent white or light-gray gills completes these simple patterns. Fish them in the surface film with a "static retrieve"—meaning dead slow or full stop.

For larvae use the classic "blood worm"—a simple, thin, wormlike form in the appropriate reddish color and ribbing. For adults, a typical Mosquito pattern or small slim Tom Thumb will work as well as anything.

Terrestrial insects occurring in forested areas north of the 60th parallel are ants (Hymenoptera), beetles (Coleoptera) and grasshoppers (Orthoptera). A few standard patterns might prove useful on occasion.

Although arctic species like grayling and whitefish are dependent on various insects throughout their particular life cycles, others must gain some serious weight in order to survive the rigors of juvenile life. Although arctic char, lake trout, pike and inconnu remain opportunistic, omnivorous feeders, they shift their eating habits to include a high protein diet of sticklebacks, sculpins, cisco, smelt, plus the fry and juveniles of other fish species, including their own kind. A fly box would be incomplete without a few patterns representing these species.

Stickleback (order Gasterosteidae) are generally less than 2" (5 cm) long. They have spines on the dorsal, pelvic and anal fins, with the number of spines on the dorsal used as a species identification. Most common in the north are the nine-spined, scaleless *Pungitius pungitius*. They are unusual in that the male dominates nest building and protection of young. At that time, it develops a reddish belly and flank color which is significant to the fly tier; however, the overall color is dark and takes on the tones of its surrounding environment.

Where sticklebacks are present, try a Clouser Minnow in green and white; an olive-brown Matuka with silver body, grizzly wings dyed green and a head of soft green hackle; a Matuka with a gray Mylar body and one turn of red hackle at the base of the head to simulate a male; or a dark Zonker with a red body. All on No. 8–4, long shank, 3x hooks.

Sculpins (Cottidae) are one of the largest families of fish. Freshwater *Cottus cognatus,* a wide-ranging northern species, are generally 2–4" (5–10 cm) long. The sculpin body shape is dominated by its broad, flattened head with prominent eyes, a rapidly tapering body to a thin wrist and large tail fin, and large, almost winglike pectoral fins. They live on the bottom, hiding under stones and cover except to dart out and intercept food. They prey on invertebrates, fish eggs and fry. Sculpins are an important food source for larger predatory fish, and sculpin fly patterns are of great use to fly fishers. Basic patterns are Muddler Minnows, Mega Divers and Woolheads tied on No. 8–2, long streamer hooks.

Cisco or lake herring *(Coregonus artedi)* have a limited northern distribution, occurring in a few lakes and rivers tributary to Hudson and James bays. Where present they are heavily preyed upon by pike, walleye and char. These are large baitfish averaging ½–1 ½ lb (225–680 g), so fly representations must be large. Try white Polar Aztecs or Muddler Heads with silver bodies and palmered white hackles on No. 2–2/0 hooks. Tie them to imitate bulk, but use the materials sparsely. This will help with casting and animation of the flies.

Smelt (order Osmeridae) are river fish with both freshwater and anadromous forms. Huge schools form in the spring and move up rivers and into streams to spawn, where they are heavily preyed upon by char and inconnu. Cisco patterns work equally well for smelt, as will a String Leech, which appears large—up to 5" (13 cm)—but has little weight, casts well and is very mobile in the water.

Large fish of all species feed on their own kind. Fly patterns that represent juvenile char, lake trout, pike, grayling and whitefish are always useful. Muddler Minnows with gold or silver bodies, Jack Sprats, Dahlberg Divers and Lefty's Deceivers are just a few worth putting to the test.

The life cycle of fish includes spawning runs, during which enormous masses of eggs are deposited on the riverbeds, providing an important food source for other species. Eggs vary in size and in shades of yellow, gold, pink and red. Try Glo-Bugs or simple egg patterns in No. 14–10.

Now, if none of the above flies work—it could happen—there is one last resort: Mammalia. Small mammals like voles, mice and lemmings occasionally end up in the water, where they fall victim to predatory pike and char. A popular pattern is a mouse fashioned from spun and clipped deer hair. If you are really desperate, you might even consider a duckling pattern—which requires a very large fly box and a sense of humor.

Dr. Martin Lamont's Must-Have Patterns for General Use on Trout, Char and Whitefish

- Dry: Blue-Winged Olive, Elk Hair Caddis, Humpy
- Wet: Carey Special, Gold-Ribbed Hare's Ear, Halfback, Muddler Minnow

CHAPTER II

BROOK TROUT

Ken Robins

B ROOK TROUT, OR AS SO MANY KNOW IT, SPECKLED TROUT—
how many anglers have fallen in love with this beautiful little coldwater
salmonid? There will always be trophy northern pike, lunker bass and
exciting Atlantic salmon, but when trout anglers speak of brook trout, it is with
care and love. It is a special species on our continent.

The native range for brook trout is the northeastern quadrant of North
America, where they live in the cold waters of the Hudson Bay and Atlantic
watersheds. When explorers and settlers arrived in areas that are now the
Maritime provinces and New England states, they found an abundance of this
tasty fish in the streams, lakes and rivers. Pushing farther west, settlers found
them in all tributaries of the Great Lakes system. This colorful little fish so
much resembled the brown trout they knew in the old country, they erro-
neously called it a trout. The truth is, there were no native species of trout in
the eastern half of this continent, only various species of char—but who could
have known that back in those days?

Brook trout and the closely related lake trout are actually members of the
char family, which also includes arctic char in its anadromous and landlocked
forms, bull trout of the Rocky Mountains region and Dolly Varden of the West
Coast (these last two species overlap into each other's territories). Recent

attempts to change the common name of brook trout to brook char have failed. After all, it was the speckled "trout" that past and present generations of anglers came to love, so "trout" it will be.

There are several strains of brook trout, almost as many as the major watersheds they inhabit. Settlers and early sport anglers were treated to brook trout of considerable size. One hundred years ago and more, Ontario's Nipigon River system boasted a great abundance of big brookies, many in the 10–14-lb (4.5–6-kg) class. The world record, a 14.5-lb (6.5-kg) fish caught by Dr. W. Cook in 1916, was from the Nipigon.

When I was a boy, the advertised place to go for trophy trout was God's Lake and God's River in northern Manitoba. Overfishing soon pushed that name into extinction. Then it was the Broadback River and its source, Assinica Lake in Quebec, that promised brook trout of 10 lb (4.5 kg) or more. That area, too, lost its appeal as the numbers of big fish declined, but big trout still swim in these and many other waters in the arctic watershed. Anglers still fly or canoe in to enjoy catching these trophy fish, and often, when they move on to new hot spots, the trout populations rebuild to levels where they can withstand limited or controlled fishing pressure.

Today, our provincial governments, with pressure from sportsmen's associations, are trying to manage this species more carefully. Many years ago the Newfoundland government, with the help and encouragement of fly-fishing pioneer Lee Wulff, acted quickly to limit the kill and the number of camps on the now famous Minipi River system in southern Labrador. There, anglers can still catch the pure strain of large, dark-colored brook trout that have been there since the Ice Age. Each angler may kill only one trout per week. Nearby, upper reaches of the Eagle River provide similar fishing opportunities, with brook trout of 5–10 lb (2–4.5 kg) fairly common. In Quebec, anglers in search of big brookies head for rivers in the Ungava Bay region, while in northern Ontario, rivers like the Winisk, Sutton and upper reaches of the Albany, still promise a large beautiful strain of this magnificent fish.

Fly fishers need not go into remote camps to find good brook-trout fishing. Roads through northern Ontario, Quebec and the Maritimes cross many productive trout rivers. In fact, a road now crosses the upper Broadback River, once accessible only to floatplanes. Even some Albany River tributaries that flow from the south cross Highway 11. Using such roads, we have walked from our car and caught 2- and 3-lb (1–1.35-kg) trout. With a little effort, anglers can travel by canoe from these road accesses to find brook trout that have endured very little fishing pressure. District offices of the Ministry of Natural Resources will direct anglers to good waters and provide maps to help make their adventures even easier.

Unfortunately, much of the original brook-trout range has been reduced. Agriculture, mining, logging, power dams and overfishing have destroyed their habitat or reduced numbers in some rivers to mere remnants of former populations. The efforts of conservation groups in southern parts of their range have restored some habitat, but changes in the overall picture are still slight. It will take many generations of effort by those concerned to undo the lack of forest cover, silted bottoms and warm water that now exist. In addition, the overkill of every large trout caught has dwarfed the strain in many streams throughout their southern range. This genetic depletion of fast-growing large fish may never be reversed, for in some streams brook trout mature and spawn at just 7–8" (18–20 cm). Fortunately, there are still many river systems with good populations that will now be preserved for future generations of anglers.

Knowing that brook trout are a char helps anglers understand where they can be found and what their habits are. Char prefer colder water than true trout. Brookies favor temperatures in the 50–60°F (10–16°C) range and need water with a high oxygen content. As many of our streams and rivers now warm up in the summer, they become marginal for brook trout. Anglers must locate suitable water if they hope to find them and do so bearing in mind that some sections may be devoid of fish while others may have good numbers. Coldwater spring sources usually make a big difference to nearby sections of a trout stream.

A significant characteristic of this stream char is its need to be under cover at all times during daylight hours. You must hunt for the sort of intimate places that might harbor them. In smaller streams they may hide beneath undercut banks or overhanging grasses, and they love the cover of brush or logs. Fishing a bright bucktail or streamer fly along the edges of such cover will almost always cause these aggressive fish to dart out and take a swipe at it. Using a bright fly, especially one with a white wing, allows you to watch the fly while maneuvering it in and around the shadowed areas of cover.

Another great source of cover is the broken surface of heavy riffles or rapids. Here brookies have cover, a continual source of drifting food and an increased oxygen supply compared to quieter sections of the river. Hunting for these microhabitats adds to the lure and fun of brook-trout fishing.

When the water is cold, brookies can be found searching for food virtually anywhere it is available. When the water warms, anglers must search pockets at the top end of rapids, where there is more oxygen, or hunt for cold spring sources, where brookies will congregate in great numbers. Unfortunately, this characteristic makes brook trout vulnerable to fishing pressure. Too often, summertime anglers have wiped out all the brook trout in several miles of river by finding them huddled and hungry in a few tiny sanctuaries of cold water. Special regulations and reduced limits are helping to protect brook trout from this kind of carnage, but these laws will never be enough. Anglers must learn— or be taught—to respect the vulnerability of these fish in such times and to avoid them until the waters cool and they spread out once again.

A major disadvantage of fishing brook trout in streams is their desire to strike at almost anything that moves—they always seem hungry and are rarely selective. They not only take natural or imitation baits well, but also attack flashy lures or flies with color and glitter that do not resemble anything which looks remotely like natural food. This fact allowed early fly fishers to create the beautiful attractor flies that were so popular 50 to 100 years ago, when Silver Doctors, Parmachene Belles and Brook Trout Fins were commonly found in their fly boxes. Other brightly colored patterns that most present-day anglers still carry are Mickey Finn and Royal Coachman wet flies or bucktail streamers. A first cousin to the latter, the Royal Wulff, is a great dry fly for brookies.

A dry fly that my wife, Sue, uses almost exclusively is the Trude. This western pattern is a caddis imitation that works whenever brook trout are rising to any type of insect. Its white wing makes it very visible on dark water and in the dull light of late evening. The hair wing also makes it quite buoyant, even on rough waters.

Another semi-attractor pattern I use for brook trout is the Skunk, which I have borrowed from West Coast steelheaders. It works well as either a small wet fly or as a larger bucktail.

Everyone has their favorite flies, and the list is never the same for two anglers. Success always convinces us that a successful fly must have some superior quality; however, when someone asks, "What works best for brook trout?" the most truthful answer is "Anything."

Fly fishers should be constantly observant. As well, they should not always stay with the routines of camps into which they go. Vivid in my mind is a late August trip that a friend and I made to the Minipi River many years ago. The routine was to get up leisurely for breakfast around 7:00 A.M., then canoe from camp to the section of river we were to fish. We carried a box lunch and fished until late afternoon when everyone returned to camp for supper. The evenings were devoted to tying flies, relaxing and telling tall tales.

We saw few flies over the water and dry flies were not effective. We did catch what we thought was our share of big brook trout—two or three each per day—but for such a remote haven something was missing. One day I noticed some of the back eddies were matted with caddis shucks—empty skins of the pupa stage. I knew that caddis hatched in the early morning and laid their eggs at dusk, so we were obviously missing both activities. The guides had no idea what happened at dawn or dusk because they had never been on the river then!

Bill and I convinced our guide to eat supper early and head back down for the evening fishing. What occurred was an experience that I do not expect ever to repeat. We went to the most likely pool for this kind of activity. A riffle poured over a gravel bar into the left side of the pool, and then the water became slick and glided in a semi-circle past big boulders and left the pool at right angles to the way it entered. The evening sky was heavily overcast when great numbers of caddis adults in three different species came out early to lay their eggs. Trout started rising everywhere.

We gave our spare rod to the guide and asked him to join in. The fish were not selective, so we all ended up using a Royal Wulff dry fly. Its white wing made it very visible on the dark water in the dull light. It was absurd! Rising trout everywhere—fighting, big fish—and us upset that they fought so long because we wanted to get our flies back onto the water to catch another giant. When darkness set in after almost two hours of frantic fishing, the three of us had landed 24 brook trout that were all 18–22" (45–55 cm) long.

Fishing in still water is more challenging, for the trout are usually well fed and not so eager to rush at anything that moves. Flies must match natural food sources in the waters to be fished. It might be minnow imitations in one place, damsel fly nymphs in another or egg-laying spinners of some insect at yet another location. Timing is also important. Fishing is better when light conditions are dull, whether dawn, dusk or just a heavy overcast. There are more hours of good fishing in the spring, when waters are cold right up to the surface. In summer, brook trout venture from the cold depths to the warmer surface only at dark, when available food sources become abundant. There is nothing like casting a large, bushy dry fly into the silent darkness when hefty brook trout are loudly slurping up big may fly spinners.

One fly pattern has withstood the test of time as both a bucktail streamer and a dry fly. Created many years ago on Ontario's Nipigon River, the Muddler Minnow is one of the world's best-known flies. Invented to imitate a sculpin, this fly has been used to imitate just about every minnow that swims. As well, in smaller sizes it can be dressed and floated as a dry fly to imitate everything from big may flies and moths to grasshoppers. I can't imagine a brook-trout angler who is not carrying at least one style of the Muddler Minnow. All season, I carry them in sizes No. 12–2. They are wonderful to use while searching the waters for big, nocturnal fish that feed only at night. The pattern's effectiveness was demonstrated one spring night. It was dark, almost 10:00 P.M. as I slowly fished a long No. 2 Muddler through a quiet pool. A fish hit, and after a very brief struggle, I landed a 5" (13-cm) brook trout—less than twice the length of my fly. To my way of thinking, there is no limit to what a Muddler Minnow can accomplish.

The equipment required to catch brook trout varies considerably, due primarily to the vast differences in the waters they inhabit. The Albany River, which you can't yell across in most sections, requires different tackle than a tiny meadow creek you can jump across. We have worn chest waders, hip boots and even running shoes—the latter being great in warm summer weather to keep cool. A very important part of your footwear on almost all freestone streams and rivers is felt soles. The round, polished stones and boulders develop an algae coating that makes walking on them treacherous. Even if an injury or a dousing doesn't occur, your ankles and feet will always end up bruised and sore if you wade without felts.

The rods and lines we use vary a lot. On small streams Sue and I use short,

7–8' rods that take 4–5-weight lines. We sometimes use 8 ½–9' rods with 8-weight lines on large northern rivers, especially in foul weather when the winds really pound us in those wide valleys. Overall though, the one I use most and recommend as a single rod for anyone is a 9' one that takes a 6-weight line. Its action is soft enough that I can use a 5-weight line for dry-fly fishing on finer waters. I could successfully fish this one rod everywhere I have been.

A weight-forward floating line will be used almost all of the time. Our lines are all loaded on single-action fly reels, and we carry a spare spool with a high-speed, sink-tip line. In heavy spring runoff or in the deep runs of a northern river, it is sometimes necessary to get down to the fish. If they are feeding on the bottom, your fly must also be there, which might even require some weight attached to the leader or the fly itself. Anglers must be observant and willing to experiment to find ways to reach the fish. A trout will almost always take a fly, but it must be close enough for the trout to see or hear.

We normally use 9' tapered leaders, but exceptions to this rule are two feet shorter on sink-tip lines and a few feet longer when casting over still waters. As brookies are not usually leader shy, the tippet needn't be very light; however, it should match the fly to ensure that it works properly. Most of the time, we use 5x tippets of 4–5-lb test. These work well for most dry flies and small wets or steamers. We rarely use a tippet that is 2x or larger, except when night fishing—when the largest fish of your life might try to rip the rod right out of your hand.

One item every angler must carry is insect repellent because brook trout, mosquitoes and black flies live and eat together. However, be careful of your choice and use of repellents. The liquid used to carry the actual repellent is usually very corrosive to paint and plastics. Fly lines in particular are vulnerable. Try to find a repellent in stick form which can be applied without getting any on your palms and fingers. If you use a liquid, wash your hands after applying it and accept the bites you get there. There has to be one negative feature to brook-trout fishing, and this is surely it.

Brook trout deserve respect because their beauty and, unfortunately, delicious taste, are a match for any fish. But more important, no matter where or how they are fished, anglers usually leave the water with a sense that something special has happened that day. Pike, bass or salmon anglers rarely go home pleased and satisfied that their best catch of the day was 8" (20 cm) long, but brook-trout aficionados do so regularly. Size is rarely their goal; rather, it is aesthetics, scenery, solitude, the drift of a fly line through the air and presenting their fly with delicate accuracy in some tiny, dark, difficult pocket of water. It is enjoyable, but there is also something intimate about it. I think these are the reasons we who fish for brook trout feel so very close to them and why we elevate them to such high levels in our minds.

KEN ROBINS' MUST-HAVE PATTERNS FOR BROOK TROUT

- Dry: Royal Coachman, Royal Wulff, Trude
- Wet: Mickey Finn, Skunk

CHAPTER 12

PRINCE EDWARD ISLAND'S BROOK TROUT

Paul Marriner

W HILE PRINCE EDWARD ISLAND (PEI) OFFERS LIMITED fishing for rainbows, steelhead and Atlantic salmon, its native brook trout are widespread, both resident and sea-runs. The island bubbles with cold springs, and some amazing fishing can be found by merely dropping a fly beside many roadside culverts. Larger streams like the Morell and Dunk Rivers are also productive.

"You've done a tremendous job here," I said to Dave Biggar as we walked along Trout River in May. Digger logs, deflectors and overhead cover structures were in evidence in every section of the stream. In addition to habitat rehabilitation, Dave and his volunteers must cope with a perennial Prince Edward Island problem: bank erosion and runoff from agricultural operations.

"You'd catch lots of small trout if you fished today," Dave said, "but our season really begins when the sea-runs start arriving in a month or so."

Tom Corcoran had voiced these same sentiments when we fished the Morell together, so off Dave and I went to the estuary to search for bigger brookies in the salt.

Although "salter" is one of several colloquial names given to sea-run brook trout, I'll co-opt it for the quarry in salt water. On Prince Edward Island, a combination of flat countryside and rock-free soil resulted in the formation of extensive, relatively shallow inlet bays. These are often spanned at a narrows by a combination of causeways and low bridges, which create significant tidal currents. Salters congregate in these flows and in the nearby shallows.

As is true for virtually all inshore saltwater fishing, knowledge of the tides is critical. On the Island, the hot time at the bridges is the last three hours of the ebb tide. Once the tide turns, the flow quickly becomes heavily loaded with vegetative debris. Near high tide, while the water is clear, it's too deep for effective fly fishing.

At other tide times, it's more productive to fish in the bays themselves. This is best done from a boat, but there are a few places where cruising trout are regularly found along the shorelines that are suitable for wading. Such spots are best found by conversations with local anglers or by watching the shoreline closely while exploring an area.

Most residents fish for salters with bait, the favorites being a sand shrimp and a local minnow known as "gudgeon" (the proper name is mummichog). The few local fly fishers try to match these species with shrimp imitations like Lester the Lobster (derived from the Squamish Poacher pattern originating on the West Coast) or an orange Whiskers, and with a variety of small streamers. Archie Clark, an experienced island fly fisher, doubles his odds by tying a streamer on the point and a shrimp imitation on a dropper about 18" (46 cm) up the leader. "While I catch most trout on the dropper," Archie told me, "enough take the streamer to make me keep it on."

Just at dusk one evening, I saw dozens of sand shrimp leaping across the surface of a shallow beach area. The occasional splash and wake confirmed that they were under attack by trout. A half-dozen casts before the action stopped yielded nothing. Later, over after-dark coffee, an experienced local angler told me that this is a common occurrence, but that no fly fishers he knew of had ever solved the puzzle. Sand shrimp are about 2" (5 cm) long, and a little research turned up the interesting fact that they exhibit bioluminescence.

Armed with this knowledge, I hope to return to Prince Edward Island with several new patterns, including a few tied with phosphorescent materials. In the meantime, if you happen to get there before me, bear this information in mind. It could make for some memorable fishing.

PAUL MARRINER'S MUST-HAVE PATTERNS FOR PRINCE EDWARD ISLAND BROOK TROUT

- Lester the Lobster
- Orange Whiskers

BROOK TROUT WITH PECAN BUTTER

Turns brookies into a marvelous meal.
(Makes four servings)

4—brook trout
Salt and pepper to taste

PECAN BUTTER

¾ cup—toasted pecans, divided—175 mL
5 tbsp—butter—75 mL
2 tbsp—chopped onion—25 mL
Pinch—cayenne pepper

1. Brush trout with olive oil, salt and pepper, and then broil until cooked through. Measure fish at thickest part and allow a cooking time of about 10 minutes per inch (4 minutes per cm). Once flesh is opaque, it is done.

2. For pecan butter, place ½ cup (125 mL) toasted pecans in food processor with butter, chopped onion and a pinch of cayenne pepper. Pulse until well blended.

3. Spoon pecan butter over fish. Coarsely chop remaining pecans and sprinkle over the top. Serve with half a baked yam, sweet potato or squash drizzled with maple syrup and cherry tomato gratin.

–Wayne Phillips

CHAPTER 13

FLY-INS

Dr. Martin Lamont

A FTER MANY HOURS OF PONDERING OVER 1:250,000 FIELD survey maps, I decided on a new destination for a river fishing trip. Ahh, the best-laid plans . . .

My route involved many miles of lonely driving along the dusty Dempster Highway, which was under construction at the time. After driving as far as I could, it was evident that I was short of my destination. Although I could see the remote Peel River valley by the contours of the land, my optimism faded. Obviously, hiking through the bush from road's end would be hazardous, with every possibility of my becoming disoriented. With no alternative plan, I cursed my bad fortune and wasted time, then retraced my route along that damned gravel road.

In those days, my backyard play areas were sparsely populated northeastern British Columbia, Yukon and the western Northwest Territories. Although the local fishing was good, it still necessitated driving long distances. The logical progression to greater fishing experiences was to fly in.

Anglers are always seeking adventure in new, unexplored locations, and Canada's vastness offers some real challenges. It is 3,400 miles (5,400 km) from the Atlantic coast to the Pacific, and if a latitude line were drawn at a northerly 55°, there are approximately 2.7 million square miles (7 million square km) filled with fish above and beyond any roads.

Considering that the majority of Canada's angling population lives close to the 49th parallel, thoughts of northern fly-in fishing trips are compelling; however, in some cases, the prospect of visiting a remote lodge may seem intimidating. Ontario, for example, has some 2 million waterways in the form of creeks, rivers, ponds, lakes and inland freshwater seas. Where does one start?

It should not be surprising that world-class fly-fishing locations in Canada have been "discovered" by countless adventurous explorers. Many now operate air charters, lodges and wilderness camps, and there are lots of knowledgeable people in those groups who are willing to help you plan a successful trip.

Maximize your fishing time by contacting the tourism office in the province or territory in which you are interested and ask specifically for information on fly-in destinations. Talk to as many sources as possible, asking where to catch the fish you seek, the best times to go, how to get there, what special equipment is required and the costs.

Timing is critical. Some areas cater heavily to hunting, so air charters are prebooked each year with hunters, guides and outfitters. In such cases, charter services prefer accommodating anglers at either end of the hunting season.

Fly-ins require lots of preparation and a firmly committed group of fellow fly fishers. All should be willing to contribute their fair share after determining what is required by way of transportation, maps, camping equipment, food supplies, boats, motors, fuel, canoes—all of which may take months to organize.

There is effort and cost in planning an extended stay or extensive overland or river trip, so your group should have a flexible time frame, say more than two weeks.

Consider hiring a large aircraft; in the long run it may prove more economical. Small aircraft may carry only one canoe strapped to its pontoons, and its limited internal cargo space also affects a party's size. A slightly larger, twin-engine plane may carry up to three canoes and all of the camping equipment for six anglers. Thus, splitting the costs six ways makes sense.

If the destination is remote, the pilot must be familiar with important details like whether the water is deep enough to land safely and whether one can beach on a gravel or sandbar for easy unloading and loading. Equally important, the pickup area should be predetermined and plans made for an alternative pickup location if necessary.

Canadian aviation history is closely linked to the development of northern communities. Anglers, lodge owners and outfitters owe much to the bush pilots who flew floatplanes like the classic de Havilland Beavers, single and twin engine de Havilland Otters. More common these days are Cessna 185 and 206, and Bell Jet Ranger helicopters. Although some lodges and logging or mining camps have remote dirt landing strips, there is far more need for floatplanes.

For extended trips, choose your fishing companions with care. Some should have wilderness experience, so their skills can be used to help out. Otherwise, consider hiring an experienced camp boss.

Inform several people of your intended destination, the expected length of time you intend to be there and your return date. The Royal Canadian Mounted Police (RCMP) can provide a Wilderness Trip Registration form to officially record your plans.

While summer tent camping on the tundra near the outlet of Kathawachaga Lake in the Northwest Territories (NWT), I set out early one morning to fish by boat. Passing a nearby island, I spotted a large group of people vigorously waving at me. I went ashore and discovered they were canoeing down the Burnside River to Bathurst Inlet, which was still three days' travel. After battling constant strong headwinds on the open waters of Contwoyto Lake, they were behind schedule and had run out of food. This sorry group had put up camp the night before, unaware of my presence. They were invited to my camp and soon revived by a large breakfast. Reluctantly, they continued their journey later that day, but fully provisioned from my supplies.

Ensure you have enough food, spare parts, boat props and fuel. Thorough preparation pays off; alternatively, a resupply flight is very expensive.

It pays to start off with a group of healthy, low-risk companions, but a comprehensive first-aid medical kit and a bush radio are also essential.

Tents should be lightweight for hiking or canoe trips, but for site-specific summer camps used for prolonged periods, use quality canvas tents. When camping in bear country, fortify the cooking tent with "bear boards" (nailed 4 x 8' plywood sheets), and use all other recommended bear-avoidance tactics.

Surprisingly, fly-fishing equipment is not very important, so keep it simple. Limit yourself to pack rods and a couple of reels, lines, a selection of flies, lightweight (and reliable) waders, self-inflating personal flotation devices which are not too bulky and spare waterproof bags in which to keep a change of clothing and your sleeping bag.

Getting to these last frontiers starts with international carriers delivering anglers to airports at Winnipeg, Saskatoon, Vancouver and Whitehorse, with Edmonton and Yellowknife serving a wider northern distribution. From these centers, scheduled carriers fly to smaller towns, most of which have nearby float-plane facilities. These charter operators provide fly-ins to full-service lodges, drop-off and pickup services to remote tent camps, day trips to alpine lakes, lake hopping, and camping and heli-fishing on some rivers.

Northern wilderness trips are confined to a short season, mostly July, August and September; however, some western locations open in the spring.

I will share a few of my experiences, but bear in mind that there are many more excellent locations.

The Coastal Islands and Saltchuck Floatplanes

"SPECTACULAR" DESCRIBES FLY-INS throughout British Columbia, there being a great variety of terrain and fish species. Flights which originate in Vancouver and Victoria connect with peripheral areas closer to the action, places like Campbell River, Prince George, Fort St. James, Smithers, Burns Lake, Nimpo Lake and Fort Nelson.

Small floatplanes are perfect for exploring remote coastal rivers on the Queen Charlotte Islands, a land of permanently green trees and undergrowth dripping wet from constant, moisture-laden weather fronts blowing in from the Pacific Ocean, where misty landscapes merge with the sky and rich marine environs embrace the archipelago.

We touched down with a watery swish as the pilot dump-landed onto a small coastal tarn and then beached. It was only a short forest hike to reach the open river estuary where smells of salt and seaweed blended with cries of the gulls. It was late fall and vast schools of coho were advancing with the incoming tide, waves of fish pushing upstream. Coho broke the surface with their backs, and out in the surf occasional fish hurtled into the air to avoid pursuing seals.

Our group split up, some to the river, others to the beach. There was no need for deep wading on the beach; knee depth was enough to avoid the narrow seaweed line which so annoyingly fouls leaders and flies. We used intermediate sinking lines to cast No. 8 flies with silver bodies, sparse white hair wings and fluorescent green heads. Fishing was hot—about 20 hook-ups, some bright silver fish, others with the pinkish purple color of early ripening fish, all 5–15 lb (2–7 kg).

In the river, our companions were casting No. 4 Purple Egg-Sucking Leeches with equal success. Coho after cartwheeling coho, hard-fighting, were more out of than in the water. At one point the density of fish was astonishing; the water went dark as they swam by the anglers. So many fish, so much fun— a rare utopian occasion. I stopped fishing, content to sit back and simply watch the arcing fly rods as others played and released those wild salmon.

Coastal Inlets and Heli-Fishing Day Trips

I AM NOT GOOD AT WAITING when I want to go fishing. On this gray spring dawn, standing in an empty municipal airport while waiting for my three tardy fishing buddies, I was restless and impatient. The lights of the little Cessna finally appeared on the horizon, and as it descended my spirits rose. Our party now complete, fly-fishing gear was transferred into a Bell Jet Ranger and the day's adventure began.

A chopper is quite a contrast to a fixed-wing aircraft, and my Cessna pilot friend was thrilled at the vertical lift-off and maneuverability. In no time we were heading east toward the sunrise still beyond the Coast Mountains, which were blanketed with fresh snow. The flight was spectacular. Under an hour's flying time took us over glaciers and snow pinnacles, past white mountain sheep high on patches of alpine pasture, and then a rapid, slightly scary descent down a U-shaped valley to where the Homathko and Southgate rivers flow into Bute Inlet.

The green river water was low, clear and very cold—as was the early morning air. It is surprising how quickly enthusiastic anglers can prepare their equipment—rods with sinking lines and fly patterns resembling emerging salmon fry still with their yellow-pink yolk sacs. We knew there were big sea-run cutthroat trout and Dolly Varden targeting chum fry on their outward migration to the ocean.

All rods were soon bent into strong, fighting cutts and Dollies to 5 lb (2 kg), beautifully colored with pale silver tones of fish fresh from the sea. After fishing through one section of accessible pools, it was easy to board the chopper and quickly relocate farther downstream. We covered a lot of water that day without any need for strenuous hiking through rough country—lazy fishing at its finest.

As the day progressed, the sun warmed the snowfields higher up. As snowmelt increased the volume of flow, the water lost its clarity, clouding slightly with glacial silt. By early afternoon the bite slowed; then with cold downdrafts off the mountaintops, the fishing abruptly stopped. Nobody cared. The day was already complete and our homeward helicopter flight happily anticipated.

The Chilcotin Fly-In and Rainbow Paradise

THE CHILCOTIN, a vast plateau surrounded by the lofty Coast Mountains, has Nimpo and Anahim lakes at its center. They are 250 air miles (400 km) north of Vancouver, and over 180 miles (300 km) by road from the city of Williams Lake. Nimpo Lake is an active aviation center, servicing the local area and points north. It is home base to many lodges that provide good local fishing and daily fly-ins to remote outpost camps, some with cabins that have full-service, boats and motors. There are several charter services and all resorts operate their own floatplanes. In the northeast arm of the lake, those with private floatplanes will find moorage facilities and aircraft services including fuel, oil and servicing. Anahim Lake, just 10 miles (16 km) away, has a 3,000' (900 m) airstrip for wheeled planes.

This area offers exceptional wilderness fishing for rainbow trout in lakes and rivers. The Dean River is world renowned for summer steelhead, as are the Atnarko and Chilcotin rivers, and the Blackwater River for its wild rainbow trout. Lakes like Eliguk, Kappan, Hotnarko, Crazy Bear and Gatcho are all rainbow trout paradises, and Knot Lake yields Dolly Varden to 10 lb (4.5 kg), as well as coastal cutthroat trout.

Fly fishing is best in spring and fall, but some big trout are regularly caught during the summer by fishing deep with fast sink lines, usually with black Doc Spratleys or Olive Scud patterns. When colorful rainbow trout that average 2–3 lb (1–1.5 kg) catapult high into the air, you understand why this is considered a fly-fishing paradise.

The Northwest—Yukon Klondike Charters

LIKE ITS PEOPLE, there is a youthfulness in this northern land, which has more square miles per angler than the rest of Canada. Travelers are tempted by excellent fly-fishing opportunities for lake trout, pike, grayling, Dolly Varden and whitefish—including inconnu. Transected by the Alaska Highway and only a few side roads, fly-ins are essential. Whitehorse has waterfront floatplane facilities on the Yukon River. Many fishing destinations are within 50–200 air miles (80–320 km), so it is only a few hours' flying time to various full-service lodges and wilderness camps.

The bright yellow Super Cub made a long approach, then descended onto the remote Yukon lake and touched down smoothly. After we disembarked near the lake's outlet, I quickly decided to split from the group as they paddled in their float tubes across the flat, calm lake. Exploring the outlet river was made easy by its low water, and the large boulders were great for walking on. The first few pools were crystal clear, and fish shadows were visible in the depths. Looking closer, I identified them as Dolly Varden.

It was frustrating as fish after fish followed my flies out of the depths, almost into the shallows at my feet, but refused to take. I accidentally hooked a small fingerling, and when it started darting about, it was instantly consumed by a 5-lb (2-kg) Dolly which set my rod to bucking and throbbing. When I finally brought it into the shallows, I discovered the Dolly was not hooked, merely clamped tight onto the now dead and badly mutilated fingerling. The almost grounded Dolly eventually opened its mouth, and slowly departed for deeper water. Clearly, Dollies prefer meat to feathers.

Farther downstream, where feeder creeks were slightly coloring the main stem, I found a midstream school of feeding grayling. They were holding in fast water and constantly rising to small blue-gray ephemeroptera. They were very selective and required constant changes of flies. A small Gray Wulff worked for a few fish, then a Gray Hendrickson started more hook-ups. I realized that as the grayling became familiar with one pattern, a change provoked more strikes.

The next half mile of river was white water. There I dredged the deeper pockets with a big, ugly, ultra-fast-sinking black Hellgrammite pattern to take grayling to 3 lb (1.5 kg). Below that section, the river again formed deep, isolated pools, and the rock formation changed to brown, broken sandstone. Fishing with Glo-Bugs, Mickey Finns and Sculpin patterns constantly produced smaller, darker Dollies with bright scarlet spots, strangely different from those caught in the outlet's clear water.

My return to the lake revealed that my companions had found good fun in the shallow bays catching pike on streamer flies. The aroma of filleted and cubed "Yukon gold pike" sizzling in the frying pan was a harbinger of one of the finest of wilderness meals.

Alberta

ALBERTA'S FLY-OUT CENTERS are widely separated. The southwest Rocky Mountain area is served by Calgary and Canmore which, being major tourist centers, have aircraft for heli-hiking and fishing in the high mountains readily available. To the northeast of the province, in the boreal forests and to some extent in the northwest Caribou Mountains, are about 10 fly-in lodges with fishing for lake trout, pike, walleye and whitefish. Some are the original full-service fishing lodges like Andrew Lake and Christina Lake, while others are tent camps. Northern Alberta fly-in operators use Edmonton, Cold Lake and Fort McMurray as home bases.

The Rocky Mountains and Alpine Adventure

SITUATED AMID THE WESTERN SLOPES of the Rocky Mountains is Golden, British Columbia, a good departure point to remote, spectacular

Fortress Lake. The only access to the lodge at Fortress is by a long hike in from Alberta or a short hop in a 185 Cessna floatplane from Golden. The latter is the choice of most anglers.

Located in British Columbia, just west of the Alberta border, Fortress Lake is a narrow body of water about 7 miles (11 km) long. It supports large native bull trout to 15 lb (7 kg), lake trout to 20 lb (9 kg) and brook trout, which were mistakenly planted between 1920 and 1930 by Alberta Fish and Wildlife personnel who thought the lake was in Alberta. The brookies are now naturalized and grow to 5 lb (2 kg).

One fall, when a friend visited from Italy, we decided to hike in on a route starting at the southwest corner of Jasper National Park. We were well prepared with hiking gear and camping equipment for our 16-mile (26 km) jaunt, including multiple freshwater fishing licenses for Alberta, British Columbia, and Jasper National Park. We drove Highway 93, the Icefield Parkway, and left our vehicle at the Honeymoon Lake campground.

The hiking trail starts close to where the Sunwapta River meets the big Athabasca River. The Sunwapta is part of the upper Athabasca drainage, and here we fished the confluence for bull trout, brook trout, whitefish, and occasional rainbows to 3 lb (1.5 kg). Luckily, it was late summer, so the river was finally running clear of silt from high altitude snowmelt. Our trek was delayed by many fine fish.

Our plans included taking pack rods. My favorite for small lakes and rivers is an old fiberglass fly rod—a 7', 2.5-weight, sturdy enough to handle the abuse encountered in camping situations. It works great with a shortened 5-weight shooting head, performs well for close-river casting, and attached to a light running line, it can be cast a mile when necessary on the lakes. A 7-weight, 9' rod which breaks down to 18" (46 cm) was in reserve for the big lake.

The trail followed southward along the Chaba River and required a challenging fording of the river to eventually reach the remote back-country campsite at the lake's east end. On the trail we heard and saw several helicopters in the distance. They were flying out of Canmore, Alberta, with heli-hikers and anglers. Westward down the long lake, Serenity Glacier and the Hooker Icefield dominated the scene, and to the north, Fortress Mountain rose over 3,000' (900 m).

Upon reaching the lake we pressed on to comfortable Fortress Lake Lodge, where we were made welcome in tent-camp accommodations and provided with good food and the latest fishing reports. Our hosts said fish were present in several feeder rivers and creeks and at the outlet. We were told that fishing is best right after ice-out in June and that the overall drift of schools of brook trout was from the east end in the spring and to the west by season's end.

The following day we were provided with a 14' aluminum boat and outboard motor to search out the schools. We boated all over the lake, checking for shoreline cover such as submerged logs, trees that had blown down along the shoreline, points, bars and drop-offs, plus any inlets that looked like holding water. Using fast-sinking lines we tried No. 6–2 Leeches and Woolly Buggers in black, olive and yellow, and a few sculpin and fry patterns.

Once fish were located there was a tendency for sudden action at each location. Brook trout do not show at the surface, so we kept scanning the lake for physical characteristics that might prove attractive to them. Growing whitecaps blew us off the lake in the late afternoon, by which time we had a few good fish to our credit.

Around midmorning the next day, a floatplane from Golden arrived with a new party of anglers. The return flight was not booked—a perfect opportunity for us "hike-in–fly-out" lazybones. The floatplane was buffeted violently on the trip, but the bumpy air time was well under an hour—hardly long enough to reflect on our wonderful alpine fishing adventure.

Northwest Territories—Piscatorial Penultimate

VISITORS TO THE YELLOWKNIFE AIRPORT are familiar with the large mural of an *inukshuk* painted by Ontario artist Ken Kirkby, an avid angler and steelheader. The *inukshuk* is symbolic of the arctic tundra, a stone way-marker for ancient and modern travelers. Coincidentally, its protruding arms closely resemble the shape of an aircraft, leading one to wonder if the ancients foresaw the day when air travel would dominate transportation in the north.

Although enjoyable, my visits to Yellowknife often made me feel the need to leave the large hotel's comfort for some outpost camp. It is only a short downhill walk from the city center to the lakeside floatplane staging area.

Morning rush hour is evident as taxiing floatplanes await their turn to take off for points west, north and east.

It was a sunny morning when my teenage son and I left Yellowknife for a three-hour charter flight into the central coastal Arctic. We flew over an extensive expanse of forest which eventually gave way to a seemingly endless blanket of tundra, sun-dimpled by countless lakes and rivers. Our bird's-eye view enhanced the sinuous eskers, scoured glacial bedrock and drumlins, pointing out the path of an ancient, vanished ice field.

On previous trips we had successfully caught lake trout, grayling and freshwater char on flies. This time our tent camp was located on high ground near a sizable coastal river. After disembarking on the gravel beach, we met with the camp boss, who had spent most of his working life in the Canadian Arctic, and his Inuit assistants. Leisurely, we discussed our strategies, for there was no rush to go fishing in the northern summer when day merges into the twilight of night only briefly. Arctic char was our target species, and I reflected on the Inuit wisdom of following the rhythm of the seasonal timetable. After the inland passage of migrating caribou herds, the Inuit headed for the coast to make a fishing camp at the same site. They were good fishermen. As soon as the river is free of ice, char that have overwintered in fresh water head downstream to salt water, and then later in the year, other year-classes of large, anadromous arctic char return to the river to spawn.

Using heavy 8- and 9-weight rods with fast-sinking lines, we cast No. 6–2/0 streamer flies—Polar Shrimps, Mickey Finns, Marabou Streamers, Woolly Buggers in orange, chartreuse, and silver and blue. These flies attracted fresh, fighting, sea-run char. They took gently and rarely jumped, but they ran—deep and fast like silver torpedoes—and did not give up easily. We were occasionally blanked when the fish went off the bite, but never for long. The runs in that area are strong and large in volume. The world record of 32 lb 9 oz (14.8 kg) was caught just 125 miles (200 km) north, and it will be broken. It is only a matter of time.

Dr. Martin Lamont's Must-Have Patterns for Fly-Ins

• Fry or Alevin patterns

- Glennie's Green 'n' Silver
- Hellgrammite
- Mickey Finn
- Polar Shrimp
- Purple Egg-Sucking Leech

CHAPTER 14

LAKE TROUT

Dr. Martin Lamont

T HROUGHOUT NORTH AMERICA, LAKE TROUT *(Salvelinus namaycush)* are known by a variety of names: laker, gray trout, mackinaw and togue being most common. To confuse the issue further, the misnomer "trout" is widely used by anglers and fisheries biologists despite the fact that ichthyologists have classified lake trout as char, members of the genus *Salvelinus*. Related members include arctic char, Dolly Varden, bull trout and brook trout.

Physically, all char have similar characteristics—deeply forked tails and large heads—but there are variations in body shapes, coloration and size. Largest of the genus, lake trout attain impressive weights—up to 100 lb (45 kg). They are the least colorful, typically an overall bronze, and a green-gray dorsal area overlaid with whitish or yellow markings that blend as spots or vermiculations. The belly is creamy white, and the pectoral, pelvic and anal fins are orange and have the distinct white leading edge common to all char.

Sexual maturity varies from twelve years in the north to six in the south, dependent on water temperatures, productivity of the lake and the trout's rate of growth. Lakers are "fall spawners," but far northern stocks spawn in late summer and southern stocks in November. Spawning is often a nocturnal event, with fish moving up onto the shallows before sundown and then retreating to deeper water by daybreak. Eggs are deposited randomly over clean, rocky bottoms, settling in crevasses between the gravel. Fertilized eggs incubate at a rate dependent on water temperature, hatching anywhere between two to four months. After fry emerge, initial growth is slow as they feed on invertebrates like mosquitoes, black flies, caddis, may flies, scuds and worms. When they attain some size, approximately 2 lb (1 kg), their appetites are insatiable. They are omnivorous, but consumption consists almost entirely of fish. Any fish! They have evolved into free-swimming predators at the top of their food chain.

Lake trout are dependent on cold, unpolluted water, and do not tolerate temperatures greater than 50°F (10°C). For almost half of the year, their metabolic rate slows, remaining in a state of dormancy under the winter ice as they await the renewal of spring. Shortly after ice-out, they move up into shallow water to feed, but later they avoid the warming shoals of summer by moving back into deeper water.

Although anglers often encounter concentrations of fish and assume abundance, population densities are not great throughout their range. Lake trout are very vulnerable to overfishing, so catch-and-release should be considered in coldwater fisheries. If you wish to take fish for consumption, make them small ones, not large, sexually mature specimens.

Although lake trout range across the top of North America, their distribution is not homogenous. In Canada they are found in southwestern Nova Scotia and New Brunswick; several areas in Labrador; Quebec and Ontario, but not through the Hudson Bay and James Bay lowlands; the Manitoba, Saskatchewan and Alberta boreal areas; and northern British Columbia. Yukon, the Northwest Territories and Nunavut offer prime lake-trout waters, including world famous Great Bear and Great Slave lakes and their vast chain of interconnecting waterways. These complex hydrological systems drain large areas of mountains and tundra bog, rivulets, creeks, rivers and smaller lakes.

Many famous rivers flowing north to the Arctic Ocean—Mackenzie, Coppermine, Burnside, Back, Tree, Kazan and Thelon—have lakes in their systems holding lake trout. The northern limit of their range are the Arctic Islands of Banks, Victoria, Southampton, King William and Baffin.

Most anglers troll spoons or plugs for lake trout, often employing heavy sinkers, downriggers or wire line to present their lures. However, when conditions are right, lakes and rivers offering fly-fishing opportunities for lake trout are found across Canada from the Pacific to Atlantic coasts. The best times are spring, right after ice-out, and fall, when lake trout frequent the coldwater shallows. Between these periods, summer water temperatures warm up and fish move into the depths seeking the comfort of colder water, rendering them unavailable to fly fishers.

There are, however, locations in the far north and occasionally at higher altitudes where water temperatures scarcely vary throughout the summer season. Fish in these locations remain accessible to fly fishers, so—in some areas—it is true that lake trout can be caught on the fly in almost every month from May to October.

Fly Fishing for Lake Trout from Spring to Fall

I WAS ABOVE THE 60TH PARALLEL, standing on the frozen shoreline of a northern Canadian lake. The afternoon sun was very warm, and reflected light glaring off the ice-covered lake stung my eyes. There were telltale signs that the long winter was finally over and the almost symbolic but natural event of ice-off was about to happen. The ice looked crumbly, with blue pools of the clear, thin ice and visible cracks propagating in the warming shallows.

There was a sense of excitement in anticipating the breakup, and thoughts of rigging up my tackle for the next morning to fly fish on the lake could well be a reality. Later, the paling of the northern evening brought down from the nearby mountains a strong catabatic wind. Sleep that night was disturbed by the noise of ice cracking and finally by the constant tinkling of millions of ice candles colliding.

Early morning found me on the lake shore, fly rod in hand, scanning the shallow, extremely clear green water for cruising fish. The far shore, by the outlet, was impossible to reach. Ice had blocked the outflow, and strong winds had piled heaps of broken ice particles high onto the shoreline, making it impassable by foot. The only option was to fish the open water on the lake's leeward side.

Just offshore floated a large ice pan. Below it, in the dark green shade of its edge, fish forms cruised to and fro, targets easily identified as lake trout. After a few diligent false casts, my line, leader and fly were dropped onto the ice pan. A gentle retrieve brought the fly to the edge of the ice, where it dropped into the water. The fly, a nondescript fry pattern, was instantly seized by a gray-green laker, followed by a solid hook-up like attaching to an inanimate log. The log woke up. What ensued was a strong, deep-running fight typical of lake trout.

That morning many other fish fell for this unorthodox "off the ice" fly delivery. All were released into ice-cold water which chilled my hands almost instantly. Recovery treatment that consisted of sticking my hands under my outer coat was necessary before I could continue casting. The largest lake trout that day was over 10 lb (4.5 kg).

Spring brings lake trout out of their dormancy. After spending six months locked under the ice, they are ready to feed, grow and reproduce during the short arctic season. They avoid deep, cold water by moving into the warming shallows and margins of the lake, where they feed. A fly fisher walking the shoreline should take advantage by seeking positions where the light is from behind. This allows visually spotting cruising fish, often close to shore in knee-deep water. Occasionally, fish reveal their location by attacking baitfish and driving them onto the surface.

When blowing winds create ripples on the water's surface, it is more difficult to spot the cruising lakers. Concentrate on looking through the window of a wave as it rolls over to break. This part of the wave is clear when viewed directly at 90°, and fish forms can be seen at close range.

At this time of year, flies imitating small baitfish are useful. If you can spot a local species, so much the better. Copy it by size and color; otherwise, use generalized smolt patterns like the Gray or Black Ghost, Black-Nosed Dace or Alaska Mary Ann. I prefer Aztec-style polar bear hair streamers tied in larger sizes—No. 4–1, 3x–6x, long-shanked barbless hooks with a straight eye.

Naturally, a matching rod weight should be chosen to handle big streamers when chucked at big fish. Expect lakers from 5–20 lb (2–9 kg) in this spring fishery. A 7–8-weight rod in combination with a large capacity reel will do well. Intermediate- or slow-sinking lines are suitable for shallow water, and the reel should carry a good supply of backing. Lake shorelines usually have lots of open water without snags, but trophy-sized lakers have a tendency to run deep and long. Without a boat to follow them, having lots of backing gives you the confidence to handle those larger fish. They aren't leader-shy, so attach a standard 6' level leader of up to 10-lb test.

Lake trout are predators and baitfish are their preferred meal. Opportunistic feeders, they hang around feeder creeks and streams flowing into the lakes. At times lake trout follow grayling spawning runs right up into these very small, shallow streams. These big fish seem out of place as they invade the small creeks, but they take advantage of the situation by feeding on adult grayling and particularly on juveniles.

At these times you must approach a small creek with stealth, casting a large streamer fly down and across into the larger, deeper pools. Keep well back from the water's edge and maintain a low profile. You will only get a few casts before the big fish are spooked, and usually the first cast offers your best chance. It may result in an explosive hook-up with a laker that runs so violently in the restricted space, it virtually runs out of water and ends up flopping high and dry on the boulder-strewn margins of the creek.

As summer advances, the long northern days rapidly warm the waters. In more southerly lakes thermal stratification of the water develops. The warming surface drives most fish species into deep, colder water, where they are not easily accessed by fly fishers. However, lakes farther north tend to stay cold and can be fly fished throughout the season.

Smaller lake trout hang around the stream inlets and outlets, plus stretches of fast rivers connecting the lakes. Large fish out in a lake's deeper water can be caught from drifting boats by using deep-sinking lines. Concentrate on areas that have specific fish-holding structures like islands, narrows, bars and drop-offs. There are generally three prime fish-holding areas in a lake: the inlet, outlet and any narrows. The latter are often associated with an offshore island and underwater bars or eskers. Other locations worth investigating are wherever you detect a rapid change from shallow to deep, or over reefs, points and outcrops where there is a detectable current. Water flowing over or around these structures attracts baitfish like grayling, whitefish, sticklebacks and sculpins, which in turn attracts predatory lake trout.

A long line cast in the direction of the drift will sink rapidly as your boat's forward motion moves over the line. By using a mid-thwart drogue or sea anchor setup to drift a boat sideways onto the bars or drop-offs, two fly fishers can efficiently deliver their flies deep by making long casts with very fast-sinking lines. The trick is to use a large, fast-sinking, "pulsating action" fly like a String Leech or Woolly Bugger with a marabou tail.

By doing a countdown as each angler works a different depth, it is possible to determine how deep the feeding laker trout are located—sometimes as deep as 30' (9 m) or more. An almost vertical, rapid-line retrieve with fishlike jerks will often induce strikes. Lakers frequently follow a fly for a long time before striking close to the surface. Don't hurry the retrieve near the end; fish it out right to the boat before preparing for the next cast.

Productive fly patterns are Muddler Minnows with gold or silver bodies that imitate deepwater sculpins, Zonkers and Matukas to simulate nine-spined sticklebacks, String Leeches as grayling and whitefish, Jack Sprats and Dahlberg Divers as lake-trout fry, and Woolly Buggers as leeches. Try a variety of colors, especially later in the summer as the fish become more aggressive with the approach of their spawning time. This late in the season, lake trout lose the selectivity of spring feeders. Try large, gaudy attractor patterns like Woolly Buggers, Egg-Sucking Leeches, Silver & Red Flash Flies, and Bunny Flies in outrageous colors like red, yellow, purple and pink. Experimentation is fun.

Good rods for boat fishing the lakes and big river sections are 7–8-weight, preferably in lengths of 9–10'.

Lake trout are opportunistic feeders, and on many twilight summer nights, just after the sun sets beyond the horizon and before it returns, char—lakers and nonmigratory arctic char—anticipate surface-emerging insects. Enormous numbers of caddis or chironomids will emerge in northern lakes. The volume of flying insects can actually be a hindrance to anglers who have a hard time keeping them out of their mouths, noses and ears.

During these hatches I have witnessed both species of char right on the surface with their backs out of the water, mouths open, scooping up the abundance of emergers. During times such as these, anglers should be in an anchored boat at a lake's outlet, where flowing water acts as a funnel for the surface feed.

Using a lighter 5–6-weight rod with a floating line, present dry flies like caddis and high-floating deer- or elk-haired patterns to fish cruising on the surface. The tactic is to cast out and observe the position of the closest approaching fish; try to anticipate its speed and line of travel. Adjust your fly's position by pulling in enough line that they should intercept; then let it drift, and await the outcome. Most times a fish will turn to the fly and consume it. Now comes the difficult part. Do not strike. Wait for that cruising hulk to turn and impale itself on the hook, and then hang on.

Lake trout frequently move into the interconnecting rivers between lakes. Good locations for fishing from a stationary boat are at anchor midchannel in a river or off and above the seams that form between a fast midriver flow and the slower back eddies closer to the bank. Lake trout hold on the edge between fast- and slow-flowing water. Using a full, fast-sinking line and a short leader, cast down and across, allowing your fly to swing deeply from the fast into the slow current. Lakers will often follow a fly right down to the final swing across to a position directly below the boat, and then a hook-up occurs.

Working from a boat allows more coverage of water than could be possible from shore. Also consider that wading is dangerous in water that is very cold and swift, and the rocks are often slick and slippery. Don't take chances, even though wearing a personal flotation device. If you go in and don't drown, hypothermia can be a killer in northern waters.

There is no perfect boat for northern waters. Broad-beamed aluminum skiffs with rounded bows and flat bottoms are stable, making them great river boats, but they are rough-riding when pounding on the choppy surface of wind-swept lakes. Deep-V hulls with pointed bows are best for lake use, but downright dangerous in fast-moving flows when running upstream.

Know what your boat and motor are capable of doing. With a heavy load on board, an outboard motor may not be powerful enough to advance upstream through heavy flows. Anticipate such water before you try it. Better to drop off a couple of anglers onshore and have them hike above a stretch of rapids, than to risk an aborted try in difficult water. Equally, on the return downstream through thin water, it is best to line a boat downstream from shore. Always overestimate your daily fuel requirements and take lots of spare props, pins and spark plugs.

Places To Go, Best Times and How To Get There

LAKE TROUT ARE INVARIABLY in remote places, so it pays to maximize your fishing time by a well-planned trip with professional guided assistance. Many outfitters are available, and a good starting point is to contact provincial or territorial tourist information offices, fishing lodges and guiding associations.

Here are some names of bodies of water synonymous with good lake-trout fishing, going from west to east:

- Yukon: Aishihik, Kluane, Teslin, Quiet lakes
- British Columbia: Atlin, Babine, Dall, Moberly, Muncho, Shuswap, Tochodi lakes
- Alberta: Cold, Grist, Namur, Peerless, Rock, Swan lakes
- Northwest Territories: Colville, Contwoyto, Dubawnt, Great Bear, Great Slave, Lac la Martre, Trout lakes
- Nunavut: Dubawnt, Garry, Contwoyto, Pellatt lakes
- Saskatchewan: Athabaska, Lac La Ronge, Reindeer, Wollaston lakes
- Manitoba: Athapapuskon, Clear, God's, Vanderkerkhove lakes
- Ontario: Great Lakes, Lake Simcoe
- Quebec: Mistassini Lake
- Labrador: Albert, Dyke, Kepimets, Lobstick lakes
- Nova Scotia: Lake Pochwock, Sherbrooke Lake, Dollar Lake

Looking at the broad picture, there are obvious best or well-known destinations in each province; however, any list would be incomplete, merely scratching the surface of a wide range of possibilities which should be researched.

In general fishing terms, the farther north the better for all-season lake-trout fishing, which means starting in July at ice-out and finishing in September—a short season. Although they can be caught on cast flies in the far north during each of those months, the window of opportunity is very narrow farther south. There, fly fishing is only an option for a few weeks right after ice-out and then again for a few weeks in the fall just as the spawning runs develop.

Dr. Martin Lamont's Must-Have Patterns for Lake Trout

- Bunny Fly
- Polar Aztec
- Silver & Red Flash Fly

- String Leech
- Woolly Bugger

Baked Lake Trout with Mushrooms and Red Pepper Sauce

An elegant dish to impress dinner guests
(Makes four servings)

4 6–8 oz—lake-trout fillets—4 170–250 g
1—roasted red pepper
Fresh lemon juice, divided
½ cup—fresh tarragon leaves—125 mL
or 2 tsp—dried, divided tarragon leaves—10 mL
Olive oil
Salt and pepper to taste
2–3 cups—mushrooms, thinly sliced—500–750 mL

1. Roast whole red pepper until skin is charred. Place in a paper bag until cooled. Remove skin and seeds and discard. Chop, then pulse pepper in a food processor until smooth. Add 1 tsp (5 mL) lemon juice, a pinch of tarragon and 2 tbsp (30 mL) olive oil. Season with salt and pepper to taste. Pulse until well blended.

2. Brush olive oil over fillets, sprinkle with tarragon, salt and pepper. Bake in a 400°F (200°C) oven until done, usually 10 minutes per inch (4 minutes per cm) at thickest part.

3. Sauté mushrooms in 1–2 tsp (5–10 mL) olive oil in a nonstick pan. Add ¼ cup (60 mL) water to assist cooking mushrooms and prevent burning. Cook mushrooms over low heat until dry. This makes them far more flavorful. Arrange a bed of mushrooms, place a fillet on top, then ladle red pepper sauce over the fish.

–Wayne Phillips

CHAPTER 15

THE BLACK CHAR

Bob Rife

A CCORDING TO THAT MOST HONORED SOURCE, *Funk & Wagnalls Standard College Dictionary,* Canadian edition, char means to burn or scorch the surface.

Well, that wasn't what it was about, not at all—a fly fisher many hours and dollars from home—a stranger in a strange land was not looking for something black and burned. No, the target was the grand and gloriously colored *Salvelinus alpinus.*

Now you're talking—Latin?

Yep! It's the technical name for arctic char, indicating, as it does, a close relationship to brook trout *(Salvelinus fontinalis)* and lake trout *(Salvelinus namaycush).* In fact there are only minor differences in the fish. Something to do with mouth parts distinguishes them. And, despite how my friends from Alaska twirl it out to charr, literally, I will stick with the one "r" char spelling.

The word *char* is derived, the good book relates, from the Scottish Gaelic *Cara*—blood red. That has to do with the fish's flesh which is often that color, depending on its diet and on its magnificent spawning colors. In parts of the extreme north of La Belle Province, Nouveau Quebec, they go so far as to designate it red trout.

It has other names. As a staple in the diet of the Inuit, they have many words to describe it, always depending on the size or sex of the specimen or the season. The most common is *ilkalupik*. Another is *ekaluk*. It is called *bleikja* in Iceland, *roye* in Norway, *roding* in Sweden, *paliya* in Russia and *omble chevalier* in France. Remember, it is circumpolar in distribution.

Whatever you want to call it, the char is also not black—in fact when sea-run fish return to spawn in all their finery, they are almost beyond compare. Then, the back is a dark green with silvery blue sides dotted with brilliant large dashes of red, orange or pink. The belly is whitish to orange, even red. Sometimes the flanks and bellies are fully red. To top it all, the leading edges of the pectoral, pelvic, anal and often caudal fins are sharply defined in immaculate white. It's a magnificent trophy.

In Canada there are two kinds of char—landlocked (isolated populations living in freshwater lakes) and the anadromous or sea-run fish. The latter move downstream to salt water before or during ice breakup in spring. The runs are usually completed by the end of July.

After a summer offshore and in estuary pools, the fish congregate at the river mouths to begin the return journey upstream to spawn—that process happening in early winter. The females, which spawn only every second or third year, produce from 3,000 to 5,000 eggs. And oddly, anglers find that male char are often slightly larger than females.

The usual weight of a sea-run char taken by rod and reel will run from 2–8 lb (900 g–4 kg). If it's record weight you're after, consider the world all-tackle mark that was established July 29, 1981. Jeffrey Lee Ward landed a char weighing 32 lb 9 oz (14.8 kg). He was fishing the Tree River in the Northwest Territories.

The U.S. National Freshwater Fishing Hall of Fame's listed record weight for fly fishing with 2-lb test leader is 14 lb (6.4 kg) taken by Roy McGraw from that same Tree River on August 11, 1992. Ed Rice landed a char weighing 20 lb 4 oz (9.2 kg), again from the Tree River, Aug. 4, 1993. He used a fly rod, but no listing for leader test has been volunteered.

The fish entered in the records were all what you might call elderly. Research friend Dr. Ed Crossman, who with Bev Scott wrote the authoritative *Freshwater Fishes of Canada*, notes that char grow slowly, reaching commercial size of approximately 10 lb (4.5 kg) in the central Canadian Arctic at about age 16.

But on to the black char and the angling thereof.

Char fishing is all about timing—getting to remote visible-flight-rule places in a specific time period. Lousy flying weather has stranded many a would-be, color-char angler. But poor weather is also a good time for char fishing—more about that later.

Although char are at their peak in a color sense when they begin their run from the sea in late summer (August) to early fall, that's also when writer-angler and streamside friend Ernest Schwiebert calls them "hardware" fish—easy prey for a spin fisher pitching a shiny spoon. Then they jostle each other in teeming schools, jumping and rolling and porpoising in the tidal waters as they get their first taste of the freshwater home they left in the spring. After a summer dining on silvery capelin and other baitfish, they are suckers for the spoon and may seem to ignore offerings by the fly angler. Char are never a wary fish and the fall-run schools are in shallow pools, 2–4' (60 cm–1.2 m) deep.

At these times a fly fisher needs some patience. I watched a fish follow my fly lazily for more than 50' (15 m). Then, as I was prepared to call it quits, ready to lift the rod tip and start again, the char struck.

Its move startled me, but not as much as the charging run after the strike that sent line and then backing screaming off my reel. Its run was a flat-out sprint downstream and deep. I slip-slopped on the stony bottom, racing after my quarry, rather like a perambulating, water-logged scarecrow, arms and rod held high, hoping to keep something on the reel's spool—anything.

Ernest had given me ample warning. "The first run by a fresh, sea-lice-covered char is stronger than that of a grilse (an Atlantic salmon youngster of about the same size, six pounds in this case)." He compared it with the well-documented first-run challenge of a bonefish.

The sea-run fish begin their downstream movement when the ice breaks up. It may even occur under the ice. They may start the return journey for the spawning grounds as early as late July. The freshwater diet—the part that interests fly fishers—is mostly midges in the larval and pupal forms. And the midges—no-see-ums—as arctic travelers are well aware, are plentiful at that time of year. As they emerge, they get aggressive. I can still hear the yelps from skeeter and black fly attacks.

Now to that bad weather oddity. Char are not active on sunny days—I assume like all arctic dwellers they just like to lie around and bask in the warmth. Schwiebert first noticed this on the Laxa River in Iceland. "A series of sunny days makes them sluggish, reluctant to feed." When it turns brisk and nasty with rain or even sleet, they get very active.

He suggests bright, wet flies and Mylar marabou and polar bear streamer patterns—all fished near the bottom. Among the wets I tried were some Scottish trout patterns, a streamer and a black midge.

Dave Little, an angler with the Northern Labrador Outdoors, goes along with our suggestion of tiny midges: "The char here (in northern Quebec) seem usually to feed on tiny black flies, so I find Black Gnats work well, hook size 12 or 14." He reiterates Schwiebert's comment about reel backing: "Use a reel with lots of backing—they are fighters!"

That brings us to tackle selection. A solid 8 ½'-rod, probably a jointed one (you are flying to your fishy destination, remember), 6–8-weight. Always the paranoid one, I took two rods—both jointed, one boron, the other graphite—a 6-weight for the fun of lighter equipment and challenge, a 7-weight for tackle-busting runs of record hunters.

On the reels, try a selection of floating, sinking and sink-tip lines in lighter colors—visibility always helps and the char could care less. Spare spools are a great idea.

Leaders: 9–12', 4-lb test or greater. Use 2-lb if you want that world mark, but don't forget those bone-rattling runs!

Ernest added a footnote to our conversation from his *Trout,* a definitive, two-volume set: "They are surprisingly strong fighters and superb table fare."

As a tried and true piscatorial trencherman, those final words "table fare," especially when matched with "superb," really turned me on. And that's where black char entered the picture.

We had slogged back to the camp, rods angled over the shoulder. I happily carried the night's dinner, a fish fresh from the salt. Charlie, my guide, rolled his eyes under the brim of his slouch cap: "Ah, monsieur, it will make a fine meal! You'll see, I have the recipe!"

So we gathered around the campfire where Charlie began his magic. First into the big frying pan, the inevitable butter. Then the big slabs of red char were gently placed, not crowded, into the butter. The sizzling began and our mouths watered in anticipation. Then came the surprise. Charlie whipped a bottle from under his squall jacket and began dousing a thick, brownish sauce on the fish. The pan soon was a roiling cauldron of frothing bubbles.

"There, that should do it!" said the magician.

He was right. On each hungry angler's plate, he placed a big BLACK char—what looked like charred char!

"HP Charlie strikes again," yelped a guide from another firepit.

We gingerly tasted the black—blackened?—char. It took a little courage; black is not a great food color (I know, technically black is not a color).

But it wasn't bad. In fact, it was pretty good. Tangy. However, I hate to spoil HP Charlie's delusions of cookery grandeur—it was not something for a "ristorante" in the Big Apple. His char reminded me of the way Alaskans tend to spell the fish's name: charr—acceptable, according to the dictionary, but a second choice.

I still prefer a pan-fried fillet au naturel, or perhaps for a change, this broiled-in-foil dish:

1 3–4 lb—char—1 1.4–1.8 kg
1 ½–2—cups of cooked rice—375–500 mL
char roe (if available)
Chopped celery, tomato, parsley and onion (flakes will do)
Lemon juice to taste
Salt and pepper to taste

Combine the rice with the roe and spices, and stuff the mixture in the cleaned fish carcass. Wrap in foil and cook slowly over the coals (or on a barbecue), turning occasionally.

Now that ain't black!

BOB RIFE'S MUST-HAVE PATTERNS FOR CHAR

- Black-Nosed Dace Streamer
- Montreal
- Thor

UNGAVA'S ARCTIC CHAR

Kenneth Coupland

THE WORDS *arctic char* BRING TO MIND A RIVER—SWIFT, cold, rock-strewn—a background of 15' (4.5-m) black spruce, and beyond, a range of low mountains. This is what John and I encountered when we arrived at Kanniq (Helen's Falls) on the famous George River, intent on fishing for Atlantic salmon.

Like many fly-ins, our starting point was Kuujjuaq (formerly Fort Chimo). The flight eastward, 60 miles (97 km) or so, terminated on a small landing strip near the camp. We were thankful our pilot knew what he was looking for, as the terrain all looked the same to us.

Weather in the Far North is always a consideration, especially in the last part of the season. Fishing trips to these types of camps are usually of seven days' duration, which allows for weather changes and variations in fishing conditions. Caribou are migrating as the salmon and char fishing draws to a close, so it is common to find hunters and anglers in camp at the same time. If so inclined, you can book a combination trip, fishing and hunting on alternate days. In fact, when you arrive back in Kuujjuaq, it's common to see large piles of caribou antlers sitting on the tarmac, waiting to be loaded along with the hunters and anglers.

In our case, the weather was cooperative, and after the river had yielded some fine salmon, we decided to spend one day on our own to try for arctic char. They are something of a mystery. Of the same family as brook trout and lake trout, arctic char have the same need for pure, cold water, but unlike their relatives seem to be found mostly in rivers. Anglers often become frustrated with them, especially when nothing seems to work—which can probably be attributed to the fact that we seldom devote much time to them, preferring to pursue Atlantic salmon which, after all, is what attracts us up there in the first place.

Excellent fishing for char of 8–10 lb (4–5 kg) is found in many rivers flowing north into Ungava Bay. Commercial camps located on rivers like the Payne, Tumulik and George usually concentrate on salmon throughout the short summer. However, some also offer char fishing and in a few cases brookies and lake trout.

Initially, our quest proved easier said than done, for the char were definitely not where our guides had said they should be—about 2 miles (3 km) downstream from camp. Puzzled, we pressed on. Our perseverance paid off, for 1 mile (1.6 km) farther downstream we found the hot spot. It lay right in the main river—a fairly fast, even flow, roughly 3' (90 cm) deep over a gravel bottom.

At our guide's insistence we had taken spinning tackle, which is legal there for char, but the heavy lures produced frequent hang-ups. It was obvious that fly tackle would be more effective, so we switched to our light salmon outfits—a prudent move that led to a memorable day of fishing.

I have heard that arctic char on some rivers may make extended runs, perhaps right into the backing, even punctuating them occasionally with a jump when the run ends. I have never seen this on the George River. Unlike salmon, which dissipate their strength with long runs and repeated jumps, a char's fight is more remindful of a large, dogged, brook trout. I suppose it's possible that this particular strain is unable to jump, for except when they are on their spawning run, we tend to find them in calmer stretches of the river and never below the falls or rapids where salmon congregate.

Medium-weight tackle is recommended. My favorite char rod is a 10', ⅞-weight that easily throws large No. 8–2 streamers. Almost invariably you will find yourself in situations that call for casting a fair distance into a strong wind, which is, of course, probably what you were doing all along while salmon fishing.

Char have no experience with fly hatches; consequently, until they run upstream their only food will have been creatures like capelin and shrimp. Flies are usually bright and flashy—red and white or blue and white—with a silver-tinsel body. I originally decided on using a blue and white streamer since it resembled a Blue Fox spoon that the Inuit were using successfully with their spinning tackle.

After John and I tired of fishing, we poked around and eventually found ourselves looking down at 10 char busily performing all the gyrations associated with spawning. We were dangling a large fly just over their heads, unsuccessfully, when they all disappeared in a flash. As we wondered what had happened, a lake trout, fully five feet long, cruised slowly through the pool. It wouldn't take our fly, either. However, it was a good note on which to end our day and walk back to camp.

Incidentally, if you intend to save some char to take home, we found the plainly hued ones were the best choice. Those in full spawning regalia were quite soft and unsuitable for the table.

CHAPTER 17

DREDGING FOR WALLEYE

Russ Swerdlyk

THE PILOT OF OUR FLOATPLANE POINTED HIS FINGER OUT the window of the lodge, shook his head and remarked, "There's a hill on the other side of the lake with a giant spruce tree on it. If I can see the tree, we fly. If I can't see it, we don't."

A heavy fog had settled in during the night, and as I looked in the direction he had pointed, the scene was a major disappointment. The pilot's words confirmed it.

"It looks like you two are stuck on the ground until tomorrow morning." He added, "I'll try to reschedule for an early flight in the morning."

Gord Ellis and I were at Miminiska Lodge on the Albany River in northwestern Ontario, and our original plans called for a floatplane to fly us to a tributary of the Albany and a 12-mile (19-km) canoe trip for trophy brookies. Weather has a way of quickly changing one's plans in the north, and occasionally these changes can lead to some new and thrilling adventures.

My repertoire of fishing experiences was about to have a new chapter added. I'd always wanted to catch walleye on a fly rod, and since my fishing partner and I were eager to get out and do some fishing, we looked at each other and instantly made our decision.

Within the hour we were in a boat, drifting along a foggy, rock-studded shoreline with several wave-swept points extending into the deeper water. I rigged up my 7-weight rod with an extra-fast, 10' sink-tip line. My terminal tackle consisted of a 4', 6-lb test leader, and a white, rabbit strip Muddler Minnow I christened the Muddler Zonker.

On my third cast toward one of the protruding rocks, I hooked a solid fish. Its black and gold hue identified the fish to be a walleye, and my fly-fishing life list was about to grow by one more species. Despite a determined battle to get free, the walleye's runs became progressively shorter. My first walleye on a fly, a respectable 2-lb (900-g) fish, was victoriously held up for a photo, unhooked and released.

With the aggressive strikes, sharp, razorlike teeth, and determined fight of those Albany walleye, my first fly managed to last only a bit over a half hour. Take plenty of flies for walleye fishing was the first lesson of the day.

Gord and I caught and released walleye that pulled my hand scale past the 3-lb (1.4-kg) mark. Catching walleye on a fly turned out to be not as difficult as one might have assumed. The deep, dog-fighting style and tenacity of the walleye was enhanced by the use of the fly rod, and I found the action quite exciting.

Since that first Albany walleye on a fly years ago, I have jumped at the chance to fish this warmwater species whenever the opportunity arises. Walleye and fly fishing appears to be an oxymoron, but the truth is that if you can get a fly down to the bottom, the walleye will do their bit to cooperate.

With the technology in sinking fly lines today, getting a fly down to 12–15' (3.6–4.5 m) is no longer a difficult task. My present pick for walleye—a high-speed, high-density, extra-fast sinking shooting head—gets the job done without much of a wait for the fly to get down to fish-holding depths. With this line, I even manage to get hung up on the rocky bottoms common to walleye hangouts. Getting hung up while walleye fishing is a fact of life—and a positive sign that the fly is in the right place. The nature of the fish is to stay on or close to the bottom structure near rocky points and shoals. To catch fish, the rule is simply to get the fly down to those fish-holding depths.

When walleye are in deeper water, I will go to a full-sinking line, a class 4 or more, depending on how patient I feel. Waiting for the line to sink is one of the more difficult things to do when fish from a school are hitting. Keep in mind that really fast sinkers like the lead core that many steelheaders use are difficult to cast all day long. What you gain in sink rate, you lose on comfort of casting. I try to fish with the fastest sinker I can be patient with, without sacrificing too much comfort in casting. The idea is to enjoy the outing, not build muscles.

Using weighted flies helps to get down more quickly, however, the casting becomes more of a chore. My preference is to let the fly line pull down the unweighted fly rather than use lead-filled flies. Unweighted flies tend to have a more seductive action, and can be fished more slowly to entice strikes from slow-moving walleye. This means being patient while the line sinks; however, if casting weighted flies is not too annoying, they will sink faster and stay in the fish-holding area much longer.

Leaders for walleye are simple to rig. I use ordinary monofilament from three to four feet in length. The short leader is used to keep the fly near the bottom, and walleye do not seem to be too sensitive to this setup. Longer leaders can belly up and keep a fly away from the fish. In amber-colored waters, which are common to many walleye habitats, the use of amber versus clear-colored monofilament for the leader is a bonus.

A wire leader is not necessary for walleye. If an angler is willing to sacrifice the occasional bucktail or streamer to a deeply hooked pike, then a metal leader can be eliminated. If, on the other hand, an angler is also interested in landing pike, which often inhabit the same lakes as walleye, either a heavy leader of 30-lb test or more is required, or some other type of tooth-resistant leader material. If you don't like wire, there are several ways to go, depending on your own personal choice. The simplest is to use heavy monofilament. Pike will still bite off occasionally, but this is the easiest material to cast.

A second choice would be the use of tooth-resistant leader material made especially for fly fishing. I've used a Fenwick product which is made especially tough for toothy critters, and found the ability to tie knots with this material a welcome way to save flies from being bitten off. It also casts well.

Another option is to purchase regular wire leaders and modify them for fly fishing. I use wire cutters to cut the snap and swivel off, leaving a length of wire leader with a small loop at each end. This leader system is one of the most efficient for keeping flies on the line, and the casting remains reasonable. For this system, flies must have large eyes in order to get the leader material through it.

As the sun makes its way across the sky, walleye tend to work into deeper

water. A change in tackle can improve your odds of success. My 10-weight, 9'
graphite rod with an extra-fast-sinking shooting head gives me longer casts, a
faster sink rate, and results in more of the larger walleye coming to hand. The
deeper an angler can go, the more options become available for searching and
finding fish with the fly rod.

Rods for walleye should be on the heavier side, not so much for playing the
fish but for casting as far as possible with the larger flies. A 9- or 10-weight
graphite rod is ideal for shooting line out the distance required to work a shoreline efficiently. I find my longer casts work a fly through the fish-holding zone
more effectively, and the longer casts also provide opportunities to manipulate
my fly more enticingly by twitching and varying its speed. Extra slow retrieves
seem to produce more strikes from the slower-swimming walleye.

Reels for walleye need not be high tech. Single action models like the Hardy
Marquis series are more than sufficient for playing walleye and light enough to
match up well with the larger graphite rods.

Walleye flies should lean toward a long profile rather than short, stubby patterns. Walleye feed on smelt, herring and whitefish where available, and these
baitfish tend to be long and skinny. White flies with some type of flash will produce where these baitfish are present. In order to fish these longer patterns, the
use of tube flies can be a real help, especially on windy days. Flies tied on plastic tubes and fished with a small hook are much lighter than those tied on long
wire hooks, and they can be cast more easily.

In waters where several types of baitfish are available, the best flies for walleye remain minnow or leech imitations like Muddler variations and Woolly
Buggers. A good producer in the waters I fish is a Black Zonker tied with a
Muddler Head. A black Woolly Bugger with pearl Flashabou stripes is another
of my top producers. Black seems to be a universally attractive color to walleye
no matter where anglers encounter them. Because walleye are not anywhere
nearly as selective as trout, most minnow, sculpin, or leech-imitating streamers
and bucktails will produce fish.

An important piece of equipment that makes a big difference in hooking
fish is a diamond-grit hook sharpener. I find myself constantly sharpening
hooks while walleye fishing, primarily because of the constant bumping of the
rocky bottom with the fly. Dull or bent hooks add up to missed strikes that can

be easily avoided with the use of a clip-on hook sharpener. Compared to fish in the trout family, the mouth structure of a walleye is much more bony, so sharp hooks are a must.

Equally important are surgical forceps or needlenose pliers for releasing walleye. Their sharp teeth can quickly turn fingers into raw, bleeding flesh, and without some kind of a hook disgorger the walleye would be impossible to release quickly, efficiently, and without harm. Forceps allow an angler to work out, carefully and more precisely, deeper-hooked flies without doing more damage to the fish and without risk to the angler's own safety. I keep a pair clipped to my vest and find them to be absolutely the best and fastest way to release fish. A pinched-down barb is another way to make releases faster.

Walleye action comes in waves. Whenever a school of fish is located, anglers will be able to pick out a half-dozen-or-so fish before the rest of the school gets lockjaw. This is typical walleye behavior. To capitalize on this, it is best to work a shoreline until fish are located, fish the area until the action dies off, then resume a steady shoreline hunt.

Although walleye prefer rocky points and shoals, trophy fish can be found in deeper, mud-bottom flats at times. Exploring middle-of-the-lake flats with a fly rod can appear to be an overwhelming job; however, a patient systematic search can be the key to success when all else fails. Once a fish-holding depth or pattern has been established, it pays to keep an eye on the fish-finder to maintain that contour.

Walleye become more active as the light fades. Night fishing can be very productive for this species because of this characteristic. Staying on the lake for a few hours after sunset can produce some of the best and biggest fish in relatively shallow water. By putting in the added effort after dark or for a few hours before sunrise, an angler may latch onto some trophy walleye that have moved into shallow water under the cover and security of darkness.

Since adding walleye to my life list of fly-rod-caught fish on the Albany so many years ago, I've spent many enjoyable hours fly fishing for them whenever summer circumstances have dictated a trip for a warmwater species. Walleye on a fly provide a unique set of problems to overcome, a different set of conditions to adjust to, and deepwater fishing tactics to develop. If you're up for the challenge, give walleye a try.

Walleye Shore-Lunch Fish Sandwich

The perfect shore-lunch sandwich
(Makes four servings)

Walleye fillets

Salt and pepper
2 tbsp—margarine, plus extra for frying—30 mL
Lemon juice (optional)

Bannock

1 ½ cups—flour—375 mL
1 ½ tsp—baking powder—7 mL
1 tsp—salt—5 mL
2 tbsp—margarine—30 mL
½ cup—water—125 mL
Margarine for frying

Dill mayonnaise

4 tbsp—mayonnaise—60 mL
1–2 tbsp—chopped fresh dill—15–30 mL
or 1 tsp—dried dill—5 mL
Lemon juice to taste

1. Dill mayonnaise should be prepared at home and carried in a cooler, along with tomato slices, lettuce and thinly sliced sweet onions for the sandwiches.

2. Take premixed dry ingredients for bannock in a heavy plastic bag. Work margarine into dry bannock ingredients, and then moisten with enough water to make a dough.

3. Build a fire and let it burn down to coals. Heat a pan over the coals, melt some margarine in it, place dough in pan and flatten with a fork. Flip bannock over when browned on first side. (It's done when it sounds "hollow" when tapped on the bottom.)

4. Pat walleye fillets dry. Remove cooked bannock from pan, return pan to coals and melt more margarine. Add fillets and season to taste with salt and pepper. When browned, flip fillet and add a squeeze of lemon if desired.

5. Break or cut bannock into 4 pieces and slice each in half. Everyone makes their own walleye sandwich by placing a fillet between two slices of bannock liberally coated with dill mayonnaise. Add tomato, or onion slices, and lettuce if desired.

–Wayne Phillips

CHAPTER 18

OUANANICHE!

George Gruenefeld

FOUR TIMES MASSIVE GLACIERS RUMBLED ACROSS THIS LAND. Four times they have retreated to their arctic lairs. The first three rumbled elemental bedrock, roughing out the fire-formed face of the Precambrian Shield. The last one, Wisconsin Glacier, rumbled southward about 100,000 years ago and held the land in its tenuous grip for 60,000 years. When it withdrew around 38,000 B.C., it had put the final brush strokes to the land of the ouananiche.

It was Wisconsin Glacier which molded the Laurentian Hills, scoured out the St. Lawrence riverbed and shaped the magnificent fjords of the Saguenay Valley. And on the ice-bridge created by the Wisconsin Glacier, Paleolithic hunters followed mastodon from Asia to North America.

Legend suggests that the retreat of Wisconsin Glacier trapped anadromous Atlantic salmon in many lakes and rivers of northeastern North America. That legend stands on shaky ground since throughout its natural range, and especially in the case of Lake St. Jean at the head of the Saguenay River, there were historically no obstacles capable of shackling the irrepressible spirit of *Salmo salar*.

At its core, the conundrum is whether *Salmo salar* is originally a freshwater or saltwater fish. The accepted theory is the latter, that salmon of the Atlantic seaboard are fundamentally marine fish which choose to spawn on the sun-warmed riffles of coastal rivers rather than in the hostile environment of the sea. If this is the case, then the freshwater variation can indeed be called landlocked.

However, I'm not entirely convinced that this is the case. *Salmo salar* strikes me as a freshwater creature, a denizen of brawling rivers and clear, crystalline pools. Could it be that this fish once lived, fed and procreated entirely in the freshwater rivers of eastern North America and western Europe? It's entirely plausible that the advance of the last Ice Age created conditions in the rivers unsuitable to large populations of salmon, and in order to survive one segment remained landbound while the other drifted downstream toward river estuaries and the sea.

The salmon retreating before the encroaching ice gradually adapted to a marine interval with physiological modifications which made it possible to survive in salt water. A period of 60,000 years—the life of the Wisconsin Glacier—is more than sufficient for such an evolutionary change. Yet, as long as runoff from the leading edge of the ice field provided suitable, though restrained freshwater-spawning habitat, there was no need to evolve a marine reproductive strategy.

Hence, we have sea-run or anadromous salmon which live in the food-rich Atlantic Ocean by choice and fight their way up to the shallow headwater riffles of freshwater rivers to procreate. And we have freshwater salmon which live in inland rivers and lakes by choice, not because Precambrian upheavals have barricaded their access to the sea. They are landlocked only because nature has not adapted them to live in salt water.

At one time scientists regarded freshwater salmon as a distinct species, or at the very least subspecifically distinct, and named those found in the Lake St. Jean watershed *Salmo ouananiche*. The rest were listed as *Salmo sebago*, after the Maine lake in which large freshwater salmon were abundant. Size seemed to be the major differentiation between the two, and ouananiche originating from north of the St. Lawrence were considered the smaller of the two subspecies.

Although the distinction is still discussed as an academic exercise by taxonomists who write the reference books, they unanimously accept the assertion made by D.G. Wilder in 1947 that freshwater and anadromous salmon both belong to one and the same species—*Salmo salar*. That stand is further strengthened—and also confused—by the successful introductions of salmon fry from anadromous parentage in landlocked freshwater habitats.

In any but the most remote limits of their range, it is difficult to find pure strains of landlocked salmon since biologists have pandered with geographically foreign strains for more than a century. As early as 1877, they stocked Lake Memphremagog with the offspring of Lake Ontario salmon and in 1902 with the offspring of anadromous salmon. Somewhere along the line, Lake Memphremagog was also stocked with fingerlings of Lake Sebago origin. Even Lake Sorcier in Mastigouche Wildlife Reserve, known as the home of truly wild ouananiche, was actually stocked with the progeny of anadromous salmon. The same is true for lakes Tremblant, Kenogami and Mekinac.

Lake Tremblant, beyond any shadow of doubt, was the crowning glory of experimental colonization of salmon in previously uninhabited waters. A deep coldwater lake, Tremblant was originally home to big lake trout along with some brook trout, but foreign species—primarily coarse fish like rock bass, sunfish and yellow perch—found their way in and multiplied. These fish fed heavily on lake-trout eggs, and as the number of lake trout diminished the smelt population mushroomed. Convinced of the need to intervene, biologists launched a two-pronged counterattack by introducing muskies to deal with the overpopulation of coarse fish and salmon to stabilize the smelt population.

Both introduced species did better than hoped. Each settled into its own ecological niche. Muskies lurked in the shallows and gorged on nuisance fish and in doing so became a prized sport fish for local anglers. The salmon, meanwhile, grew fat on vast banks of smelt which inhabit the depths of Lake Tremblant. Within a decade of the initial introduction, anglers were catching landlocked salmon weighing over 10 lb (4.5 kg). Top catches include one of 19 lb 10 oz (8.9 kg) by Michel Rouday on May 23, 1976, and 21 lb 6 oz (9.7 kg) caught by Jean-Guy Lefevre of St. Jovite on 18 May 1982, which stands as Quebec's record. Biologists monitoring Tremblant salmon on the Caché River spawning beds say they have seen 30 lb (14 kg) fish.

These Tremblant fish, like most other salmon introduced to freshwater areas of Quebec these days, would do their seafaring parents proud. They look remarkably like anadromous salmon caught in Gaspé rivers, except their coloration in May has the same reddish hue as a sea fish after two months in fresh water. The similarities between fresh and saltwater salmon are, without question, sometimes stunning, especially when transplanted populations are involved. Yet at other times the differences are apparent as well, particularly in the case of native populations.

A few years ago, while fishing the Big River north of Goose Bay in Labrador, I was able to compare native landlocked salmon and fresh, sea-run Atlantic salmon first-hand. Although primarily a grilse river, the Big nonetheless provides excellent action on salmon 3–8 lb (1.4–4 kg) in size. A rugged river, its drainage basin consists of tendrils that reach deep into the heart of the Labrador Plateau although salmon can access only the first 20 miles (32 km) in from the sea. Beyond that point, the Big is a mile-long (1.6 km) cataract which roars its way down the flank of a high ridge in a long, straight ribbon of white water. Above that lies White Bear Lake.

Although they nose their way into the pocket water at the base of the cataract, none of the sea-run salmon can find their way up the torrent. Above, however, White Bear Lake has a large population of landlocked salmon which frequently make their way downstream. Near the river mouth, within earshot of the mighty rollers of the Labrador Sea, Big River rushes headlong into a deep, wide pond—perhaps better described as a lake since it is big enough and calm enough for single-engine floatplanes to land with their cargo of anxious anglers.

At the phalanx between the pond's calm water and the rush of the current, hovered legions of fish. A Muddler Minnow, No. 6 or 4, cast into the heavy water to drift out into the calm was deadly. While every second cast produced fish, the trouble was you couldn't predict which kind of fish—at times it would be a hefty, sea-bright sea trout of 4–5 lb (1.8–2.3 kg); at others a grilse or salmon still bearing sea lice; and now and then you might hook a landlocked salmon.

The difference between the anadromous salmon and their smaller freshwater brothers is startling. Scale readings suggested that landlocks were of the same age group as the 3–4-lb (1.4–1.8-kg) grilse, yet a big landlock barely tipped the balances at 2 lb (900 g). Furthermore, the landlocked salmon had proportionately large heads and gaunt bodies, much like slinks (kelts), while sea-run fish had proportionately small heads and sleek, full bodies. In color the anadromous fish were typically silver-flanked, while landlocked fish had golden sides like those of well-colored walleye.

Most interesting of all was that the landlocked fish shunned salt water. From the pond near the river mouth, it is just a short swim to the freedom of the open sea, yet they chose to remain in fresh water. This example once again drives home the point that these fish are landlocked by nature rather than by some insurmountable obstacle.

And, if this is indeed the case, then even the Montagnais Indians of Quebec's north shore might have been in error when they called the fish *ouananiche,* a term which by a popular interpretation derives from the Montagnais word *aonanch,* supposedly meaning "landlocked." I doubt that they would have made so obvious an error, so the alternative suggestion that the word *ouananiche* means "little salmon" is far more plausible. However, I believe that the derivation of the word is *ouana,* which means "look there." Early European settlers might well have taken the expression to be the name of the fish which their Montagnais guides were trying to point out; later, the explorers themselves added the diminutive suffix *iche* meaning "little" in Montagnais. Hence the term *ouanan-iche,* "little salmon."

I don't accept the explanation that little salmon is a direct translation from the language of the Montagnais since the Montagnais term for salmon is *ou-sha-shu-mak.* Considering this, the direct translation of "little salmon" to Montagnais would be *ou-sha-shu-mak-iche,* an unlikely root for the word *ouananiche,* no matter how badly it's mispronounced.

No matter whence the word *ouananiche,* which flows so gentle and clean off the tongue, its pedigree is best discussed by pundits, along with the conundrum of whether the landlocked salmon preceded the anadromous salmon or vice versa. Blue skies, errant breezes, tumbling waters and the truth of a well-placed cast, rather than the musty depths of some forgotten tome, are the realm of anglers. I'd rather work the east bay of Lake Sorcier or the reservoirs of the Peribonca with a silver-bodied, minnow-imitating streamer when the fish are up and the air carries the scent of a million spruce trees, than find myself stuck in some stuffy library.

Lake Ontario was at one time the westernmost reach of landlocked salmon, and fish weighing 30 lb (14 kg) and more were said to choke tributary streams like the Ganaraska, which is today choked by over 100,000 steelhead every spring. Wanton genocide, the construction of dams and the destruction of their habitat wiped out Lake Ontario's landlocked salmon populations, and current restoration attempts receive only token support from an angling community infatuated with western interlopers like chinook salmon and steelhead.

Eastward, we come to landlocked salmon waters worth marking on the map: lakes Tremblant, Chaud and Sorcier. All three have landlocked salmon by the hand of man rather than the design of nature. The same is true of Lake Mekinac north of Grand-Mère, and Memphremagog in the Eastern Townships. And to the south, the states of Vermont and New York have succeeded in reestablishing a landlocked salmon population in Lake Champlain. Many of its tributaries on both the New York and Vermont shores offer excellent stream fishing for landlocks. Tops among these is the Bouquet River, where a fishway was built to provide salmon with access to virtually the entire stream bed.

Lake St. Jean was at one time the landlocked salmon fishing capital of the world. Even before the opening of the Quebec and Lake St. John Railway in the early 1880s, anglers were drawn from the United States and Europe to tackle the lake's feisty ouananiche, which, according to sporting literature of the day, were considerably smaller but stronger fighters than landlocked salmon of Maine's Lake Sebago. By 1895, the Ashuapmushuan, Metabetchouan, Mistassini and Peribonca river systems had been explored, and the Grande Decharge of Lake St. Jean into the Saguenay River had become a major sport fishing area.

In those days H.J. Beemer ran two hotels on Lake St. Jean (one at Roberval and the other at the Grande Decharge) in addition to holding the lease on "almost all ouananiche waters within a radius of several days' journey" from the lake. Guides could be hired at $1.25 a day each, two to a canoe, or the hotel would provide a package deal which included tents, bedding, provisions, utensils and guiding services at "hotel rates." The ouananiche fishery of Lake St. Jean became a major tourism industry for the region.

Unfortunately, other industries in the region cared little for the well-being of the ouananiche. Lumber drives scoured out the riverbeds, hydroelectric dams blocked access to the spawning beds, and the pulp and paper mills stole water from the rivers. Lake St. Jean populations of ouananiche were being strangled to death by industry, poaching and overfishing. Concern over the decline of these fish triggered the construction of fishways, restocking programs and restoration programs in major tributaries of the lake, but it will be a tough battle to bring the numbers of ouananiche back to levels known in the heyday of sport fishery.

Lake Kenogami, to the south of Lake St. Jean, is historically known as a place to catch big brook trout, but since the early 1980s it has emerged as a prime landlocked salmon spot, thanks to extensive stocking operations. Eastward, native populations of ouananiche still thrive in more remote reaches of the St. Lawrence north shore. The Manouane, Outardes and Manicouagan watersheds are prime ouananiche waters in Quebec. Many Labrador rivers also support heavy populations of ouananiche, especially in their headwaters. The Hamilton River, which flows eastward from Churchill Falls to Goose Bay, is one of Labrador's best-known landlocked salmon streams.

Many of the rivers draining northward into Ungava Bay harbor native populations of landlocked salmon as well, notably the Caniapiscau. Its headwaters, once accessible only by floatplane across countless miles of tundra and taïga, is now accessible by road via Matagami and Radisson.

No matter where you find them, landlocked salmon are, without equal, the finest, most demanding denizens of our coldwater streams. It is an accepted fact that in all but the most remote waters, some 98 percent of the ouananiche caught are taken by no more than 2 percent of the anglers. Quite simply, successful landlocked salmon fishing demands skill, dedication and experience. A case in point is Lake Tremblant, where every account of its big salmon in the media precipitates a flurry of angler interest, a flurry which dwindles just as quickly because the fish are extremely difficult to catch. So, season after season a small group of knowledgeable anglers—no more than a handful—ply Lake Tremblant's waters and take fish consistently.

The lessons Lake Tremblant has to teach, however, are valuable, and the techniques apply on most other southern lakes. While any available leisure time is a good time to fish, most of the big landlocks are caught during five or six days following the smelt run peak. During this period salmon can be found actively hunting in shallow waters, but since the concentration of forage fish is fast disappearing, they are more prone to attack an angler's offering.

Minnow-imitation patterns which resemble smelt are highly effective during this period, and the secret is to troll them on a very long line at a faster speed than used for most other game fish, except muskies. The reason for the long line is that these fish are easily spooked by boats, so as you proceed you create a wide swath in which there are no fish. The long-line technique places your fly far enough behind the boat to reach the zone where fish have forgotten the disturbance and begin to move freely once more. Furthermore, instead of trolling in a straight line, try a lazy zigzag or serpentine course so the lure, which travels in a straight line, cuts across undisturbed water.

Another technique which can be used where smelt are absent originates from Lake Memphremagog, where runs of these forage fish usually occur before the season's opening. For a two-to-three-week period, depending on how quickly the sun warms the lake, landlocks work the shoreline in search of baitfish. The technique for catching these salmon consists of simply trolling a short, shallow line right in close so your rod tip almost touches the shoreline foliage. Initially we used small minnow imitation plugs, but quickly found that streamer flies like the Magog Smelt—or one of its many subsequent modifications—were even more effective, especially when trolled with a full-sinking line extended. Again, the secret is to troll at a fairly fast clip.

A fast trolling speed, combined with a short line is also used on Lake St. Jean, although I've spoken to other anglers who had excellent results using the long-line techniques. I ran into problems every time I tried it, however, because pleasure boaters on Lake St. Jean seem to derive great satisfaction from veering close behind fishing boats and cutting their lines.

For river fishing I prefer fly gear, partly because streamers or wet flies work better than lures in fast-flowing water, and partly because I feel the full power and speed of a landlocked salmon. Streamers like the Nine Three, Black Ghost, Gray Ghost, Supervisor, Edson Light Tiger and Edson Dark Tiger rank among the top landlocked salmon flies, but I always carry a few Muddler Minnows as well. On magical summer evenings when the lake surface is flat, mirroring the surrounding shorelines, I've seen ouananiche on both Lake Sorcier and Lake St. Jean take surface flies. I have caught them with fairly large Gray Wulffs on Lake Sorcier as well as on hinterland rivers. The technique for fly fishing landlocked salmon on flowing water is identical to that used for sea-run salmon.

A ouananiche is different from every other game fish. It embodies the spirit of freedom, of wilderness and of wild places. It is a spectacular fish, hard-fighting, acrobatic and bold. In its genes can still be heard the rumble of retreating glaciers, and in its leaps is the quicksilver glint of sun on ice.

George Gruenefeld's Must-Have Patterns for Ouananiche

- Dry: Gray Wulff
- Streamer: Black Ghost
- Edson Dark Tiger
- Edson Light Tiger
- Magog Smelt
- Muddler Minnow
- Supervisor

CHAPTER 19

THE HARRINGTON FISH & GAME ASSOCIATION

Dave Smallwood

T HE WOOD STOVE WAS ANTIQUATED AND SIMPLE, MUCH LIKE
the membership which was enjoying its warmth at the moment. Our
president, Clarence P. Henderson, was leaning against the podium at
that particular time, the bar at others, beginning his version of the State of the
Union Address.

"Gentlemen, you are a sorry-looking lot and the financial statement I hold
in my hand says you're cheap as well!"

Clarence had a way of glaring over his bifocals when he chose to berate the
membership on its lack of morals, money and manners. The fact that he stood
6' 4" and weighed around 240 lb helped as well. "We have agreed, as a membership, to stock eight lakes with ten thousand fingerlings this spring. In case
you haven't looked at a calendar lately, that is approximately THREE MONTHS
AWAY!" His jowls now oscillating rapidly, he continued, "The Trout Stocking
Fund is empty and we need to come up with $800 in short order so, pursuant
to The Harrington Fish & Game Code of Ethics, Article 26, subsection 9, para-
graph 2A, I am implementing a surtax that will apply to all items sold in this
bar. Furthermore, all bar tabs and moneys owing will be marked for immediate
payment—and all subsequent financial transactions in this establishment will
be on a CASH BASIS ONLY!"

We sat in stunned silence. Did we actually have a Code of Ethics? From over my left shoulder, Yves, a French Canadian who lived down the road in Hawksbury, whispered, "No money, no trout?" I nodded my head slowly in the affirmative. *"Pas l'argent, pas biere?"*

I turned my head slightly and whispered back, "That's right. No money, no beer."

By this time Clarence's glare and imposing physical attributes had us writhing uncomfortably in our seats. I think we all felt somewhat akin to my old tomcat the time he realized that our neighbors' two dogs, which he had taken great pleasure in tormenting, weren't tied up—and there wasn't a tree within 50 yards.

"And Article 26 is effective immediately!" Clarence drove home his finishing blow with as much finesse as Muhammad Ali in his prime. We were beaten and knew it. Since cold hard cash among the members was as fleeting as full-time employment, there was nothing else to do but head home and consider the evening's repercussions.

It's not that the Harrington Fish & Game Association members were a bunch of debauched, incorrigible fly fishermen with little or no means of visible support. Absolutely not. That's simply the way things worked out and, well, we were as comfortable with it as we were with our mission statement, which in actual fact was as nonexistent as our Code of Ethics. We had simply set out wanting to have some high-quality trout lakes where we could fish and not pay exorbitant club fees. The fact that we couldn't pay the fees, anyway, or that none of the clubs would have us, was irrelevant.

The idea was simple. North of Hawksbury, between Harrington and Lost River, were numerous small lakes far back in the Quebec forest. After locating prospective bodies of water on a topographical map, forays were organized to scout out the most likely locations for a stocking program of brook trout or "Quebec Reds" as they were called locally. We even had the services of a legitimate fisheries biologist to help us along—Jean-Yves Menard. Mind you, I think he was more interested in keeping an eye on our antics than being an actual member. He became an "associated" member shortly after Serge Beaulieu suggested stocking the town's water supply with brookies. Serge wasn't much on hiking and thought this was a good idea for the association's older members.

That idea had no sooner got loose when we had Jean-Yves parked on our doorstep, no doubt at the urging of the provincial fisheries office.

As the list of selected lakes was narrowed down, Jean-Yves would take us along for some testing, and then let us know which waters had the best chance of producing trophy trout. It worked beyond our expectations. After that, each spring the hatchery truck would arrive at the clubhouse, and the driver would typically refuse to turn off the ignition until the order was paid for in cash. We were always short but the money always materialized, covered by some "anonymous donor." We all suspected our president, but he would never admit it.

The clubhouse, actually Clarence's one-room bar, was perched down a dirt road right on the forest's edge. From there, each member would hoist a couple of large plastic bags containing trout fingerlings into his backpack, and then strike out for his designated lake with Clarence's orders ringing in their ears: "Be careful with those trout! Don't bounce around like that, Serge. They're fragile! And don't you clowns be stopping off to fish before you release those trout or you'll die of thirst if I have anything to do with it."

I think that if Clarence could have arranged it, we would have tiptoed up to the lakes so as not to disturb the tiny fish. We quickly learned that the trick to stocking trout was to be the first in line. It was infinitely better to depart for your assigned lake with the president's nattering growing ever fainter with the distance than going with the president in tow. That was the "luck" of the last person in line.

I'm sure it was Fate that delayed me that morning. First, an alarm clock went off 20 minutes late, plus my truck, which rarely did start on command, took twice as long to coax into life. When I finally skidded to a stop in front of the hatchery truck, Clarence was waiting impatiently beside three plastic bags full of trout. I was caught. It would be me and the president and three hours of hiking. And dividing two into three, I knew whose pack would be heaviest.

Our destination was McPhee Lake, high in the hills on the west side of Riviere Rouge. The spring day was already hot, the trail's clay surface was playing havoc with my footing, and the president was in rare form—meaning he managed to stay within 50 yards behind me, all the while his booming voice berating "the youth of today" for being out of shape.

When I stopped to catch my breath, I heard the sound of dripping water. I looked at the ground behind me. A puddle! Gently lowering the backpack, I was inspecting the plastic bags when Clarence ambled up beside me.

"Problems?" he asked, crouching down on one knee.

"I've got a leak in one of these bags . . . and there it is!"

Clarence had about the most solemn face I have ever seen. To lose so much as one fingerling was unthinkable. In his mind they were almost like his own flesh and blood.

"Take off your hip waders!" he barked. "I have an idea!" One never argued with Clarence, so the words *Why?* or *No!* never entered my mind.

"Now, we'll just pour them into your waders and top them off with water from the other bags."

He held the waders as I poured—carefully. Then we set off once more, each carrying a water-filled hip wader with the top rolled down to help contain its precious load, a rather cumbersome load but it worked.

Fortunately for me, the trail wasn't rocky, so despite the fact I was in my stocking feet, we made good time. About 40 minutes after discovering the leaky bag, every fingerling swam out of my wader into the shallows of McPhee Lake. Clarence watched this event from atop a half-sunken log, not uttering a word; then he handed down my other wader. When the last fingerling had departed from the final bag, I climbed slowly back up onto the bank. As Clarence had vacated his stage and was nowhere to be seen, I flopped down under a big maple tree, leaned back and closed my eyes. The coolness of the ground soothed my aching body, and I could almost feel the earth absorbing three hours of sweat.

The hiss of a fly line startled me from my self-imposed dormancy. I sat up and glanced to my left. It was Clarence making a succession of tight, liquid casts that culminated with his fly alighting daintily on the water's surface. In all the time I had known the man I had never seen him fish, let alone cast a fly. I couldn't believe what I was seeing. He was pure poetry in motion, each cast an identical imitation of the last—deft and purposeful.

I lurched to my bare feet and walked closer to watch. I announced my presence by stubbing my toe on an exposed root and yelping with pain. Clarence glanced at me and smiled, not in amusement, but a warm, gentle smile that indicated he was in his glory at the moment.

"They like to circle from right to left in this lake," he announced. "Beats me as to why." His bamboo rod quietly creaked and groaned as he sent his fly out to a chosen spot known only to himself. "Watch carefully. Leave it on top of the water, and then raise the tip so as to move the fly ever so little."

As the No. 12 Adams moved almost imperceptibly, the largest brook trout I had ever seen swirled at the fly, took it and was off to the depths. It was a grand battle on the fish's part, but despite its size and strength, Clarence was the eventual winner. When the brookie finally came to hand, we briefly admired its deep, beautifully marked body. Then Clarence removed the hook and watched as the trout slowly finned back to the deep water. Clarence looked out over the lake, studied it for a few moments, and then indicated by a quick movement of his head to the left that it was time to head back.

After donning my socks and my still-wet waders, I found Clarence once more gazing at a lake which, like the others under our jurisdiction, was stocked by anglers with little else but a love for fishing and for their quarry.

Late one fall evening I left the Harrington Fish & Game Association headquarters, not knowing it would be for the last time. Life had caught up to me, and fate was leading me westward to my destiny.

The phone call came on a Saturday night, three years after I left Quebec. "Clarence died yesterday," Serge said quietly. "He went to get some firewood for the wood stove and didn't return. He had a heart attack out by the wood pile."

Serge had other calls to make, so we said our good-byes. Truth was, neither of us wanted to talk at the moment.

I sat back and thought about the man who had spearheaded the association from the outset, stocked lakes with his own money, and introduced so many of us youngsters to the art of fly fishing and the beauty of the back-country. How do you thank someone who has given you such a large portion of your life? Who quietly cleared your bar tabs when you were broke? Who left money on the front seat of your truck because he had heard college books were expensive—but who would never admit to the deed? Perhaps by just passing on the love of the sport that he gave each of us.

So, if you see a fly fisherman sitting by himself, hoisting a beer and quietly proposing a toast to the Harrington Fish & Game Association, please allow him his moment of silence.

CHAPTER 20

MOUSE ON WATER

George Gruenefeld

IN THE FINAL MOMENTS OF DUSK, IN THE SUSPENDED TIME WHEN the last of the daytime predators find sanctuary and the first nocturnal hunters emerge, the water's surface turns to the color of molten lead. It is a promised moment of truce, an interval when the peace of the moment insinuates that no harm can befall earth's creatures.

In the corner of the small bay, a spruce blowdown lists far out over the lake's surface; the soil around its roots inexorably washed away during the storms of autumn past, yet still the softwood clings to life with just a few bare strands. And, if you could hear with the ears of a night hunter, you'd catch the faint sound of miniature paws scampering nervously over the rough, resinous bark of the fallen spruce.

Its courage bolstered by the deepening grayness of dusk, a vole has ventured out, almost to the vertical crown of the spruce. As it turns to scamper back to the cover of the forest floor, the vole misjudges its footing and falls with a Lilliputian splash to the water's surface. Momentarily confused, the creature swims away from shore. Then, realizing its error, it sets out valiantly for the bank. Its progress scores a tiny V across the flat surface of the bay.

With landfall near at hand, a muted splash suddenly interrupts the silence, and when the ripples subside, the vole has disappeared and the implied truce of late evening is restored. Nature quickly glosses over the drama of life and death; the surface of the bay is once again flat and the color of molten lead.

It happens so swiftly and so unobtrusively that we humans are rarely aware of what has transpired, yet if the truth be known, the scene is repeated frequently during the course of a summer. Perhaps we labor under mistaken concepts of predator–prey distinctions and have been lulled into believing that land creatures devour land creatures and that fish feed on other fish, on aquatic nymphs and, occasionally, on some terrestrial insect that ventures away from the safety of shore.

The fact is that fish can, will, and do readily feed on small birds and mammals whenever the occasion presents itself. The list of finned predators runs virtually the full gamut of freshwater game fish from brown trout to gar. It comes as no surprise that pike and muskies consider mice, ducklings and even small muskrats as choice items in their diets, but few anglers realize that trout also feed readily on small mammals. Yet feed on them they do.

According to W.B. Scott & E.J. Crossman in the 1973 *Freshwater Fishes of Canada* from the Fisheries Research Board of Canada, Ottawa (212), brook trout devour, without hesitation, small mammals that stray from shore. They write that "larger trout, particularly in northern waters during summer, are known to eat numbers of small mammals, mainly the field mouse, *Microtus,* but also the redbacked vole, *Cleithrionomys,* and shrews" (225). The authors also cite lake trout as being partial to mice and shrews.

Bass—both largemouth and smallmouth—will take mice, voles and shrews with scarcely a moment's hesitation. Harry Murray, in his book *Fly Fishing for Smallmouth Bass* (Lyons & Burford, New York, 1989, page 31), states that "Mice provide such a large meal for the smallmouth that once the fish is big enough to handle one I doubt that any poor creature that finds himself swimming past a smallmouth's feeding station ever makes it all the way across. Although mice can swim they have no affinity for the water and in most cases are taken by bass by accidentally falling from the banks. Their method of swimming is much like a dog's paddling."

Murray also states, "A deer-hair pattern, fished in close to the banks with a slow, steady retrieve, will take many nice bass."

It might be that anglers have not realized—or perhaps do not want to acknowledge—that their favorite game fish will readily devour small mammals, but in relation to the number of other lures on the market, few are made to imitate mice. Even bass anglers, who are aware of the penchant both largemouths and smallmouths have for mice, carry only a token selection of imitation mice in their tackle boxes. Since both the stores and the tackle manufacturers are driven by the whims of the consumers, the selection is understandably scant.

Yet if more anglers understood when, where and how fish take small mammals, and used mouse imitations accordingly, the demand would be a great deal higher. It stands to reason, for instance, that you'll catch few, if any, bass, pike or trout by flinging a mouse imitation around in the middle of a lake; nor will fish rise out of 30' (9 m) of water to grab it from the surface, no matter how enticingly you twitch it across the water. To be effective, you must absolutely present your offering at a time, in an area, and in a way the fish expects to see it.

A mouse swimming more than a stone's throw from shore is immediately suspect; a fish expects to see the small, hapless mammal in water close to shore where it might have fallen from an overhanging bank or vegetation. And the fish expects it to be swimming toward or possibly parallel to shore, rarely away from shore. Keep your casts fairly short, if possible.

If you're fishing for pike, you'll likely get the best results during the brightest part of the day when they are on the prowl, but for most other game fish, dawn and dusk are the best times—in fact the darker the better—since this is when they venture into the shallows to hunt for food. For evening fishing the time to start is after the last rim of the sun has disappeared below the horizon, and the time to stop is when you can no longer tie a knot in your line. In the morning start at the first hint of dawn and stop when the first rays of the sun begin burning off early morning mists.

Imitation mice will produce fish, whether you use spinning gear or fly rod. Naturally, with spinning gear, a lure must provide the weight to carry it to its target, and top water plugs like the Creek Chub Mouse and Shakespeare Swimming Mouse provide just that. However, fly fishers have a great deal more versatility in weight, shape, size and materials, since the line carries your offering to its target. Deer-hair bass bugs, cork-bodied poppers and even big Muddler Minnows can all be fished to imitate a swimming mouse trying frantically to reach the safety of shore. Beyond these recognized patterns, fly tiers are limited only by their own imagination and skill in creating realistic fly dressings from spun deer hair.

Essentially, all you really need to achieve is a believable shape and let your skill as a fly fisher do the rest. I use an elastic band and natural deer hair to fashion effective mouse flies. First tie a length of elastic band onto the hook so it extends three fingerwidths beyond the hook bend. Spin on a medium bunch of deer hair, and then tie in two short pieces of elastic band to emulate the back feet. Spin on two or three more bunches of hair and attach two additional short sections of elastic for the front feet. Spin on two more small bunches to reach the hook eye.

Now, trim the spun hair into the shape of a mouse, being careful not to cut off the feet or tail in the process. Lastly, trim the tail and legs to an appropriate length—I like to leave the tail fairly long so it trails in the water, while the feet should extend only a short piece beyond the belly so they have a degree of rigidity while retaining flexibility.

At first I added eyes and ears to a fly to produce, in my own mind, a realistic mouse, but then it occurred to me that a fish looking up will never see either of these decorations. They impress the angler more than the fish! Now I completely bypass this time-consuming step and have yet to find it makes any difference in the effectiveness of my offerings.

Of course, other tiers have their own thoughts on the subject. Murray, in *Fly Fishing For Smallmouth Bass,* for instance, does not bother to tie in any kind of material to represent feet. In fact he prefers a totally unadorned belly profile and uses chamois leather to fashion the tail. On the other hand, Murray applies a spot of black paint on either side of the head to represent eyes, and he trims the deer hair in such a way as to leave ears.

Far more important is the way a fly is fished. No fly will tempt fish if you belong to the fling-out-and-crank-in school of angling. To use an imitation mouse effectively, you must, in your own mind, become that creature. You have no fear of swimming, knowing that the air bubbles in your fur will keep you afloat, but you're acutely aware of the unseen danger from below, so you dog-paddle frantically to safety. Retrieve your line in continuous one-inch spurts and, after about two feet of steady "swimming," stop two or three seconds to rest, to let the panicked creature catch its breath before continuing its desperate bid for safety. If you have trouble empathizing with such a mouse, imagine instead, how you would feel after being tossed into shark-infested waters about 300 yards from shore and having to swim for safety.

Murray's technique is similar: "I get my best results by working the Deer Hair Mouse in close to the bank with a line-hand twisting technique," he states in his book. "I seldom fish it out more than ten feet from the bank before picking it up to recast back tight to the shore about five feet above or below the first spot."

Prime spots to fish for bass are along the edges of docks, next to semi-submerged blowdowns, and beneath overhanging brush or trees. In areas frequented by brown trout, blowdowns and overhanging vegetation are also productive areas to cast mouse imitations. For brook trout, the shorelines of headwater lakes can be effective. In streams, cast your offering into the fast water, and then start it swimming to shore as it reaches the pool so it imitates a mouse that has been swept down by the current and is trying to make its way to shore in the calmer water of the pool. Walleye will also respond to flies when they enter shallow bays to forage for food, usually late in the evening.

As I write these lines, my mind returns involuntarily to images etched into my memory—images of the Sainte Marguerite River in late evening, a September chill already in the air and dusk settling in over the solitary pool. Gone are the salmon anglers of summer. The season has been closed for a week and the handful of sea trout anglers with whom I share the river are congregated on a more popular pool downstream. For all I know I'm the only human being left on the darkening planet.

The winds that bent high branches earlier in the day have completely subsided, and in the calm semi-darkness I savor the ease with which I can cast the outrageously large, bulky Muddler Minnow out into the fast water and marvel at how much it looks like a living thing as it bobs down into the pool. It and the river seem to be the only living entities in a microcosm shrinking with every passing minute. My attention is riveted on the bobbing fly. I'm mesmerized as it swims to shore, obediently following the undulations of the fly line. I forget that the creature is a fly, that it is attached to a wisp of barely visible leader. I forget why I'm there. And the night creeps another step closer.

Again I lift the fly line skyward, then forward, and again the strange, disembodied creature floats down through a sluice into my pool, and somehow I'm unaware that its life, its frantic bid to reach shore, is a mechanization created by my own hand, by my own thoughts. A dozen times, perhaps more, perhaps less, it floats down through the sluice and swims across the pool, for all I know, of its own accord. And night comes closer yet.

Mechanically, I prepare to cast again. As I do, a big fish swirls almost at my feet, and I catch a glimpse of a white-trimmed fin. I feel the rod tip come up solid against the pull. I sense that the jolt is too hard even before the leader snaps, and within seconds the river regains its composure. It's as if nothing has happened. No trace, no evidence. The river flows on inexorably and the night deepens.

And I stand at the water's edge, fly rod tucked under an elbow, staring down at the broken leader in disbelief.

GEORGE GRUENEFELD'S MUST-HAVE PATTERNS FOR WARMWATER FISHING

- Cork-bodied Poppers
- Deer Hair Bugs
- Deer Hair Mouse
- Muddler Minnows

CHAPTER 21

WHITEFISH

Dr. Martin Lamont

THE DISTRIBUTION OF WHITEFISH, WHICH BELONG TO THE family Coregoninae, is widespread throughout the northern hemisphere, including Canada, Asia and Europe. When the last polar ice cover started melting and the process of glacial retreat was in full swing, there were rapid changes in the waterways. With these changes whitefish expanded into new environments, and their rapid colonization brought about morphological diversity of the species. There are many variations, from giant to pygmy forms, but three basic classifications are of interest to Canadian fly fishers: lake whitefish, mountain whitefish and inconnu.

In body form whitefish are salmonid, characterized by a small head and mouth, and a forked tail. Their scales are almost herringlike, cycloid and large, giving an overall silvery color with hints of purple-pink iridescence on the sides. The dorsal is darker, blackish with tones of brown, green or blue. The whitefish can only inhabit coldwater environments and does not tolerate pollution.

Spawning can occur at any time of the year but most are fall spawners, from September to December. Unlike salmonids, whitefish do not form redds; they generally deposit eggs randomly on rocky and gravel areas with some water flow.

All species of whitefish tend to school up in deep to midwater levels, where they feed on plankton, fish eggs and bottom invertebrates such as scuds and larvae. When an insect hatch occurs, whitefish rise to the surface to intercept the emergers. In the north these are typically chironomids, mosquitoes, caddis or may flies. The rise form is distinctive, with only the tips of the dorsal and tail fins breaking the surface as the whitefish roll over while taking insects just subsurface or in the film. The reason for this is that the mouth of a whitefish is under its snout, so it takes an insect by sucking it in.

Lake Whitefish *(Coregonus clupeaformis)*

LAKE WHITEFISH are the most abundant and widespread, occurring in most Canadian provinces except the Arctic Islands, Nova Scotia, Prince Edward Island and Newfoundland.

Their body form is deep and slightly flattened laterally. They average 2–4 lb (900 g–1.8 kg) in weight, but occasionally are larger. Most anglers catch lake whitefish while winter ice fishing with baits and jigs. Although fly fishers can also intercept them in lakes, they are seldom deliberately targeted. Most often they are hooked accidentally while seeking other species; however, having been surprised by the scrappy fight, many anglers start wondering about how to take them consistently.

Lake whitefish are often available early in the season as the water becomes ice free, feeding and become more active somewhat earlier than trout. In some southern locations they are available as early as March. As water temperatures warm with the approach of summer, whitefish seek deeper water and scatter over wide areas. Although juveniles prefer the warmer shallows of lake margins, which are more productive in the spring, later on they move to cooler depths as littoral water temperatures increase.

During fall spawning runs, lake whitefish move into shallow waters and tributary streams, again making them accessible to fly fishers. They also migrate in and out of lakes, and can be found between lakes in interconnecting rivers. Occasionally they even migrate into brackish estuaries and Arctic Ocean inshore areas.

Mountain Whitefish *(Prosopium williamsoni)*

MOUNTAIN WHITEFISH occur on both slopes of the Rocky Mountains. In British Columbia, watersheds like the Skeena, Nass, Kootenay–Columbia, and Thompson–Fraser systems have sizable populations. In the mountains and foothill areas of Alberta, they are found in watersheds of the Waterton, Highwood, Oldman, Crowsnest, Castle, Athabasca and North Saskatchewan rivers. Further stocks occur in the northeast watershed of the Rocky Mountains Cordillera, in the Liard and Peace systems, and other Mackenzie river tributaries. Populations also occur farther south in Washington, Oregon, Idaho, Montana and Wyoming.

Mountain whitefish have a more pointed head with a prominent bulbous snout, a cylindrical body shape, and a large adipose fin. They are rarely large, but up to 2 lb (900 g) is possible. Of interest to fly fishers is the mouth structure—as it is small and overhangs the lower jaw, fish ingests their food by sucking rather than biting. This often results in short takes and requires finesse in approach. Ultra-fine leaders and tippets such as 2–3-lb test fluorocarbon are a good choice. Take care while playing these fish as the mouth is soft and tears easily. Lightweight tackle and rods—something around a 3- or 4-weight—will also help.

As some southern and western rivers stay open and ice free in late winter and early spring, some of the best fishing is available in January, February and March. Following a cold spell, rivers are often low and clear, and at such times whitefish school up.

To hook these cautious biters, fish fine and use small patterns representing hellgrammites, stone flies, caddis larvae, nymphs and fish eggs. Being weighted, small wire worm flies sink well. Tie them in gold, copper, bronze, yellow, orange, red and green, and fish them deeply by bottom-bouncing. Takes are virtually imperceptible, almost requiring a sixth sense to tell the difference between a fish and touching the bottom. They take with a gentle pull, and your strike should be rapid but with minimal movement of the rod tip.

Spring fishing can also be dangerous. I recall as a young man fishing for mountain whitefish in the Toad River, a tributary of the Liard. The river ice had just started breaking up in the middle of the channel, and the water was clear, not yet colored by the silt that occurs at full ice-out. Conditions were ideal for fishing; however, reaching the open water required some ingenuity. I found two blown-down aspen trees, which I dragged out onto the unreliable ice in hopes that if it gave way the trees would support my weight.

The whitefish action was fast and wonderful, but I was so nervous that I cautiously retreated to the bank. No sooner had I reached shore when the whole ice pan gave way and began tumbling downstream in large chunks. Firmly engraved in my mind is the fact that fly fishing can, at times, be a dangerous sport and that one should not take unnecessary risks.

Mountain whitefish do not like or inhabit lower elevations and gradients, where a river builds in size and slower currents result in increased temperatures. Neither do they take to high-alpine lakes or the uppermost tributaries of river system. The areas most suitable for mountain whitefish are main streams and larger midsection tributaries. Flat valley sections where a river breaks into braids is especially useful for rearing young fish. The juveniles prefer slower side areas of a stream.

In warming summer temperatures, whitefish move into and hold in fast-flowing, riffled sections or drop back into big, slow, deep back-eddies which tend to retain food that passively drifts in. At these times it pays to try tiny No. 28–18 dry flies, nondescript black or gray patterns with no hackles, which sit deep in the surface film. Alternatively, try drifting deeply sunk weighted nymphs into the back eddies.

Late summer offers some of the best fly fishing opportunities as fish begin concentrating in schools, preparing for their fall spawning runs. This, however, can be inconsistent as the schools are constantly moving, foraging in different river sections on a daily basis.

Inconnu *(Stenodus leucichthys)*

FRENCH VOYAGEURS NAMED these giant, fish-eating whitefish *inconnu*—meaning "unknown"—and they are also called sheefish.

In Yukon they are found in large river systems like the Yukon, Kluane and Teslin; in British Columbia in the Liard; in the Northwest Territories in the Mackenzie, Anderson, Taltson and Big Buffalo rivers of the Mackenzie Delta,

Hay River and Great Slave Lake. Being in remote areas and in large river systems on which travel is often difficult, inconnu are rarely targeted by anglers.

In appearance, an inconnu is somewhat tarponlike. Its overall color is silver and it has large, bright scales, an elongated, streamlined body, and a large mouth with an extended mandibular jaw. Its jaws contains small teeth, which seems appropriate for the only fish-eating member of the Coregoninae. It is also the largest whitefish, attaining weights of 50 lb (23 kg) plus. However, 10–15 lb (4.5–6.8 kg) is more common.

There appears to be two types: one entirely confined to fresh water, the other anadromous, wintering and living in estuarine brackish areas to feed and returning to fresh water to spawn during late summer or early fall.

Right after ice-out, lots of inconnu are on the move inland from their brackish wintering areas, following schools of baitfish on their upstream migration. Early season water flows are heavy and silted from snowmelt, so fishing can be impossible for fly fishers.

Around midseason—perhaps late July and August—water levels are lessening and inconnu become easier targets. As they are still feeding heavily on baitfish, they are in prime condition. They target whichever species are present: whitefish, cisco, grayling, char, salmon fry, suckers, smelt, sticklebacks and sculpins. The best fly-fishing opportunities are the mouths of clear-running tributaries feeding onto main-stem rivers and areas with slower flows.

In September and October, when inconnu ascend clearer creeks to spawn, they stop feeding. They are midwater, broadcast spawners, depositing eggs onto rocky and gravel substrata of the riverbed. Following spawning they rapidly return to the main-stem rivers, where freshwater inconnu seek out deep holes for wintering over, and anadromous types return to the estuaries. Many survive to repeat spawning annually.

The fry develop rapidly and by two years, after juveniles adopt a piscivorous appetite, growth rates are accelerated. Adults are almost exclusively fish eaters, living for up to 20 years and reaching weights of 50 lb (23 kg).

Fly patterns for inconnu should represent baitfish. Many that work for pike or lake trout will do. Generally, a white-bodied fly with a two- or three-color wing of polar bear hair or FisHair (blue, yellow and green) are often productive, some weighted, some not. Use large hooks in No. 2–4/0, and add a little

Flashabou for added visibility. Also try patterns like the Zonker, Matuka, Thunder Creek, Deceiver, and Mickey Finn.

Because of their migratory nature, inconnu are constantly on the move—here today, gone tomorrow. It requires a boat and motor to follow their daily movements, so you should hire a local guide who knows a river's most likely locations. As inconnu avoid fast flows, concentrate on quieter, more protected holding water. Cover the slower-moving inside bends and areas close to the openings of sloughs. Look for river obstructions, drop-offs, or holes behind bars and ledges, and fish any large back eddies.

Flies must be presented deep by using a full-sinking or sink-tip line. When your fly is close to the bottom, imitate the slow, intermittent swimming action of a baitfish moving along the bottom. Experiment by varying your retrieves, but keep that fly deep and slow.

Surface disturbances created by inconnu chasing food close to the surface often gives away their location. At these times it pays to cast down and across with a floating line and an unweighted fly. Stripping the fly back fast in the surface will trigger strikes. An inconnu hits a fly hard, and then follows up with some spectacular aerial acrobatics.

An 8-weight rod is the minimum for casting large flies, and the longer the shaft, the better for mending line when fishing flies deeply. A reel with good line capacity is also necessary. These fish are not leader-shy, so it pays to fish short, 4' tippets of 8- or 10-lb test.

Flies for Coregoninae

IN-SURFACE FILM EMERGERS: Small "nonfloating" dry flies or subsurface "dry flies" with no- hackle. No. 18–14 Blue-Winged Olive or Hendrickson and emergent chironomids.

Nondescript no-hackle midge patterns: Black or gray, No. 22–18 "dry/wet flies."

Emerging caddis: A good generalization is simple patterns of soft hackle (very sparse—two turns) nymphs based on the Partridge and Orange, Yellow, Peacock Herl, and Olive. No. 18–14.

Wire Worms: With or without brass bead heads. Wire colors in gold, bronze, copper, yellow, orange, red and green. No. 20–14.

Egg patterns: Any Glo-Bug in small sizes, No. 14–10.

Baitfish patterns: Whitefish occasionally strike small streamer patterns fished with a long, slow, steady retrieve through deep, dark eddies. Try small Muddler Minnows with a touch of yellow in No. 14 and 12.

Another midwater tactic is to fish with a tandem setup. Any of the above flies with a plastic egg or two positioned 20" (50 cm) up the leader. This additional weight helps swim the fly deeper.

To present a deeply sunken fly, present a combination of a heavily weighted Gomphus with no hook or barb, plus a small trailer or dropper pattern which could be any of the above mentioned flies positioned about 20" (50 cm) from the "sinker."

For inconnu, use large No. 2–4/0 baitfish pattern. The basic fly could be a white chenille body with a silver rib. Add a white polar bear hair wing and red hackle fiber tail. To finish, tie a teal body feather as a hackle at the head. Other patterns include variations of the Zonker, Matuka, Thunder Creek, Deceiver, Mickey Finn, Polar Aztec, Alaska Mary Ann, Bumble Puppy, Flash Fly and String Leech Fly.

Dr. Martin Lamont's Must-Have Patterns for Whitefish

- Partridge Series
- Wire Worms

Baked Stuffed Whitefish

Moist and flavorful
(Makes four servings)

1 2–3 lb—whitefish, or equivalent of smaller fish—1 900g–1.4 kg
1 tbsp—olive oil—15 mL

1 cup—diced cooking onion—250 mL
1 cup—diced mushrooms—250 mL
1 cup—diced celery—250 mL
2 cups—diced fresh bread crumbs—500 mL
3 tbsp—fresh tarragon—45 mL
or 1 ½ tbsp dried tarragon—22 mL
Zest and juice of a lemon
Salt and pepper to taste

1. Scale whitefish, remove dorsal fin, entrails and head. Make a few slashes on sides to prevent fish from curling during cooking.

2. For the stuffing*, sauté onion, mushrooms and celery in oil until nearly soft. Add bread crumbs and cook for a minute or two. Place in a bowl; season with tarragon, lemon zest, salt and pepper. Allow to cool.

3. Salt and pepper inside cavity and spoon stuffing inside. Place fish in a baking dish and squeeze fresh lemon juice over it. Bake in a 350°F (180°C) oven until cooked through, about 10 minutes per inch (4 minutes per cm) of thickness, or less if cooking smaller fish.

You may use your favorite stuffing recipe for chicken or turkey, but use milder herbs like dill, tarragon or basil as whitefish has a delicate flavor.

Serving each person a whole fish is wonderful. Surround whitefish with a mixture of stir-fried red and yellow peppers. Creamy mashed potatoes also complement the sweet, mild-flavored flesh.

–Wayne Phillips

CHAPTER 22

SAILFIN OF THE TREE LINE

Bob Rife

THE ARCTIC GRAYLING *(Thymallus arcticus)*, A SPECIES OF FISH you could label Sailfin of the Tree Line, carries a ponderous load of myth beneath a colorful, grand dorsal fin. Prized by fly fishers for its beauty, grayling surprises many for not only its sporting character, but its delicious taste.

Izaak Walton, in *The Compleat Angler,* probably was responsible for the first, and longest-standing of the untruths about the fish, one that has led anglers astray for 300 years. He described grayling as soft-mouthed, and fly fishers, myself included, reacted softly and carefully to strikes, not unlike the tactics used for whitefish. Invariably, this technique resulted in disappointing getaways and prolonging of the myth.

Truth to tell, the grayling's lip is more like an old leather belt—pliable, but tough and once the hook is planted, difficult to lose. Credence for the soft-mouth fable was also abetted by two other details—the puny size of the creature's mouth and the manner in which grayling take a fly. Compared to a trout of similar length, the mouth of a grayling truly is quite small and unless anglers are prepared with flies ranging from No. 20–10, they may experience nudges rather than strikes and blame it on that supposedly soft mouth, when it was merely because the hook was too large.

The strike itself is another grayling peculiarity. They often lie deep in clear, cold runs, most often in water so clear you can look down and see the school. They rise swiftly to the fly, moving like an express elevator straight up to the target, unlike other species that rise in long slants to eye the bait from behind. After a speedy attack, the grayling may then either roll like a salmon to take the fly, or in bass fashion, leap from the water over the fly to complete a splashy downward take!

My first encounter with this exotic (it earns the designation, if for nothing else because it dwells in far-off, hard-to-reach and therefore expensive places) was on a trip to the Northwest Territories, an area north of Manitoba, which on April 1, 1999, became Nunavut ("Our Land" in Inuktitut). I was wandering a portion of the Wolverine River, well above the tree line, almost to the Arctic Circle.

My gear was simple: a No. 6 floater on my favorite boron, a fairly stiff 8 ½' rod. Since this particular spot, as I found out later, held only average-size grayling, I might have tried a 5-weight rod (there was little wind in this protected bend of that river). I could also have selected a sink-tip line—and I did just that later from the shore of a nearby lake, successfully tossing a bedraggled Hare's Ear Nymph. I suppose I could even have tried a sinking line to get right down and work the bottom to seek out trophy fish.

Surface fishing on a lake may require a long rod (9' or 10') to deliver searching casts, especially if you don't see any dimpling. Even if you do, approaching by boat is difficult. Wind is an ever-present casting hazard though it can put a hatch into windrows along shore for a real grayling bonanza.

The sinking presentation in more shallow locations can give you a "second chance" on each cast after the initial pass. Use a hand-twist retrieve to bring the fly back to the target. Should you feel a tap, but no strike, stop the retrieve. That cease in the action will almost certainly bring on a hit—they truly are an inquisitive fish.

Be that as it may, I like working the surface—I want to see all the fun I can. As a result of this preference I've come to realize arctic grayling are not as leader-shy as internationally known author and personality Charles Ritz would have it in his *A Fly-Fisherman's Life*. He really warns you off—advises very long leaders plus an ultra careful presentation. Mind you, he was tackling the European cousin of *arcticus,* and more to the point, was working the heavily angled waters of the Traun River in central Austria. Any game fish worthy of the name, and *Thymallus* is surely that, gets the smarts and can become exceedingly wary under those conditions.

For my first try at grayling, I selected one of my personal favorites, a dark Whitlock Muddler, putting it on a 5' 4x leader. Next was positioning for the cast. Of course, when you can see the target, as I could, it is much easier. The idea is to get either upstream or across stream and cast so you can drift your offering over the fish, being careful to have a little slack line.

I was fishing at the top of the run from a boat maneuvered by my guide who was using a long pole. I cast downstream, and then waited as my fly caught the current. It was a fortuitous float—the attraction brought on a bump-and-roll strike. Of course I was startled! Of course I was excited! Of course I struck too soon. It was similar to my initial experience with Labrador salmon—too anxious. I had to learn to wait until the grayling got the fly fully into its little mouth.

Arctic grayling don't get to see that many anglers in their far northern home, so they aren't at all shy. But be assured, they are precise. Cast a foot to either side of their station and the presentation will be ignored. More often they take a fly at the head of a run rather than at the tail.

At times they also can be picky about fly selection. Sometimes floaters are their thing—other times it's nymphs. They seem frivolous in their mood changes. The change is sudden, giving the stream an almost inexplicably deserted aspect. Yet a switch in tactics may bring it all to life again.

"You may come face-to-face with a grayling and be ignored; yet it will study every fly as though trying to help you find the right one," former executive editor of *Field and Stream,* Al McClane wrote some years ago.

Not to be forgotten is that insatiable curiosity. An oddball choice from the fly box could restart the action.

My guide brought up another point. "Watch them dimpling—the rises. If it stops, they could be gone—the school could move. No point in sticking around. They just won't be hitting here then. What's good, is that they stick together. If that happens, we'll go look for another feeding run—when we find one—see them rising, we're back in business."

For the moment I could still see fish dimpling the glide in the river, so I shot another cast. It was hardly classic, but I was a yard or so above the target and the next thing I knew there was a burst from the water and whammo! I had hooked my first grayling.

This time no premature strike, no worry about a set hook or the supposedly soft mouth—the fish darted to the side and then plunged deep, moving aggressively from side to side—then it was over. It wasn't a prolonged fight, but it was interesting. I pulled the 1-lb (680-g) grayling over the side and glowed with pride. And I got a whiff of what startled Walton: "Some think he feeds on water-thyme, for he smells of it when first taken out of the water. . . ."

It's an unusual odor—neat—giving one a sensation similar to the moment when you smell freshly caught smelt. And, as if you hadn't guessed, that smell of thyme is what prompted the scientific Latin moniker *Thymallus*.

On first glance away from the graceful dorsal fin, you'll notice grayling have large scales, not unlike a whitefish—but much more vibrant colors! I stretched out that amazing fin. Every first-time grayling angler does it—check any catch pictures. But it is wonderful. Keep your eyes on the fish, for the colors fade quickly. The rows of spots, black on tinges of pink and white and purple and greenish iridescence make for a never-to-be-forgotten moment. Ray Bergman, the author of *Trout,* said it well: "When you looked at them in the water preparatory to landing them, they looked like fish-shaped, animated purple flowers."

So why that huge fin? Ernest Schwiebert, architect, angler, author *(Match the Hatch, Nymphs,* among others) and a charming river companion of mine, always recognizable for his wide smile and trademark red neckerchief, called the fin a part of the grayling's nesting business. In his monumental, two-volume treatise, *Trout,* he explained: "While the male hovers protectively near, the female sweeps the coarse, bottom gravel free of silt. Their exaggerated dorsal fins are part of a ritual territoriality, and are raised like hackles on a gamecock when another male approaches the female." Sounds reasonable.

The elegant *arcticus* is of the genus *Thymallus.* That latter grouping includes the European grayling, as well as the arctic and subarctic (not *arcticus*) strains found across northern sections of Asia and Europe. Among other subspecies is the now extinct Michigan grayling, after which the town and township in that state were named. Tales of the timbering era of Michigan relate how dozens of wagons loaded with grayling made daily trips to railhead towns so the grayling could be distributed to Detroit and Chicago restaurants. Sadly, they also tell that if the transportation was not on time or unavailable, tons of fish were left to rot.

While this catching was going on, logging stripped the forest cover, poisoned streams and created dams that choked off spawning runs. Despite amazing fecundity—thousands of eggs per fish—the Thymallus tricolor was gone in about 30 years.

Happily, there's still an abundance of arctic grayling in the northern reaches of North America. Nearly all large oligotrophic lakes and their tributaries in the region are its home. Good examples are Great Slave and Great Bear lakes.

But something to keep in mind when you plan that big trip is to realize that it is not found, so far as can be proved, in the rivers flowing into Hudson Bay or the rivers that drain northern Quebec or Labrador. Biologists feel this absence has something to do with events during the age of glaciers.

For those of a scientific bent—the grayling's flamboyant dorsal fin carries more than 17 rays—those bony extensions like ribs in an umbrella. It spawns in the spring, March and April, with as many as 13,000 eggs per fish.

Their diet varies with the location, but does include small stone flies and may flies. However, please note, a major portion of the diet—more important by far than insects are invertebrates—scud and shrimp. The former are found along shorelines when the grayling tour those areas in the spring during spawning. The shrimp in the diet are mainly a deepwater variety—some living as far down as 1,000' (300 m).

Later that memorable day on the Wolverine (ah, how long those arctic days . . . they almost never stop, literally), I had the opportunity to dispel yet another grayling myth. Somewhere I had picked up the notion that grayling were a second-rate food fish—bony with an easily forgotten taste. Now I know why the restaurants in Detroit and Chicago were so eager for catches in those bygone days. Grayling has firm, white flesh with both a delicious, delicate flavor and aroma.

The best ways to prepare it are pan frying or poaching. Another method to delight the palate is to smoke the flesh. Connoisseur Ritz loved them that way.

Barbecue fans can try broiling them in foil with, say, a slice of tomato and a lit-tle green pepper or celery wrapped in to enliven the mix.

For frying, pan dress the fish as you would a brook trout, making sure to carefully remove all of those large scales. My wife's revered Uncle Percy, who taught me to enjoy pickerel (walleye) fillets at the campfire, would surely have placed half a pound of butter in the pan to assure all went well in the cooking. It was his way and the result was fabulous. However, in these more fat-conscious times, a dollop of vegetable oil will serve the purpose. Don't overcook any fish—a minute or so on each side until golden brown, then . . . aaah! Some writers say it is the best-tasting of fish. I'll leave that to you.

To poach, place the fish (dressed and descaled as above) in a court bouillon with some suitable herbs (Thyme? Why not?) and poach lightly until it meets the taste test.

Having enjoyed this feast, the obvious task at hand is to pinpoint what to use and where to go to find more grayling and perhaps tap into a record fish next time out.

The usual catch is 1 ½–5 lb (700 g–2.3 kg). The current world all-tackle mark, and one that has been around since August 16, 1967, is the fish taken by Jeanne Branson (the name has a familiar ring—former lodge-owner's family?), a 5-lb 15-oz (2.7-kg) beauty from the Katseyedie River.

Top weight in the fly-fishing category is a 3-lb 12-oz (1.7-kg) fish taken by Dr. Paul Carpenter from Great Bear Lake on August 5, 1982. He was using a 2-lb test leader. A number of grayling weighing 4–5 lb (1.8–2.3 kg) have been land-ed by fly anglers from Great Bear in the past few years on leaders from 4- to 8-lb test. Generally, the recommended size is a tapered 3x (about 5-lb test) to 5x (2 ½-lb test) and 5–9' in length.

About the cast—better get used to a slack-line effort for surface and just-below-the-surface work in rivers and on lake shorelines. Offshore lake casting is usually with a sinking line unless you see the fish rising.

The slack-line cast, for those unfamiliar with it, is a method of throwing more line than necessary to reach your target. That way it will absorb some of the force of the stream's current and allow you a few extra seconds of drag-free float where the grayling will see only the fly, not the leader or line.

Practice this cast. Just before the loop straightens out over the target, pull back on your casting hand, and do it abruptly. This causes the line to jerk back toward you and fall in folds on the water. Varying that sudden movement of the casting hand changes the amount of slack line formed. It does take a little practice, though the resulting opportunities are well worth the effort.

In deep runs I found that the normal nymphing technique—short, stop-start retrieves on a sink-tip line—brought on solid takes.

As far as fly selection goes, these could serve: Black Ant, Black Gnat, Elk Hair Caddis, Gold-Ribbed Hare's Ear Nymph, Humpy, March Brown and Muddler. Almost any small, dark, stone fly, nymph or midge would probably work. A Black Ant filled the bill for me; there were no giants, but lots of curious fighters. This list was compiled from my trips and from the likes of Art Flick, Ed Koch, Lefty Kreh, Schwiebert, Ritz, Charles Wetzel and Dave Whitlock.

Bob Rife's Must-Have Patterns for Grayling

- Black Fur Ant
- Black Gnat
- Early Brown Stonefly Nymph
- Hare's Ear Nymph

CHAPTER 23

PANFISH AND THE FLY

Steve Galea

I F I WERE A GAMBLING MAN—AND I'LL BET YOU TEN TO ONE
I'm not—I'd risk a box of fine flies backing up the proposition that most of
us began our angling careers by catching the lowly panfish. Furthermore,
I'd suggest that even now, every time we pass a freckle-faced kid fishing off a
dock, a smile forms and there is a strong temptation to stop and join in the fun,
or at the very least, to watch and coach as that time-honored red and white bobber gets pulled under again and again. In fact, I'm so sure of those two statements that I'd hazard to call it gambling at all. Such is the ageless appeal of panfish—those lively little gems that represent our Canadian angling roots.

Panfish—meaning rock bass, perch, crappie, bluegill, and pumpkinseed—
are the Rodney Dangerfields of the Canadian fly-fishing scene. They get no
respect at all, which is a shame, because they can teach even the most skilled of
us a thing or two, as well as offering us fine and varied sport from before black
fly season to well past the dog days of summer when mosquitoes and deer flies
jump into the fray.

What can we learn from a fish that's been caught by every youngster who
ever set bare feet on a dock? Well, it's like that saying, "Everything I ever needed to know about life, I learned in kindergarten." Consider this a fly-fishing
kindergarten, for panfish will remind you of those long-forgotten fundamentals.

The first and most important one is: We are doing this to have fun! The second: Never underestimate anybody.

The real significance of these fish lies in the fact that they are ideal tutors for new fly fishers. They are not hard to catch and are about as forgiving as your mother, yet they can be selective.

Catches will get progressively better as the fundamentals are mastered. Teach a person to fly cast in the morning; then watch them glow as they tussle with panfish that afternoon. This enjoyment and success will encourage new anglers and simplify the sport to a level proportionate to their development. It provides them with an on-the-water classroom to try out the techniques learned from books or video—fundamentals that are not so easily grasped without real honest-to-goodness practice. It gives good experience on the important skills of watching the line and hook-setting, as well as line management and fighting the fish. And it's much easier on the heart to lose a 2 ½-lb (1.1-kg) rock bass than an 11" (28-cm) brookie.

It is for these reasons I believe panfish were put on earth to make anglers of us all. But, more than that, they are yet another perfect opponent for the fly rod. They are prolific, scrappy, aggressive and sometimes fussy, yet take everything from dry flies to nymphs. Seasons are long, and they live in waters ranging from the smallest pond or creek to the Great Lakes. They can be found in one form or another across most of southern Canada. In a word, they are accessible and often save the day when all else fails. In fact, panfish are so hardy and adaptable that fish and game departments across Canada encourage us to catch them by providing extremely generous limits and lengthy seasons.

Which came first, panfish or the pan? Hmmm . . . I suppose the former. Yet it's easy to imagine that these two institutions evolved side by side, or that if the inventor of that cooking utensil was a Canuck, he enjoyed perch as much as back bacon. Panfish make a tasty meal, fit perfectly in the pan, and come in numbers that prevents anyone from going hungry. A shore lunch of crappie or perch ranks right up there as a genuine culinary delight, and they are so prolific that we can enjoy taking limit catches without feeling guilty.

To me—issues of the stomach aside—the beauty of fly fishing for panfish lies in the chance to experiment with things most of us wouldn't want to try on a crowded trout stream. Long ago I improved my nymphing skills on a creek where a hoard of considerate, if not intellectual, rock bass gave me private lessons. After a few of their insightful examples, I felt very comfortable taking the lessons to the rainbows and brookies, with great success I might add. I still go back and enjoy that spot; success hasn't changed me.

As easy as they can be to catch, to hook panfish consistently requires an understanding of their ways and habitat; they should not be underestimated. Naturally, each species is unique, but as a group we can make a few general statements that will help load up your stringer.

They are schooling fish. This is important for their survival and also holds significance for the angle. If you catch one, you will catch others—often a multitude, in fact. Besides that, they generally roam in packs of like sizes, so if you land a big panfish, stay put and you'll likely catch more. Conversely, if you find yourself catching stunted fish and it's the big ones you're after, move on.

Panfish require cover to ambush their quarry. Typical cover includes stumps, rocks, sunken trees, the shade of overhanging trees, weed beds, dock pilings, buoys and the like. From these underwater hangouts they chase minnows, small frogs, surface insects, nymphs, crustaceans, worms, leeches and emerging insects. This evidence that they are aggressive opportunists permits us to fish a wide variety of flies, but generally patterns that work best by dead-drifting in the current or making slow retrieves will provide the most action.

Panfish are fairly low on the aquatic food chain. Everything from seagulls and herons to fish ducks and larger predatory fish seeks the pleasure of their company at dinner. As an example of the adversity they face, consider the fact it is estimated a yellow perch has a 1 in 5,000 chance of surviving its first year. Other panfish have it worse. Often, the last thing a panfish sees is the toothy grin on a pike's face. On rare occasions that crooked smile might be worn by a fly fisher.

Their defense lies in the use of cover, the numbers in a school, and speed, although as fish go they are not particularly fast. For them it's sort of like the old joke where the fellow says to his buddy, "I don't have to run faster than that grizzly—I just need to be faster than you." The shade and shelter extended by cover help create a preferred temperature and valuable shelter from danger that lurks above, hence, the importance of these locations to the angler seeking panfish action.

Earlier it was noted that panfish take flies with surprising regularity. Although they can be selective about the lure that is offered, the real key to catching them is to slow things down considerably. Quick motions tend to frighten them. If a fly can be brought within their line of sight by a dead-drift or a slow hand-twist retrieve, you stand a good chance of drawing a strike. With poppers or sponge spiders, the idea is to pop or twitch the lure, and then let it sit for an agonizing few seconds. These fish spend a good deal of time scrutinizing their next meal. Often, especially with pumpkinseeds, the strike will come during this quiet time. The nice part of this is they often do it within plain sight, so anglers with polarized glasses can see how a fish responds, approaches and takes their offering. Having an understanding of all these things is, of course, invaluable on the trout stream.

Einsteins these fish are not. Still, they have their preferences and can be surprisingly selective. As a case in point, I recall camping on a point overlooking a Haliburton area lake one summer. Shortly before dusk perch began rising to the bay's surface with such regularity that the rings made it appear as if it were raining. Having been skunked for splake all day, it seemed these easy pickings might be a welcome break. My brother and I rigged up our fly rods and commenced chucking every dry fly in our box at them, but to no avail. Undaunted we desperately fumbled with smaller and smaller flies in the fading light. Finally, we discovered the ticket—a No. 18 Griffith's Gnat! With this diminutive classic we caught perch on almost every cast until they stopped rising with the onset of darkness. This worked the next night as well and remains as one of the unexpected highlights of that week-long trip.

Generally, though, it isn't that complicated. Hooks No. 12–8 are more than adequate on most occasions. Personally, I prefer barbless No. 10s. You'll catch lots, so why waste time unhooking them?

Size issues aside, the choice of flies in panfishing is largely a matter of individual preference and esthetics. But, as in other types of fishing, certain flies have gained a reputation as consistent producers. Foam Spiders, small poppers, Woolly Buggers, Woolly Worms, moth patterns, crayfish patterns, small Dahlberg Divers, Partridge and Yellow soft hackles, Black Gnats, Light Cahills, Black-Nosed Dace, Muddler Minnows, flashy streamers, and the like have all been used with good results. I can personally attest to the fact that small Clouser

Minnows, brown stone fly patterns, Bead Head Prince Nymphs and Parachute Adams dries can be deadly as well.

Strike indicators can be a useful tool when fishing in and around cover such as brush piles, or when dead-drifting wet flies or nymphs in currents. They also have their place when trying to detect the delicate take of a crappie. Watching the end of the fly line where it connects to the leader also works very well and is infinitely more instructive when a novice is learning to recognize the subtleties of a take. I have used both methods extensively and prefer the latter, but you know what they say about opinions. Try both and decide what works best for you.

There are two schools of thought when it comes to equipment for these little guys, and I guess it is really a function of your own thoughts on why you fish for them. If you fish panfish for fun, the obvious choice would be a lightweight rod, say a 1- or 2-weight with a floating line and light leaders and tippets. You don't need to fish fine and far, but the practice and sport inherent to that approach can be virtuous things.

On the other hand, using your regular trout rig has advantages as well, especially when fishing from shore on big lakes or ponds. Casting distance is improved, poppers are easier to throw, wind is less of a problem, and you are fully prepared if you run into some different, larger, toothier species. Besides, it gives you experience with your trout rod. All of these things have merit. Catching 1,000 trout in a season is a real feat. Catching 1,000 panfish in a week is an attainable goal. Get the picture? It's all experience to the good.

As for clothing, nothing prevents you from using your good old vest and waders if you want to get right in there although this is generally summertime fishing and a sport that can be handled nicely from shore or a canoe. A wide-brimmed hat and polarized glasses are always a good idea, too. A small net can come in handy for those "surprise fish." On really hot days a float tube is an absolute treat, but be sure to use adequate sunscreen as low-angled rays bouncing off the water can fry you up more quickly than you'd think.

One very effective way of fly fishing for panfish entails a three-level approach, which is a prospecting method I have come to rely on. Using this common sense approach allows you to carefully tailor the flies in your panfish box, and an organized box facilitates more fishing time. It's also a genuine phenomenon that you can show off at the fly-fishing club. I suspect that not many of us have ever seen one up close.

Begin by casting a popper, dry fly or Foam Spider out to likely stretches of water. If the fish are active and striking, the action is absolute pandemonium. The advantage of starting on top is easily understood if you are casting around weed beds, logs, downed timber, or other potential underwater snags. It should be stressed that the top-water retrieve is very much stop-and-go stuff—more stopping than going, in fact. Letting ripples from the lure die down to nothing is a good rule of thumb before twitching or popping it again. Waiting even longer wouldn't hurt. If a current is carrying the lure, twitch or pop it when it passes over high percentage spots.

Failing to get action on slow top-water retrieves, or if the fun has died down to nothing after a few fish (which is often the case), proceed to a midlevel streamer or wet fly like the well-respected Woolly Bugger or a Partridge and Yellow. Cast out to the same spots and bring the fly back with an extremely slow hand-twist retrieve. If a strike indicator is used, keep an eye on it; otherwise, pay close attention to the end of the fly line. A gentle tug or hesitation in the line is all there is to indicate a take. In some cases, though, the takes are anything but subtle.

Once all the possibilities from the previous two approaches have been exhausted, the next step is to cover the same water with a weighted fly like a Bead Head Prince Nymph or a small Clouser Minnow. After the line is laid on the water, let the fly sink while watching the indicator or end of the line. Strikes often come as the fly is descending. If the fly makes it to the bottom, then a slow, jigging retrieve will often be just what the doctor ordered. Where rock bass are common, this also brings in smallmouths very effectively.

If none of these methods produce, move on to a different location or try again with a new selection of flies. Color changes often make all the difference. Switching a black Woolly Bugger for one of olive has often saved the day for frustrated anglers. Yellow or black are well received in most Ontario waters, but may be different in your area. Experiment. It's good, clean fun.

The nice thing about the method just described is you cover all of the water thoroughly, and if everything goes well you will experience three very different techniques—and generally hook fish each way. This is one reason why I believe panfishing is the way to introduce newcomers to the sport. A dedicated panfish angler will gain a wealth of experience over the course of a season.

Another pleasant spin-off of this, or any other kind of panfishing, is the nontargeted species that often join in the fray. When fishing my favorite panfish creek for rock bass, I often catch a limit of smallmouth as a bonus, for they enjoy the same habitat. Pike and walleye have provided me with similar surprises.

When fishing creeks or rivers for panfish, read the water as you would a trout stream. Anything that causes a break in the current, or any drift that carries food toward fish waiting in ambush positions is prime, especially around the cover of stumps, fallen trees, rocks and weed beds. Deep holes and undercut banks work just as well for panfish as trout.

Cast dries and Foam Spiders upstream and across. Poppers can be retrieved against the current, and then twitched over likely spots as they swing. Streamers can be fished traditionally—hung in the flow and swung across as well—and wets by casting across and drifting down, then retrieved with a slow hand-twist. Nymphs can be deadly when drawn in against the current, or fished upstream in the traditional manner using a high stick and that magical touch that skilled nymphers develop. This is, in fact, a great place to learn and practice difficult nymphing techniques. All of these methods are effective ways to catch panfish in flowing waters.

When fishing lakes and ponds, bear in mind that most panfish are comfortably within easy-casting distance from shore. Find cover within casting range, then work it by moving along the shoreline until you connect and can fish the area thoroughly. Wading works, but so does fishing from small punts, canoes or float tubes. During springtime, fishing spawning beds is almost a no-brainer and is permitted in most jurisdictions.

As mentioned previously, the larger fish tend to go slightly deeper. Shoals anywhere in a lake are good bets, as are the mouths of feeder streams and the fringes of weed beds. The characteristics of specific fish also help determine where to wet a line.

Bluegills are a form of sunfish that thrive in quiet, weedy waters near docks and along shaded shorelines. Larger fish school together and inhabit slightly deeper water. They feed only in the daytime, probing the shallows in the mornings and evenings to feed on insects, crustaceans, worms and the like. When hooked on a fly rod, they resist by swimming at right angles to the pull of the line but give up after a short, vigorous battle. They are easily duped by dry flies, especially may fly and damsel fly patterns. Spawning beds are made on sandy or gravelly bottoms and guarded by the male, which is particularly aggressive at this time. This happens in springtime when water temperatures hit about 67°F (19°C).

Rock bass are one of my favorite summertime targets. These scrappy, little, red-eyed sunfish thrive in areas that have rocky bottoms and fallen trees—the more rocks the better. They are aggressive and take little poppers with gusto and gobble up undersized Clouser Minnows as well. A short but lively fight is the result. They will also feed at night with great enthusiasm. Inhabiting the same waters as smallmouth bass, mixed catches are quite often the norm. Rock bass spawn in areas similar to other sunfish, also in the spring when water temperatures hits 60–70°F (16–21°C).

Yellow perch are the fish that save some outings when all else fails. When found, perch bite all day long, especially around noon and toward evening, and then shut down at night. They move in schools of like-sized fish throughout a lake and can be found in deeper water during the day, then shallower as evening approaches. Perch are not much as fighters, but if jumbos are encountered, things are very different for fly rodders. These fish average 1–2 lb (450–900 g) and are full of fight.

Perch can be found in creeks and rivers, but lakes are their natural habitat. They prefer colder lakes with rocky and sandy bottoms and extensive weed beds. As indicated by their coloration, they are denizens of the weed beds which they use for cover. Perch are generally caught where the water is 3–15' (90 cm–4.5 m) deep, so split-shot or sink-tip lines can be useful. They have a penchant for yellow flies. Like crappies, they are prized for their table value.

Both black and white crappies are pursued by an army of devotees. The challenge of catching these paper-mouthed fish and the reward they provide in the pan are enough incentive for most anglers. When a school is found and the bite is on, they are excellent quarry for fly fishers. They will do best in the afternoon with small bucktails and other flies that imitate minnows, the preferred food of both white and black crappies. Preference is given to white and red colors with a bit of flash. They can be taken up top with small poppers and dry flies, but not nearly as effectively.

Like other panfish, crappies are creatures of cover. In springtime they come in shallow to spawn, and nests are protected by the males. Prior to spawning, crappies gather in large schools. They are vulnerable from this prespawn stage through to the spawn. As summer approaches, they roam deeper waters. Black crappies, which are most common in Canada, prefer clearer waters than their white counterparts and also prefer more vegetation and quiet waters.

Pumpkinseeds are one of the most beautiful of all sunfish—or of any fish that swims for that matter—so it's fitting that wherever present, they are probably the fish most of us cut our teeth on. They are perfect in that they are generally close to shore, preferring docks, weed beds, buoys and other cover, usually over soft, silty bottoms. Their spawning habits are very similar to bluegills.

Pumpkinseeds take flies very well all year round but even more so in the spring. Wet flies and small dries are very effective at this time, but dries can be quite productive on still waters in the summertime. Although yellow and black are preferred colors, I have had great luck with a Partridge and Yellow, Black Gnat (wet and dry), Leadwing Coachman, and damsel fly dries, to name a few. But with these fish, almost any appropriately sized (No. 14–10) fly will likely get some results. Even so, fine tuning and experimentation will produce further success. Where legal, a dropper fly can double your action.

So there you have it—maybe not everything you ever wanted to know about panfish, but enough to get you started. Rig up for them on those hot summer days when other action has slowed down to nothing, and you'll not regret it. Well, you just might complain a touch about your jaw hurting from all that laughing and smiling, but hey, that's the price us panfishermen are willing to pay.

STEVE GALEA'S MUST-HAVE PATTERNS FOR PANFISH

- Dry: Foam Spider
- Griffith's Gnat
- Wet: Bead Head Prince Nymph
- Black-Nosed Dace

Bluegill Crepes with Spicy Chili Garlic Sauce

Spectacular, but not difficult. Make crepes ahead of time and keep
warm in the oven or reheat just before serving.
(Makes four servings)

2–3 cups—cooked bluegill—500–750 mL
½ cup—diced onion—125 mL
½ cup—diced mushrooms—125 mL
½ cup—diced celery—125 mL
½ cup—diced red pepper—125 mL
1—Clove garlic, finely minced
Butter or oil for cooking vegetables
2–3 tbsp—chopped fresh tarragon —30–45 mL
Salt and pepper to taste

1. Remove fish head, entrails, scales and discard.

2. Lightly salt and pepper fish and sauté, or roast in 350°F (180°C) oven until no longer translucent (about 10 minutes). Skin as soon as possible; remove flesh and reserve. Ensure no bones remain in flesh. Break fish into pieces.

3. Dice onions, mushrooms, celery, red peppers, garlic. Season with tarragon, salt and pepper and cook in butter or oil until softened. Combine with fish.

White sauce

(Makes about 1 ½ cups / 375 mL)

3 tbsp—butter—45 mL
3 tbsp—flour—45 mL
1 ½ cups—milk—375 mL
Salt and pepper to taste

1. Place butter in bowl and microwave. Stir flour into melted butter and

microwave briefly to cook. Add milk and microwave until thickened, stirring occasionally to keep sauce smooth.

2. Gently fold white sauce into fish mixture. Add salt and pepper to taste. Keep hot in oven until you stuff and roll the crepes.

3. Spoon ⅓–½ cup (75–125 mL) of the fish and white sauce mixture onto center of each crepe and roll sides around filling. Top with band of chili garlic sauce.

SPICY CHILI GARLIC SAUCE

Combine ½ cup (125 mL) white sauce with ½ tsp (2 mL) hot chili garlic sauce.

–Wayne Phillips

CHAPTER 24

ONTARIO STEELHEAD

Andrew Somerset

A
S TROUT SEASON WINDS TO A CLOSE EACH FALL, YOU WOULD expect Ontario's fly fishers to sigh, mope about, and wipe down their rods with misty, nostalgic expressions on their faces—but they don't. Instead, they are overtaken by an odd, feverish condition. Their hands twitch, they mumble to themselves irrationally, and they toss and turn in their sleep— it's steelhead fever! Trout anglers get excited about opening day, but dedicated steelheaders get bouncing-off-the-walls pumped when the first cool, wet days begin to rattle leaves from the trees.

I'm sure that some future graduate student will unlock the cause of all this. The proximate cause of the steelheader's apparent fever, our future student will postulate, is imminent contact with steelhead. The ultimate cause, however, is that the steelheader needs the fever to keep warm in the coming months as icy rain dribbles down the back of his neck and his toes go numb.

The most telling symptom of the fever is The Stare: at once empty and penetrating, intense and bored, it is the final symptom of steelhead fever. More than the hunched shoulders, the reddened fingers, and the icy drip hanging from the end of his nose, The Stare symbolizes the steelhead fanatic's unfortunate addiction. It is a look of both determination and resignation, the look of someone who is cold and wet and bored, but is damn well staying until he catches a fish.

As it rains and blows and spits wet snow, the steelheader retracts into his neo-prene shell until only his eyes remain alive, eyes that continue to pierce the veil of blowing wet flakes, ever hoping to catch a sliver of silver—until a voice floats across the water, calling, "This sucks. Let's go home."

Steelhead in the Great Lakes are contradictory fish. We love them and hate them, get pumped up for the run and then die of boredom fishing it. On one day, they are easy to catch; for the next 10 you get blanked. Some days you'll believe they are great game fish; on other days—usually snowy ones—they just aren't worth the pain. They are among our most sought-after game fish, and—among anglers—our worst understood. Most strange of all is that in Ontario, a country characterized by flat cornfields rather than the fir-covered mountains of their native range, steelhead now sustain stronger runs than in many West Coast rivers.

One of the most common steelhead misconceptions is that the Great Lakes steelhead fishery is put-and-take. While this may be true in some states, it is not the case in Ontario. For the most part Ontario's steelhead are wild fish, except in rivers with high fishing pressure where wild runs are supplemented by stock-ing. In fact, Ontario had "wild," or naturalized steelhead runs created by American stocking programs before stocking ever began in the province.

Seth Green, the American hatchery pioneer, stocked the first steelhead in the Great Lakes in the mid-1870s. By 1882 at least one tributary on each of the Great Lakes had been stocked with rainbows. On the Canadian side of the lakes, however, only three plantings took place before 1900 although strays from the U.S. side were already establishing runs. Those strays received an enthusias-tic welcome from Ontario anglers. By 1912 pressure from anglers led to stock-ing on Ontario's side of Lake Superior.

Steelhead were established in Ontario tributaries of Lake Huron and Georgian Bay by 1920, and the Ontario government began stocking in 1922. Lake Erie followed in the late 1920s, but stocking on Lake Ontario did not begin until the 1940s. In each case the fish soon established naturalized runs, and today steelhead are found in many Ontario streams where they were never stocked.

Although most anglers loved the new fish for their fighting qualities, some expressed concern over effects the introduced species might have on native brook trout. That concern persists today. Many anglers complain that the introduction of rainbows to their favorite streams has ruined the trout fishing. Although there is evidence that steelhead may out-compete brook and brown trout in high-gradient streams, this does not seem to be the case in Ontario. When they do "ruin" the trout fishing, it is because large numbers of juvenile rainbow trout take dry flies more readily than browns or brookies, forcing the stream trout angler to change tactics.

Except perhaps on Lake Superior, Great Lakes tributaries are quite different from West Coast rivers on which steelhead evolved. Nevertheless, Ontario steelhead runs are strongest on the lower lakes. Their success in Ontario rivers should not be surprising, for they are supremely adaptable. In their native range steelhead inhabit streams ranging from frigid Alaska to the Californian desert. Their anadromous lifestyle helps insure them against drought and disaster, and they are more tolerant of warm water and less dependent on ground water than either brook or brown trout. Steelhead are a natural fit for marginal Ontario streams that can't support brook trout.

Why have steelhead been so successful in the Great Lakes? Ontario rivers, thanks to a combination of geology and land use, are far more productive than West Coast rivers, thereby producing more smolts for their size. Those smolts also have higher survival rates in the Great Lakes than in the ocean, thanks to a notable lack of killer whales, seals and other large predators. Pressures such as commercial by-catch, clear-cut logging and the like are also less significant. The result is steelhead runs that can dwarf runs in West Coast rivers of similar size.

Today, Ontario steelhead runs are sustained mostly by natural reproduction with supplementary stocking in some heavily pressured rivers. Their numbers are limited mainly by climate and habitat quality; dry summers and cold winters cause fluctuations in year-class strength. Unfortunately, many anglers respond to fluctuating numbers by calling for more stocking. But stocking sometimes does more harm than good as bucketloads of rubberlike hatchery fish swamp runs of naturalized fish that have become adapted to their adopted rivers.

Are Great Lakes rainbows steelhead? Some anglers claim that they are just rainbow trout, and deride the notion of "Great Lakes steelhead" as romantic twaddle. In fact, steelhead and rainbow trout are the same species, with some strains showing more migratory tendencies than others. The distinction between the two exists only in angling usage. The argument that Great Lakes fish are not "steelhead" because they never enter salt water is the kind of legal hair-splitting that only highlights the childishness of the argument. The best answer is that a fish that behaves like a steelhead is a steelhead; Great Lakes fish grow to large sizes, mature in large bodies of open water and migrate up rivers to spawn. Close enough.

Certainly, the fish stocked in the Great Lakes over the years were predominantly from "steelhead" strains, rather than resident rainbow strains, which may account for their migratory tendencies. Although many sources name the McCloud River rainbow strain as the first to be introduced to the Great Lakes, in fact the first eggs shipped to Seth Green were of steelhead from the San Francisco Bay area, with McCloud River fish not following until three years later. The McCloud strain, also called the Shasta or Californian strain, actually consisted of the offspring of an indiscriminate mix of steelhead and resident rainbow eggs. The Redwood Creek steelhead strain was also stocked in Lake Superior before the turn of the century with great success.

Ontario reared the McCloud River strain at the Normandale hatchery until the 1930s when the Kamloops rainbow strain and a fall-spawning strain were added to the mix. The resulting Normandale rainbow was a mongrel. In 1981 an outbreak of disease at the Normandale hatchery forced Ontario's Ministry of Natural Resources to eradicate the Normandale strain, which in the long run was probably a good thing. Ontario's standard hatchery fish is now the naturalized Ganaraska strain, and wild Ganaraska River fish are mixed into the brood stock periodically to prevent the strain from becoming too "domesticated."

The hodgepodge of different strains stocked into Ontario waters has created a fish that is somewhat different from its West Coast cousin. Most anglers agree that the "best" Ontario steelhead are Lake Superior fish, which are also genetically closest to West Coast fish. Stocking and genetic tinkering on the lower lakes has resulted in lower quality fish, but where steelhead are allowed to establish unique local stocks, the quality of the fish improves.

Steelhead can be found in Ontario rivers 10 months of the year. A short-lived and probably ill-advised attempt to establish summer runs by stocking the Skamania hatchery strain met with little success. Fall runs vary in strength from one river to the next and begin as early as the first of September on some rivers. Fall runs peak in November on most rivers. Winter steelheading is usually impossible because rivers are frozen over in January and February. Steelhead in Ontario spawn between February and early May, and some remain in rivers until the beginning of June. However, while steelhead are available for most of the year, it seems there is never enough time to fish for them.

Conventional wisdom holds that steelhead are among the most difficult of freshwater fish to catch, ranking alongside muskellunge and Atlantic salmon. This is only partially true. Dedicated muskie hunters will tell you that they are fairly easy to catch—once you know where to find them—and steelhead are little different. Catching steelhead is a two-pronged problem: first, you have to find the fish, and then you have to catch them. Then there's a third prong—you also have to land them.

No book or magazine article has yet told the secrets to finding steelhead. Locating them is a matter of experience and local knowledge, and even steelhead gurus who seem always to catch fish may not be able to explain how they do it. The general advice is deceptively simple: fish around obstructions. Fish migrating upstream stop when they meet an obstruction, which may be as obvious as a dam or as deceptive as a shallow riffle. Fish stop below obstructions and above them, and such locations may often hold pods of fish. But any steelhead river is a maze of obstructions. Guessing how far upriver the fish may be and which obstructions will hold the greatest numbers . . . as I said . . . experience and local knowledge.

Finding fish is the larger part of the problem in steelhead fishing, for they are not particularly hard to catch once you have found them. Techniques for Ontario steelhead differ from those used on the West Coast. Ontario steelheaders are more likely to favor nymphs and egg flies than hair-wing wet flies and Speys, and they will dead-drift flies under indicators more often than use the wet-fly swing. In part, the difference in technique reflects the fact that steelheading in Ontario evolved from trout fishing, whereas West Coast steelhead fishing is the child of Atlantic salmon fishing. However, some of the differences are a result of different physical conditions.

Generally, Great Lakes rivers are smaller and get colder in winter than their southern British Columbia counterparts. By late October water temperatures on southern Ontario rivers may be above 85°F (30°C), and the mercury remains there until April. For much of Ontario's steelhead season, winter steelhead tactics will be more successful. Fish are reluctant to move to the fly, so you must move the fly to them. Pools and runs on Great Lakes tributaries are often short and deep, requiring weight to sink flies quickly to the bottom and keep them there. The reasons for an Ontario steelheader's preference for nymph fishing is clear.

Still, the swinging fly can be deadly for Ontario steelhead if used properly under the right conditions. The wet-fly swing, often dismissed as a technique for beginners, is actually one of the most difficult to master. To provoke a steelhead into swatting a wet fly, you must first present it at the steelhead's eye level and then conspire with the current to pull it away just as it approaches the fish's nose. Catching trout on wet flies is like teasing kittens—they'll swat anything. Catching steelhead on wets is more like teasing an adult cat. You have to work your mouse-on-a-string just right, and even then you won't get anywhere unless the cat is awake. Small rivers and cold water make the swing difficult, but when it works, it is one of the most exciting ways to catch steelhead.

The key to catching Ontario steelhead—provided you first find fish—is to understand how conditions change through the season, and then adjust your tactics to match. Ontario's steelhead season can be divided into five distinct phases: early fall, late fall, winter, early spring and late spring or the drop-back season.

Early fall fish are strong and aggressive but unpredictable. The strength of early fall steelhead runs varies from one river to the next and from year to year. Some rivers have comparatively strong early fall runs with fish entering early in September. On most rivers, however, the early run is weak with small numbers of fish following chinook salmon upriver.

Water temperatures in early fall are still within the preferred range for steelhead, and the fish are active. On rivers with strong runs, they can be caught on swinging wet flies and even (according to a lucky few) on waking dry flies. The same tactics would probably succeed on other rivers, but with smaller numbers of fish, most anglers prefer to use proven methods. The most popular approach is to fish egg flies behind chinook salmon redds, where steelhead wait and pick off eggs. Nymphs also are effective, since hen salmon cutting redds will dislodge large numbers of aquatic insects. While you might not expect steelhead to show any preferences, float fishers say that when the fish are on spawn, eggs work best. Since float-fishing accounts for many more steelhead than fly fishing, I'm inclined to take their word for it.

The greatest problem in early fall fishing is spotting fish. Clear water promotes sight fishing, and it is always most tempting to fish for what you can see rather than what you can't. The dark, easily spotted shapes of spawning chinooks are distracting, "training" the eye to see darker shapes. The far paler and less numerous steelhead are often harder to spot among them. Chinooks are obvious—fresh steelhead are ghosts.

The late fall season begins as leaves drop from the trees, sometime in mid- to late October on the lower lakes. By this time the chinooks are mostly finished spawning, and carcasses litter the river banks and shallows. On many fall steelhead rivers, this is the prime steelhead season when larger fish begin running upstream.

In late fall, water temperature drops to 40°F (4°C) and lower. Steelhead become less active, and even anglers who favor the swing switch over to standard Great Lakes steelheading tactics: dead-drifting nymphs and egg flies on a long leader under an indicator. However, hardware anglers take fish on spinners, and some late fall fish will still chase a swinging fly. These are the most aggressive and fight the hardest—one good reason to consider fishing wet flies.

Regardless of whether you fish nymphs or wet flies, the watchwords for late fall fishing are low and slow. Even the most active fish will rarely chase a fly very far, so you must drift it almost right onto a steelhead's nose to provoke a response. The success rate of fly fishing drops off dramatically compared to float fishing once the water temperature drops, because getting a good drift with a fly rod requires excellent line-control skills. But these alone are not enough to catch fish in late fall. Concentration and perseverance more than ever are critical to success. My favorite times are cold, snowy November days when snowmelt discolors the water, and a raw wind saps the strength from your fingers. It's tough fishing: the combination of slow action and frigid weather can quickly turn you into an automaton, repeatedly casting and drifting through the same part of the same run instead of methodically searching the water.

Steelhead rivers in Ontario freeze over through the coldest winter months.

When the ice melts, the winter steelhead season begins on river mouths with year-round open seasons. On the lower lakes the ice melts any time from mid-February to early March. During the thaw, snowmelt runs off rapidly over the frozen ground, and the rivers usually blow out, becoming too fast, too deep, and too dangerous to fly fish until water levels drop. When the floods recede, winter flows are normally low and clear, and getting a fly to the bottom is not difficult.

Getting to the bottom is only part of the problem. Steelhead fishing during this period is colder and more difficult than at any other time, often serving as little more than casting practice and a way to scratch the fly-fishing itch. Water temperatures through February, March and early April hover just above freezing. My "coldest" fish came from the Maitland River in mid-March when my stream thermometer registered 30°F (−1°C). Even given an inaccurate thermometer, that's cold weather.

Fish in frigid water will not chase a fly, and fly fishing in these conditions is a slow and brutal business. Float fishers, as always, are more successful, partly because bait offers the additional enticement of smell. Yet they remain even more successful when they run flies under their floats. The reason is simple: float tackle allows anglers to get a longer drift, putting the fly in front of more fish.

To the fly fisher this means two things. First, line control is of paramount importance. Second, concentration is even more important in the winter season than at any other time of year. Running a fly repeatedly and randomly through a run is a waste of time. Identify the areas where steelhead might hold and cast and mend so your short dead-drift hits that area.

In the preseason, egg flies are again popular. Although few steelhead spawn in the sections of river open to preseason fishing, the spawning runs of white and longnose suckers take place in March and April, and steelhead eat their yellow eggs. Small black nymphs, which imitate winter stone flies, also produce fish. Winter stone flies provide the fly fisher's first hatch of the year and can be seen crawling over snowbanks on sunny days. Whether steelhead actually prefer to eat sucker eggs and black stone fly nymphs over other food is irrelevant. When the water is only a couple of degrees above freezing, and your toes are only a couple of degrees above that, anything that increases your confidence and helps you stay focused is worth believing in.

Early spring, regardless of the dictates of the calendar, begins some time in April as the snow disappears, the ground turns to mud, and water temperatures slowly begin climbing toward civilized levels. Although heavy spring rains can still raise rivers to flood levels, most of the year's major flooding is over. Most steelhead spawn during this period, and opening day falls somewhere toward its end. This time of year brings more anglers to steelhead rivers than any other, and on the more popular southern Ontario steelhead rivers, contending with crowds can be a challenge.

Rising water temperatures means more active fish and higher success rates. Various nymphs, Woolly Buggers and Egg-Sucking Leeches take fish, but egg flies are still often the most productive patterns. A simple chenille egg—little more than chenille wound around a hook—is easy enough to tie so that losing them on bottom by the dozen is almost painless. In clear water, natural shades of yellow, orange or pink are most productive. As the water turns color to "steelhead green," chartreuse eggs account for more fish, and fluorescent orange and hot pink eggs work best when the water turns downright murky. The same applies to the color of the egg on an Egg-Sucking Leech. Sometimes, having the right color seems to make all the difference.

Shortly after opening day, early spring blends into late spring or drop-back season. Steelheading tradition frowns upon fishing for kelts, but in the fertile rivers of the Great Lakes, fish quickly recover condition after spawning and provide an unmatched, highly sporting fishery. Best of all, many anglers are unaware that steelhead remain in Great Lakes rivers until the end of May or even into early June, and the opening day crowds quickly thin out.

Drop-back steelheading is the easiest fly fishing of the year. The fish are hungry, and the spring fly hatches are beginning. Nymphs, Woolly Buggers and Egg-Sucking Leeches become the most effective patterns. Swinging flies work, but during heavy hatches steelhead begin behaving like overgrown, supercharged resident rainbows, and trout-fishing methods take over. Dead-drift nymphs through likely pools and runs, and always allow your fly to swing up like an emerging insect at the end of the drift—just don't use your 6x tippet.

Finding steelhead kelts can be difficult. Like fresh steelhead running upstream, they tend to concentrate. Finding a pod of fish is the most important step to success. Unlike fish running upstream, drop-backs moving down don't have to contend with obstructions, so they don't hold in the same places. Look for them in relatively deep pools above long, shallow sections of river. Fish often hold in these locations, waiting for high water before navigating the long stretch below. They also congregate where spring seeps and coldwater streams enter the river. The slightly colder water attracts kelts as the river warms throughout May.

Ontario's "name" steelhead rivers, such as the Ganaraska, Saugeen or the St. Mary's Rapids, are well-known for producing large numbers of fish, and they also attract large numbers of anglers. However, steelhead in the Great Lakes run everywhere they can, from small streams dumping into Lake Erie to large, warmwater rivers with only few coldwater tributaries. Almost any Ontario river that flows into the Great Lakes is a steelhead stream. The question is rarely whether steelhead run a river, but how many.

Fly fishing is not the best way to catch steelhead, and the action is often slow. Ontario rivers run cold when the steelhead are in. Rain beats the brim of your hat and drips occasionally down a sleeve or the back of your neck. Your hands become reddened claws, and your toes ache from the chill of the water. But then—your line stops—and the dark surface shatters in an eruption of steel and silver. In that instant, all of the cold and pain disappears. Is it worth it? Oh, yes.

ANDREW SOMERSET'S MUST-HAVE PATTERNS FOR ONTARIO STEELHEAD

- Egg-Sucking Leech
- Flashback Stone
- Flash Fly
- Sydenham Peacock
- Woolly Bugger

CHAPTER 25

AN ANGLER MOST BLASPHEMOUS

Kevin Fancy

I AM A HEATHEN AMONG FLY FISHERS. YES, TO SOME I AM A sinner of hell-bound proportions because, despite tradition, I will use any legal fly-fishing method to catch fish. Is this morally wrong, or am I just an opportunistic angler with some mighty powerful techniques under my fishing vest? I prefer to think I'm simply versatile, with a few years of logic and experience on my side, but other anglers have been less kind.

My first experience with nonconventional fly fishing was, coincidentally, my first fly-fishing experience. It was a fine spring day when I was taken to the backwoods by a fishing buddy who goes by the moniker of "Mac" (this because he has one of those old, oddly spelled Scottish names that no one can pronounce without someone offering to perform the Heimlich Maneuver). At Mac's suggestion, I had armed myself the day before with a brand new 8-weight rod and a sink-tip line.

Our destination was a small lake, maybe 1–2 miles (1.6–3.2 km), west of Ottawa, Ontario. Our quarry were the elusive (or so I was led to believe) brown trout. We slipped our boat into the water around 9:00 A.M. only to find a couple of others had beat us to this remote lake. By 11:00 A.M. there were six boats stirring up the lake, including ourselves.

It is a well-known fact that while hunting the wily brown in The East, there is no need to get up early as they seldom bite before 10:00 A.M. As I recall, the occupants of two boats were trolling gangs, one with minnows, the other with worms. Anglers in two other boats were still-fishing in likely areas with unknown baits, and the other boat was drifting as its two occupants worked plugs willy-nilly.

We all bucked and weaved, doing our best to offer space to each other, and when the opportunity arose to survey the luck of each other, we did so as friendly anglers do. We discovered that by high noon, none of the others had managed to bag more than a few sunfish. Conversely, Mac and I, who were trolling flies, had taken our first trout around 10:00 A.M.—an eye-pleasing brown of 3 lb (1.4 kg) plus. By 11 we had missed several strikes but had boated another brown almost identical to the first.

About the time the sun hit its apex, the mini-armada started closing in on us. Having noticed our luck, they watched what we were doing, trying their best to find out what kind of bait we were using. There was nothing secretive on our part; we were simply so busy catching (and missing) fish, we didn't take time to explain.

Soon, a line of boats was trailing us like a string of baby ducks following their mother. Some drew so close to our stern that we knew they were riding directly over our flies. It didn't matter. In full view of everyone, Mac and I nailed two more fish, one right after the other. That seemed to be the proverbial straw, for the other boats pulled away one by one and headed for shore.

We followed soon after so we could grab a bite of lunch at the truck. Only one other boat remained in the water when we arrived, for the others were all being packed out. While our boat was pulled onto shore, there was quite a commotion as 11 curious anglers descended upon us like black flies to see if we would willingly share our secret.

We showed them our fish, the flies we had used and the way we rigged them. We even offered some of our more successful patterns for them to try, for the true spirit of good sportsmanship is helping out others whenever you can. Only two anglers took us up on our offer. They immediately launched their boat again, and, in full view of everyone, proceeded to catch a nice brown not 50' (15 m) from shore. After that, our fly boxes were quickly picked clean. We prudently kept our best patterns for the day, offering our doubles or whatever other patterns the anglers thought might work. Later as we sat in the shade and ate our lunches, the newly initiated anglers gathered around us while Mac and I lectured them about the acquisition and various uses of flies.

This happened 20 years ago, when the art of trolling flies seemed to have been forgotten by all but the most seasoned of fly fishers and was against everything fly-fishing purists held sacred. Today, fly trollers are still looked down upon with disdain by those in tight rubber suits with frozen nether parts and wet feet. However, a wise man once said, "Necessity is the mother of invention," which is why I troll flies and still spread the word today.

Although Canada has thousands of streams and rivers which can be plied the "acceptable, old-fashioned way," it also has multitudes of large lakes holding big fish which can't be caught using traditional fly-fishing methods. Not one to miss good fishing opportunities because of archaic traditions instituted 200 years ago and on another continent, I use what works. And trolling flies for lake-dwelling trout outperforms standard methods hands down.

Trolling with Traditional Gear

IN THE SPRING, I head out on my favorite waters with a 7-weight rod armed with a quick-sink-tip line. At the right speed, this means that 90' (27 m) behind the boat my fly is traveling 2–5' (60 cm–1.5 m) below the surface, a perfect depth for foraging fish.

My choice of bait is something meaty like a Black-Nosed Dace or a Muddler pattern. If the water is still and I see phantom midge larvae floating by, I will even try a Zug Bug (although the two are not related, seeing the former is a good indicator the latter will work). This is not a traditional Zug, but one tied on a No. 2 Mustad 9671 or 9672. These are very effective patterns in the early to midspring, and they have regularly helped me catch browns, rainbows and brook trout. Later in the season I add to my arsenal leech patterns like the Woolly Bugger and my favorite—the Nine-Three with another nontraditional addition, a stinger hook.

As spring turns to summer, I change my line and flies. Fish go deeper at this time of year, so it is necessary to get down to where they are actively feeding. I still use the 7-weight rod or drop to a 5-weight for brookies, but change to a 5-weight, triple-sink line, which allows the fly to sink easily 10–12' (about 3.5 m). There is no need to match your rod with the line while trolling. A 5-weight line is best for going deep as its small diameter creates less water resistance, while a 7-weight rod has the backbone needed for the intense strikes you will get—and the large fish you will be horsing in. Don't worry. Once a fish is hooked, the fight is the same as if you were standing on the stream bank, fighting the old-fashioned way with matched gear.

I find trolling a great way to break in new or potential fly fishers for two reasons. First, there is nothing to teach about casting because they simply feed out line as the boat moves along. We all know some would-be newcomers avoid the sport just because the thought of learning to cast can be intimidating—this avoids that bugaboo. Second, once a fish has been hooked and a novice has the chance to play it with the fly rod, he or she will also be hooked. There is nothing like catching a fish on a fly, and sooner or later a novice develops the itch to learn to cast. But at that particular moment they are involved with catching a fish and enjoying the feel of a fly rod in hand—living life as it should be.

Lead the Way

Come late summer, trout can only be found deep during the day. Of all the lakes I have plotted, I have found few in Canada with a thermocline deeper than 25' (8 m), a depth around which fish seem to hold during hot weather. No fly line in the world will reach that depth while you are trying to maintain any sort of forward motion, so it's time to change gears again. Once more I ignore tradition, this time taking a page from the book of lake-trout fisher folk—not a whole page mind you, just a line or two. My rod becomes a 9-weight and out comes the lead-core trolling line. Onto my fly reel I spool about 20' (3.6 m) of backing, followed by four colors of lead-core—each color is 30' (9 m) long—then 20' (3.6 m) of 8-lb test monofilament, which is used as a leader. This outfit has served me well on the lakes I fish, but if trolling for Great Lakes steelhead or large western rainbows, you might consider more backing and a slightly heavier leader.

A rod holder is definitely a plus with this outfit as dragging that much weight around all day will take its toll on your arms. My favorite, a model known as a "Down Easter," employs gravity to lock the holder closed until the rod handle is lifted up.

Deep fishing means less light penetration, so I switch to streamer patterns in attractor colors. Yellow Marabou Muddlers work well as does a Doc Spratley (a popular West Coast fly that is little-known east of the Rockies), tied with an attractive orange waistcoat. In fact, almost any orange or yellow fly performs well wherever the water is cloudy or light penetration is at a minimum. When it works, I even have a special fly called the "Fancy Sunrise" that knocks 'em dead.

To get down to the fish, I start at one and a half colors, then two, etc., until I find the fish. Now, fishing with lead-core is nothing like using traditional fly line. Believe it or not, there is a better connection to your fly, so if you bump bottom you can tell by the feeling if it's rock, wood or marl—a great advantage in unknown waters. And when a fish hits, you will also notice the difference. Imagine tying a bowling ball to a length of wire, and then holding one end as you drop the ball off the roof. When the ball reaches the end, you know it pretty quickly. It's the same with lead core and fish. When a fish hits, it's like a jolt that will pull your arm out of its socket if you aren't paying attention. After that the fight is a tad sluggish as the fish has to fight you, the rod and the weight of the line—but you will catch fish when others are not. And isn't catching part of the game?

Other Nontraditional Presentations

I ONCE INTRODUCED FLIES to a Great Lakes charter boat captain, who tried them every which way before relegating them to his downrigger. Now he always puts down one fly among his other hardware and sometimes switches to all flies when the fish are "on." Keep in mind that this fellow makes a living from fishing, so if it works for him, it will work for you too. Other than the downrigger, no special equipment is needed.

Another option with which you can experiment will, under some circumstances, improve your success, but only if you are willing to try it. Take a spoon that is known to be productive, remove the hooks, and fasten it backwards on your line. To this, tie in an 8–12" leader between the spoon and your fly. As the spoon is backwards, rather than wobbling as it moves through the water, it swishes from side to side, giving your fly the action of a wounded minnow. Neat trick, eh?

This is also the greatest way to present a fly when using a spinning outfit should a friend not own any fly gear, or if (heaven forbid!) you wish to cast from shore into a stiff wind or longline troll behind your boat. Yes, you can use a fly with spinning gear—at least you can if you want to catch fish and traditional methods are impossible. The trouble is getting your fly or your fly-spoon combination down. For this, use a small keel sinker with a swivel at both ends to avoid line twist. Just cast out as far as you can, and then let it sink a bit. When the line levels off, let out a little more until you think your fly is 100' (30 m) behind the boat, lock your bail, and then hang on.

I Rest My Case

Now you know why fly-fishing purists think of me as a blasphemous, devil-worshipping angler bound for hell. I dare to break the "rules" of fly fishing and never hesitate to try something new—assuming of course, that it's legal. I know I'm not the first to troll a fly and won't be the last. In my opinion a fly is no better—or worse—than a spoon, spinner or jig. All are simply different types of lures, and some combine the best of both. For years lure manufacturers have known the effectiveness of dressing the hooks of spoons and spinners with "flies" of squirrel tail, deer tail, feathers and rubber skirts.

Don't be blinded or hog-tied by tradition. Every once in a while someone comes up with something new or rediscovers something old—like trolling flies. Not all ideas are worthwhile, but every so often some real innovations are made or uncovered. Don't be one of those stubborn fishing folk who cling to the old ways no matter what. Summon the courage, curiosity and open-mindedness that made you an angler in the first place and strike a new path for yourself. It may lead to a dead end—or you might just find yourself in the legendary "Fiddlers Green."

KEVIN FANCY'S MUST-HAVE PATTERNS FOR TROLLING

- Canadian Nymph
- Doc Spratley's Intern
- Fancy's Sunrise
- Nine-Three with stinger
- Yellow Marabou Muddler

CHAPTER 26

LEAD-CORE BRITISH COLUMBIA STYLE

Robert H. Jones

O NE OF THE MOST PRODUCTIVE LAKES IN BRITISH COLUMBIA'S Cariboo region is Sheridan Lake—4,098 acres (1,658 hectares) of spring-fed water filled with rainbows, many topping 10 lb (4.5 kg). Their size is attributed to the abundance of freshwater shrimp. Two-year-old trout stocked as fry usually weigh over 2 lb (900 g), and some three-year-olds hit 6 lb (2.7 kg).

The office porch at Sheridan Lake Resort is lined with "brag boards" listing the names of hundreds of anglers who have caught 5-, 6- and 7-lb (2–3-kg) trout. Inside are more boards showing larger fish in the mid and high teens. According to owner Bob Leith, the resort record is 17 ½ lb (8 kg).

In a typical season, ice-out is by May 1st, with the turnover between June 2nd and the 7th. Fishing is excellent right after ice-out as the trout are ravenous. Shortly afterward the chironomids come on slowly, followed around July 1st by may flies and sedges.

When the shallows warm during the summer, trout seek cooler temperatures at 45' (13.5 m) or more. With an ample supply of cool water, they remain in peak condition. When the doldrums end toward mid-September, trout return to the shallows and fishing can be outstanding right through until early November, weather permitting.

Fishing tactics range from casual bait plunkers to obsessive fly-flingers. The latter use mainly shrimp patterns like a Doug's Drifter, Werner Shrimp or Baggy Shrimp and, when appropriate, various chironomid and bloodworm imitations and big, bushy dry flies. A group of anglers who account for many of the big trout use lead-core line to troll large flies. Some use 8-weight fly rods and reels, while others favor 7–9' casting rods and level-wind or single-action reels.

A typical setup consists of four "colors" of 18-lb test lead-core—each color representing 30' (9 m)—and 100' (30 m) of 4- to 6-lb test monofilament. The amount of backing depends on the reel's line capacity, but should be a minimum of 100 yards (90 m) of 15-lb test braided Dacron.

Two must-have trolling patterns are the Horsehair Nymph, originally tied with horse hair or black bear hair, and the Slim Pickin's, fashioned entirely from pheasant tail fibers. Of the latter, Bob Leith said, "It's the number-one fly all year round. Sometimes chironomids are outstanding, sometimes Mikulak Sedges and Tom Thumbs, sometimes leeches, but day in and day out there's your Slim."

Because of the water's clarity, trout in the shallows are boat-shy, which accounts for those 100' leaders. Troll dead slow—less than a foot per second. Generally, each half color of lead-core takes the monofilament down 4' (1.2 m), double that depth for one color, and so forth. A depth sounder is the quickest way to determine the best depth at which to fish, but don't hesitate to ask for advice. Sheridan Lake regulars are among the friendliest, most helpful anglers you can ever hope to meet.

BOB JONES' MUST-HAVE PATTERNS FOR LEAD-CORE TROLLING IN BRITISH COLUMBIA

- Horsehair Nymph
- Slim Pickin's

CHAPTER 27

BROWN TROUT

Chris Marshall

THE FIRST REAL FISH I CAUGHT WAS A BROWN TROUT. THAT wasn't surprising as brown trout were the only real fish around in the place where I grew up—the east slope of the Pennines in Yorkshire, England. I didn't catch it on a fly. In fact, I didn't even use a rod and line; I caught it with my hands by "guddling." Eventually, however, I was initiated to the fly rod, but only after progressing through the various and mandatory apprenticeships from a penny hook and line attached to a sycamore stick to an Allcock's split bamboo rod and a center-pin reel.

But at every stage, my quarry was the brown trout. Other species—grayling and coarse fish were found only in the flatter, gentler lands to the east beyond the industrial blights of Bradford, Leeds and Huddersfield. Eventually though, in my midteens, I was able to reach these by bike or bus, and I temporarily neglected both brown trout and fly fishing as I pursued more exotic quarry—carp, tench, bream, chub, and barbel.

It wasn't until I emigrated to Canada soon after my 21st birthday that I rediscovered the delights of brown trout and fly fishing for them. For even in arid southern Saskatchewan where I lived when I first arrived, there were brown trout—or, at least I was told there were—up in the lonely, wind-swept headwaters of the Swift Current River. I searched for them, but never found them. It wasn't just because they were the only real game fish within reasonable driving distance of Swift Current 40 years ago, it was because, like many immigrants, I was drawn to things which reminded me of home. Like me, the brown trout is an immigrant.

It was that same longing for the familiar that generated the diaspora of the brown trout from its native Europe in the mid-19th century. As the British built their empire, they took with them those things they considered essential for civilized living: roses, cricket, gin, fly rods and brown trout. While it was a simple matter to transport the former, shipping brown trout across thousands of miles of ocean was a formidable task in the days of sail. There was no mechanical means of refrigeration or aeration, so the only possible chance of success was to pack fertilized eggs in ice and hope the ice lasted until the voyage ended.

In the face of this, it's rather amazing that in 1852 the first attempt was not aimed at eastern Canada, which was a relatively short voyage over cool water and offered a climate eminently suitable for browns, but at Australia—on the other side of the world and across the equator. No wonder it met with failure. So did the second and the third attempts. But in 1864 the clipper Norfolk arrived in Melbourne carrying 90,000 Atlantic salmon eggs and 1,500 River Itchen brown trout eggs. Thirty percent of the salmon eggs and 20 percent of the trout eggs survived. Some of the latter were transferred to the Plenty River in Tasmania and thrived, providing progeny which became the wellspring for the spread of brown trout throughout the Antipodes.

The Australian success was followed by a successful planting of trout in Madras, India, from Loch Leven in 1868, and by two failed attempts in South Africa in 1875 and 1882 (the first successful attempt in South Africa was in Natal Province in 1890). But it was not until 1883, 30 years after the first Australian attempt, that the brown trout finally emigrated to North America—and it had nothing to do with the British Empire! They were a gift of German fish from Baron Lucius Von Behr to American ichthyologist Fred Mather. But British trout were hot on their heels, with a batch of eggs from Loch Leven fish arriving in 1884. These were reared successfully in hatcheries in New York State and Michigan. From there they spread rapidly across the continent.

The first Canadian stocking was not far behind—a batch of eggs from Loch Leven fish arrived in Newfoundland in 1886. Four years later, Quebec imported stock from New York. The spread westward was much slower in Canada than in the U.S.: Ontario in 1921, Alberta and Saskatchewan in 1924, British Columbia in 1933 and then Manitoba, but not until 1943. The vast majority of these came directly or indirectly from U.S. hatcheries. The ephemeral browns of the upper Swift Current that eluded me in 1960 were descendants of these, their ancestors having preceded me by almost four decades.

Brown trout are found in every province. They finally arrived in Prince Edward Island around the late 1980s and were most likely an anadromous strain which strayed over from the rivers of Tatamagouche Bay across the Northumberland Strait. They have, however, found a major niche in only four provinces—Newfoundland, Quebec, Ontario and Alberta. In some cases, they simply took over from the less aggressive native eastern brook trout, but in most, they moved into streams so degraded by human activity that brook trout could no longer tolerate them. Here, brown trout thrived and multiplied.

This is particularly the case in southern Ontario, where fly fishers in pursuit of resident trout find mainly browns. Apart from a few exceptions, brook trout have retreated to the tangled refuges of the headwaters streams—places that fly fishers usually avoid. However, on some streams, such as those east of Toronto where I do most of my fishing, brook trout can be plentiful in the first two weeks of the season. In fact, I'll often catch twice as many brookies as browns. I suspect this not so much that they temporarily outnumber the browns in the stream, but that they are so much easier to catch, and as soon as the water begins to warm up, they have headed upstream where cool springs keep the temperature more to their liking. The browns are far less sensitive and hang on through the summer heat and low water.

This means that in southern Ontario after the middle of May, fly fishers interested in fishing for resident trout in streams close to home must be prepared to deal with finicky, wary brown trout.

They aren't easy. When they were first stocked over here, anglers grown used to the uninhibited and undiscriminating native brookie cursed these elusive European immigrants. Fortunately, attitudes have changed radically over the last 100 years, especially among fly fishers. Now, we welcome the challenge.

Most of the brown trout streams and rivers in southern Ontario are located south–southwest of a line drawn between Wiarton and Belleville. Most of these are relatively small, but there are a few, such as the Saugeen, Nottawasaga and Grand, that are substantial rivers. All run north and west into Lake Huron or Nottawasaga Bay. The Grand, which runs south into Lake Erie, is the only significant exception. The Grand is also exceptional in that it is a tailwater fishery, kept cool by bottom draws from the Belwood Dam just upstream from Fergus. The stretch of water from the dam downstream almost as far as Waterloo, is one of the most productive brown trout fisheries in the country.

However, while thousands of fly fishers might flock to the Grand each season, it is the scores of smaller rivers and streams scattered throughout the region that provide regular sport for fly fishers in pursuit of brown trout. In the southwest, there are middle and upper sections of tributary streams that run into Lake Erie and the southern end of Lake Huron—a number of them being delightful spring creeks, running through gentle valleys, crystal clear and edged with clumps of watercress. Around Kitchener–Waterloo are tributaries of the Grand River, and immediately west of Toronto, rocky streams cascading in pools and riffles from the slopes of the Niagara Escarpment. Stretching eastward from Toronto are a succession of gravelly streams running through the eskers and moraines of Durham and Northumberland counties. Yet farther east are a handful of tributaries of the Trent River, nutrient-rich, spring-cooled, flowing gently through woodland and pasture. But these are the last, for east of Belleville the streams are too warm and susceptible to drought. Only in the tiny, secret channels of the headwaters—overhung with ferns and underbrush, canopied in dense cedars—are the waters cool enough in high summer to support trout. It is in such places that the remnants of the wild, native brook trout still thrive, as well as the occasional brown. But these are not waters for the fly fisher—even the bait fisher finds them formidable and impenetrable.

Because I live at the extreme eastern end of the good brown-trout waters, this is where I do most of my fishing. My favorite stream is a tributary of the Trent River. It's a good size—20–30' (6–9 m) across—and with a good flow. It runs west to east, and for much of its length skirts the edges of eskers where numerous, constantly cold springs maintain the flow and keep the water relatively cool, even in deep summer. A rich stream, high in pH and heavily weeded in places, it's the nearest thing I have to a spring creek within comfortable driving distance. Let me take you there. . . .

Early Season

WE'VE ARRIVED MIDMORNING. There's really no need to come earlier as the fish are rarely willing to move for a fly until the day warms up and the aquatic insects become active. Even now, in water still cool from the vestiges of spring run-off, it seems dead and we are reduced to drifting a weighted nymph along the bottoms of the deep pools where most of the trout are holding.

At noon we break for lunch. By now the sun has warmed the air. Waxwings are gathering in the cedars on the opposite bank, and a pair of kingbirds are perched expectantly on a fence post just upstream—infallible signs that the hatch is about to begin. Sure enough, there's the first Hendrickson rising slowly off the water. It doesn't get far. In a flurry of wings, a waxwing intercepts it before it reaches the sanctuary of the bushes. Now there's another—and another—until the air fills with delicate gray shapes lifting off the water and swooping birds feasting on them.

At the head of the pool—a swirl—just where the flow begins to slow as it enters the pool, I wait, focussed on each fly that drifts over the spot. Twenty seconds later, a trout engulfs a fly.

Like the birds, we have anticipated the hatch and have already changed our gear for dry fly-fishing: a 5x tippet and a No. 14 dry Hendrickson. Now I approach the stream, slowly and stealthily. I kneel 5' (1.5 m) back from the bank, keeping my profile low. By now three trout are rising regularly in the pool, and there are others in the next pool upstream.

There's a fish rising just across from us, tight against the far bank, alongside the red twigs of a dogwood. By the lightweight, splashy rise, I can tell it's not a big fish—perhaps 7–8" (18–20 cm). The two fish rising at the head of the pool are considerably bigger, but I decide to use the little fellow as practice. As long as I play him carefully, it won't disturb the others.

Still rusty from the long winter abstinence, I flub the first cast, but within a couple of minutes, the fish is rising confidently again. This time there's no mistake. The fly lands a couple of feet above him, drifts drag-free, and he grabs it. I was right—a brown about 7" (18 cm). We admire his silvery, green-gold flanks, mottled with the faint purple smudges of lingering parr markings. Seems there's more of Loch Leven in his genes than the Black Forest. Then I let him slip back into the water.

The two fish upstream are still rising steadily. One is holding about 3' (90 cm) below the other. The heaviness of the swirls indicate that both are good-sized fish, but the farthest one looks substantially larger, maybe as large as 20" (50 cm). He's selected the best place in the pool so that he's first in line for intercepting the flies as they come down the riffle. However, if I cast to him first, I'll inevitably disturb the lower fish, which is also a good one. So I decide to go for the lower fish first.

He ignores the first drift. Perhaps I put the fly over him too soon after he'd risen. Sometimes trout get into a rhythm of rising, taking flies at regular intervals, ignoring those that drift down between. So I wait, timing the gap between rises—about 12 seconds. On the next cast, I drop the fly a couple of feet above him, just nine seconds after his previous rise. And he takes it! He dashes for the dogwoods on the far bank, but I manage to turn him and he runs downstream toward us. Finally I have him close to the bank, and I slide my finger and thumb down the leader to hold him for a moment in the shallows. He's not a he, but a she—and no Scottish silver like the previous fish, but glorious German gold with the characteristic large red spots. I grasp the shank of the fly and deftly twist it loose. She hangs in the current for a moment, then darts back into the pool.

Upstream, the larger fish is still rising. I dry off the fly with a few fast false casts and watch the fish for a few minutes before casting. It doesn't pay to rush, for that's a sure way of making a botch of things. I decide to move a couple of yards closer. When trout are intent on feeding, they tend to be less wary, especially in the early season. It's also good to have as little line on the water's surface as possible as this allows for greater line control and ensures a drag-free drift of the fly. We crawl together along the bank and hunker down beside a scraggly alder. The fish is only about 25' (7.5 m) away, across and upstream at an angle of about 45°—a relatively easy cast.

He takes it on the first drift. I set the hook—but too quickly—and the fly and line come back, falling in a tangle in the alder beside my shoulder. I grin sheepishly and shrug off my disappointment. I take time to refill and relight my pipe, but he doesn't rise again. That's par for the course in dry-fly fishing for browns. So we move on, for there are other fish rising farther upstream. Moreover, the big one will most likely have regained his composure and be feeding again when the spinners fall in the early evening when we come back downstream.

Late Spring

LATER IN THE SPRING, the hatches of flies become more complex. Once the Hendrickson hatch is over around the middle of May, a number of other ephemeral varieties appear in quick succession. Some streams have significant hatches of the huge green drakes; all have hatches of tiny blue-winged olives (BWO), which are less intense but last through the summer and are equally attractive to the trout. There is also a succession of caddis hatches on all the streams. On many, in fact, these are more significant for the fly fisher than the may flies, particularly on those waters which are more extensively degraded.

As the weather warms, the hatches of may flies occur increasingly later in the day, with spinner falls coming hard on their heels and eventually, by the end of May, mingling with the hatching flies. Some of the caddis hatches, however, occur in the morning and trickle off throughout the day, providing excellent sport from midmorning to dusk. Often the fly fisher is faced with a number of different species hatching at the same time, presenting an intriguing challenge in pattern selection.

Tactics in the late spring are similar to those used earlier, except that as the water warms and flows decrease, dry fly and emerger-fishing become increasingly more appropriate than fishing streamer flies or deepwater nymphing. It's also best to fish a lighter line (3- or 4-weight) and a lighter tippet, often as fine as 7X, especially when fishing No. 20 and 18 BWOs. Stealth also becomes increasingly important as lower, clearer water makes the trout more wary and enables them to detect an approaching angler more readily.

Summer

MANY FLY FISHERS in southern Ontario abandon the trout streams to fish for bass and other warmwater species after the last weekend of June—and for good reason, as on most streams even the brown trout rarely feed in the middle of the day. There are exceptions, such as the Grand River tailwater fishery, where the bottom draws from the reservoir maintain relatively cool water temperatures for a number of miles downstream from the dam. But even here, the best fishing is in the early morning and late evening, for the photophobic brown trout shuns bright sunlight, especially in low, clear water.

Fishing a streamer fly from dawn to sun-up can provide some exciting moments with big browns. Some streams, especially the Trent River tributaries, have huge hatches and spinner falls of tiny trichorythodes (No. 24–22) from around 8:00 to 10:00 A.M. every day from July to September. These are not easy to fish, and the bigger trout don't always feed on them, but they can frequently trigger tremendous activity.

Evenings, from just before sunset to dark, can usually be counted on for some sort of hatch activity—always some species of caddis and the ubiquitous BWO. At the end of June, the less degraded streams have good hatches of *Isonychia,* and some have massive spinner falls of *Siphlonurus* (the "phantom hatch") from late dusk on into the dark. The latter has to be one of the most challenging and exciting situations facing a fly fisher. With the air filled with dancing, mating flies and the water alive with the splashes of rising fish, most of the time it's impossible to see the artificial on the water. This means that an angler is compelled to set the hook whenever there is a rise close to where he thinks the fly might be. Sometimes there is a connection.

Fishing terrestrials can be quite productive, especially in the dark, when a big hair bug dragged across the head or tail of a pool can conjure up some of the bigger browns in the stream. But terrestrials can also work well if fished during the day—the exception which makes the rule. Windy days are the best time for this. Browns will often hold beside cover close to the bank, waiting for beetles, ants and other insects to be blown out of the littoral vegetation onto the water. Some of these offer juicy mouthfuls, but none more so than grasshoppers. Where streams run through meadows and open land, grasshoppers often swarm in August, and when the wind blows there are always a few drifting downstream.

Tactics for hopper fishing are rather different from normal dry-fly fishing, for although it's still necessary to practice stealth, the presentation should be anything but delicate. Hoppers are big, fat creatures, and when they hit the water, they do so with a resounding smack. That's how the artificial should be presented, for lurking browns are used to the sound and home in on it. Hoppers are also vigorous creatures. When they hit the water, they struggle to get out, kicking with their long, hind legs like a swimmer on an inflatable raft. The trout respond to this, too. This means that rather than allowing the artificial to drift passively, it should be given frequent, erratic twitches to simulate the struggles of the natural. When trout take them, the effect is often explosive.

It's now more than half a century since I reached beneath a flat rock on that tiny moorland brook, wrapped my fingers round a 6" (15-cm) brown trout, grasped its slippery flanks, drew it out of its element, and looked in wonder on its gold-vermilion-silver dappling. And here, half a world away, on richer, gentler streams, and far more amply equipped, each time I bring a trout to hand and gaze upon it, the gulf of time and space contracts. The moments become one—Yorkshire moor and Ontario valley are joined—and I am richer for it.

CHRIS MARSHALL'S MUST-HAVE PATTERNS FOR BROWN TROUT

- Blue-Winged Olive
- CDC Waterhen Bloa
- Green Drake
- Hendrickson
- Hopper

BROWN TROUT GRATIN

Covered with bread crumbs and baked until golden brown
(Makes four servings)

16 oz—cooked, flaked brown trout—500 g
1—large cooking onion, diced
1–1 ½ cups—mushrooms, coarsely chopped—250–375 mL
1 ½ cups—white sauce (recipe below)—375 mL
1 cup—fresh bread crumbs—250 mL
Olive oil or melted butter
2 tbsp—fresh tarragon —30 mL

or 1 tbsp—dried tarragon—15 mL
Zest and juice of one lemon
Salt and pepper to taste

1. Bake trout whole. While still warm, remove and discard the skin and flake the flesh with a fork.

2. In a skillet, fry onions and mushroom until they are softened, and then add to flaked trout. Gently mix white sauce into the trout and onion mixture. Pour into baking dishes. You may use a large baking dish, but individual dishes make a great presentation.

3. For topping, place fresh bread crumbs in a bowl with a tbsp or two of olive oil, some lemon zest and juice. Toss lightly until all crumbs are moistened. Flavor the bread crumb topping with tarragon. (Basil or dill also complement fish.) Bake in a 350°F (180°C) oven for 30 minutes or until heated through.

WHITE SAUCE

(Makes about 1 ½ cups / 375 mL)

3 tbsp—butter —45 mL
3 tbsp—flour —45 mL
1 ½ cups—milk —375 mL
Salt and pepper to taste

1. Place butter in bowl and melt in microwave. Stir in flour, and then microwave briefly to cook. Add milk and microwave until thickened, stirring often to keep sauce smooth.

–Wayne Phillips

CHAPTER 28

GORILLAS AND HAWGS!

Bob Rife

"**L**OOK AT THAT MOUTH! YOU COULD FIT A WHOLE GRAPEFRUIT in there!" My son's eyes were almost as wide as the bass's gaping maw. It was his first look at a largemouth, up close and awesome.

My thumb was tightened on the big hen fish's lip, immobilizing her against the clenched fingers of my left hand—the weight of the bass pulling back and down. *Micropterus salmoides,* the largemouth, is named for the fact that the crook of its jaw extends back beyond its eye (unlike the smallmouth's). It is not a handsome fish in the sleek, small-scale trout way, but it is an ambush brawler, ready to do battle—and along with the smallmouth, probably the most sought-after fish in North America.

And gorilla? Well, my brother-in-law George says they used to call 'em hawgs down there because they grow so big in his deep south state that at dusk on some back ponds you could actually hear them snort like a hawg. But recently a lot of snowbirds have taken to using the hawg nickname, so the locals, perforce, have adopted a new name, calling monster bass gorillas—bigger and uglier.

Fly fishing for largemouth wasn't all that popular until 1913, when a Tennessee tier by the name of Ernie Peckinpaugh put it all together with the first cork-bodied bass bug. He was looking for something that would keep his big flies floating. The floating aspect, he thought, and obviously proved, was the key to making the flies become truly bass-seductive. A cork body solved his problem—he found the imitation was deadly when cast softly near a bass hangout at dusk.

The heaviest largemouth ever taken (the all-tackle record) was 22 lb 4 oz (10.1 kg). George Perry made the record books with his fish taken from Montgomery Lake, Alabama, on June 2, 1932. The world mark for fly fishing is 13 lb 8 oz (6.1 kg) by George Zanata with a catch from Lake Tarpon, Florida, on March 16, 1996. He used a 6-lb test leader. The champion in the class for the lightest tippet, 2-lb test, is Donnie Thomas, who caught a 6-lb 8-oz (2.9-kg) bass from Eden Pond, North Carolina, on May 30, 1985.

In Ontario the all-tackle record is a 10-lb 6-oz (4.7-kg) largemouth. No other information is available and no records are kept for fly fishing in the province. One must remember that largemouth in the northern fringe of their distribution grow very slowly—in Canada, a 5-lb (2.3-kg) specimen is always a lunker. It might take six years to reach 15" (38 cm), while a cousin from the Deep South would do that in two years.

Lefty Kreh (author, artist and angler) was watching me bending a rod one day. I was trying a new rod-and-line combination. I'm a southpaw, too, and casting mentor Lefty was looking on. He took time out to relate his philosophy on bass. "Hawgs like big, long, fat, wavy patterns. Smallmouth go for more direct imitations of their food."

"It's the old imitation-versus-attraction thing," I suggested. Possibly.

Along those lines, he said, is the Pencil Popper, designed by yet another artist, author and angler, Dave Whitlock. It has a long, thin body with a small fluff of marabou for a tail.

It's a killer. With its small face you can snake it among lily pads and thick grasses and not get snagged. Dance it and then make it act like a wounded minnow. Of course, tying on a piece of monofilament as a weed guard is almost a prerequisite when gorilla fishing.

My favorite largemouth fly is Lefty's Bug. It isn't as hard to cast as most big bass flies. It has a lot less air resistance, so you get it where you want to throw it—a little open spot of water near the junglelike den of the largemouth. Once there, you wait for a slow 10 count with the fly sitting up so temptingly nice (the cast got his attention, now the wait makes him extra anxious). Kreh points out that it takes only a little line twitch to get either a loud or soft pop, bringing on

Mr. Anxious's smashing strike. Woweee! There is nothing like that heart-stopping, surface strike—FEErocious!

To get down to other particulars—differences between largemouth and smallmouth—one must reiterate that this country is on the northern edge of all bass habitat, particularly largemouth. So there are only a few places in the so-called banana belt of Ontario where the big guys live. They cohabit with smallmouth, in the sense that you can find them in the same river or lake, but at that point the differences begin.

Smallmouth love rubble, rocky bottoms and underwater cliffs. Largemouth are the jungle cats. They hang out in and along the edges of weed beds, cattails and lily pads, near or under stumps, logs and docks.

Remember the largemouth is an ambush addict. Look for places where they can hide and wait for dinner, deep in the shade and shadows where passing baitfish won't suspect trouble.

Watch the interiors of these dark and weedy spots, but keep an eye on the outer edge of them, too. Largemouth hold where the striking range is short. They are blunt and fast, not maneuverable. They want to hit and win—suddenly.

Perhaps they'll wait under a slanting shoreline tree, basking in the late-day warmth, watching patiently for unwary ants or other insects to take a wrong step and fall to the surface. They may be under a low bank where the grass hangs invitingly down, providing shade and a hangout where again an unwary insect or small animal might come a step too close.

Having found the lair, it seems all so reasonable to cast into it. Not so—you'll put down the big ambusher. Instead, flip the cast 6' (1.8 m) or more from where you suspect the ambush. Then begins the waiting game. I suggest a very slow 10 count, but I've seen some great tournament bass fishers wait as long as a minute, sometimes five, quietly biding their time. They know the bass knows the lure is there. They want to make her (big bass are usually females) get anxious about the territorial invader, to make her wonder why it is waiting there, to make her feel almost compelled to strike.

That's when you twitch the fly. She'll bash it—maybe not to strike, perhaps to defend her domain.

Patience is the key now, too. Wait for her to inhale the fly—a taut line is vital before your strike. Reel in gently until there's no slack.

When you feel a steady pull, she's made up her mind. That's when to set the hook. Strike and strike hard. Don't lift the rod—yank back on the fly line to set the hook. Lifting the rod makes it bend, gives slack line and allows the bass a chance to spit the hook before it is set in its jaw.

Of course there are times, and you'll get to know them, when you can just feel the bass has the fly in its mouth and is ruminating about it, wondering just what has been inhaled. That too is the time to strike. Don't give the bucket-mouth time to decide negatively. Strike hard.

I know it sounds as if you have to read the mind of a bass, but in a sense that is what you do with today's ultra-sensitive tackle. Even so, don't go too light. The necessity of heavier equipment to handle the fish under tough conditions means a choice that includes heavy-duty, bass-bugging rods or even light-duty saltwater fly rods. Use something with enough muscle to horse a good-sized bass out of a tangle of weedy cover. I like an 8 ½' graphite rod with a weight-forward floating line.

As it turns out, all of my bass have ripped from their cover, leaving me with a relatively simple job of hook setting. I haven't had to fight saw grass, as I've seen happen too often in tournaments in the south.

When bass feel the bite of that hook, they hightail it for cover with an unbelievable burst of energy, a try for safety. You must snub that attempt and have the tackle to handle it, which is where short, tapered leaders of 5–7' come into play. I like a 6' leader. And don't go much under 10-lb test for relatively clear water. They turn over big flies very well. Where the water is greenish or stained brown—whatever—you can go even heavier. If the water is gin-clear you might have to go drop down to lighter test, past 10, but that situation is unusual.

Naturally, big bait brings big fish—the old saw holds true—so experiment with big streamers. I've tried long slabs of rabbit fur, so heavy that it made for such ugly casting I thought the commotion would ruin all chance of a hit. But it is the wait after the cast that does it—patience. The bass is watching for sure. Outwait her.

A dedicated southern fly rodder I know uses nothing shorter than a 6" streamer. He likes black and works the thing along the bottom like a worm. The hook size is no mean thing, a No. 1 or 1/0. Some poppers he has go 2/0.

And, I can't say it often enough—you need sharp hooks. I carry both a small hone and a small mill file and use them after each fish or foul-up. The bony cartilage in a big bass's mouth is nothing to play games with. You must strike fast and hard when the time comes, and you want a hook point that bites deep.

That southerner feels, as I do, that a buggy head on the fly is vital. Since bass inhale flies, often so lightly the angler doesn't know what's going on, the rough head allows for a little confusion time on the part of the bass. She doesn't know what she has, and hopefully the angler feels something and strikes before the bass figures it all out.

It's just another reason why, at times, I have resorted to different types of big-headed Muddlers—they add to your fishing senses. And they do work.

There's also the matter of more colorful flies. As the night comes on, I move to more color. It seems to go against another old saw: bright day—bright lure; dark day—dark lure. However, color seems no problem for bass as night falls.

There's a little, old, yellow popper with a pair of big, red, bulging eyes that both the bass and I love. Bright colored flies certainly give me a better idea of where things are. I like to put the popper close to the weed edge before the wait and my eventual retrieve.

Poppers are, of course, most effective on calm water. Around dusk, just as the sun dips behind the trees on the edge of the lake, I begin casting around docks and such. The boaters and swimmers are less active and the bass are getting in a feeding mood. The spot I enjoy working is a submerged weed bed not far from a dock. I'll cast, wait the required time, and then begin a slow pop, pop retrieve with a lot of big pauses.

That brings me to another reason I like poppers. For no reason I know, you can cast them again and again to the same spot and not put the fish down. It seems ridiculous, but ol' Gorilla just ignores cast repetition when it comes to this fly. The old pause-and-twitch may be part of it, who knows. I've taken fish after I had all but given up.

The casts need not be long—50' (15 m) or less. It is easier to set the hook on shorter casts; the longer the cast, the more slack line you have to contend with before setting the hook. Oddly, even within short-casting range, I like the way a weight-forward line performs. For some reason they cast more accurately for me, and accuracy is important. It's a good idea to keep the rod tip low and pointed right at the target as you start the retrieve—again you reduce the amount of slack line.

My fly line for bass is a light orange color—very visible for me at all times and just great in failing light. I watch it for any sign of movement that isn't telegraphed by the line to my hand. I watch for rise forms—any surface motion that might be a prestrike key. It is a time of high concentration and intense quiet. Bass hear very well—any untoward noise can put them down. Remember that as it gets past dusk. Make your retrieves at night a matter of timing, making the pops as regular as clockwork. That will help the ever-vigilant bass home in on the sound of the lure. Change the cadence and the bass can miss.

As for the eating, bass taste great! Don't listen to the stories of muddy fish. It usually means the catch has not had proper care—has been left on the dock in the sun or on a stringer hanging in the water. All fish must be cleaned and the flesh cooled as quickly after being caught as possible. Live wells do help.

In the case of bass, a member of the sunfish family, the matter of filleting is simple and can be accomplished in minutes. Cut down along the backbone and carefully feel for the rib cage, paring off the fillet from the gills to the tail. Skin the fillets rather than using descaling methods. That eliminates one source of any off taste.

I use a two-bowl method to get a simple batter on the flesh. In the first bowl pour some milk. If you wish you can beat in an egg. In the second bowl sift some flour with goodly amounts of pepper and your favorite spice (paprika?). By the way, I don't use salt—it's not necessary and tends to break down the fish's flesh. It's bad for your diet, anyway.

Now dip the fillet in the milk and then roll it in the flour mixture. Next, pop it into the pan. Use a light oil for frying and turn the fillets after a minute. After a minute per side, test for doneness. Aaah, that testing! Scrumptious!

But back to the catching. . . . Among the many flies that attract largemouth are big streamers, big bugs and poppers. Pick any color, as they all work. Bass bugs, for instance, imitate just about every type of food a bass would find interesting: frogs, mice, moths, dragonflies, your choice.

The flies listed below are some of my favorites.

Lefty's Deceiver: As Lefty Kreh says on the tying of his great fly: "It needn't be fussy, just fishy-looking. Tight lines, Bob, but not too tight."

Gray Ghost: J. Edson Leonard, a well-respected angler and writer of *Flies and the Essential Fly Tier,* says this of streamers: "In the longer streamers, color combinations seem to be important. Largemouth are more responsive to some color mixes than they are to others—yellow-black, red-gray and red-white are the ones most cited. I certainly do not disagree."

Irresistible: Eric Leiser, author of *The Complete Book of Fly Tying,* makes his version of this fly with a tail of woodchuck hairs. He thinks they look better— "the markings are more prominent, better defined. But, no matter what material you use for the wing and tail, the pattern remains effective, for what really makes the Irresistible is the clipped deer hair body."

BOB RIFE'S MUST-HAVE PATTERNS FOR LARGEMOUTH BASS

- Gray Ghost
- Irresistible
- Lefty's Deceiver

CHAPTER 29

EXOTIC ALTERNATIVES

Chris Marshall

I T WASN'T ALL THAT LONG AGO THAT "ALTERNATIVES" IN freshwater fly fishing referred to popular game fish—smallmouth bass, largemouth bass, pike, bluegills and crappies. Now, most fly fishers, especially in southern Quebec, Ontario and Manitoba, frequently target these species in the summer when trout streams warm up and become less predictable. Consequently, they have forfeited the label alternative and handed it over to some new species. The new alternatives are much more exotic. For the most part, they are species which anglers infrequently or never fish for deliberately. Many rarely take hardware, and some are despised as trash fish; however, all can be taken on flies. Some present fascinating challenges, and I consider one of these exotics to be one of the toughest-fighting fish in fresh water.

River Exotics

THE TRIBUTARIES of the lower Great Lakes, which run too warm in their lower reaches to support resident trout, tend to have good populations of smallmouth bass. However, many have much more to offer fly fishers.

Walleye are one of the most popular game fish in central Canada. Although not generally regarded as being of interest to fly fishers, they take flies readily. I took my first on the fly by accident one summer evening at dusk on the Moira River, a few miles north of Belleville, Ontario. I'd been fishing for smallmouths in a deep pool just below a long riffle, and I was refilling my pipe prior to quitting for the day, letting my line, with a big chartreuse Woolly Bugger on the end, drift through the pool. When I came to reel in, something hit. Hard! It fought deep and doggedly, but didn't have the quickness or vigor of a smallmouth.

I wasn't particularly surprised when I saw the dusky gleam of gold and green of a walleye, for the Moira is a productive walleye river. But what did intrigue me was that it was relatively large—over 4 lb (1.8 kg)—and that I'd caught it in a pool in the middle of a long stretch of fast water, over a mile (1.6 km) from the slow water where walleye are usually found. In the spring, walleye run from deep, slow stretches into the shallower riffles to spawn, but few stay there after the middle of May, and those that do always appeared to be immature fish. My catch wasn't a fluke, for I took another that same evening.

Later, I discovered that this pool and a number of others in the middle reaches of the river, have cool springs upwelling from the bottom. This could be the reason for decent-sized walleyes holding in them through the summer. But whatever the reason, those fish provide excellent sport on a Woolly Bugger fished slow and deep, especially at dusk.

This phenomenon is not confined to the Moira River. Where similar conditions exist on other rivers harboring walleye, they can be taken regularly on big Woolly Buggers and marabou-winged streamers throughout the season, provided they are fished slowly and close to the bottom.

Sheepshead are the bane of tournament bass anglers. Nobody fishes for them deliberately; however, anyone who's caught one will acknowledge their impressive fighting qualities. Red drum, their cousins which live in brackish waters of the southeastern coast of the U.S., are prized as game fish. Sheepshead are also worthy of the same designation.

The best time to fish for them is in June when they enter the lower reaches of rivers to spawn. They tend to hold in deeper pools and riffles, just off the edges of the current, and they take flies readily. The technique is simple—a teasing, slow-drift retrieve close to the bottom. To achieve this, it's essential to ensure that the fly sinks to the bottom quickly. This means the fly or leader—or both—must be weighted. In deep, swift water, a sinking or sink-tip line might be necessary. The cast should be made somewhat upstream to allow the fly to sink, then retrieved slowly on the downstream swing.

The best flies are big (No. 2–2/0) Woolly Buggers in chartreuse or white. My favorite, the Moira River Bugger, has a white body and tail, black hackle, a fluorescent red head and lead dumbbell eyes tied on a No. 2/0 Bartleet hook.

Large catches are rare—three or four sheepshead in a three-hour session is par for the course, but in rivers I fish most of the time, the Moira and the Trent, there are bonuses: walleye and pike, making for some interesting mixed bags.

It's not necessary to use particularly heavy gear as long casts are rarely necessary. All that's needed is an outfit with enough backbone to throw big, heavy flies and weighted leaders—a stiff 7-weight is usually sufficient. Nor do you need a big reel with lots of backing, for while sheepshead are powerful fighters, they never seem to take off for the lake as do steelhead and salmon.

Lake whitefish are great sport on big, bushy dry flies during Hexagenia hatches in June. However, they can also be taken on nymphs when they make their spawning runs up rivers during the fall.

Many anglers believe whitefish are impossible to catch at this time, except by illegal snagging. However, while it's not easy fishing, it is possible to take them on nymphs, provided they're presented properly. The secret is getting your fly to dead-drift right onto their noses. It helps tremendously if you can see both the fish and the fly, enabling you to set the hook when you see the fish take, but this is often impossible. In such cases you must watch the end of your fly line. Whitefish take subtly, and the indications are correspondingly subtle, often no more than a slight hesitation of the drift or an almost imperceptible tightening of the line. The hook should be set on the slightest suspicion of either of these. Most times it will be nothing. Sometimes you'll snag fish as whitefish tend to pack closely together, but you will hook a number in the mouth—not many, but enough to make all of the hard work worthwhile.

A 6-weight outfit is ideal for whitefish as they rarely run over 4 lb (1.8 kg), with the average around 2 lb (900 g). They're not too fussy about flies: any natural-colored nymph pattern, such as a Hare's Ear or a Casual Dress in No. 14–12 will suffice. Weighting both fly and leader is essential for getting down to the fish.

Redhorse suckers *(Moxostoma)* are represented by seven species throughout their range: black, copper, golden, greater, silver, river and shorthead. One of the largest of the genus—14–18" (36–46 cm)—and most certainly the most widespread, is the shorthead redhorse *(Moxostoma macrolepidotum)*, more commonly known as the northern redhorse. A sleek fish with blood-red fins, it is found from brackish waters on the East Coast, right through to clear, clean rivers originating in the Rockies. It's also one of the most challenging fast-water species for fly fishers.

Because redhorse feed almost exclusively on invertebrates along the bottom, they are prime targets for nymph fishing. Moreover, much of the time they feed in shallow, clear water where they are very visible, so it's easy to see when they actually take your fly. There are two things which make this challenging. First, it takes pinpoint accuracy to get your fly in the right place, just upstream of a feeding fish so it drifts down naturally right onto its nose. Second, because redhorse are extremely spooky, you have only one chance to get the cast right— meaning you must ensure your approach is sneaky enough that they don't detect you and take off. In this respect, they are far more spooky than brown trout. Redhorse are the ultimate challenge for fast-water nymph anglers.

Because stealth and gentle presentation are so important, a light outfit (5- to 6-weight) is preferable. Any flies which suggest the small invertebrates on which they feed will work well. Impressionistic nymph patterns in No. 14–12 on fine (4x or finer) leaders are the order of the day.

Chub and fallfish are as generally despised by fly fishers as sheepshead are by dedicated bass anglers. There is some justification for this as they can be a considerable nuisance on trout streams, especially to anglers lacking the experience to distinguish between a trout and a chub rise. However, on streams too warm for trout, they can provide fast, furious sport, especially on a summer midday while trout are sulking. And because their feeding habits are so similar to trout (without being so finicky), they are an excellent target for beginning fly fishers seeking to practice their skills and have fun at the same time.

There's not much difference between creek chub *(Semotilus atromaculatus)* and fallfish *(Semotilus corporalis)*. Most anglers simply lump them together. In fact, in parts of the country, the regional name for fallfish is chub. There is only one clear distinguishing feature between the two: Creek chub have a dark spot at the base of the dorsal fin; fallfish do not. Fallfish also grow larger, occasionally reaching 18" (46 cm), but creek chub rarely make it to 12" (30 cm).

While neither species can match the wrist-jarring dash of a resident trout, they put up a spirited fight. Getting into a school of fallfish 12" (30 cm) or longer can be a memorable experience.

Besides dry flies, fallfish and chub also take nymphs and wet flies readily, and larger individuals will also hammer streamer flies and bucktails. On days when the trout are lying low, or when you just feel like wetting a line without the complications of switching into the stealth mode of trout fishing, chub and fallfish offer a stress-free alternative. Just take along your trout gear and persuade yourself that you're really fishing for trout.

Stillwater Exotics

IN CANADA, our still waters range from Lake Superior to farm ponds and prairie dugouts, and conventional fly fishing is practiced on all of them. The species of interest are varied, depending on location, but two which provide some very unconventional fly-fishing opportunities are longnose gar *(Lepisosteus osseus)*, commonly called garpike, and carp *(Cyprinus carpio)*. The Canadian range of garpike is limited to the Great Lakes region and southern Quebec, but carp are widespread from southern Quebec through Saskatchewan and in parts of southern British Columbia. Both species spend much of their time in shallow bays along the margins of lakes and along the edges of rivers. In these circumstances they offer the Canadian equivalent to wading the bonefish flats.

My first fly rod encounter with garpike was in a backwater of the lower Trent River in the mid-1980s while I was wading the shoreline for smallmouths. I came across a school holding in a slow, deep pool where a tributary entered the main river. They were cruising slowly up and down the pool, frequently breaking the surface with their long noses.

I couldn't resist a cast. Two garpike followed the streamer, and one even gave it a couple of bats with its snout. The same thing happened on the next cast—and the next. Changing flies made no difference; whatever I threw at them and however I varied the retrieve, the most I got was mild curiosity.

It wasn't until about seven or eight years later that I finally learned how to get garpike to hit a fly—thanks to a youngster whom I'd taught to fly fish a few years earlier. We discovered that garpike in still waters, like shallow margins of the Bay of Quinte, were much more inclined to hit flies than those in rivers. I'm not sure why this should be, but perhaps it has something to do with differences in feeding habits between river fish and lake fish. Then again, it could be nothing more than our failing to fish for the river populations when they were actively ready to feed.

However, when garpike converge in shallow bays in the warm waters of July and August, they readily hit big, gaudy streamer flies. The water where we fish is too shallow for a boat or float tube, but the bottom is firm enough for easy wading. The secret to success lies in spotting garpike before they spook. Frequently, they'll show themselves by sticking the ends of their snouts out of the water, and at times you'll see a swirl and fry scattering as a fish feeds.

Once you spot a fish and get within casting distance, flip your fly beyond and ahead of it and begin an erratic retrieve right across its nose. Speed things up when the fly is closest to the fish.

Hits are usually sudden and savage. Hook-ups can be infrequent due to the garpike's hard, bony mouth although a small double or treble hook tied on as a stinger improves the ratio. Sometimes garpike (especially the smaller ones) will come in after no more than a couple of head-shakes, but often the fight is spectacular with wild tailwalking and strong runs. As the bigger fish are well over 3' (90 cm) long at weights of 10 lb (4.5 kg), this can be a breathtaking and memorable experience.

Gear for garpike need not be super heavy. A 7-weight outfit will serve quite well, provided the rod has enough backbone to cast big, heavy streamers. I prefer a 10', 8-weight, as the extra length helps me keep that double-hooked streamer well above my head. A short wire leader helps prevent bite-offs. These can be tied right into the fly. Garpike don't seem to be too fussy about fly pattern. As long as it's bright, gaudy and big (No. 2–2/0 long streamer hooks), it will work.

When we first began catching garpike, the water of the Bay of Quinte was still colored and relatively weedless. Now, thanks to phosphate reduction and zebra mussels, it's crystal clear and very weedy. This has made wading for garpike much more difficult. While increased water clarity makes it easier to spot fish, the dense weeds impede wading and constantly foul the hooks. Such weedy, clear water is common throughout the garpike's range, making for sometimes frustrating, but always challenging fly fishing.

Since I was a teenager, I've had this love affair with carp. In England, where I grew up, they're the number-one game fish. Imagine my delight when I moved here in 1960 and found waters swarming with them—and nobody fishing for them. "Garbage fish" was the universal attitude. How I used to shake my head at my misguided Canadian angling friends. However, the attitude is rapidly changing. Carp fishing is catching on. There is a Canadian Carp Association based in Peterborough, Ontario, and there are regular carp fish-ins and tournaments (matches, as they're called in England and Europe). Many anglers still use regular spinning gear and dough balls or corn for bait, but many are beginning to use some of the sophisticated, specialized gear from across the pond (such as bolt rigs and hair rigs), not to mention exotic baits such as "boilies." And some of us fly fish for them.

By far the best time to fly fish for carp is in the spring when they move into shallow water prior to spawning. Water warms more quickly in the shallows, and the fish bask there, soaking up the warmth, feeding on invertebrates in the newly sprouting aquatic vegetation. In these conditions they are especially partial to an artificial nymph placed strategically in front of them. This makes for what is perhaps some of the most challenging and heart-stopping freshwater fly fishing there is.

This is no delicate business. Leave your trout gear at home. What you need is a heavy-duty 9- or 10-weight rod, at least 9' long, with a fighting butt. I use a 10' rod with a WF-9 floating line—the same rod I use for chinooks. The extra length makes it easier to maneuver the line among the cattails without fouling it. It's perfect for making short flip-casts, which are what most situations demand as you must be close to a fish in order to see it take. Carp are so quick to spit out an artificial fly that the usual method of watching for the leader to twitch is useless. Most times the leader never even moves when a fish takes.

The reel should be large enough to take the heavy line and at least 100 yards (90 m) of backing, which should be top-quality Dacron of at least 30-lb test. A good disc drag is an asset but not strictly necessary. What is absolutely essential, though, is an exposed, flanged rim. This allows you to use your fingers and palm as a brake, a much more sensitive and rapidly adjustable system than a mechanical drag. The reel should also have a precisely machined spindle and sleeve, preferably of stainless steel. Ball bearings are even better, for poor-quality reels can easily seize up when these powerful fish take off on their characteristically long, blistering runs.

Choosing an appropriate leader presents something of a dilemma. For such powerful fish, a strong tippet is essential, yet at the same time it must be fine enough to allow a natural presentation of small flies. If you opt primarily for strength, you lose out on presentation. If you opt for presentation, you lose out on strength. Luckily, recent generation of leader materials designed specifically for fly fishing reduces this dilemma. For my tippet I use an Australian product which offers 3x (.008" diameter) with a breaking strain of over 8 lb and 2x (.010" diameter) of over 10 lb. In relatively snag-free water, the 3x is fine, but where fish have to be turned or stopped sharply, 2x or even 1x should be used although the latter will restrict you to flies of No. 8 and larger. In all cases, whatever size you use, a loop knot (Duncan Loop or Non-slip Mono Loop) will allow your fly to swing free, enhancing the naturalness of its presentation.

I've never known carp to become as selective as trout in their feeding; however, the best flies are those which actually imitate things on which carp are used to feeding. In some heavily fished waters where anglers regularly chum with corn, bread, or pellets, "flies" which imitate these can be very successful, especially if they're impregnated with the appropriate scents and juices—although some purists would shudder at this practice. But where I fish, carp are not used to finding food which humans throw in the water. This means that we use flies which imitate the invertebrates and crustaceans for which carp habitually forage. Most impressionistic nymphs in sizes No. 12–6 will work well. Scud, shrimp, crayfish and worm patterns are also good. All should be weighted. Crayfish patterns will allow you to fish a larger fly and a heavier leader. But, in most cases, presentation is far more important than pattern.

And this brings us to tactics. Most anglers are familiar with the popular slogan "Think like a fish!" However, when you fly fish for carp you should think like a heron. Stealth, stillness, and positioning yourself where the fish will come to you are what it's all about.

First, stalk the water's margins looking for signs of carp in the shallows. This isn't too hard in the spring. Even well before the actual spawning, there are always a few particularly randy individuals (most likely male) that will be sloshing around in the shallows. Look for these, for where there's a couple there will be more. Watch the water for a while, noting the patterns of movement. You'll find carp patrolling in schools just offshore. Once you've established the pattern, wade out slowly—sneakily—and position yourself where you are close enough to passing fish that you'll be able to see them take your fly beneath the surface. Then, just like a heron, freeze and wait.

When you see a school approaching, wait until they are within easy casting range. Then, as unobtrusively as you can, flip your fly about a foot in front of them, so it is just reaching the bottom as they approach. If they're in a feeding mood (not all are), you'll see one engulf your fly. At this point, set the hook immediately. If you don't, you'll be too late, and the carp will spit out the fly.

Once you've done this, hang on and watch that your fingers don't get in the way of the reel handle. Unless the carp is heading for obvious snags, ease off and let it run. That's what all the extra backing is for. It won't run forever. Just maintain a gentle pressure and it will eventually turn. Then be prepared to pull in line fast, as they frequently head right back at you. Whatever you do, never let the line go slack. It's also a good idea to have a big landing net with you and also a fishing buddy, so you can net each other's fish.

Chris Marshall's Must-Have Patterns for Exotics

- Dry: Hare's Ear
- Casual Dress
- Wet: Moira River Bugger

Oriental Steamed Carp

Rich with flavors of the Orient
(Makes four servings)

6–8 oz—carp per person, gutted and scaled—170–250 g

3 cups—water—750 mL

3 cloves minced garlic

2 tbsp—minced fresh ginger—30 mL

3 tbsp—soya sauce—45 mL

Salt and pepper

Minced garlic and ginger (optional)

1 bunch—green onions

¼ cup—slivered almonds, toasted—60 mL

SAUCE

¼ cup—vegetable oil—60 mL

2 tbsp—soya sauce—30 mL

1. Place water in a wok and add garlic, ginger, soya sauce and dash of salt. Place bamboo steamer over wok. Salt and pepper carp, and then place in steamer and cover. Steam 10-20 minutes, depending on size of carp. To increase oriental flavors, sprinkle minced garlic and ginger over the fish before steaming.

2. Cut green onions in 1" (25 mm) diagonal pieces. Before serving the fish, top with green onions and toasted slivered almonds. Mix vegetable and soya sauce, heat and drizzle over fish. This helps crisp the skin and adds a great deal of flavor. To reduce calories, omit the hot oil and add soya sauce; however, the skin will not be crisp.

3. Serve on a platter with steamed rice and stir-fried vegetables. Red peppers, onions and sugar snap peas are a great combination. Mild, sweet Vidalia onions are even better than green onions.

–Wayne Phillips

CHAPTER 30

LAKE WHITEFISH ON DRY FLIES

Gord Ellis

L AKE WHITEFISH ARE CANADA'S MOST OVERLOOKED GAME FISH, and for no apparent reason. They take a dry fly with vigor and fight with spirited—if somewhat spastic—determination. Whitefish are also a treat on the table, and in most jurisdictions their sheer numbers allow for a guilt-free harvest. Canadian fisheries managers have been trying for years to promote whitefish as an under-utilized species—sort of a poor man's salmon. Luckily, when taken on a fly, a whitefish will blow away a similar-sized brookie, laker or brown trout, so given the chance, a whitefish sells itself.

Whitefish aren't suckers. They're also not bony, nor oily. In fact they are few of the things that most people think they are. Whitefish are, in fact, more closely related to trout than to suckers and sport a very troutlike adipose fin. They do have large scales and a small, pouty mouth, but run a fillet knife through that body and you'll find the bone structure of a salmonid and fine, flavorful meat.

If you've wanted to catch a few whitefish but have had some difficulty in the past, there is no better time to try than during the may fly hatch. Timing the hatch in Canada varies depending on your latitude, but most hatches occur from late May to mid-July. Track down an entomologist or biologist in the area where you live, and they will be able to tell you when the peak of the may fly hatch occurs. The key to making good whitefish catches during the may fly hatch is to fish on the surface, and no technique is more successful than classic dry-fly fishing.

My first real introduction to dry-fly fishing for whitefish took place at Ivanhoe Provincial Park near Chapleau, Ontario, on Canada Day (July 1), 1990. The height of the may fly hatch usually falls on the first week of July in northern Ontario, which is why the local Ministry of Natural Resources was holding a Whitefish Weekend at the park. The may flies were going and the bite was on. Local angler John Seyler and I spent a couple of very enjoyable hours fly fishing the reedy shoreline of a point no more than a stone's throw from the Junior Ranger Camp on Ivanhoe Lake.

The bottom was dark, muddy and shallow—perfect conditions for a mega-sized may fly hatch. We started fishing the lake two hours before the main body of the hatch, yet the whitefish were already lying in wait for that magic moment. Anchored in the canoe, enjoying the muggy afternoon air, we methodically cast to the reed edges and let our flies float on the calm surface. Strikes came quickly, usually in less than a minute if our may fly imitating presentation was sitting high and dry on the water. The whitefish would erupt suddenly under the fly, causing it to disappear into a plate-sized swirl. My heart skipped several beats thanks to these surprise attacks.

At nightfall when the may fly hatch kicked into gear, the whitefish went crazy. In an effort to slurp up as many of the insects as possible, the fish became less wary of a water-saturated fly. Strikes came steadily and double headers were common. By the time it became too dark to thread a line through a hook eye, the fish were on a rampage, striking with abandon. Even a cigar butt was fair game. Seyler called it "a feeding frenzy in every sense of the word" as hundreds of whitefish turned the surface of the lake into a seething cauldron, their silver flanks flashing in the moonlight. We had a blast that night, catching and landing over a dozen 2–3-lb (900 g–1.4-kg) fish, while losing countless others due to those paper-thin mouths, slippery scales and our lack of a landing net.

As the moon appeared, the hatch slowed and we went back to camp, wet, slimy and smiling. By any measure it was great fishing, yet only one other angler had been there enjoying the phenomenal action. Since that day I have experienced similar dry-fly fishing for whitefish in several Canadian provinces, and I continue to be struck by the lack of anglers taking it in. That's a shame.

Medium-weight fly gear is all you need for whitefish angling. A 6-weight fly rod, single-action reel and weight-forward floating line will do the trick nicely. For lake fishing during the hatch, I like an 8–9' tapered leader with a 4–6-lb test clear tippet. This setup will do justice to just about any whitefish you run into, and since they can grow to double-digit proportions, a 6-weight will allow you to land any larger fish that may come along. You'll be amazed at how hard these fish pull.

A varied selection of may fly- and caddis-imitating dry flies, a hook hone and a bottle of fly flotant will round out the required equipment.

Long, graceful casts are not usually important in this game, so don't be afraid if you're inexperienced. When whitefish are biting, a short roll cast from the boat or shore is usually fine. Douse your fly liberally with flotant, or it will drown under the barrage of whitey strikes and be virtually useless. The use of flotant helps keep flies on the surface longer, but it's a good idea to carry lots of flies so you don't run out of bone-dry ones to throw. Wear a bandanna or hat and dry your soaked flies on it. Whitefish are not super discriminating about dry flies, but my favorite patterns lean toward old classics that include both the Gray and White Wulff, March Brown, and Mosquitoes in sizes ranging from No. 12–8.

Although lighter-colored flies are a little easier to see, I've found that neutral or grey-colored imitations are most attractive to surface-feeding whitefish. Occasionally, the addition of two or even three flies to a leader can create a feeding frenzy without the benefit of real may flies. This works especially well in the early part of the evening when the whitefish are "looking." Attach the flies to the leader by leaving a long tag end off the top hook eye, or just add an 8" length of leader on the hook shank of the preceding fly. Using the same size and color of fly is a good bet if you want to mimic a may fly hatch, but occasionally, adding two or three different sizes and colors of flies will allow you to figure out quickly which pattern the whitefish want. (Editor's note: Always check provincial/territorial fishing regulations to ensure whether or not more than one fly can be used, and if so, the maximum number permissible.)

When searching out feeding whitefish, watch for boils on the surface and the occasional forked tail slicing the water as signs that the silver fish are gearing up for dinner. Muddy-bottomed bays, weed beds, reed-tipped points, swimming beaches and tapering shorelines are all high-probability spots for major may fly hatches. The fish will be cruising around the reed beds and along the edges of submerged weed beds, waiting to pounce on the flies as they emerge. The splashy take of a whitefish is an exciting thing to witness, especially when it's your fly that is being whacked.

Expect to miss a lot of strikes and lose a lot of fish when fly fishing for whitefish. They have a small mouth, and the membrane that connects the jaws is paper thin. If a fish strikes your fly, wait to feel it on the line before gently lifting the rod tip to set the hook. A sharp hook really increases hooking success. Play the fish gingerly and take a net—trying to hand land a whitefish is a nerve-wracking experience as they inevitably get off due to those extremely slippery scales.

Fly fishing for whitefish during the may fly hatch is a hoot! It requires only a modicum of skill and equipment while providing maximum fun. In fact, whitefish angling during the may fly hatch deserves to become a Canadian fly-fishing tradition.

GORD ELLIS' MUST-HAVE PATTERNS FOR LAKE WHITEFISH

- Gray Wulff
- March Brown
- Mosquitoes
- White Wulff

CHAPTER 31

ALGONQUIN'S TREASURES

Kenneth Coupland

Ontario's Algonquin Park has been in formal existence since 1893; however, it was used for lumbering, trapping, hunting and fishing for many years before. The park has been subjected to many instances that could be construed as misuse throughout its lifetime but has apparently survived all of these, and with enlightened conservation policies may actually be improving.

One aspect that has changed is the increased restrictions on the use of motors. This must be considered when planning a trip.

At first glance the map of Algonquin Park can be very daunting, for it shows a vast number of lakes, rivers and streams. Where does one start? The park's location seems ideal in that all parts are fairly accessible by roads from major population areas in southern Ontario and the Great Lakes states. Highway 60 branches eastward off Highway 11 near Huntsville and actually cuts through the park's southwestern corner northeast of Dwight, then exits at Whitney. Whitney can also be reached via Highway 17 from Renfrew and Ottawa, or via Highway 127, which runs south to Bancroft.

The Highway 60 route provides several popular "jump-offs" like Canoe Lake and Opeongo Lake. There are two road-access points from Highway 17 to the northern side of the park. From Deux Riviers it's about 19 miles (31 km) south to Brent on Cedar Lake, from where you can head up the Petawawa, Nipissing or Cochon rivers. From Eau Claire it's about 16 miles (26 km) south to Kiosk, right where the Amable du Fond River drains from Lake Kioshkokwi.

On the west side, access from Highway 11 is from South River northeast to Kawawaymog Lake (known locally as Round Lake), which is outside the park boundary, but which provides access to the Amable du Fond River and North Tea Lake. A few words of warning about Kawawaymog Lake: It is large, relatively shallow, and can be rough in high winds. We try to cross it early in the day before the wind picks up. Also on the west side, Rain Lake is about 16 miles (26 km) east of Kearney.

There are many other access points, but one pretty well requires local knowledge and experience to make use of them.

Algonquin Park is far enough north that killing frosts may occur at any time during the summer. The average temperature difference between high and low is 24°F (13°C)—the greatest range in southern Ontario—which usually provides warm days and cool nights. Elevations reaching 1,850' (555 m) above sea level in some areas also greatly influences the climate. Rainfall is about 30" (76 cm) per year, with most of that during the fall months. What all of this means is that one must be ready for rather dramatic, even severe weather changes, especially in the spring when most fishing occurs in the park. Consequently, at times you might encounter solid ice, pack ice, and ice floating in high water levels.

The species most actively pursued in the park by fly fishers is brook trout, more commonly called speckled trout or specks. Also present are lake trout, found mostly in the deeper lakes, smallmouth bass in the warmer waters of the southeastern region, and walleye, pike and muskie in the extreme northeastern waters.

Somebody's questionable wisdom resulted in the introduction of smallmouth bass into Kawawaymog Lake. Now they may be found all the way down the Amable du Fond River, right through to Manitou Lake. What was once a pure trout fishery is no longer. Although smallmouths are admirable game fish, we should not deliberately mix the species.

My fishing partners and I try to keep a close eye on the weather in the spring, aiming to get in to our favorite spots about a week after the ice has gone out. If we are lucky, we can do a fast portage trip, having dodged around any pack ice, and reach the spot we have chosen as a base camp. After setting up camp, we are ready to fly fish the shoreline of the main lake for both speckled and lake trout. The rivers are full and provide excellent fishing, especially where they enter the lake. From this base camp, we always do one-day portages into any back lakes that we have found to be productive. For these outings, we take a minimum amount of equipment.

You may, of course, also fish for bass, pike and muskies as soon as their seasons open.

Summer, when children are out of school, is a grand time for tripping with your family—a fine chance to introduce them to wilderness camping, swimming, canoeing, blueberry picking, and generally enjoying life.

Fishing in the park during autumn can be most pleasant, with fall colors in evidence and NO BUGS! However, water levels may be down if the summer was hot and dry. When this happens, brook trout may be difficult to find and may actually be down deep with the lakers. As the season's end approaches, the brookies, followed later by the lake trout, will congregate in their spawning areas. Here, fly fishing comes into its own since you may cast a small streamer into 1' (30 cm) of water with great success.

After some 30 years of spending at least a week each year in the park, our equipment selection has evolved into a standard for each person, one that changes very little from year to year. When I think back to when two of us sheltered under a canoe with two ponchos snapped together as a thunderstorm raged overhead, it is obvious that we have come a long way.

A map and compass are essential, and a small, lightweight Global Positioning System is certainly worth considering. Our personal gear includes waterproof insulated boots, rain gear, light parka, work gloves, broad-brimmed hat, head net and sunglasses. You may add whatever you think is suitable, always bearing in mind that it all has to be carried over the portages.

For tackle, I consider a 7- or 8-weight fly rod about right, preferably a 4-piece model that can be fastened under the canoe gunwales. Also, after one memorable experience of trying to fish through a jungle along a small creek, I built a very short, lightweight rod using a spare, 3' fly rod tip section. This is rigged with one of Hardy's baby reels and an old Herter's 5-DT-F line. Figuring that it would not be used for distance casting, I spooled a fairly heavy line that would load the rod with barely 10' (3 m) out. It will handle more line but is obviously limited. I keep it rigged and stashed along with the other rods, making it readily available for instant action if we encounter a good piece of river as we travel.

Flies should include streamers from No. 10–4, some nymphs, and a few small, dark dries. After all, trout feed extensively on black flies.

While boats are an option in easily accessible waters, a canoe is essential if you plan much portaging. We prefer a 16-footer that is deep, stable and capable of carrying two persons with their packs and other gear. A basic consideration is whether to use a motor. We have always used a small two h.p. outboard when we plan to traverse large lakes. If you have ever made your way up North Tea or Opeongo into a strong wind, you will know what I mean. Even with a motor it can take a couple of hours—and all day without one. If you do take a motor and fuel, you will probably have to do a double carry over the portages. And remember—even small motors can be heavy and awkward and a gas can still has to be carried in one hand.

Since the park has such a variety of large and small lakes, plus rivers and streams, you may decide to concentrate specifically on lake or river fishing—but often it's a combination of both. For many years we have usually aimed at more remote parts of the park. This has meant starting off around 8:00 A.M., spending one day of fairly strenuous traveling and portaging, then finally making our base camp on the back lake just before nightfall. From this base we can fish the main lake, or do one- or two-day trips into some of the more remote lakes and streams up in the highlands. These latter lakes, which are usually unnamed on the map, are at a considerably higher elevation.

Over the years we have settled on a few favorite areas to which we like to return. Descriptions of a few of them follow.

The Petawawa River is long, with many portages, and offers much wonderful water to fish. It passes through several lakes that contain excellent populations of both lake and brook trout, and that have many good camp sites. Anglers usually leave their vehicles at Cedar Lake and may even camp there, fishing the lake itself. Downstream from Cedar, the river is definitely "big water" and should be used by only expert canoeists. Cedar Lake is a large body of water with some surprisingly deep parts, but there are excellent shoals and structure off the river mouths which offer good fly fishing for brook trout. If you decide to get out the heavy tackle and go after lakers down deep, they have been caught up to 45 lb (20 kg).

The Nipissing River is also tributary to Cedar Lake, flowing down from the most remote part of the park. In fact, it originates very close to the northwest boundary. Since our favorite fishing spots for several years were well up the river, we have tried reaching them either from Cedar Lake or by traveling downstream from its headwaters. The latter may be preferable since it avoids having to travel upstream for a couple of hours through innumerable S-turns. An interesting development occurred many years ago when the dam at the bottom of Cedar Lake went out, allowing access to walleyes from the Petawawa River. We discovered this run when we found walleyes spawning in the Nipissing, then moving on down into the river mouth. For several years we had excellent fishing, catching fish as large as 10 lb (4.5 kg) in about 6' (1.8 m) of water. We used sinking lines and large yellow streamers.

Opeongo Lake is very large, very deep, and has an extensive lake-trout population. We have never fly fished Opeongo, having used it mainly to travel north to smaller lakes like Big Crow and Big Trout. Our favorite lakes are Lavielle and Dickson to the northeast. Our usual route is to travel down the Crow River to Lavielle, enjoying excellent fishing on the Crow, and then at various spots on the main lake that have proved productive in the past. To the south we can reach Dickson Lake, which also provides all kinds of good fishing for specks and lake trout. At the junction of the two lakes is a hot spot known as the "Glory Hole," where I recommend that everyone be sure to try their luck.

Dickson Lake may also be reached directly from Opeongo by a long portage of about 5 miles (8 km). This is a tough portage and should not be undertaken lightly or without adequate preparation. I have seen people come off this one looking like "death march" victims.

Kiosk is a village on Lake Kioshkokwi on the park's northern edge. If your party has members who, for whatever reasons, are unable to handle the physical demands of canoeing and portaging, it is possible to camp here quite comfortably. You can fish the main lake and still have the option of venturing beyond into some of the other brook-trout lakes.

It is impossible in this short account to do more than highlight some of the salient points of interest to fly fishers. I continue to meet anglers who admit that they traveled into Algonquin when they were younger, but have not done so for several years. I marvel at this because the old park has never ceased to be ever-changing and interesting to my friends and me.

I recall that when a famous music critic was asked why he said that Mozart was the most under-appreciated composer ever, he replied, "No matter how much you say about him, you can never say enough." Perhaps this is the way my friends and I feel about Algonquin Park—and why we keep going back.

CHAPTER 32

GREAT LAKES, GREAT SMALLMOUTHS

Marty Roberts

SMALLMOUTH BASS ARE ARGUABLY THE FEISTIEST, MOST EXCITING game fish anglers can hook on the business end of their fishing lines. Even more exciting is having a nice 3–4-lb (1.4–1.8-kg) bass testing your abilities with a fly rod, for this little mass of pure fury provides more twists and turns than a pinball machine. Their size and shape allow them the mobility needed to run through weeds or wrap around logs in order to outsmart anglers.

With that first experience of a smallmouth exploding from the water, a dry fly at the side of its mouth as it tail-walks, dives and leaps in no particular order, it is the angler who is hooked.

Distribution

ALTHOUGH SMALLMOUTHS were originally found in eastern North America, they have spread across Canada to varying degrees. Stocking in every province has seen some positive effects in small, selected pockets in the west, and particularly on the east coast. Central and southern Ontario, where this species is highly regarded by all sport anglers, are very well populated. The average smallmouth caught in the Great Lakes system weighs 1–2 lb (450–900 g). Barely an eyebrow is raised at a 4-lb (1.8-kg) catch and 5 lb (2.3 kg) is fairly common. The North American record is slightly shy of 12 lb (5.5 kg), which was caught in the perfect habitat of Kentucky. Of course a fish of that size is a rare commodity and cannot be expected in most lifetimes, but the opportunity to hook into a few 4-lb (1.8-kg) bass in a day's outing is most appealing.

Habitat

WHERE SMALLMOUTHS LIVE is dictated by what they eat. Crayfish, aquatic insects and even small frogs top the list, but smaller species of baitfish are also popular food items. Because of this, the fish will stay in shallow-to-medium water over a rocky or sandy bottom. Favored spots are those with broken rocks and crevices in which the bass can hide. Many will also hold in small weed beds waiting for their next meal to swim by.

Where they reside has a direct bearing on their appearance. Smallmouth colors vary from shades of green for those living in weed beds to hues of brown for those on rocky shoals. In the latter case, this has led to the popular nickname "bronzeback."

As the season progresses they migrate into deeper territory, generally something in the 30–40' (9–12 m) range. As cooler temperatures return, so do the bass, heading for the familiar shallows from early summer. Spawning season—which is usually June and even early July—is when you will find fish still guarding their nests.

Seasons and other Regulations

THE TRADITIONAL OPENING DAY for Ontario smallmouth bass has always been the last Saturday of June. The season generally runs through until November 30. This holds true for all of the Great Lakes, but there are a few exceptions. Lake Superior, for instance, is open all year for bass. Anglers should take special care to study the Ontario Fishing Regulations Summary for exceptions. There are a number of sanctuaries, for example, along the shores of the

Great Lakes. Many of these areas are closed to all fishing from June 1 until July 15. The purpose of these sanctuaries is to give the smallmouth bass ample time to spawn and hatch the eggs. Because bass nest in wide-open, flat, rocky bottoms, it is easy for anglers to accidentally destroy eggs and nests while simply wading through the area.

My favorite time to fish the sanctuaries, and perhaps readers should take this as a huge hint, is right from the day they open. Not only have the fish had peace and quiet for six weeks, but in most instances, they have not seen a fly of any kind since the previous fall. In other words, they are downright voracious and readily attack most offerings thrown at them by anglers.

Populations

IF A VISITING ANGLER talked to someone who regularly fishes in any one of the Great Lakes, the message would invariably be that this specific area has the best and biggest population of smallmouth bass in Ontario. The fact is they are everywhere. Lake Superior and Lake Huron have very respectable stocks and can be extremely productive. Lake Erie is perhaps the number-one spot for both quantity and quality. Lake Ontario, at least up until the 1990s, was sporadic but is improving. In fact, I will go so far as to predict that Lake Ontario will eventually catch and even surpass all of the other lakes.

As with all of the Great Lakes, very definite cycles occur just about every decade. During the 1970s, '80s and '90s, Lake Ontario was known for its herds of salmon. I call them "herds," because any living thing that grows that big and that fast must travel in herds. It now appears, and many biologists agree, that the cycle is swinging over to smallmouth bass and they will most likely become the species of quantity there.

Erie is the lake presently setting the guidelines and should for some time. Because it is very shallow and has a very solid limestone bottom, it is an ideal environment for this species to thrive in and to reproduce in great numbers. Thanks to the foresight of Ontario fisheries biologists, smallmouth bass should be the number-one species of game fish in Lake Erie for many more years.

Getting at Them

AS WITH ANY STYLE OF FISHING and any species of fish, there are many ways to get to them. Having lived on the shores of Lake Erie my entire life, my favorite motto is: "Only a fool would take a fishing boat out on that water."

Well, we all do it, but hopefully the idea strikes home. The Great Lakes, Erie in particular, can go from mirror calm to 6' (1.8 m) waves in less than an hour. In other words, unless you have a radio-equipped 20-footer, don't risk going more than a mile (1.6 km) from shore. However, a calm day is very inviting for anglers with 12–14' aluminum cartoppers to venture out and test their skills with a few smallies. The real beauty of these lakes is that most of the good fishing is along the shorelines.

Several years ago, as a casual experiment I decided to "compete" against the participants in a national professional bass tournament. Not being a competitive fisherman, I often wondered how I would fare against the pros. My test was off the record and for my information only. What I found was quite intriguing and interesting to say the least.

After watching 100 or more boats roar into oblivion, I set out several miles down the shoreline. I couldn't help but think about those $20,000 bass boats as I tossed my $200 float tube into the water and set out with fly rod in hand. At the end of three days, matching tube against bass boat and fly rod versus hard tackle, I had my answer. My total three-day weight would have put me in the upper half of the field—not bad for an old hack. This was, of course, not due to any great feat or because I was any better at fishing. It was only because the Great Lakes are so plentiful with these fish, and pretty much any technique and presentation will work in the right conditions.

The whole point here is that if visitors to the Great Lakes want to drown a fly or two, they need not be overly prepared. In midsummer most locals venture out with only a pair of shorts and running shoes. The not-so-brave, such as I, will don waders for the occasion. My personal favorite style of fly fishing the Great Lakes shorelines is with the aid of a float tube. This is, perhaps, the ultimate fishing vessel for any fly fisher and obviously can take you to places no boat could ever go. There are always plenty of pockets for tackle, lines, reels and flies. No fly fisher on the big lakes or small ponds should be without one.

Another superb method of getting on the water is with a lightweight aluminum boat. I prefer a small, 12' model, one that can be easily flipped onto the roof of my car. With the aid of a three to six h.p. outboard motor, the sky is the limit where access to prime fishing areas is concerned.

Presentation

PRESENTATION ON THESE BODIES OF WATER is actually quite simple. There are no currents, ripples or fast eddies to deal with. Deep pools are mainly nonexistent, and only the rare undertow will dare to take your fly for an unplanned ride.

Most anglers will present their fly in a circle, covering a full 360°. The only factors to really consider are wind and direction of the waves. I find casting best when the surface is anywhere from flat to waves of 1' (30 cm). Anything beyond that pretty much negates the notion of using a dry fly.

As with most of the Great Lakes shores, and particularly Lake Erie, one can wade out as much as 200 yards (180 m) from shore and still be just over waist deep. If you manage to find a nice calm bay with little boat traffic, you will certainly have lots of water to cover and can virtually spend the day trying to do just that.

Once the fly is in the water, it is best to experiment to determine which speed of retrieve will be the order of the day. Some days fast and jerky is best; other days slow and methodical will be the answer. If using a dry fly, a slow retrieve—not much quicker than 1' (30 cm) every 5 to 10 seconds—is the best method for enticing a smallmouth to break water. Rather than pull their food under like many trout, they will make a screaming run for the surface, gulp up the food on their way by, and then proceed to put on a show that would thrill any angler.

Wet flies are also very effective, and once hooked, the bass will tail-walk and dance like no other fish in North America.

Because even a little breeze can wreak havoc on the best of fly casters, Great Lakes fishing can be a challenge at times. I have found a couple of methods that have been helpful over the years. Naturally, casting with the wind is the best advice. By getting the fly out a long way, you keep it in the water longer while drawing it back against the push of the waves. It is also quite useful to allow the waves to actually draw the bait back out again, covering the same areas perhaps where a cross-eyed bass has missed its target.

Casting into the wind is absolutely hilarious when it is hampering another angler—perhaps your partner. But when it happens to you, it can be very frustrating. I have found the best presentation in these conditions is to use a sidearm cast. It doesn't take long to develop and can be mastered fairly quickly. Keeping your fly, leader and line just above the surface avoids most effects of the wind and puts your mock insect out where you want it. This method is best accomplished from a float tube or while wading, where you are already down near water level. I have also found that keeping the fly well away from yourself is the safest method of casting. I haven't hooked my earlobe or even knocked my hat off for years now.

Tackle

THE FLY ROD OF CHOICE for the Great Lakes is generally a 5-, 6- or 7-weight. All work quite nicely, but everyone has a preference for various reasons. I prefer a 9' rod in a 5/6-weight combined with 6-weight line. This combination seems to produce the casts needed for these waters—and the most excitement when a bass is hooked. Most fly fishers carry two lines: weight-forward floating, and weight-forward sinking models. If the water is rough, a sinking line is your best bet; however, a floating model is most widely used and only on occasion is a small weight added to get the fly just a little deeper.

The range of leaders used can be anywhere from 2x to 5x, 7- to 4-lb test. My preference is either a 3x or 4x, whichever comes out of my pocket first. The important thing is that not a lot of leader is necessary, and it is recommended they be kept at or under 7 ½' in length.

Wet or Dry?

ON SOME OCCASIONS weather and water conditions dictate the choice between wet or dry flies. The rule of thumb should simply be that a dry fly be used only on very calm water, with waves just a few inches in height. Wet flies, of course, can be used in any conditions and will produce no matter what the weather. Wet flies should be retrieved reasonably fast and kept to within the upper half of the water depth you are fishing.

Patterns

THE BEST THING ABOUT FISHING for smallmouth bass, particularly in the Great Lakes, is that almost any pattern will work to some extent. There are, of course, several favorites. The number-one fly under any conditions is the Woolly Bugger. This leech pattern is most productive and seems to be on the menu of choice for smallmouths. The black version works very well, but different variations often come through with good results. Generally, I find that as long as you stick to dark colors, they work well. Combinations between body and tail using black, olive-green, dark purple and dark blue have been very successful and provide many hours of fishing fun. As a general rule it is best to use these flies in the No. 8 range. Of course, this can vary with experimentation, bearing in mind that larger bass tend to go for larger baits. Every smallmouth angler should have one fly box full of Woolly Buggers in various colors.

Another popular pattern in these big lakes is a caddis fly imitation—about No. 14 works best. Known locally as the sand fly, this insect is in great abundance and is a mainstay in the diet of smallmouth bass. If it is light brown, small and jittery, they will inhale it.

Also used quite often are insect patterns such as an ant or a large fly, much like a deer fly. Finally, if all else fails, streamers of the trout variety will work in some areas. Again, darker colors seem to be best in most conditions, provided they are not too large.

In very weedy areas, various deer-hair-bodied flies are tempting morsels for bass. These take a little more finesse to use but can be deadly when the conditions are right, meaning a calm, or near-calm surface. This allows an angler to work a fly over gently, through and around the weeds and vegetation that provide shelter for those really big fish. In these situations it is often wise to use a weedless hook, which allows you to cast your fly right among the lily pads. Try letting your fly rest on top of a lily pad for a few moments, and then pull it slowly off the edge and into Mr. Bronzeback's hiding spot. There are few times as exciting as when a smallmouth bursts from the weed beds with your fly hanging from its lip. You must then battle the fish and the weeds—a real test for any angler.

Hot Spots

THE GREAT LAKES COVER A LARGE AREA, and it's almost impossible to name every little nook and cranny where smallmouths can be found. Although just about any good-looking shoreline—which would probably be hundreds of kilometers—will likely be productive, some locations are ranked among the greatest hot spots in North America. In Georgian Bay, part of Lake Huron, the eastern shoreline is a great place to start. The vicinity of Killarney and down to the outlet of the Moon River harbors bass in good numbers. Farther south, on the same coastline, near Parry Sound, anglers have been known to catch a limit or two of wily bronzebacks, and below that, Honey Harbour is also very popular.

In Lake Ontario, the best place to try is in the Kingston area, better known as the Thousand Islands (quite aptly named). This location has been home to many bass tournaments, and the competitors always come up with large numbers. This area is not very far from the Ganaraska River, which might entice typical trout anglers to test their skills with the bass.

The Lake Ontario smallmouth bass fishery is growing by leaps and bounds. The western shore from Niagara-on-the-Lake to Toronto has already produced bass in good numbers, and it has been predicted that within the next 5 to 10 years this may be one of the best smallmouth spots on the Great Lakes.

For now, Lake Erie seems to be the leader. Just about any little bay from Rondeau to Long Point to Turkey Point will yield many smallmouths of decent sizes. The option of flat bottom or weedy bays is always there, and a fly fisher can pick and choose, never having to worry about seeing another soul.

Perhaps the best overall spot on Lake Erie is the shoreline from Port Colborne, at the Welland Canal, down to the mouth of the Niagara River at Fort Erie. This is one of those spots with a sanctuary, so boundaries must be observed. However, once anglers are permitted on these waters, they are never disappointed. The amount of access to the water is almost limitless, and with very few weed beds and mostly flat limestone bottoms, fly fishers can wade with ease. The population of smallmouth in this area continues to grow every year, and it appears they will always be there. Local anglers have kept this a secret for many years, but there is certainly enough for everyone.

Smallmouth bass are a worthy quarry for any fly fisher, and the shores of the Great Lakes provide superb habitat for them. From all indications it should be a fantastic fishery for years to come.

Marty Roberts Must-Have Patterns for Great Lakes Smallmouth Bass

- Woolly Bugger
- Roberts' Woolly Boolly
- Martin's Nasty Bugger

Potato-Crusted Smallmouth Bass

Unforgettable!
(Makes four servings)

4 6-oz—bass fillets, or equivalent portions—4 170-g
3 to 5 small potatoes, thinly sliced

Roasted red pepper sauce

2 large red peppers, roasted
1 garlic clove, minced
2–4 tbsp—olive oil, or light cream*—30–60 mL
2 tsp—lemon zest—10 mL
Salt and pepper to taste

1. Season fish with salt and pepper to taste. Slice potatoes thinly. Small potatoes with the skin left on are best. Sauté potatoes on one side only until golden brown and remove from the pan.

2. In the same pan, sauté the fish for a minute or two, and then turn. While fish is cooking on the second side, quickly arrange potato slices (golden side up) on top of the fish to look like scales. Continue to sauté fish until it cooks through.

3. For the sauce, roast red peppers in a 350°F (180°C) oven until very soft and browned, and then place in a covered bowl. When cool, remove and discard skin and seeds. Pulse in a food processor with all other ingredients until sauce is smooth. Puddle red pepper sauce on a plate and top with a bass fillet.

Light cream makes a rich, luscious sauce.

–Wayne Phillips

CHAPTER 33

MUSKIE MAGIC

Burton J. Myers

ONCE UPON A TIME THERE WAS A MUSKIE FISHERMAN ON A lake. Not a great lake, to be sure, but a great muskie lake, nonetheless. Not a great muskie fisherman, either, but a muskie fisherman to the core.

He was schooled in the stout rod, the maximum-capacity casting reel and the lure that had trophy bass cowering in their lairs. And yet, into this arena he brought a 9-weight faerie wand, a single-action reel, and a 2/0 hook adorned with a clump of deer hair and a touch of feathery fluff.

The audience—long-stemmed bulrushes, cattails, low-bush cranberries and swamp maples—waited stoically for the impending duel. While the challenger was a bit insecure, the champion was as Nature intended, a master of its domain. It had passed all challenges, surviving for more than two decades. Its very existence was a testament to that part of Nature this fisherman held in reverence. And I wanted that fish.

I had caught many muskies, more perhaps than most would believe, but only a few were truly deserved. Too many were due to the savvy and skill of a hired guide. More, still, were due to perseverance on good water rather than carefully honed tactics. But this was a lake I fished often. I had taken muskie from almost every clump of coontail and cabbage, and I knew it held a scattering of fair-sized fish.

As the first breath of early morning air caught the bow of my boat and moved it into position, I began to false cast. When 50' (15 m) of line became airborne, I stopped playing with it and let my Perch Special settle into about 15" (38 cm) of water—the "transition zone" between shoreline vegetation and submerged greenery.

I spotted the telltale V of an approaching fish the moment I began my retrieve and prepared for the strike, yet nothing happened. I continued my steady retrieve, expecting at any moment to feel the powerful surge of a taking fish. Still nothing happened. Then, 20' (6 m) from the boat, my fly now visible just below the surface, I saw her thick form scant inches below my offering. I hesitated and became so transfixed upon the fish that I failed to see the fly disappear. One moment it was there; the next it was gone. Instinct took over for my stumbling brain, and I set the hook—hard!—as only a muskie angler can.

What happened next was anything but legendary. I fell ass first into the bottom of the boat, draped in fly line and tippet, the bushy Perch Special neatly embedded in my neck. Such are the joys of muskie fishing with a fly.

Having bested muskie in just about every way possible, it was just natural that I should want to do it with a fly. My first step was an audience with the late, great Lee Wulff at the Toronto Sportsmen's Show. I remember firing off a bevy of carefully thought-out questions to the aging master before he stopped me in midsentence with a wave of his hand and a raised eyebrow. "Yes, Burt, you can catch muskie on a fly," he said. "And, yes I have. But why would you want to? A big in-line spinner works a lot better, you know."

Most of the time Lee was absolutely right, of course, but not always. There are times when a fly presented properly can spin a magical spell with muskie.

First, it's important to understand that catching a muskie on a fly can range from being a relatively easy task to an undertaking of monumental proportions. Fabled waters such as Eagle Lake, Lake of the Woods, Georgian Bay and the St. Lawrence River are capable of producing fish of record proportions, but they are few and far between, and most are pulled from depths exceeding 15' (4.5 m). Better bets are smaller lakes with numerous weed beds, shoals, and points with drop-offs and dense populations of muskie.

I also prefer clear or slightly stained water where fish can sight feed. Stony

Lake in Ontario's Kawartha Region is a good bet, as are numerous smaller lakes in the Haliburton Region. Muskie in these waters average under 10 lb (4.5 kg) and feed regularly in water that is less than 12' (3.6 m) deep, where a fly, even on the surface, is clearly visible.

Top locations to make contact with fish have clearly defined edges. While muskie are sometimes found smack in the middle of some of the thickest cover imaginable, as a general rule they hold where a weed bed ends and a mud flat begins, or where a rock shoal or point drops into deeper water. Another good indication of a location's potential is the presence of baitfish or small panfish like perch, pumpkinseeds or bluegills. The closer any of these locations are to the deepest water in a lake, the higher the potential for making contact with a trophy muskie. In most lakes that's a fish approaching the 48" (1.2 m) mark.

June and early September through until fall turnover are prime times, with summer days under a rising or falling barometer a close second. During the mornings and evenings, look for fish in water that is less than 6' (1.8 m) deep. While these are the key feeding periods, I prefer midafternoon between 1:30 and 4:30 when the fish are often roaming around in their home range. Although this movement is not connected to feeding, fish will strike when an opportunity presents itself. Pay particular attention to transition zones with water depths of 8–15' (2.4–4.5 m) where the bottom begins to disappear from sight.

Avoid fishing in hot, still weather when the water temperature exceeds 70°F (21°C). When water warms past that point, muskies don't handle the stress of even a short tussle very well, making successful catch-and-release rates nosedive. It's not that a 9- or 10-weight fly rod isn't capable of quickly subduing most fish, for even a 10-lb (4.5-kg) fish barely puts a decent bend in my 10-weight Fenwick. However, the added length of fly rods in these weight classes adds more leverage than the standard casting rods used by most muskie anglers. I consider the use of lighter-weight rods as irresponsible. Besides, they won't handle the big, bulky flies you will usually require.

Marry your rod to a reel with a good drag and don't get hung up on stories about fish that empty spools. I've never had a muskie get more that a few yards into my backing. Muskie are sprinters, not marathoners. They aren't particularly leader-shy either. Seven-foot leaders of 20-lb test mono with 20-lb or better wire tippets are my choice for most conditions. I prefer a loop-to-loop system that allows me to prerig a dozen flies with 12" wire leaders.

Fly selection for most muskie fishing is fairly spartan: tarpon-sized Deceivers in yellow, red, white and black are top choices. Other productive patterns include the Bunny Leech, the Dahlberg Diver, and various rat imitations. In truth, just about any big bucktail fly will work, particularly if it features large eyes, preferably held in position and protected by an epoxy head. One of my favorites is the previously mentioned, one-of-a-kind, Perch Special—a 6" tube fly crafted by Bob Jones. Its yellow bucktail dressing has Magic Marker highlights that give it a perch look.

Besides your basic outfit and a few flies, you'll need a set of large needlenose pliers, a jaw spreader (one of those spring-wire contraptions that hold a fish's jaws open), and a net or, better yet, a landing cradle. If you don't plan to keep a fish, leave it in the water. I go barbless on my muskie flies, and it seldom requires more than a quick twist to free a fish.

A basic stop-start-stop retrieve works well. With surface flies always maintain the speed of your retrieve, even when a fish appears. However, with streamers such as a Deceiver, let the fly sit motionless in front of the fish. Big deer-hair streamers are almost neutrally buoyant and often just too tempting for a fish to pass up. There is nothing in my overstuffed trays of muskie lures that can quite match this magical tactic, nor can they imitate the natural look of a deer-hair surface pattern.

No, you won't find my mountain of muskie rods and tackle boxes out in a yard sale, at least not at any time in the near future. But when visible fish ignore just about everything else in my tackle box, I switch to one of my bits of feathers and fur. On too many occasions to be an accident, these same finicky fish have become clueless rockets that smack my offerings with wild abandon. That's why I always keep at least one fly rod rigged and close at hand.

I'm also a realist—fishing for muskie with a fly seldom produces the numbers or sizes that make legends of anglers, but watch one of those animals dance across the water at the end of your fly line, and you'll soon learn why the real legends of this game are these very special fish.

Burton J. Myers' Must-Have Patterns for Muskie

- Bunny Leech
- Dahlberg Diver
- Lefty's Deceiver
- Perch Special

CHAPTER 34

FLATLANDS JACKPOT

George Will

As oxymoronic as it sounds, there is some terrific trout fishing in the Keystone Province. World-class trout waters, both still and flowing, scattered over the prairie landscape? Yes, you read correctly—world class. Still you scoff? Well, I know of at least a half-dozen lakes where one can expect to regularly hook rainbows and browns of more than 20" (50 cm) and a couple of others which produce monsters in the 30" (76-cm) range. The huge brook trout of God's River have been the stuff of legend for decades, but there are several freestone streams in southern Manitoba that easily match the productivity and beauty of such better-known waters as the Madison and Ausable. And the best part is, there are relatively few fly fishers. It seems most Manitoba anglers would rather chuck hardware or bait for walleye and pike than toss a Woolly Bugger at a trout as big as their thigh. Go figure.

Let me step back a decade or three to the 1960s. While I was attending university in Winnipeg, a friend of a friend, who happened to be a fisheries biologist, told me of a stocking program that had been initiated by the Fisheries Branch of the Ministry of Natural Resources. Selected streams and lakes throughout the province were being heavily augmented with various species of trout. The idea was to create alternative fisheries to take pressure off smallmouth bass and walleye, which were receiving some heavy pounding. I was able to finagle a stocking map and took special note of the Whiteshell district in the southeastern part of the province. There, several lakes were being turned into trout waters, as were a couple of streams in the Duck Mountain area to the west. The program also included various other small lakes and ponds scattered all over the place. I obtained the relevant topographic maps and started making plans. As far as I knew, at the time I was the only fly fisherman in Winnipeg, having never met another.

But let's step back a bit further in time. While most of the contributors to this tome were possibly born with fly rods in their hands, my transmutation from hardware tosser to hackle jockey occurred despite some formidable obstacles. By my late teens I had grown increasingly disenchanted with heavy-duty bait fishing and spin-casting, so I became a devotee of ultralight spinning. In a place where 20-lb test line was regarded as gossamer, and a rod that actually bent under the weight of a fish was thought to be defective, getting my hands on such gear was difficult to say the least. But ultralight fishing led me to trout and from there to fly fishing for trout. Why? The discovery of several books on fly fishing in the library and two in particular—one by Joe Brooks, the other by Jim Quick—described in great detail the how-to's and where-to's of fly fishing. I was hooked.

Imagine the difficulties faced when I started trying to put together the necessary gear. I scoured every outdoor store in Winnipeg looking for fly tackle. Most carried none, and many store owners had no idea what I was talking about. Why would I want to use anything other than a pickerel rig and minnows or a Dardevle?

It took over a year to assemble an outfit which, in retrospect, was quite laughable. Amazingly, I found a very good fly rod, a Browning Silaflex, which had been languishing on a rod rack at the downtown Sidney I. Robinson store for years. The reel, a British Condex, came from a dusty box located at Market Sales on Main Street. The rod cost an exorbitant $40 and the reel $15. I even discovered a genuine wicker creel and bentwood net, just like the ones on the cover of Jim Quick's book. Fly lines and leaders were harder to come by. The only mail order catalogue available at the time was from Herter's in Minnesota. It was 99 percent hardware, but did have a small assortment of fly-fishing tackle. I ordered my first fly line, an HCH floater of indeterminate brand, some 7 ½' leaders, and one of their fly assortments—$12.95 for 100 flies ranging from No.

12 dries to huge streamers. It was a good thing they were so cheap, for the life of a fly during those early days was short.

Then came the really hard part—assembling the gear and learning to cast, using only the instructions and pictures in books. Following the directions in Brooks' book, I wound my line onto the reel (there was no room for backing), formed a whipped loop in the end, connected the leader, then tied a fly to the tippet. Learning how to tie Blood Knots and Perfection Knots from books was a slow, frustrating process, but I was finally ready.

I still recall that first time on the lawn with my assembled gear and Brooks' photos of the casting process and the loud snap heard as the end of my leader exploded and my fly vanished. That first session produced a much-shortened leader that would not fit through the eye of a hook, a dozen lost flies and several pitiful fits of temper. It took some time before I acquired the timing and technique to lay out 30' (9 m) or so of line with my fly still intact, but I was eventually ready to hit the water.

I chose the Whiteshell River, which I knew had been stocked with trout. Unfortunately, I had not factored in such things as bushes and trees, slippery rocks and strong winds; therefore, my first effort was a catastrophe. Every fly I possessed was attached to a willow branch or pine limb, my leaders were balls of wind knots, the first 20' (6 m) of my fly line was shredded, and I was hypothermic—and almost catatonic with frustration.

For a time I reverted to hardware, but eventually picked up the fly rod again. It helped when I was able to obtain some leaders which lacked the physical properties of watch springs and actually straightened out, and that, fortuitously, my next fly line actually matched the rod, thereby making the mechanics of casting much simpler. I also discovered a nearby gravel pit by the name of Moosenose Pond, which was full of trout and devoid of vegetation. I caught my first trout on a fly there.

For the next few years I made regular trips to the Whiteshell, fishing the river and various lakes like Lyons and Star near Falcon Lake. Either wading wet or fishing from my canoe, I learned the secrets of matching the hatch—or at least of tying on a fly that resembled something the trout might eat. Hooking and playing fish was another part of the learning curve, but eventually I was able to land fish on a regular basis.

By the time I discovered the Pine and Steeprock rivers in western Manitoba's Duck Mountains—that would be in the late 1960s—I could cast with accuracy and had assembled a collection of flies that resembled various insects and other critters I had observed as being part of the trout diet. I had even stopped carrying an ax and saw as part of my outfit (to cut down the brush which often snagged my back-casts and to recover flies from trees). In those days the Pine and Steeprock rivers were totally unknown. Access was a problem, but I was not afraid of bush-bashing to reach those classic freestone streams that tumbled cold and free from the Duck Mountains, for I had learned they were heavily stocked with rainbows and brook trout.

There were endless riffles and pools, boiling rapids and numerous beaver ponds. The brookies were especially abundant in the beaver ponds and weren't particularly selective about the flies they attacked. The rainbows tended to favor the riffles, and it was there I discovered the intoxication of dry-fly fishing. I remember with vivid fondness many days of spectacular fishing in that pristine, untouched wilderness. I rarely saw another angler and never another fly fisher.

When I left Manitoba in the early 1970s to attend graduate school in British Columbia, there were only two things I regretted leaving—duck hunting in the fall and fly fishing on the Pine and Steeprock rivers. However, with year-round fishing for steelhead, salmon and Kamloops trout, I quickly forgot about Manitoba.

Fast forward, now 20-odd years later, near the close of the millennium, when I found myself back on the Flatlands, facing the prospect of unlimbering my fly rods with some trepidation. Spoiled from years on the West Coast, I feared that instead of flinging flies I would be dusting off the bait-casting gear and buying frozen minnows. However, before reverting to hardware I checked around the local tackle stores and picked the brains of some biologists at Natural Resources. Amazingly, there were still plenty of stocked trout waters within easy striking distance of Winnipeg. Most were ponds or small lakes, but as I was to find out, they provided spectacular fly fishing without the crowds which often characterize angling experiences in most parts of the country.

What was even more surprising was the scarcity of other fly-flingers. Almost without exception, every time I ventured out in my float tube I had the entire pond or lake to myself. While I pounded trout with flies, the odd worm-drowner would plunk from the shore. This was especially true at the Reynold's Ponds about 30 miles (48 km) east of Winnipeg. Once the road was passable during the first spring after my return, I drove in from the Trans-Canada Highway to check them out. I saw immediately from the number of rises that there were plenty of trout in attendance. These former gravel pits had been differentially stocked with rainbow, brook and brown trout. The browns really interested me. In one of the smaller ponds right beside the road, I couldn't help but notice heavy, swirling rises in the weed beds. I knew immediately that it was brown trout foraging for large may flies *(Hexagenia limbata)*, known locally as fish flies. Feeling that kind of sweet panic known only to anglers, I fumbled to cut my leader back to about 8-lb test, then tied on one of the biggest, bushiest dry flies in my box—a No. 8 Tom Thumb.

A 60' (18 m) cast was necessary to drop my fly at the edge of the weeds. It was as if a depth charge had gone off beneath it. A monster brown launched upward with my fly clamped in its jaw. It hit the water with a huge splash, dove into the weeds and promptly broke off. It all happened so suddenly, I didn't have time to set the hook.

When I stopped shaking and could breathe again, I tried tying on another Tom Thumb, and it was all I could do to thread my leader through the hook eye. Then, the same savage hit—same result. Eventually, I managed to stay connected to one of the smaller fish. I measured its length against the ruler on the front of my float tube before releasing it—19" (48 cm). Holy smokes! I thought. That meant some of those that broke off were much larger—10 lb (4.5 kg) plus.

That was quite a day—as good as I can remember, even when compared to fishing some of the fabled trout lakes south of Kamloops. And the best part was that I was able to repeat the experience several more times over the summer and early fall on a number of the ponds with rainbows and brook trout. At no time did I ever see more than a handful of other anglers, and they were always plunking worms and gear from the shore.

On one late September afternoon, I fished a boatman pattern in one of the ponds, hooking and releasing over 50 rainbows up to 3 lb (1.4 kg). Some guys on shore remarked that it was like watching an episode of *The Real Fishing Show.* I would wager that within days there were some serious inquiries at the local tackle stores concerning fly-fishing tackle and float tubes.

It was ironic that just as I was about to leave the Flatlands again, I learned of a spectacular fishery for truly monstrous trout in Manitoba's Parkland area. I have not personally experienced this fishery, and I can only report second hand. A local angler by the name of Bob Sheedy (yes, there is another fly fisherman in Manitoba) has specialized in fishing the lakes of the Parkland, which he calls the Big Seven—those lakes which produce trout of at least 25" (64 cm) and occasionally over 30" (76 cm). His web site is definitely worth a visit: www.completeangler.net/bspicks99.htm. There are photographs of trout from those lakes that must be seen to be believed, and best of all, the waters appear as if they were designed with float tubers in mind.

Sheedy points out that the reason for this spectacular fishery is a "vigorous stocking program . . . cold water . . . highly fertile lakes." The large size of the trout he attributes to healthy scud populations, a situation not unlike some of the well-known trout factories south of Kamloops in British Columbia. He claims that the chances of hooking a trout over 30" (76 cm) are high in the Big Seven lakes, but landing one of these monsters is a real challenge because water clarity makes fine tippets a must.

Here is the condensed version of what Mr. Sheedy has to say about fly fishing in western Manitoba, beginning south of Brandon with Lake William, right on the border in Turtle Mountain Park. The best periods are right after the ice goes out and just before freeze-up. For flies, try Woolly Buggers and Sheedy's Pheasant Tail Crayfish. Nearby Bower Lake, described as "home of the Shamu, the 27" (69-cm) -plus rainbow," is extremely fertile and darkly stained. Aquatic life includes scuds, bloodworms, leeches, dace and fathead minnows. Try Wiggle Bugs or bushy Egg-Sucking Woolly Buggers.

Tokaruk Lake, 4 miles (6.5 km) north of Oakburn on PR 566 (just south of Riding Mountain National Park), has produced 30" (76-cm) -plus fish, but is now well known. As there is increased pressure, especially on weekends, stocking has been accelerated, so other size peaks should occur in the future. Plenty of the trout are 25" (64 cm) plus.

Again, just south of Riding Mountain Park is Silver Beach Lake, 7 miles (11 km) north of Angusville on PTH 476. Sheedy said he and others regard it as best of the best, claiming it may produce the largest nonsteelhead trout in Canada. Heavy weed growth makes fishing difficult for nonfly-flingers. There are some very large browns, but monster rainbows are the main draw. Sheedy measured one at 31" (79 cm) in the summer of 1996 and reports that a man living on the lake claims to have caught two which taped out at 34" (86 cm). Yikes!

Spear Lake, a reservoir near Russell, is another of those ice-out and ice-up lakes, which is the common pattern for most of these lakes because of dense summer weed growths. There was also a perch problem, but steps were being taken to eradicate them.

A number of the Big Seven lakes are found in Duck Mountain Provincial Park. They include East Blue Lake, which produces most of Manitoba's trout records. As the water is very clear, it is popular with divers (easy to hook but real buggers to land). This clarity makes for challenging fly fishing, so Sheedy advises night fishing or using deepwater techniques with fast-sinking lines. West Blue Lake shares a campground with East Blue. Nearby Perch Lake contains large browns and is a designated trophy lake (catch-and-release). It also contains smallmouths up to 6 lb (2.7 kg) plus and rainbows to over 10 lb (4.5 kg), so, as Sheedy points out, "You never know what is going to take your fly or what it will weigh."

A short distance away, Laurie Lake is renowned for 30" (76-cm) -plus splake, as well as 10-lb (4.5-kg) browns and rainbows. Gull Lake is the Duck Mountain hot spot. It offers large rainbows, splake to 30" (76-cm) -plus, brook trout and lake whitefish. Other Duck Mountain waters include Two Mile, Beaver, Shilliday and Black Beaver lakes. It doesn't take a rocket scientist to figure out that the Duck Mountains offer a great deal of fly-fishing opportunity with relatively little pressure, plus a wide range of species and loads of trophy potential.

Sheedy also extols the virtues of fishing in the Pine and Steeprock rivers. He likens the Pine to a quiet, little Appalachian stream tucked away in the north woods, but laments the increased pressure. Nevertheless, there are many large rainbows and brookies in the upper reaches where there is little or no pressure because of restricted access. As for pressure, perhaps Mr. Sheedy should try some of the rivers flowing into Lake Ontario or streams like the Vedder in southern British Columbia

When referring to the Steeprock River, Sheedy waxes poetic about its still pristine state: "No campsites. No trails. No roads or human presence. Wild and virgin canyon country. Fast crystal water. Natural spawners. I have never seen another human footprint on the gravel bars save mine on the way out." It's good to know that it still remains virtually untouched in the 20-plus years since I last fished there, for it truly is a gem in the wilderness. If you don't mind camping rough and doing a little bush-bashing, it is the river to visit. There you can truly experience things the way they used to be.

There you have it—some of the amazing trout fishing to be had in Manitoba. Who'd a thunk it? In fact, those who spend thousands of dollars to fish the waters of Argentina, New Zealand or the Douglas Lake Ranch in British Columbia might well consider a pilgrimage to western Manitoba. Just close your eyes and pretend that you are not in the heart of the prairies, then tie on another fly as Shamu makes off with your last offering.

GEORGE WILL'S MUST-HAVE PATTERNS FOR MANITOBA

- Bug-Eyed Crystal Leech
- Pheasant Tail Crayfish
- Prince of Darkness
- Psychedelic P-Quad
- Tokaruk's Special

CHAPTER 35

STILL WATERS, FLOAT TUBES AND BIG TROUT

Wayne Phillips

J ANELLE WAS STILL TRYING TO FIGURE OUT HOW TO MANEUVER her float tube when a rainbow slammed her fly. Since it was my wife's first tubing experience and she had only been in the water five minutes, she assumed fly fishing in stocked trout waters was not all that difficult.

That weekend it wasn't, as it turned out. Five of us caught and released at least 50 rainbows in two days of fishing. Few showed themselves with rises, but we discovered them cruising at about 10' (3 m)—where they devoured our leech patterns. All it took to get a hit was a short cast with a sink-tip, then a couple of strips. To top it off, not a single trout was under 5 lb (2.3 kg) and most were over 10 lb (4.5 kg).

Some trips work out perfectly and trout willingly strike your flies. But what do you do the next time when the lake seems completely dead? Catching trout consistently from stocked waters can be more than challenging, but there are ways to increase your chances of success. A float tube, a handful of proven flies, an eye for observation and a couple of different techniques are just the ticket to help you tie into some tackle-busting monsters.

My first years of fishing for stocked trout were hit and miss. After a glorious day of fishing, I thought I had discovered the secret to success. However, assuming that conditions would be the same on a return trip often resulted in little or no success. It became obvious that changing conditions, the availability of different insects, and the fickleness of trout made fishing for them a series of ever-changing problems that required solving if I hoped for success. Poring over my fishing journal revealed no distinct patterns to help build any consistency, but as time passed, and usually while driving from lake to lake, my fishing partners and I started piecing together techniques and tactics that worked time after time. Developed over many years, these practices still continue to evolve and be improved upon.

The best way to fish most stocked lakes in the southern Prairies is from a float tube, a remarkable craft that lets you move without alarming trout. Regular boats put you on top of the water, not in it. When you are down in the water, it's almost like wading a stream, and being closer to the fish's level makes your angling more thrilling and immediate. From this stable fishing craft, you can cover brushy shorelines, drop-offs, deep water, and the shallowest bays holding the spookiest of trout.

There are dozens of different models to choose from, so study as many as possible before selecting one. I prefer using a traditional float tube over a pontoon boat on lakes. Besides, a regular round float tube is lighter to portage into those wonderful stocked lakes located away from roads.

While fishing from a tube, being comfortable is essential. A well-designed model should include pockets to hold fly boxes, tippet material and a spare reel or two. There should also be a large back pocket for storing a rain jacket, a fleece vest or jacket for added warmth, a water bottle and your lunch. After a long day of paddling, you will appreciate having a full back rest, one which also serves as a back-up floatation device should your main tube fail.

When float tubing, a well-fitting pair of neoprene waders keeps you dry and warm. They should be on the snug side rather than loose fitting, for the more bulk, the more drag as you move through the water. Talk to other anglers before buying flippers. Bigger is not always better, as oversized fins are very tiring and the extra speed they provide is negligible. Paddling around all day is tiring on your legs, so adding huge, heavy flippers only wears you out sooner.

Along with a float tube, using the right fly line can help spell success. On many western waters, there is so much food that stocked trout grow fat on nymphs, gammarus, leeches and other subsurface insects and rarely feed on surface insects. As this forces anglers to fish their flies below the surface, a full-sinking line is essential—and far more pleasant to cast than a sink- tip.

A full-sinking line featuring a tip that sinks faster than the main body enables you to keep your fly down near the bottom. It also allows you to fish from shallow to deeper water because, as you slowly retrieve your fly, it continues to sink. A regular full-sink line often curves upward near the tip due to surface tension from the water pressure, which lifts your fly away from the bottom.

Sink-tips can be used when fishing shallower water, or if you want to keep your flies near the surface. Intermediates have proved their worth only occasionally. When spring or fall fishing, floating lines with very long leaders and weighted flies often work. The ease of lifting them off the surface and their castability make floating lines a delight to use.

Short leaders are best when fishing full-sink lines, as surface tension tends to lift your fly off the bottom when using longer leaders. Vary tippet sizes according to the size of the trout. When using nymphs, you can get away with using heavier tippets like 3x or even larger.

Since you sit low down in a float tube, a 10' rod with a fast action and a strong butt helps pull a sinking line from the water and keep your back-casts high. The wind blows in our prairie provinces, so 6–8-weight rods are preferred. Going for a heavier rather than lighter rod is a good idea, for after a day of casting you will experience less arm fatigue because it is easier to pull sinking lines from the water.

Reels that wrap line quickly—either large arbor or large diameter—are worth considering. It's a good idea to keep the drag settings light, for when a trout hits and runs, the pressure against the fly line as it cuts through the water can cause break-offs. The tighter the drag, the more frequent the break-offs. In cooler weather, full-sink lines develop a tendency to tangle on your float tube apron, so taking care while stripping in line is a wise precaution. By using a larger reel, you can get all those loose coils on your reel more quickly and avoid lost fish.

Once in your float tube with the right fly line, you are still a long way from catching trout. Even though many lakes appear to be similar, all have unique characteristics. There are a number of basic techniques you can start with to locate feeding trout. For example, there are often denser insect populations in shallow water, so beginning near the shoreline increases your chances of finding trout.

Before starting to fish, turn up your powers of observation and look for any details that might provide clues to what is going on below the surface. Newly hatched dragonflies or damsel flies mean trout will be in the shallows near the reeds and cattails, feeding on the moving nymphs. Swirls that just break the water's surface could mean water boatman or backswimmers are active and trout are inhaling them as they rise to the surface for air.

It takes a long time to become fully aware of all that is going on around you. In fact, rather than just tying on your favorite nymph and starting to cast, simply paddling around for a bit without fishing is a good way to force yourself to study and observe. This is difficult to do, but it often pays off handsomely with more fish. Walking the shoreline is another option when it comes to finding out what is happening.

Should you come up blank when looking around, there are several general ways to attack a lake. Always alter your tactics for each specific lake. If on a familiar lake, recall past trips and begin from there. On new lakes, never take anything for granted. The trout could be anywhere and feeding on who-knows-what.

Casting in toward shore and slowly drawing your fly back to deeper water puts your offering in front of many fish. Keeping casts fairly short allows your fly to sink quickly and be pulled along the bottom where there are plenty of insects. Spend extra time working areas with fallen trees, points or beaver lodges. If this tactic doesn't produce any action, place a few casts parallel to shore and work your fly back in short, erratic strips. By moving in closer or farther from shore, you effectively fish areas with similar depths.

On a small rainbow trout lake in Manitoba's Duck Mountain Park, while casting over a shallow area off a point, it seemed the trout could not leave my small, dark leech alone. They hit it after it sank 3' (90 cm) in the shallower water off the point itself or when I let it sink on my side of the point. I just worked my way up and down the point, catching and releasing rainbow after rainbow. The whole evening I never strayed from that one area.

Working the edges of drop-offs is a good idea. You can move your fly from shallow to deep water, or move in closer to shore and pull it slowly up the drop-off into the shallows. This can be difficult because your fly will hang up on the bottom until you work out the correct speed to keep it moving along without snagging. Pay close attention to any channels or areas that have deeper holes. Beaver runs near lodges can be very productive, but you do risk snagging sunken tree limbs. Trout often roam around areas like these, and a well-placed fly will draw a strike.

In Alberta I discovered that trout can be suspended midwater just like any other fish. The shallows had produced nothing, so I decided to paddle across the lake. Trolling a large bushy nymph, I was going full speed when the first trout struck. After netting it, I noticed it had strange ridges on its belly. Since it was destined for dinner, I killed the trout and found it full of snails. The bushy nymph took many trout that afternoon, all in the lake's central section.

This technique of trolling while moving between locations can be very successful. Keys involve varying your speed and the length of line in the water. A sudden burst of speed followed by coasting often brings on a strike—then another burst of speed and so on until you are across the lake. Trout seem to strike when the fly slows or speeds up. When you begin trolling, cast out a short length of line, then increase it if you get no action. The most successful troller I know fishes a short line and uses varying speeds to catch trout.

If you find suspended trout, go back to a cast-and-retrieve tactic. Counting down the time you allow the fly to sink lets you keep your fly at the trout's depth more consistently. When the wind is blowing, you can drift in one direction, then paddle back against it. On calm days, simply move around once you have taken a trout or two.

Shallow, gently sloping bays that lead to a drop-off some distance from shore are difficult to fish. Trout tend to be spooky in shallow water, so try to remain as inconspicuous as possible. Slow movements and delicate casts are critical, which is why a floating line works best under these conditions. Cast well ahead of any fish you spot, then tailor your retrieve to make it as slow as possible. In situations like this, pay extra attention to the drop-off since it is likely to hold several trout which have not yet moved up onto the flats.

A tactic that has taken many trout for me involves moving from deep water across a drop-off and into a bay. Paddle over a bit and move back out to the deep water. You can do this across the whole width of the bay. As you move from shallow to deeper water, adjust your fly's depth. This method has yielded fish from the shallowest to the deepest water on the drop-off's other side. You can often use the same fly since the fish have only moved into the shallows because there were more of the particular insects they were feeding on.

Reading rise forms on still water is very tricky. If you only spot sporadic rises, it's often best to ignore them if you are already catching fish. If you are not catching fish, stop and study the rises. Sometimes you will get lucky and be able to learn the direction the fish was going. Then it is only a matter of casting ahead of its line of travel. But usually you hear only the splash, and upon turning you are too late to learn anything other than a trout just rose. Don't despair if you don't pick up the trout's direction. Use what I call the "compass attack." First, cast to the right of a rise form, then to the left, then cast short of it, and finally cast over it. This lets you cover all the possible directions the trout could go. Just remember to cover the four major compass points. If you cover them again, lengthen your line and cast farther from the rise form.

In the Prairies, water boatman and backswimmer patterns can prove deadly when these insects are available, for trout gobble them up with wild abandon. In the fall it's common to see boils on the surface without actually seeing any trout. Chances are they are feeding on water boatman or backswimmers. The boils form as trout take these insects near the surface when they are rising to replenish their air bubbles. This is when you turn to the compass approach, but at times, especially when the insects are particularly active, just casting and retrieving is most effective. Hang on to your rod tightly and fish out each cast until only the leader is in the water. The strike usually comes when the fly is within inches of the surface.

One fall, while fishing in Saskatchewan, I saw the small lake was almost blanketed with boils. Finally one of my companions landed a fish, and while removing the fly, he noticed a water boatman in the fish's mouth. Using small Al's Peacock Nymphs we were able to interest the trout, but once back home we took to our vises in hopes of developing more effective patterns. One that has done very well for us is the Dynamite Boatman.

Anglers often ask what time of day the trout are most active. Since they generally feed below the surface on western waters, I feel there is no distinct, best time of day. From my fishing journals I know that dawn and dusk are good times, but they point out that my best fishing has actually been from 10:00 A.M.

until 6:00 P.M. This could be because the light penetration is greatest during these hours, so the fish can feed more efficiently. The last hour before complete darkness can be terrific as well.

In northern Saskatchewan you can fish all night long from mid-June until the end of August. The lakes come alive with trout rises as they sip in may flies, caddis flies or midges. However, in the central regions of the Prairie provinces, the trout are not nearly as active during late-evening and early morning hours. This is probably due to the incredible food base existing in our lakes.

The last key to fishing stocked trout waters involves fly selection. It is difficult to know which fly to use if you have no idea of what the trout are feeding on. This is why it is so essential to keep a fishing journal in which you note where and when each fly produced. In a few years you will have a priceless source of knowledge that you can apply to your trout fishing. Not only will you know which pattern worked, but also the weather conditions, time of year, and if there were any visible insect hatches.

It is more important to imitate carefully the insects' movements and sizes than their colors. Most stocked waters are very rich, almost turbid, so light penetration is often restricted. This means that while trout can't pick up exact colors, they can easily spot size or movement differences. Measuring a few nymphs or checking an aquatic entomology book makes matching their sizes fairly simple.

Getting a particular insect's movements down requires more effort. Begin by trying to observe them as they move in the water. Have a fishing partner work a fly where you can see it and compare how closely it resembles the live insect. Leeches tied with a few wraps of lead wire seem to dance more seductively than those tied without. It is often easier to work an unweighted nymph just above the weeds on the bottom. Getting an insect's movement patterns down is far from easy, but once you do, catch rates will soar.

Some general patterns that work are nymphs which imitate may flies, caddis flies, dragonflies and damsel flies. Keep a variety of sizes and colors that correspond to the nymphs in the location you plan to fish. I used to believe that the bigger the nymph the better, but now I feel smaller is often more effective. Tying general nymphs with some flashy material helps draw attention to them. Flashback patterns that feature some tinsel or Flashabou for a wing case are especially productive.

Many longtime favorite nymph patterns are especially effective on stocked trout: Doc Spratley, Carey Special, Prince Nymph, Pheasant Tail, Soft Hackle Streamer and Hare's Ear Nymph are a few that usually bring on strikes. Woolly Buggers of all sizes and colors will interest trout, and include a couple of dragonfly and damsel fly patterns to round out your selection.

Over the years I have developed a nymph that utilizes the filoplumes from pheasants. These soft, webby feathers seem almost as irresistible to trout as peacock herl. Work up patterns that are plain and simple, but also tie some with lots of flash for times when the trout aren't slamming into any fly you offer.

In Saskatchewan few trout anglers are ever caught without an O'Keefe Special. Developed by Brian O'Keefe, it is simplicity itself—a few dark-brown hackle fibers for a tail, some brown mohair wool for the body and an overwing of black bear hair with a few turns of brown hackle. Few trout ignore it.

Jeff Shepherd, who ties the most effective leeches I have ever fished, might have explained why trout love them so. He believes there is a 24-hour leech hatch all year long. There is no doubt that if I were limited to a single pattern, it would be a leech. Jeff's leeches are small and very sparsely tied. Remember that when tying leeches, smaller is often far more attractive to the trout. Tie some without any sparkle to keep them subtle rather than flashy.

An essential fly in any successful trout fanatic's box is one that imitates water boatman and backswimmers. These need not be complex—just a peacock herl body with a light-colored belly and a strip of black plastic-bag material for a wing case. Tie in either white or black rubber legs and you are done. Heavily weighting the flies helps imitate their up-down swimming motion.

Even though our lakes are full of gammarus, or freshwater shrimp as they are commonly called, shrimp patterns do not prove very effective. This could be because there are millions upon millions of shrimp in most waters, so trying to interest a trout in your pattern has a slim chance for success. Since the trout feed heavily on them, they might find another food source tantalizing. They might think, why not munch that leech swimming by while I'm feeding on these shrimp?

Do not let the challenge of fishing still waters intimidate you. A float tube, a sinking fly line, a few proven fly patterns and some observations will be all you need to get started. Trying some of the tactics and techniques I have outlined will help you on your way to success with trout. Soon, you too will be raving about the fishing you enjoyed on a stocked trout water near where you live or are visiting. You have nothing to lose—and a whole new way of fishing to gain.

WAYNE PHILLIPS' MUST-HAVE PATTERNS FOR SOUTHERN SASKATCHEWAN

- Dry: Comparadun
- Griffith's Gnat
- Sparkle Elk Hair Caddis
- Nymph: Al's Peacock Nymph
- Dynamite Boatman
- Fabulous Filo Nymph
- Flash in the Pan
- O'Keefe Special
- Flashback Hare's Ear
- Streamer: Shepherd Leech
- Chartreuse Caboose
- Woolly Bugger

CHAPTER 36

SASKATCHEWAN'S NORTHERN BOUNTY

Dave Smallwood

Q UERYING ANOTHER ANGLER ABOUT PLANS FOR THE
coming season is as much a matter of etiquette as an exercise in
information gathering. With recreational time dwindling these
days, the choice of a fishing destination is well thought out and
researched, yet a specific spot may not be as important as the direction one
intends to travel.

"Fishin' any place special this summer?"

"Oh, probably spend a couple of weeks in the north country. Saskatchewan
most likely."

Silence as they recall past forays into that fishing paradise—the aroma of a
canvas tent mingling with freshly brewed camp coffee and frying bacon as the
haunting call of a loon drifts through the morning mist—a land of myths, misconceptions, placid lakes and wild, unexplored rivers. A land that entices novice
and expert alike to explore and experience, yet rarely to understand, and never
to control—northern Saskatchewan.

Originating at the southern terminus of Prince Albert, Highway 2 has been
the gateway to northern Saskatchewan since the 1950s. Travelers driving northward make the transition from farmland to aspen parkland to boreal forest.
More important from an angler's point of view is the fact that this route offers

such a smorgasbord of fishing opportunities, it creates a dilemma in deciding where to start.

A great primer is Narrow Hills Provincial Park, approximately 75 miles (120 km) northeast of Prince Albert. With 25 bodies of water and another 30 small lakes and ponds within an hour's drive, this region offers the greatest variety of fish in the province—pike, walleye and whitefish, in addition to rainbow, lake, brook, tiger, and brown trout, plus splake and kokanee salmon.

While a few lakes offer boat access, a float tube allows you to sample some beautiful ponds located just off to the sides of various hiking trails. The Cub Hills, located within the park, offers five streams containing self-sustaining populations of brook trout to 1 lb (454 g). My favorite is Mossy Creek, where lightweight tackle and a selection of No. 20–14 patterns imitating caddis larvae, pupae and may fly nymphs can provide many enjoyable hours of fishing.

About two hours farther north along Highway 192 is a mecca for large fish and lifetime memories: Lac La Ronge. While driving along this gravel byway, you become aware of the first misconception about the north. After being surrounded by boreal forest since Prince Albert, you pass through the geographical center of the province. In truth, fully half of the province is covered by forest and one-eighth is fresh water, increasing to almost 50 percent in northern areas. There are, in fact, over 100,000 lakes from which to choose.

Numerous motels in La Ronge enable anglers to diversify the waters they fish, such as Doughton Lake for large rainbow trout or Nemeiben Lake, 12 miles (19 km) north of La Ronge, for pike, lake trout and walleye. Late fall also provides an excellent run of lake whitefish in the nearby Montreal River.

Considered one of the north's crown jewels, Lac La Ronge has several fully serviced fishing camps, and there are houseboat rentals for those who wish to explore this approximately 39 square mile (100 square km) lake at their leisure. Carpeted with a myriad of islands, the northern portion is noted for the rugged beauty of its scenery, and its fishing has attracted anglers for over half a century. Pike, walleye and lake trout abound in those clear, cold waters. Shoals and reefs are abundant, creating excellent habitat to explore with a fly. However, anglers should bear in mind that abundance does not necessarily guarantee success. A fish on every cast, as is portrayed at times, is rare in the north. Yes, it does occur on occasion, but to be consistently successful you should have a solid understanding of the species you are seeking.

Most anglers who ply large northern lakes feel that deepwater tactics like wire line or downriggers are the only methods that will take lake trout. Found in depths of over 100' (30 m) at times, they are a coldwater species from start to finish. Many anglers attempt catching lakers only when warm weather forces them deep below the thermocline, but in doing so they miss many fine days of fishing.

As the spring sun begins working its warming magic on the lakes and ice starts receding from the shorelines, a prime time for lakers is at hand. Preferring a water temperature of about 50°F (10°C), they begin cruising the shallow reefs, searching for their primary food source—cisco *(Coregonus artedii)*, also known as lake herring or tullibee. These 8–12" (20–30 cm), silvery members of the whitefish clan also favor cold water, which accounts for their symbiotic relationship with lake trout.

Lakers can be large, so arm yourself with 8–10-weight rods, weight-forward floating and sinking lines, and 10' leaders with 20–25-lb test tippets. Flies like the Gray Ghost, Black Ghost, Nine Three, Lefty's Deceiver and Clouser Minnow are good imitations, but keep in mind that length is the key, not necessarily color.

Casting amid reefs, shoals and rock-strewn bottoms generally ensures hook-ups, as does trolling flies through these areas. Then, should you connect with a lake trout, please bear in mind that in northern waters a 20-lb (9-kg) trout may be 20 to 25 years old. Obviously, proper catch-and-release techniques are essential to ensure their survival and conserve this vital resource.

The arrival of September is a wondrous time for anglers. Lake trout begin schooling for their spawning period, the males changing from silvery-dark shades to vibrant golden and reddish hues. Again, as in spring, rubble-strewn shallows are the places to be. It's not uncommon to select visually the fish you will cast to, or to watch a 30-lb (14-kg) specimen fin lazily past your boat. This is a time when frustration, anticipation and euphoria are rolled into each cast, when you experience a feeling that your fish of a lifetime may be just the next cast away. The same flies used during the spring will be effective, with points of rocky islands and reefs the most likely spots to explore.

Fall also brings rough weather, and while a tranquil autumn day may be memorable, it can easily be followed by a day of high winds and big waves. Go prepared for the best and worst the season has to offer.

Although lake trout are found throughout Lac La Ronge, the number-one location is at the east end where Hunter Bay's viridescent waters yield many of the 40-lb (18-kg) trophies taken each season.

Pickerel Bay, on the east side of Hunter Bay, is tremendously fertile walleye habitat. Although not flashy fighters, they provide an interesting diversion, and their succulent taste during a lakeside shore lunch more than makes up for their lack of tenacity. Try 6–8-weight rods, weight-forward floating lines and 7–10' tapered leaders with 0x–3x tippets, and sinking lines with short 1–2' leaders. For flies try Crayfish, Zonkers, Clouser Minnows (red/white, chartreuse/white), and Lefty's Deceivers.

About a 20-minute boat ride from the entrance of Hunter Bay is Mitchell Bay—Pike Valhalla! Shallow and weed-filled, it produces some of the largest pike taken on Lac La Ronge. Fishing these quiet waters can be mesmerizing, for you may find yourself watching a cow moose and her calf feeding in the shallows or a bald eagle lofting lazily overhead, not paying attention to the fly you are absentmindedly retrieving until the tranquility is suddenly shattered by the savage, arm-jolting strike of a "great northern pike."

Voracious and belligerent, pike simply ooze bad attitude and willingly take on any angler who wishes to do battle. Challengers come from around the world to match their skills and tackle against these toothy water wolves, sometimes victoriously, but often not. Weighing 30–40 lb (14–18 kg) with lengths exceeding 50" (1.3 m), these trophy-sized beasts have the heft and strength to provide some truly memorable moments after their surface-shattering strikes. Yet as powerful as this fish is, it has also solved a dilemma for fishing parents—providing a child's first fish. A pike's penchant for food starts as soon as it hatches, and an abundance of small "grass pike," found in most shallows during periods which happen to coincide with school summer vacation periods, has been the salvation of many family fishing trips.

Springtime is trophy time. Spawning pike head for shallow flats and bays where the water temperature has reached 40–52°F (4–11°C). After spawning—having just lost 20 percent of their body weight—the big females disperse immediately and seek a place where they can recuperate. The prime prerequisites are shelter, warmth and some easy meals to aid in their recovery. They tend to move deeply into flooded flats, lying in water so shallow that their backs are exposed to the air, boosting their heat-induced metabolism. When this is the case, fly fishing is the most effective method for targeting these often large fish.

For equipment, an 8–10-weight rod is recommended, a weight-forward floating line (I like the Pike/Muskie Rocket Taper), a sinking line like the Teeny 200 or 300, a leader with a 15" wire tippet, and a selection of weedless patterns like the Dahlberg Mega Diver and Rabbit Strip Diver. The most weedless of spoons on the market can't approach the high-floating, weedless characteristics of a well-designed-and-tied deer-hair or foam-bodied fly. When it comes to producing strikes, they are the fly-fishing equivalent of the venerable Len Thompson Five of Diamonds and Daredevle. Although totally different in action, they yield the same result—success! If weeds aren't a problem, big baitfish imitations like the Deceiver and Gray Ghost in No. 1/0–5/0 are good choices.

Shallow water is an obstacle to larger boats, so a canoe and a pair of neoprene waders (3–5 mm thick) are a definite asset. The key is to float along the weed beds and flats, then wade the best-looking ones and cast far back into them. How far? Very far. I once tried explaining this to a friend while we were fishing for spring pike. "Cast beyond that second log in the flat," I suggested, "then slowly pop the fly towards you."

He gave me an incredulous look. "I'm fishing for 'northerns,' not bears!"

"Fine," I said. "Then fish for bears."

He sent his next cast beyond two logs lying at the rear of the flat, just where the aquatic and terrestrial vegetation met. He popped his fly over the first log, then, just as it started easing over the second log, the surface exploded from the strike of what eventually proved to be a 26-lb (12-kg) pike.

"Nice looking bear," I commented. His only response was a smug, Cheshire-cat grin.

As summer's warmth increases the water temperature, there is an interesting occurrence that has fueled a common myth for eons. Lake trout are coldwater fish, walleye are warmwater fish, and pike are a conundrum that do quite well at either extreme and anywhere in between. From the time they hatch until reaching about 5 lb (2.3 kg), they inhabit the shallows. Pike weighing 6–10 lb

(2.7–4.5 kg) seek depths of around 10' (3 m), and larger fish will descend to where temperatures are in the range of 50°F (10°C). This explains why so few large pike are caught during the summer doldrums—not because they lose their teeth. A mature pike has over 3,000 teeth and canines that rival those of a fair-sized dog, and their dental structure remains intact year round. Doubtful? You pick the month, I'll catch the pike, and then you put your hand in its mouth and let me know if it still has teeth.

Autumn brings cooler weather and a bulking-up time for pike. They must eat 5–6 lb (2.3–2.7 kg) of food to gain 1 lb (450 g) in body weight. As a 20-lb (9-kg) pike can swallow an 8-lb (3.6-kg) fish in one gulp, nothing you can throw with a fly rod will ever be too big. Concentrate your efforts around rocky points and reefs, for these are prime areas for fall pike.

Pushing northward from La Ronge, Highway 102 leads toward the fabled Churchill River system. Its headwaters start in Lac La Loche and flow over 930 miles (1,500 km) to Hudson Bay, Manitoba. Although the Churchill traverses a great deal of the north country, the only bridge spanning it is at Otter Rapids, 50 miles (80 km) north of Lac La Ronge. There are two campgrounds along the river with boat access at Devil's Lake campground, 1 mile (1.6 km) north of the bridge. Cabins, boat rentals, guides, licenses and groceries are available at Missinipi, 2 miles (3.2 km) south of Otter Rapids. This northern hamlet offers everything from a world-class lodge to simple campground facilities, fly-ins, and outfitting for month-long wilderness canoe trips. With so much variety to offer wilderness seekers, one word sums up this region—choices.

Small lakes and ponds in the surrounding vicinity offer excellent fishing for various species of stocked trout, but the Churchill system is a justifiably world-famous pike, walleye and lake-trout fishery. Its pristine lakes, connected by tumultuous rapids, offer wilderness fishing at its best for those willing to meet the north on her terms. So numerous are this region's aquatic byways, wilderness canoe travelers can make their way from Otter Lake to the Arctic Ocean, with occasional portages, of course.

Is this region solely for canoeists? Hardly. With pike and walleye the predominant species, the bays, nooks and crannies of Otter Lake beckon anglers to explore and test her waters. Johnson Bay offers excellent walleye fishing, as does Norris Bay for pike, and the rapids connecting the lakes provide the sort of surreal beauty for which the north is famous, as well as excellent walleye fishing. Twin Falls and Robertson Falls, approximately 20 minutes by boat from Otter Lake, succeed admirably at both. Tiered ledges guide cascading water down into the deep pools below, creating a wilderness scene somewhat akin to an experienced sommelier executing a frothy champagne glass pyramid while pouring from a bottomless bottle of bubbly. Yet another dilemma presents itself. Does one fish, or simply sit and revel in the beautiful images nature has provided?

If the former, then a few words about the walleye in these waters may be helpful. As spring spawners, they seek the rapids to reproduce. Once spawning is completed, they move into deeper water. Fly fishers will do well working the weed beds with nymph imitations prior to the heavy hatches of brown drakes and "giant" may flies, also known as fish flies and Hex.

Pools and pockets of the rapids are excellent choices for a Woolly Bugger or Clouser Minnow, especially during early mornings or late evenings. Probably the most underrated fly is a crayfish imitation. The Churchill is inundated with these nocturnal crustaceans, and when an imitation is cast into the tail pools, it produces amazing results. Let it sink, then raise your rod quickly, drawing the fly upwards, and then allow it to settle back again. More often than not, strikes occur on the way back down.

Coupled with warm days and cool nights, fall brings the golden brilliance of aspens and tamaracks to make this a magical time of year, especially for anglers. The walleyes are large and energetic, the days are comfortable, and there is little, if any, fishing pressure.

Fishing in the north country is synonymous with adventure—a canoe, backpack and fishing rod are the means with which to pursue it to the extent of one's desire for unfettered freedom and solitary enjoyment. Although many are passionate when it comes to canoes, I am pragmatic, for the access into the back country they give anglers is second to none. Upstream from Otter Rapids, the river is inundated with forks, channels and falls, the sort of waters which stymie power-driven boats but are a haven for canoeists. With many portages well marked and maps available locally, even the most diffident novice can negotiate this water system. The prime advantage for anglers is the ability to ease one's canoe onto shore, then cast into endless numbers of pools and falls, often right from the bank in front of a chosen campsite.

Highway 102 continues through the Precambrian Shield and boreal forest, past lake-trout havens like McLennan Lake, and crosses the 56th parallel. Then, 80 miles (129 km) north of Otter Lake, you are at Reindeer Lake. Its deep, clear waters yield sizable lakers year round and provide anglers with their first opportunity for arctic grayling. At 2,600 square miles (6,733 square km), Reindeer is Saskatchewan's second largest lake, Canada's ninth largest and a top destination for anglers seeking a "Grand Slam" on lake trout, pike, walleye, grayling, and lake whitefish.

Well before the pike's propensity for flies was discovered, grayling were the sole recipients of fly fishing in the north. Their penchant for small dry flies is legendary among fly fishers, and they are definitely the most acrobatic species the north country has to offer—and the most accommodating. They also take nymphs and small spinners, allowing anglers to come as close as they ever will to holding a rainbow in their hands.

Try 4–5-weight rods, weight-forward or double-taper lines, 7–10' tapered leaders with 3x–6x tippets and flies like No. 18–14 Black Gnat, Adams and Light Cahill. For subsurface use an intermediate-sinking line (2–3 ips) and a Hare's Ear Nymph.

Some may consider lake whitefish the grayling's ugly cousin, but pound for pound they are the strongest fighter in the north and provide many hours of angling pleasure. They are found around river mouths, and in the late evening they can be seen dimpling a lake's surface in search of emerging caddis and may flies. The same flies that attract grayling succeed with whitefish, but up your rods to 5–8-weight, with weight-forward or double-taper lines.

At Reindeer Lake, Highway 102 ends and Highway 905 begins, leading travelers through eskers and sand dunes on their way to the Geikie River, about 125 miles (200 km) north. This system empties into the south end of Wollaston Lake, providing access to top lake-trout waters, plus pike and walleye in the river. Nine miles (14.5 km) upstream from its mouth, the Geikie tempts anglers with grayling-filled waters that extend downward from its source at Big Sandy Lake.

Always bear in mind that the farther north you go, the fewer amenities you will encounter. This area is no exception. A campground is located on the north side of the Geikie River bridge, and northward . . . ? There exists the stuff of anglers' dreams and countless places to make them a reality—Saskatchewan's north country.

Dave Smallwood's Must-Have Patterns for Northern Saskatchewan

- Dry: Adams
- Black Gnat
- Brown Drake
- Light Cahill
- Wet: Hare's Ear Nymph
- Crayfish
- Streamer: Black Ghost
- Candied Whitefish
- Clouser Minnow
- Gray Ghost
- Lefty's Deceiver
- Nine Three
- Pop-Lips
- Woolly Bugger
- Zonker

CHAPTER 37

BEAUTY'S BUT SKIN DEEP

Dave Smallwood

I N THE CENTRAL PART OF NORTHERN SASKATCHEWAN, EARLY June is much like early March farther south. Mornings are cool and odds are even with regard to rain or snow. However, after eight months of winter, weather was of little concern as we made our way down a portage trail to the Churchill River.

When we reached Otter Rapids, Kevin waded knee-deep into the current where a swirling back eddy curved upstream. His first two casts went unheeded. Repositioning himself, he laid his Bead Head Nymph gently beside the rock face, then let it sink and drift for a few seconds in the eddy. As he began a very slow hand-twist retrieve, his sink-tip line suddenly snapped taut, took a hard right and accelerated into the rapids, all of it, plus a large portion of backing as well.

It was a glorious battle. Before the fish succumbed, my partner had suffered two icy dunkings while clambering up and down the river bank, dunkings which I thought served him right for getting the first hook-up. Finally, there in the eddy's backwater lay one of the finest-fighting fish, pound for pound, that a fly fisher has ever seen—*Catostomus catostomus*—the longnose sucker. Honest, folks, I'm serious.

Bear with me as I introduce you to a species that will test your tackle to the utmost and turn otherwise unsuccessful days into memorable ones. Two main prerequisites we seek in game fish are that they take a fly and fight well. Aesthetics shouldn't factor into this formula, but let's face it, suckers are, well, homely. Cylindrical body, bulbous head, a large, rubbery-lipped mouth devoid of teeth (hmm . . . sounds like me). However, Mother Nature did endow them with a reserve of sheer strength, so once hooked they take the shortest route to fast water, and there's not much an angler can do about it. That's power! If these fish could jump, they would probably become an endangered species. No, suckers are not pretty, but think back to those days when pike were considered little more than garbage fish. They were unworthy of our attention—until we discovered that they willingly take flies. Amazing how quickly our attitude changed, wasn't it?

Longnose suckers are circumpolar, and in Canada are actually more prevalent than lake trout and pike. They are not found in Newfoundland, Prince Edward Island, the Arctic Islands, or any offshore islands along the West Coast. Although white suckers *(Catostomus commersoni)* are confined to North America, they are found in many of the same waters. Although whites are abundant in warmwater lakes, both species thrive in cold, fast-flowing rivers like the Churchill.

The spring spawning period is best for locating large concentrations of suckers. They spawn mostly in streams and rivers, but shallow areas of lakes also suffice. Longnose suckers enter the streams once water temperatures exceed 41°F (5°C), usually mid-April to mid-May. Thousands may ascend, with up to 500 passing a given point in 5 minutes. Their runs peak several days before white suckers enter the streams when temperatures reach 50°F (10°C). While spawning periods offer the largest concentrations, relatively large numbers occur almost anywhere there is clear, cold water.

Fishing pressure is light, which may explain their forgiveness of splashy approaches and poor presentations. However, a shadow cast over a pool will cause them to scatter. Their diet consists mainly of invertebrates found along the bottom, predominately scuds, caddis, chironomid larvae and pupae, and may flies. Although once considered predators of trout and char eggs, this theory has since been dismissed.

For lake fishing, a 5–7-weight rod will suffice, with line choice depending on the situation. I use a weight-forward floating line with a 10' tapered leader and a 5x tippet. Patterns I find successful are No. 18–12 Hare's Ear Nymph, Zug Bug, Pheasant Tail Nymph, Caddis Pupa and Gary LaFontaine's Deep Sparkle Pupa series. Some days they rise readily to dry flies.

In rivers I prefer an 8-weight rod with a Teeny 200 or 300 line. Their combination of a 24' sink-tip with sink rates of 5.5 ips and 6.5 ips respectfully are just the ticket for cutting through fast currents and reaching the bottom. Shorter, heavier leaders work best. I favor 1 ½–2' 2x or 3x leaders as these fish may weigh up to 7 lb (3.2 kg).

Whichever retrieve you use, think "slow." Allow enough time for your fly to sink to the bottom, then use a slow hand-twist retrieve. The take is not particularly gentle, but the fight is awesome. Two quick suggestions: Once a sucker takes your fly, be patient—it's going to be a long fight. Don't touch the reel—the handles will be a blur at this point and will hurt your "fingies." As your fly line streaks out through the rod guides, remember the words of John Davies of Herford, who in 1616 penned these immortal words: "Beauty's but skin deep."

DAVE SMALLWOOD'S MUST-HAVE PATTERNS FOR SUCKERS

- Caddis Pupa
- Deep Sparkle Pupa
- Hare's Ear Nymph
- Pheasant Tail Nymph
- Zug Bug

SUCKER STIR-FRY

A sweet, succulent flavor combination
(Makes four servings)

1–1 ½ lb—sucker fillets, deboned, cut in strips—500–750 g
½ cup—cornstarch—125 mL

Salt and pepper to taste

2 tbsp—peanut oil—30 mL

1 large onion, coarsely chopped

2 cloves garlic, minced

1 tbsp—fresh ginger, minced —15 mL

or 1 tsp powdered—ginger—5 mL

1 yellow or red pepper, coarsely chopped

1 cup—mushrooms, sliced—250 mL

1 cup—snow peas, left whole—250 mL

2 tbsp—soya sauce, or to taste—30 mL

1 cup—fish stock (or chicken stock, wine or water)—250 mL

½ cup—peanut oil—125 mL

2 tbsp—cornstarch mixed in a bit of water—30 mL

¼ cup—peanuts, garnish—60 mL

1. Cut sucker in strips and lightly coat with cornstarch. Season with salt and pepper to taste. Cut all vegetables in same-size pieces.

2. Heat 2 tbsp peanut oil in a wok. Add vegetables in the following order: onions, garlic, ginger, peppers, mushrooms and snow peas. Stir as they cook. Add soya sauce and fish stock. Season with salt and pepper if required. Cover wok and allow to steam until vegetables are done.

3. Cook fish separately while vegetables are steaming. If you attempt to cook it in the wok, it falls apart. Place ½ cup peanut oil in a sauté pan and heat. When oil is hot, fry sucker strips quickly, taking care not to overcook.

4. Just before serving, add cornstarch and water mixture to the wok and stir immediately to prevent lumps from forming. Cook until stock thickens. Serve stir fry mixed in pasta, over steamed rice, or with Chinese egg-nest dry noodles. Top with sucker strips and garnish with peanuts.

–Wayne Phillips

CHAPTER 38

PROSPECTING FOR PRAIRIE POTHOLE PIKE

Clive Schaupmeyer

P URSUING PLUCKY PRAIRIE PIKE WITH FLIES IS A FLY-FISHING
bonus, a practical remedy—and blessing—for many of us who want to
fly fish often, but do not live close to trout streams. Our prairie lakes and
reservoirs may not have the allure of mountain streams or pristine northern
lakes, and there may not be quite as many pike—or as many big pike—as up
north, but the waters are close, the action can be hot, and many prairie waters
actually do contain trophy pike.

If you live anywhere in Canada where there are pike and have yet to try
them with fly gear, you are in for a treat. They can be electrifying on a fly rod,
especially in the spring when their metabolism and fighting spirit are at their
peak. Or, if you've been thinking of flying to a northern lodge for early season
pike action, then wait no longer.

Pike readily take flies and are rough-and-tumble fighters. Battles are usually down and dirty, and big fish can be difficult to land. They'll make short, line-
hauling runs, often spinning a float-tube and angler. Seeking refuge in deeper
water or weed beds, pike pull doggedly and double over the strongest of fly rods.

My passion for fly fishing began years ago when I started chasing trout in
streams. But when I lived in Brooks, Alberta—a genuine prairie town—it was a
two- to three-hour drive to my favorite mountain and foothill streams. However,

several reservoirs containing pike are within 20 minutes of town, so friends and I could fly fish after supper on warm spring evenings. Or, we could do yard chores and attend to family duties on weekends and still get out fly fishing for a few hours. Thus, we were socially responsible and still fly fished all we wanted.

I started wading after prespawn pike in shallow bays on local lakes a few years ago. It's something I'd contemplated for a while but, well, you know . . . I was a trout fisherman. Then one April evening I was photographing a pair of Canada geese paddling lazily in a shallow, cattail-lined bay. Suddenly the couple were startled by a nearby swirl in the water. A muskrat, I thought. But the swirls repeated again and again. Pike!

A few days later I was standing in the bay casting gaudy flies to sex-crazed pike. In the first two or three years a few pike were caught in that bay, but the inlet has since grown in with cattails so they no longer spawn there. I've also learned that trying to attract pike in the throes of courtship is not as productive as waiting for the post-spawn action.

Each May and June, friends and I spend many days in our pontoon boats or float tubes on local reservoirs catching lots of feisty 2–5-lb (900 g–2.3-kg) pike. Catches weighing 6–10 lb (2.7–4.5 kg) are not uncommon, and each year a few trophies are caught. (These trophies are caught by my friends, as I seem to be forever cursed against catching a real wall-hanger pike over 20 lb / 9 kg.)

In addition to being closer to home, there are other practical reasons to fly fish for pike. The early season pike frenzy coincides with spring runoff in many of our foothill and mountain trout streams. Some trout streams don't legally open for fishing until mid-June, and pike waters are still relatively uncrowded compared to many trout streams.

The Fish

PIKE *(Esox lucius)* ARE NATIVE to the northern hemisphere, ranging from northern United States through most of Canada and Alaska, Europe and Asia. Pike live in lakes and in slow, meandering streams and rivers throughout a large part of Canada, but not in Nova Scotia, Prince Edward Island, Newfoundland and all but northern British Columbia.

Pike in southern Alberta typically weigh 2–10 lb (900 g–4.5 kg), with the majority in the 2–5-lb (900 g–2.3-kg) range. Females 36–45" (90 cm–1.14 m) in length, weighing 10–30 lb (4.5–14 kg), are occasionally brought to hand. Ken Zorn currently holds our local fly-fishing pike record at 43" (109 cm), while my personal best is 38" (96.5 cm).

I've fly fished in northern Alberta where the average size of pike is larger than ours in the south. Northern pike average 5–10 lb (2.3–4.5 kg), the majority being 6–8 lb (2.7–3.6 kg) and many over 10 lb (4.5 kg). More secluded lakes in northern parts of the Prairie Provinces typically produce higher numbers of trophy pike over 20 lb (9 kg). The record weight in Manitoba is 42 lb (19.1 kg), 43 lb (19.5 kg) in Saskatchewan and 38 lb (17.3 kg) in Alberta. There are some big pike out there, folks—and they eat big flies.

Pike are piscivorous, aggressively attacking and consuming any fish smaller than themselves, including other pike. Large streamers that imitate the color and action of resident baitfish will catch pike; however, many popular patterns are gaudy and flashy, and it's not always clear what they are actually supposed to represent. Possibly those garish flies imitate young whitefish, but more likely pike attack because they are opportunistic feeders that can be lured by anything flashy, or by anything that remotely resembles a meal. I've caught 10" (25-cm) pike that attacked 5" streamers. It's not something I like to talk about, but it illustrates how fierce these finny critters can be, no matter what their size.

Equipment and Rigging Up

AN 8–9-WEIGHT FLY ROD with a fighting butt is required, even if the pike where you fish are not very big. Heavier rigs help cast big, heavy streamers, and the extra power helps control even a midsized pike when it's buried in dense weeds. A 7-weight rod may be suitable if there's no chance of hooking a trophy fish, but definitely leave your new 5-weight trout rod at home, even if it has a great guarantee. Pike don't usually make long runs, but when they go they are unstoppable, and a feisty 12-lb (5.5-kg) pike will likely explode a light trout rod. In addition to the practical need for heavier gear, there's an ethical demand. A moderate-sized pike will take far too long to land with light gear and likely be too tired for successful release. Match your gear to the fish.

A standard weight-forward, floating line will do for pike fishing and that's what I used for several years. In 1998 I finally broke down and bought a floating Musky/Pike Taper and found it superior for casting heavy flies. Normally, flies attached to a floating line will naturally sink down 2' (60 cm) or more and if the pike are deeper, one or two split shot can be added to the monofilament leader. Later in the summer when pike are down deep in cooler water, a sink-tip or full-sinking line may be required. Pike put a lot of stress on reels. Their short runs are unstoppable, and sooner or later you'll have your knuckles severely rapped by the reel handle. This high-speed stress is hard on reel innards, so buy one of good quality with a positive drag system that will help control hard runs. Add 50 yards (45 m) or so of 20-lb test braided Dacron backing to build up the line's diameter on the spool. This mainly is to speed up line retrieval, for it's unlikely you'll see the backing very often when pike fishing—but it can happen.

Attach 4–6' (1.2–1.8 m) of 10–20-lb test, level, monofilament leader to the fly line with a loop-to-loop connection or Nail Knot (tapered leaders are neither necessary nor desirable for casting big flies). Loop-to-loop connections make for fast leader changes on the water. I use level monofilament, no more than 6' (1.8 m) long, so I can maneuver the pike in close without worrying about the loop connection hanging up in the top guides—which could happen with a leader longer than the rod. For those of us who are not powerful casters, the shorter leaders also result in better line and fly turnovers. However, some fly anglers prefer longer leaders during the later part of the season when pike are more cautious.

There are several combinations of materials and methods to connect flies to the end of mono leaders. Each has advantages and disadvantages, and different anglers have their own preferences. Like most fly-fishing techniques, there are few right or wrong methods. I like to keep things simple and prefer attaching about 8" (20 cm) of nylon-coated braided steel leader to every fly I tie. The steel fly leader is connected to the mono leader with a loop-to-loop connection. I've never had a steel leader break, changing flies is fast, and other than simple end loops, no knots are used.

Attaching an 8" coated steel leader to every fly at home is more work (and more expensive), but it's a simple system and worth the small effort and cost.

Occasionally steel leaders kink and twist, and since they are impossible to straighten, must be replaced.

Steel leaders are attached to flies by threading 2" (5 cm) of leader through the eye and then twisting the tag end around the main section several times (similar to the initial twists on a Clinch Knot). The twists are then fused together with the open flame of a match or lighter. The twisted loops are briefly heated until they bubble and turn white, but not so long that they burn. A similar loop is formed at the other end of the steel leader to attach to the mono leader—which also has a loop. Steel leaders can also be attached to flies by crimping on metal sleeves. The sleeves and crimping tools are available at most tackle shops. Finally, flies can also be attached to steel leaders using a Figure-8 Knot.

Some pike anglers prefer using hard, tooth-resistant 20–30-lb monofilament leaders and tying on their flies—usually with a Clinch Knot—without steel leaders. Fine. I tried this the first time I fly fished for pike and lost a fair-sized fish because it hit from the side and sheared the leader. However, monofilament leaders may be an advantage in heavily fished water where pike are leader-shy.

Special pike leaders that have a section of braided steel at the fly end are available. I found them inconvenient for changing flies, so continue using mono leaders attached to the fly line and steel leaders attached to my flies. It's simple and it works.

Other Tackle You Will Need

THERE ARE NOT MANY PIECES of pike fly-fishing equipment that are as mandatory as jaw spreaders and either long-nosed forceps or needlenose pliers. Occasionally, pike will take the hook quite deep, so the jaw spreader and long forceps are a must for hook removal without hurting the fish—or yourself. Many jaw spreaders have pointed hook ends which can damage pike jaws. To prevent them from piercing the jaw tissue, I slip a few inches of thick surgical tubing over the sharp ends. Others wrap the pointed ends with electrical tape.

Also handy for making on-water adjustments and repairs are an extra spool of monofilament leader, steel leader, a cigarette lighter, split shot, a hook sharpener, wire side-cutters and needlenose pliers. Light cotton gloves help to grasp slippery pike. Chest waders are required for spring wading in shallow bays or paddling around in a float tube or pontoon boat. On most lakes, a small personal float craft or boat is required to get to the pike-feeding grounds after they leave the shallow breeding bays.

Flies

THERE ARE MANY PUBLISHED fly patterns for pike, and most fly shops carry a few local designs. Any number of streamers 4–6" (10–15 cm) long, of colorful synthetic hair and flash filaments, will catch pike when they are feeding. My two favorite color combinations include gold flash filaments mixed with orange artificial hair, and chartreuse and yellow artificial hair, again with a few flash filaments. Red and white, and yellow and red are also popular colors for pike flies. Streamers that look more like baitfish such as shiners and whitefish are also used. They have light-colored undersides, dark backs and silvery flash filaments.

Some anglers prefer long streamers 8–10" (20–25 cm) in length, but such large flies tied with artificial fibers can result in false hookups—a fish is on for a few seconds, then gets off. Apparently the teeth temporarily tangle in the long fibers, then pull free because the jaws aren't anywhere near the hook at the head of the fly. A common solution for this problem is to add a second hook (called a trailer or stinger) to the back end of the fly. However, it is more difficult to remove a fly with two hooks, and there's a greater chance of an unsuccessful release. I've tried huge flies and find that more pike stay connected to smaller streamers—meaning no more than 6" (15 cm) long. Again, my ideas differ from many pike pros, who insist that big 8–10" (20–25-cm) flies are a must for catching trophy pike, so maybe big streamers are worth tying and trying. Perhaps this is why I have never landed a trophy pike, but my friends who do catch big pike also use smaller flies. Besides, is a 5–6" (13–15-cm) streamer really that small?

If possible, tie or buy pike streamers with artificial fibers as they do not hold as much water as some natural tying materials like rabbit fur and marabou feathers. These natural materials look great below the surface, but they absorb lots of water and can be quite difficult to cast because of the added weight.

Most of my pike flies are tied on No. 2/0 and 3/0 short-shank hooks. Others use long-shanked hooks down to No. 2. Weed guards made from thick monofilament are helpful when fishing through weed beds, especially later in the year. Some patterns use stiff bucktail hairs that cover the hook and reduce weed interference. Brass, steel or pearl eyes add flash, and the extra front-end weight presumably adds fish-attracting action to pike flies. And no one can deny that those eyes look so damned cute.

All hooks should be debarbed for ease of removal from pike. You will also appreciate the ease with which a debarbed pike fly will slip out of the back of your hand (the voice of experience).

When and Where

PIKE CAN BE CAUGHT ON A FLY any time the water is free of ice. Generally they are slow to bite during the spring breeding season (just after ice-out), then start feeding heavily right after they spawn. They seem to slow down again as the water warms. The action varies with the season, but pike can be caught for six or seven months of the year in most parts of Canada.

Pike move into ice-free shallow bays while the main part of a lake is still frozen. They swirl and twist (in breeding mode) when there is still floor ice in the bays and the water is ice-cold. I've caught a few pike during the height of the breeding season—but damn few. Streamers can be stripped right in front of pike floating on the surface, but when they have sex on their pea-sized brains they just aren't interested in eating.

By late April, anglers often start grumbling about the pike being off—forgetting it's the same every year. We've gone out once or twice and caught one or two pike—or none at all. We keep grumbling. Then at the end of one sunny day in early May, my phone will ring in the evening. It will be KK, and the news will be: The pike fishing is hot! (Kiyoshi, a.k.a. KK, will have spent the afternoon catching pike.)

In southern Alberta the best pike action is in May through early June, but they can be caught all summer as well. I've fished for pike in northern Alberta and northern Saskatchewan a couple of times—once in early June and once in mid-July. The action was great in early June, just two weeks after ice-out. We caught our share of pike in July as well, but the lodge owner said we had missed the peak feeding season.

Within the time window when pike fishing is generally hot, there will be ups and downs in the action as pike moods change. Around here the pike are most active (read: easiest to catch) during warm and sunny, clear-sky, high-pressure weather systems. Sure, they are catchable on cold, blustery spring days, but the catch rates usually fall off drastically.

Where are pike likely to be? Well, they are ambush feeders and live near, on, over, beside or within something like a weed bed, drop-off, reef, shallow bay or stream flow. Most often they will be caught where there is some noticeable structure or a change in water condition, such as clarity, temperature or current. Food organisms that attract baitfish—which attract pike—live in weed beds or may be carried in a slow current near an inlet or outlet. When prairie winds roil the water in shallow bays, pike will hold just inside or outside of the murky water waiting for a meal to cruise by.

Where would you hide if you were a hungry pike waiting to ambush a meal? Quietly kick your float tube near an island or point, cast to the shallow water, then control your retrieve so the fly drops down as the water gets deeper. Or, cast parallel to the drop-off and retrieve at various depths. Hold over a shallow bar or weed bed and cast out to deeper water, retrieving your fly so it travels up the slope or beside the weeds. Cast a gaudy streamer into small, open pockets along the edge of a weed bed. Try casting into flowing water that could carry food, or that might be warmer or cooler than the surrounding water. If the water has clear and murky sections, cast into or alongside of the cloudy water and retrieve your fly into or along the edge of the clear water.

Techniques

I HAVEN'T A LOT TO SAY ABOUT TECHNIQUE. Try various retrieval depths, strip speeds and actions until something works. Here's a good way to start. After casting your fly, let it sink for a few seconds, depending on water depth; then retrieve the line in short, snappy 4" (10-cm) strips every second or two.

Strip speeds don't have to be fast, but they usually need to be lively. In spring, sluggish retrieves usually don't get pike excited. Or perhaps I should say that lively strips work well in the spring, and I am not about to change a technique that works.

In midsummer, when water temperatures increase, a more sluggish fly retrieve may be required. We normally quit fly fishing for pike in June when the water gets warmer, but in the summer of 1998 some friends continued fishing and caught lots of pike in July—and the action carried on well into August. A local fly-fishing club member, Alan Kloepper, told me that he had noticed a slower recovery seemed to produce more pike.

On my first late July outing, I let the fly sink down several feet and used the faster strips—not as Alan had suggested. It worked, but not like in spring. I then tried keeping my line barely tight and pulling on it very slowly. There was little forward movement or action to the fly, but it worked well. One evening while using this retrieve, I landed five pike that had merely mouthed my gaudy streamer—not one of them hit it. I could feel there was a fish at the fly because of a slight tension, and sometimes the line vibrated, whereupon I set the hook.

Releasing Pike

DEBARB ALL PIKE FLIES! THERE—I SAID IT AGAIN.

Fly fish for pike with heavy gear that allows you to get a fish to hand as soon as possible without undue fatigue. Pike can usually remain in the water while the hook is removed, especially if lip-hooked. Sometimes they will have to be gently lifted out onto the mesh deck of a float tube or pontoon boat. Handle them carefully, trying not to damage their delicate gills nor to remove excessive amounts of mucus from their skin.

Landing nets should not be used for pike that are to be released. They twist and tangle too much, making them difficult to remove from the webbing. Many fly anglers use landing cradles (hammocks), which allow large pike to be gently controlled while the hook is removed.

Most pike are lip-hooked and the fly is easily removed, especially if it is barbless, but, as mentioned, jaw spreaders and long forceps are a must to remove the occasional streamer that is hooked down inside the mouth.

When the hook has been removed, cradle the fish in the water and move it gently back and forth until you are certain it can swim away. Usually, you will be rewarded with a spray of water in the face as the lively pike splashes its tail to escape—fair ball considering what you have just done to it.

Clive Schaupmeyer's Must-Have Patterns for Pike

- Baitfish Streamer
- Great Pumpkin streamer
- Slider Floating streamer
- Tweety Bird Streamer

CHAPTER 39

PIKE ON "DRY FLIES"

Clive Schaupmeyer

Pike eat primarily below the surface, but at times floating flies provide exciting top-water action. This is more likely to happen when the sun is low, which for most of us is toward sunset versus early morning.

Calm waters are generally best, but if it's choppy, pike will often strike floating flies that make lots of noise. Poppers with flat-faced heads are recommended as they make an audible "sploosh" when stripped.

Floating pike flies have two basic parts: a body-tail section and a foam head. The 5–8" (13–20-cm) body-tail consists of a few strands of feathers, frayed yarn, and synthetic hair or similar willowy material. If tying your own, use yellow, chartreuse or orange body materials, and highlight it with gold, pearl or silver flash strands. Local experience may dictate other color combinations. Dress them lightly to avoid absorbing too much water, which interferes with casting.

Flies are supported in the water by foam heads. They can be purchased from fly shops, or made by punching cylindrical plugs from the type of high-density foam used in knee pads and beach sandals. Use a short section of 0.5" diameter copper or brass tubing, sharpened at one end as a punch. Taper the head with a sharp knife, scissors or coarse sandpaper, and then punch a small hole lengthwise through the head to accept the hook eye.

After securing the body-tail material to the hook, wrap the shank behind the eye with a single layer of yarn and coat it with head cement, Pliobond or Goop, then push the head over the eye and onto the shank. Mount the taper forward for a slider, or flat-face-forward for a popper. Simply leave the head force-fitted, or secure it with a few wraps of thread over the tapered end.

Retrieval techniques are simple: Cast, take up the slack, then strip in a few inches every second or two. Pause occasionally and let the fly sit for several seconds. Vary the timing, speed and distance of each strip until you find a productive combination.

One clear advantage of floating flies is they can be tossed into small openings where weedless, sinking flies won't work. It can sit and be twitched, then slowly retrieved in clearings no larger than a bathtub. If they ignore your floating slider, try a larger pattern, a different color, or a noisy popper.

Strikes can be awesome—a pike may take you by complete surprise by leaping clear of the water to grab your fly on the way up or down. Most strikes are less spectacular, but still rather startling. A pike may approach from behind or the side; then its body will half emerge the instant it attacks. Then there are those heart-arresting attacks that start several feet away. . . . The water swells up from stage left and a wave races toward your fly. It's hard not to pull the fly away from these aggressive attacks, but delay striking by simply raising the rod. Most pike will get hooked on their own—or not.

PIKE CHOWDER

Drives away winter chills
(Makes four servings)

1 lb—boneless pike, cubed—500 g
4–6 slices bacon, diced
1 onion, diced
1 red pepper, diced
2 potatoes, diced
1 tbsp—fresh tarragon—15 mL

or 1 tsp—dried tarragon—5 mL

4 bay leaves

4–6 cups—milk—1,000–1,500 mL

1 cup—kernel corn—250 mL

Pinch—cayenne pepper

Salt and pepper to taste

Beurre manie* or bread slices

Fresh chopped chives, garnish

Optional—diced mushrooms, celery, carrots or squash

1. Sauté bacon, onions and red pepper in a stock pot. Add potatoes, tarragon, bay leaves and milk. Simmer until potatoes are nearly done.

2. Add corn; simmer 5 minutes. Add cubed pike and cayenne pepper. Simmer 5 minutes. Season with salt and pepper to taste. Remove bay leaves and discard.

3. Thicken chowder with beurre manie and garnish with fresh chopped chives. If preferred, mushrooms, celery, carrots, squash or other vegetables may be added.

*Beurre manie: Equal amounts of softened butter and flour creamed together. About 3 tbsp (45 mL) of each should be sufficient. If preferred, rather than beurre manie, you may place a thick slice of bread in the bottom of a soup bowl and ladle chowder over it.

–Wayne Phillips

CHAPTER 40

ALBERTA'S TROUT PRESERVE

Bob Scammell

I T IS SLIGHTLY LESS THAN 20 YEARS SINCE ALBERTA FIRST BECAME a destination for fly fishers of the world. It was in the late 1970s and early '80s that articles in major outdoor magazines—some by major outdoor writers—proclaimed that the lower Bow River offered perhaps the best dry-fly fishing in the world for trophy-sized rainbow trout. By the time I served on Canada's first team in the World Fly Fishing Championship in England in 1987, I was being asked in a dozen languages (all of which seemed to have incorporated the word "Bow") about the fishing in Alberta, how to arrange a trip and access to the water, and how it was possible that there could be any fishing at all when most of the best water was public.

That last question was easily answered with a flat "That's why," but the rest were all hard questions, even in those days, because the few dedicated Alberta fly fishers were pioneers in the sport on the vast number of rivers, lakes and streams in their huge province. Alberta is a land mass of over 260,000 square miles (673,350 square km) lying immediately east of the Continental Divide. It slopes easterly and northeasterly from altitudes of nearly 13,000' (3960 m) down to 2,100' (640 m) at its eastern boundary and 500' (150 m) at its northern border. The province contains 6,560 square miles (16,990 square km) of permanent lakes and about 12,500 miles (20,100 km) of rivers and streams located among seven drainage systems, five of which have their headwaters in the Rocky Mountains. Approximately 40 percent of the total lengths of streams and rivers—5,000 miles (8,000 km)—is capable of supporting coldwater species like native cutthroat, lake and bull trout (the latter two are really char), mountain and lake whitefish, and arctic grayling. Introduced species include brown and brook trout (the latter is also char) and rainbow trout, which is native in Alberta only in the Athabasca River watershed.

An early warning: The bull trout is Alberta's "provincial fish" and considered endangered, so there is a zero limit on this species throughout the province. Yet, strangely, bull-trout fishing can be fast and furious in certain places, so anglers in Alberta must learn how to identify them (memorize the jingle "no black, put it back") and release every one landed.

Even today, if you fly fish in Alberta, you are still a pioneer in many ways, and one of the most common sighs and sayings you will hear from resident fly fishers is "So many rivers, so little time." The answers to the "Where to go?" questions of resident and nonresident fly fishers alike became much easier with the introduction of the *1998 Alberta Guide to Sportfishing Regulations*. This magazinelike publication is given free to every angler when an Alberta Sportfishing License is purchased. The 1998 edition announced what is probably the most extensive sudden move into catch-and-release trout fishing made by any North American jurisdiction since Yellowstone National Park went fundamentally catch-and-release in 1962.

The new 1998 Alberta regulations multiplied by 8 times the number of catch-and-release waters in the province, going from 5 to 39. At one stroke Alberta became one of the great trout preserves in North America. The list of catch-and-release waters provides a rough guide as to where the best fly fishing for coldwater species of the eastern slopes of the Rocky Mountains is likely to be found. But that rough guide should always be discussed with an experienced resident fly fisher because, as is always the case with radical and sudden change, regulations hastily written are difficult to understand. Politics is involved in some of the catch-and-release selections and so is the hope that such regulations will improve some streams that have never really been first-class because of alleged overfishing and killing.

Remember those Rocky Mountains whenever trying to decide when to go to Alberta to fly fish for trout. Unquestionably, the practical season is May through September. Many resident anglers will tell you that if they had just one month, they would take June, but they would also admit that in many years the rivers and streams through June are high, muddy and unfishable due to mountain snowmelt augmented by runoff from heavy early summer rains. Other locals favor September, but the waters can often be very low and challenging during that month. Consensus dictates that the most reliable month in terms of ideal water conditions is July, which is also when some of Alberta's better aquatic insect hatches take place.

Time decided, the first destination for every fly-fishing visitor to Alberta still has to be the lower Bow River for several reasons. First is its consistency. I have fished the Bow for nearly 50 years, and it remains like whisky—it is never bad, but some years are better than others. In recent years the dry-fly fishing that made the Bow's reputation has not been as good as usual, but streamers and nymphs still produce remarkable numbers of the rainbows and brown trout that were introduced in the 1930s and, occasionally, native cutthroat and bull trout. The average size of all these species in the Bow is large, frequently 13–20" (33–50 cm) although many in the 24–28" (60–70-cm) category are taken every year.

By far the most important reason for a visitor to Alberta to start with the lower Bow is to learn what it will teach about fishing in Alberta generally and about other prime Alberta fly-fishing destinations. Although the beds and shores of the Bow are public property by Alberta law—like the beds and shores of all Alberta rivers, lakes and streams—getting to those on the Bow over extensive private land holdings is unusually difficult. Most of the lower Bow fishing is accomplished with guides rowing McKenzie River drift boats or johnboats. The Bow guides are an accomplished and knowledgeable lot who can also tell curious visiting anglers a great deal about fly fishing in other parts of Alberta.

Eric Grinnell, for example, is a fisheries biologist who has made a career of guiding on the Bow and in other parts of Alberta, particularly the very southwestern corner of the province, which is quickly becoming known as one of the frontiers of superb fly fishing in North America. Grinnell is also the only outfitter operating on the lowest of the lower Bow, from the Carseland Weir down through the Siksika Indian Nation reserve, where it is frequently forbidden to land a boat on the tribal lands. Grinnell meets this challenge by floating downstream in a jet boat and camping on islands, which remain public land even on a river flowing through an Indian reserve. On day trips, in the late evening he simply jets back upriver to the point of origin. There are very large rainbows and browns in this section of the river, and it is one of the few places left in Alberta where a person may, if desired, legally keep a trophy fish for the wall.

Base for most Alberta visitors to the Bow is Calgary, a city with a population of nearly 900,000, through which the river flows. Most visiting Bow anglers take advantage of the wide range of lodgings and restaurants the city offers. The Country Pleasures store on the south side of the city is a headquarters for anglers. Information on current fishing conditions on the Bow and other Alberta choice waters can always be obtained, and cards, brochures and contacts with reliable guides are always available, not to mention advice on fishing and fly choices from the store owners and staff, all of whom fish the Bow regularly.

At Country Pleasures there is always current information available on the second Alberta fly-fishing destination that no visiting fly fisher should miss—the Crowsnest River. About 200 miles (320 km) southwest of Calgary, it flows along Highway 3, through and by the historic mining towns of the Crowsnest Pass.

The most reliable and long-standing source of local advice on the Crowsnest—and other fly-fishing opportunities in this penultimate frontier of Alberta fly fishing—is The Crowsnest Angler, located right beside Highway 3 at the east entrance to the town of Bellevue. Proprietor Vic Bergman, an accomplished guide on the best waters of the area, books other guides through his shop for float fishing and walk-in trips on many of the area's superb rainbow and cut-throat rivers and streams. Besides the Crowsnest, which is predominantly rainbow fishing with some big brown trout below Lundbreck Falls, there is the Oldman River, including its developing tailwater fishery for rainbows below the Three Rivers Dam, and the superbly scenic Castle River with its cutthroat, rainbow and bull-trout fishery.

Bergman and his guides will also outfit forays just over the Crowsnest Pass into British Columbia's Elk River and its usually very fast cutthroat fishing. Visiting fly fishers in this area should also inquire about possibilities on the Livingstone River, a drive-in, semi-wilderness fly-fishing experience for native cutthroats and a few bull trout and rainbows. In this area there is a little-known, moody and erratic fishery for very large brown trout in the stretch of the Waterton River flowing between Waterton Lake in the National Park and Waterton Dam. This area, including Waterton Lakes National Park itself, offers some of the finest lake fly fishing in Alberta.

Bergman and his guides will take anglers on hike-in trips to some of the high mountain lakes in this corner of the province, mostly for cutthroats and rainbows, but also to a few lakes that hold achingly gorgeous but moody golden trout. Any visiting angler who decides to fish lakes for trout should act only on current information obtained on arrival, because the fishing in some Alberta lakes that was fantastic last season is frequently totally wiped out for this season by harsh winter conditions.

Most anglers visiting the Crowsnest Pass stay in one of the two or three larger motels in the Pass town of Blairmore, or in bed-and-breakfast operations that have started appearing in the area, some right on the banks of the Crowsnest. One of the favored of these is Bedside Manor, operated by Dr. William and Shirley Sara. The historic Lethbridge House was moved onto riverside property that includes hundreds of meters of superb Crowsnest water.

Where to eat in the Crowsnest Pass has been a challenge for many years. At this writing the choices of most visiting anglers are Popeil's Family Restaurant in Coleman, The Inn on the Border just off Highway 3 right up on the Alberta–British Columbia boundary, and the newer RendezVous Restaurant located on the Crowsnest bank at the east entrance to Blairmore off Highway 3.

Fly-fishing visitors to Alberta, particularly repeaters who have "done" the Crowsnest and the Bow, are now starting to venture north into central Alberta, roughly that part of the province between the northern outskirts of Calgary and the southern boundary of Edmonton. Again, most of the best fly fishing for the coldwater species in this general area will be in the foothills and mountains west of Highway 2.

A major base for food and lodging relatively near some of the prime coldwater fisheries in central Alberta is Rocky Mountain House (population 5,800) which is 55 miles (89 km) west of Red Deer on Highway 11. Visiting anglers frequently stay and eat at the Walking Eagle Motor Inn. Ram River Sports offers a full line of fly-fishing tackle, flies and local information and serves as a booking point for the few guides who work waters in this area. Another popular spot is approximately 15 miles (24 km) southwest of Rocky Mountain House—Terratima Lodge on the banks of the main fork of Prairie Creek.

Many Alberta and Montana fishing guides come to this area on their days off to fish the tiny North Raven River, sometimes called Stauffer Creek. It is approximately 20 miles (32 km) east of Rocky Mountain House on Highway 11, then 9 miles (14.5 km) south on Highway 761 to the hamlet of Stauffer. The North Raven is a spring creek, not much more than 10' (3 m) wide and so devilishly difficult that it is unofficially known to many very fine resident anglers as "The Trout Stream From Hell" because of its close quarters, thick willow jungles, and very large and wary brown trout—altogether a combination that makes the North Raven one of North America's most challenging trout streams.

Fortunately, North Haven is also a very rich trout stream featuring some heavy caddis hatches and exceptional hatches of most of the major may flies native to Alberta. Strangely, this tiny creek has massive hatches of three of North America's largest may flies: the western green drake *(Drunella grandis)*, the brown drake *(Ephemera simulans)*, and the Hex or fish fly *(Hexagenia limbata)*—also absurdly misnamed as the Michigan caddis. During these hatches, huge browns are frequently hooked but rarely landed, simply because of the close quarters. It is fascinating for most anglers to learn—whether they are able to exploit it or not—that all this richness results from one of North America's first and major moves into stream reclamation and conservation. In the early 1970s the North Raven was all but finished as a trout stream, mainly because its banks had been destroyed by cultivation too close to the water and cattle tromping. A classic stream study was done and the North Raven became Alberta's first Bucks for Wildlife project. In only 25 years, a combination of sportsmen's money, landowner co-operation and the expertise of official biologists repaired the stream so that it is better than it ever was.

One of the popular ways to fish the North Raven is to stay streamside at the Lazy M Ranch, where some heartfelt angling sympathy is frequently served along with good food, and where arrangements might occasionally be made with someone who has the courage to guide on such exacting water. Nine miles (14.5 km) south of Stauffer, flowing along Highway 54 is the South Raven River, a typical—and excellent—central Alberta trout stream. Larger and much less technical than the North Raven, it is perhaps one of the province's more underrated rivers.

While down at the South Raven, it is worthwhile to head east on Highway 54, through Spruceview, and then turn south to the Dickson Dam on the Red Deer River. A promising tailwater fishery is developing in the Red below the dam. Since the mid-1990s Alberta's largest fly-caught brown trout have been taken and released (there is a zero limit) in these waters. Generally, the word is that if fish are not rising when you get there, you should consider going elsewhere. It is always worth proceeding farther southwest to the Sundre area to try the Little Red Deer River and Fallentimber Creek, another two of Alberta's more unsung trout streams. Before doing so, it is worthwhile having lunch, dinner, even a late breakfast at the Tivoli Garden Cafe on Highway 54 at the eastern end of Spruceview. Any Danish specialty on the menu is worth trying.

One of Alberta's truly "must" fishing experiences is generally reached by driving about 60 miles (97 km) southwest from Rocky Mountain House on Highway 752, then northwest on the road from Strachan along the North Fork of Prairie Creek to the Ram River, onward to the North Ram, then to the South Ram River. The difficulty here is that there are no facilities other than a campground or two and nobody you can phone to get a current report on water and fishing conditions. Both rivers are generally in best fishing condition from mid-July through September. If they are prime when you arrive, you are in for one of the truly great North American fly-fishing experiences.

Prior to the mid-1950s, the entire Ram system upstream from sets of impassable falls was virtually devoid of fish. These waters were considered ideal for cutthroat, so in 1955 westslope cutthroats were planted and quickly took hold. The North Ram has been catch-and-release for many years now and offers the opportunity to catch and release very large cutthroats—often to 20" (50 cm), rarely to 28" (70 cm)—in the kind of mountain-wilderness environment most of us associate with this species. Strong lobbying will likely result in the South Ram also being designated catch-and-release, which will enhance a remarkable fly-fishing opportunity for those who are sound of wind and limb—or wealthy. The South Ram canyon is a hard hike down and harder up, but features deep, green holes full of the kind of cutthroat you get when they have had time to grow.

One guide knows the whole Ram system really well and can arrange many kinds of trips, ranging from day outings to "century-before" streamside camping trips to—for those who can pay the freight—helicopter transport down into the canyon and back out at day's end. There is at least one other, more recent guide on the Ram, but the one who has guided me more than once, and whom I can highly tout, is Ron Manz.

If you are the kind of visitor who likes adventure, self-outfitting and guiding, you could venture into Alberta's newest and perhaps ultimate fly-fishing frontier, the area generally west and considerably north of Edmonton, into the vicinity of the city of Grande Prairie and the towns of Grande Cache and Valleyview. There you can still experience fly fishing for native coldwater species, the likes of which we all think no longer exists anywhere in the modern world.

The Little Smoky River, which has flowed alongside Highway 43 from Fox Creek to Valleyview for several years now, has been one of the rare catch-and-release arctic grayling fisheries in North America, if not the best. The river is beautiful enough to take your breath away, rich in insect life, and teeming with grayling running from tiddlers to, rarely, 18" (45 cm). As is typical with the species, they have brief periods when they are not feeding; the rest of the time virtually any fly, generally a dry, will do. Most fly fishers on the Little Smoky routinely report 100-plus grayling days.

There are no guides on the river, so careful self-outfitting is required up there, even before making the long drive required to reach the river. For example, the Little Smoky can stay high, dirty and unfishable for long periods of time in a wet summer, so an inquiry about water conditions should be made of the Fish and Wildlife Division offices at Fox Creek or Valleyview. Asking further questions may result in a contact with someone who can give some help on the best sections of the river and directions on how to get to them.

The same cautions are in order with regard to two exceptional bull-trout rivers, the Muskeg and Kakwa, reached via Highway 40 between the town of Grande Cache and the city of Grande Prairie. Inquiries should be made of the Fish and Wildlife Division offices in Grande Prairie or Grande Cache. If you manage to talk to Shane Ramstead at the Grande Cache office, you will be fortunate indeed, for he knows as much as anyone alive about the Muskeg.

My inquiries about the Muskeg in the summer of 1998 were discouraging: a dissident Indian band was camped along the river and systematically fishing it out, killing and shipping in horse-pack boxes the magnificent bull trout on which the limit is zero for anyone else. I could believe this, as on my last two-day trip to the river, five of us took and released hundreds of bull trout up to 24" (60 cm), mostly on our special streamer fly tied to resemble a strip of raw liver. The Kakwa was still fishing very well at the same time, perhaps because it is closely monitored in connection with an ongoing bull-trout research project.

Again, be warned that you are in the last fly-fishing frontier Alberta has when you are up in the northwest foothills, muskeg, mountains and boreal forest; and know that you are on your own. As on most frontiers, the fishing can be terrible or superb beyond your wildest dreams, and which it is depends on quick-changing factors like the weather and the habits of humans who are always quick to exploit frontiers. Make your inquiries and then go—if you are an adventurous, self-reliant fly fisher. I think I still am as I enter my sixth decade, and at this time of writing, I still plan on achieving one of my wildest dreams. I am going to pick one of these three rivers, put a pack on my back, and do Hemingway's Big Two-Hearted River bit: wade, hike, fish and camp ever upstream and into the wilderness.

What to Bring

ANYONE EMBARKING FOR ALBERTA should remember the Lefty Kreh dictum: "I always pack for it's colder than anyone says where I'm going, or warmer, or wetter, or drier, or somebody forgot the lunch." All conditions are true for Alberta, except that nobody ever forgets the lunch.

If restricted to one fly rod, most Albertans would probably choose a 6-weight, 8 ½' graphite, but might also own a 7–8-weight for high winds in the south and a 4-weight just for the pure pleasure of using it on a fine day. Floating, weight-forward lines are the choice for most fishing, but fast sink-tips are often used for fishing streamers on the Bow. Full sinkers are seldom used, except on a few specific lakes.

When floating on the rivers, there will be frequent stops to fish certain runs and pools more slowly and carefully, so chest waders with felt soles are essential.

Whenever Lefty fishes in Alberta, with regard to flies he does here what he does anywhere in the word—waits until he gets here, then consults with residents about the current "hot" patterns. That is good advice, but there are old standby patterns that work just as well here over the long haul as they will virtually anywhere else in the world.

The most frequently used dry flies are of the down or horizontal wing variety, simply because Alberta trout enjoy good hatches of caddis flies, stone flies and grasshoppers—all down-wing species. This accounts for the current popularity in Alberta of the Stimulator, Elk Hair Caddis, and Letort Hopper in No. 16–6 and with varying body colors. For a similar style attractor pattern, the Royal Trude in No. 14–8 serves well.

For the dun stage of all major may fly hatches, the Adams is a generic match from No. 22–8. Many Albertans prefer the Bastard Adams, either standard or parachute, tied with a single white-hair wing, rather than the traditional wings of divided grizzly hackle tips. This provides greater durability and better visibility on our frequently turbulent and steel-grey waters.

A large, heavily weighted black nymph, like the Montana Stone or Brooks' Stone in No.10–6, is needed in those rivers and streams that hold heavy, year-round populations of immature year classes of salmon fly nymphs. For virtually any other nymphal forms, a Gold-Ribbed Hare's Ear in No. 16–8, weighted and unweighted, serves as well here as elsewhere in the fly-fishing world.

Alberta's trout respond well to streamers from ice-out to freeze-up, so well, in fact, it's a wonder there are not more original, local creations than there are. Short of tying them yourself, it's difficult to buy streamers here that are weighted heavily enough. Many Albertans do well with only two streamers—dull and bright. A black streamer, say a Woolly Bugger with a Krystal Flash or Flashabou tail, generally works well, and when it won't, a bright, predominantly white pattern like the Royal Coachman streamer will.

Required Reading

The Alberta Guide to Sportfishing Regulations, given to all purchasers of an Alberta Sportfishing License, is absolutely required reading for every angler, every year, in order to determine which special regulations apply to each river, lake or stream.

Also strongly suggested as required reading is a current edition of Barry

Mitchell's annual *Alberta Fishing Guide,* which regularly appears at newsstands, fly shops and sporting goods outlets early each April. This private publication generally contains a dozen feature articles about Alberta angling, not necessarily confined to fly fishing, including updates on expected fishing conditions for the season. Written by some of Alberta's top angling writers, it contains 1,300 carefully crafted listings of information about, and directions to, most of Alberta's finest rivers, lakes and streams. Maps are included, but many readers find them too small and cramped to be of real use, so supplement them with *The Fishin' Map* series that is available in stores that sell fishing equipment.

Several books are useful for anyone fly fishing in Alberta. Jim McLennan is a superb fly fisherman, a former Bow River guide, and one of Canada's finest angling writers. His *Blue Ribbon Bow,* the only book on the Bow and long out of print, was reissued in paperback in 1999. Jim's *Trout Streams of Alberta* is very informative and a good read, as is Chris Dawson's *Due North of Montana,* although it is somewhat quirky and personal about the waters recommended. *The Essential Guide to Fly-Fishing* by Albertan Clive Schaupmeyer is not restricted to Alberta, but does deal with many of our best fly-fishing waters and methods for fishing them.

The Phenological Fly by Bob Scammell is a vest-sized guide to Alberta's most important aquatic insects for anglers. It provides a natural method, using stream-side wildflowers as indicators, for anglers to predict what is likely to be hatching.

BOB SCAMMELL'S MUST-HAVE PATTERNS FOR ALBERTA TROUT

- Dry: Bastard Adams
- Letort Hopper
- Poly Ant
- Stimulator
- Nymph: Brook's Stone
- Despickable
- Short Black Booger
- Hot-Wired Whole Squirrel Hide
- Streamer: Royal Letort
- Purpetraitor

CHAPTER 41

PRAIRIE TARPON

Bob Scammell

OW CAN YOU EXPLAIN THE ANONYMITY ON THE TROUTLESS prairies of a fish that runs in schools, takes the dry fly eagerly, that is a spectacular jumper when hooked, and when smoked is a famous delicacy to rival smoked salmon? Yet the goldeye is even more unknown than our northern sheefish, which is so obscure that it is called "inconnu"—French for "unknown."

Prior to the completion of the Dickson Dam, Alberta's Red Deer River was one of those large, silty systems favored by the two members of the Hiodon family: many goldeye *(Hiodon alosoides)*, the western member; and a few moon-eye *(Hiodon tergisus)*, the eastern member of the family. These fish still inhabit the Red Deer tailwater—a good thing because the river below the dam can still get high and muddy, at which time the goldeye is the fly fisher's insurance fish, feeding freely, even rising to dry flies in brown water that completely puts down brown trout. These fish are common in Alberta's larger rivers after they come out of the mountains and flatten out onto the prairies. The Bow, Oldman, North and South Saskatchewan, Peace and Athabasca are Alberta rivers where good fly fishing for goldeye may be found.

The goldeye, armored with huge, hard scales, appears to be a creature from another age, ancient and prehistoric. The fish is shadlike to some, tarponlike to me, as though it would be more at home in salty than silty water. That wonderful eye, encircled with the gold ring, hypnotized me the first time I ever saw it. The sides of the fish are deep, slablike and pure silver. I have an unattributed note that says the Cree called this fish *napak kinosew,* which means "he is pressed flat, fish." If so, the phrase is very descriptive; the two members of the Hiodon family and the mooneye as well, are narrow in cross section and thin through the shoulders.

In many jurisdictions goldeyes and mooneyes are not even given the status of game fish. In that respect Alberta has been more progressive than most. Here is what Dr. Martin Paetz, Alberta's former chief fisheries biologist, has to say about the goldeye in *McClane's New Standard Fishing Encyclopedia:* "The goldeye is probably the best of the province's warmwater game fish as far as sporting qualities are concerned." Paetz goes on to note that "being insectivorous in feeding habits the goldeye provides excellent fly fishing . . . it will hit floating patterns with reckless abandon and it is not unusual for this fish to leap out of the water in trout like fashion when hooked on light tackle." It is the leaping of these big-scaled, big-eyed and silvery fish that reminds me of baby tarpon.

My father was a fan of the old *True* magazine, and in its long-gone pages I read as a kid one of the only articles I have ever seen extolling the virtues of goldeye fishing in, of all trouty places, Montana. That article made the amazing claim that goldeyes could be taken on flies. The trouble was that I did not fish flies in those days, and neither did my father.

It was not until I moved to Red Deer in the early '60s and learned to cast flies that I began to wonder whether goldeyes really could be taken on artificial flies. One June Sunday morning, the Red Deer River was in full mountain runoff, brown and cloudy, so, because I have always believed black to be the most visible color in dark water and that a little flash attracts attention, I tied on a small streamer with a black bear-hair wing and a silver tinsel body. From the first cast, I began to feel a curious pluck at the fly just as it started to straighten out in its drift below me. Now I know it was the characteristic raspy pull of a goldeye at a fly. Eventually I struck back, the waters shattered, and a live mirror flipped, shimmered and flashed in the sunshine. Before the day ended I added several more to my first fly-caught goldeye.

Now I seldom resort to streamers. Where the goldeye really shines is in the eagerness with which it will take a dry fly right off the surface. "What fly?" I am often asked, and always reply, "Any fly at all, so long as it is a grasshopper imitation." My own preference is a No. 10 Letort Hopper for its deer-hair durability because a goldeye's tongue and mouth are, in fact, like a rasp and a couple of fish can quickly reduce a hackled Michigan Hopper, for example, to a bare hook.

While a perfectly dry, dragless, float upstream often takes goldeyes, it is possible sometimes to cast too well for them. A hard thing for the expert—letting the fly drag on purpose—is one tactic that makes the goldeye such a gem of a quarry for beginning fly fishers. Purposely dragging the fly over where a fish had previously risen, then letting the fly swing around on a long line downstream and making a big wake far below, often draws slashing hits from goldeyes.

Try fly fishing for goldeye if you visit the Red Deer, or any other of the western rivers where the species is found—you'll like it. Me? Now I have the best of two worlds. One September evening I made two casts to two rising fish on the Red Deer River tailwater near the base of Dickson Dam. First cast of a No. 14 Elk Hair Caddis produced an 18" (46-cm) brown trout; the second, a 16" (41-cm) goldeye.

LARRY SALAMON'S SMOKED GOLDEYE SPREAD

One of Canada's most famous delicacies
(Makes four servings)

4 goldeye
1 egg (uncooked)
Pickling salt as needed
Water

1. Scale, gut and remove heads from goldeye. Split each fish halfway down the back, then freeze. (Freezing allows the brine to better penetrate the flesh.)

2. Place enough water in a container to cover the fish by 2" (5 cm). Place an egg

in the water and stir in pickling salt. When the egg floats, the brine is ready.

3. Remove the egg and place fish in the brine for 12 hours. Remove from brine and smoke according to directions on your "hot smoker" (True North, Little Chief, or similar). Goldeye must be hot-smoked to cook the flesh and reduce the oil content.

4. Remove flesh from fish and combine with mayonnaise for a delightful spread. Excellent with crusty French bread and a tomato and onion salad, dressed with a balsamic vinegar and olive-oil vinaigrette.

–Wayne Phillips

CHAPTER 42

WESTSLOPE CUTTHROATS AND BULL TROUT

Jim Crawford

THAT THERE ARE STILL UNFISHED RIVERS AND LAKES FULL of wild native trout waiting to be discovered in North America is a myth. While there are places where two indigenous western game fish—westslope cutthroats and bull trout—come eagerly to a fly, the simple magic of halcyon fishing days in untried waters is long gone.

One region that offers a taste of what it might have been like is that section of the Rocky Mountains where southeastern British Columbia, southwestern Alberta and northern Montana meet. Rivers like the upper Columbia, Kootenay, St. Mary, Skookumchuck, Elk, Wigwam, Oldman, Castle, Saskatchewan, North Fork of the Flathead, and the lakes and tributaries that feed them, still hold native westslope cutthroat, bull trout and mountain whitefish; and fishing can be excellent. This is considered the most productive region in North America for these species, and while there isn't room here to cover more than a fraction of the good waters available, it would take a lifetime or two just to check out the few that are mentioned. However, the methods of locating fish and the techniques, gear and patterns used to catch them, will vary little no matter where you try.

Westslope Cutthroat *(Oncorhynchus clarki lewisi)*

WESTSLOPES ARE EASILY IDENTIFIED by two bright orange or red slashes on the throat. Body colors vary from bright silver to gray to light bronze, with black spots that normally do not extend below the lateral line. River residents won't get much over 20" (60 cm) in length, and 4 lb (1.8 kg) is a heavyweight. Westslopes larger than this and caught in rivers have usually come from a rich lake environment.

Cutthroats carefully and deliberately, almost trustingly, look at a wide variety of dry flies and nymphs without showing too much concern about how they have been presented. While this might make a sloppy fly fisher look good at times, it doesn't mean you can get careless. Usually you get only one chance, and if the fish doesn't take or you miss the hook-up, don't count on it returning.

Although westslopes are strong and hard-bodied, they are not particularly active fighters—no jumping, and no long, ripping runs. The reason is that in their niche with other native species, they do not have to be aggressive to survive. Slow and gentle works fine. However, they do not compete well for food, so when nonnative fish intrude into the westslope's realm, their population quickly suffers.

The original range of westslope cutthroat extended throughout major drainages in southwestern Alberta, northern Montana and Wyoming on the eastern side of the Rockies, and on the western slope in southeastern British Columbia down through Montana and into Idaho. Today, overfishing, loss of spawning habitat and hybridization with other cutthroat and nonnative rainbows (resulting in "cuttbows"), plus the threat of other introduced species has drastically reduced pure native strains in many waters.

Bull Trout *(Salvelinus confluentus)*

BULL TROUT ARE NOT "TROUT" AT ALL. They are actually a char and resemble other members of the char family like lake trout, Dolly Varden and brook trout. While westslope cutthroats are easily identified from other trout, it's not so easy to discern a bull from its cousins. The most distinguishing characteristics are no dark spots or markings on the dorsal, and their bodies are covered with light spots, sometimes faintly colored yellow, crimson and white.

Their original range was extensive and included all but a few of the watersheds that held westslope cutthroat, plus most other major drainages throughout the west. California was the lower end of their range; the Canadian Rockies in Alberta and British Columbia their northern limit, as well as the states of Montana, Idaho, Washington, Oregon and Nevada. Today their range is drastically reduced to areas in southern British Columbia and Alberta, and northern Montana and Idaho. A few tiny remnant populations have also been discovered in northern Nevada, eastern Oregon and eastern Washington.

In addition to habitat reduction from logging and mining, overfishing and the predation of young by introduced species such as lake trout, pike and walleye, part of the reason for their drastic reduction everywhere is that bull trout were long considered to be trash fish, even by fisheries personnel. They are natural predators, so to protect the "sport fish" being introduced into their habitat, bulls were removed any way they could be.

Despite this, bull trout are survivors, albeit some live under conditions that can only be considered dismal. They are often found high up in tiny, cold mountain streams where food is scarce and the environment extremely severe. There, a 10-year-old fish might be only 8–10" (20–25 cm) long. Under more ideal conditions in lakes or big rivers where food is plentiful, some live more than 20 years and attain weights of up to 25 lb (11.4 kg).

Bulls are voracious carnivores and feed on anything that looks edible, making them exceptionally vulnerable to anglers. They can be caught on most streamers or large-nymph patterns, and once in a while will rise to big Hopper, Salmonfly or Stimulator patterns. It's an interesting situation when a 10–12-lb (4.5–5.5-kg) bull ends up on the end of your 4x tippet.

Fortunately, the U.S. Forest Service and Bureau of Land Management are cooperating with Fish and Wildlife branches in Canada and the U.S. to develop bull-trout recovery plans, and their future, although still not bright, is better than in recent years.

North Fork of the Flathead River (Montana and British Columbia)

BEGINNING IN THE ROCKIES near the British Columbia–Alberta boundary, the North Fork of the Flathead flows north, then east, and finally south for 47 miles (75.5 km) in Canada before continuing another 58 miles (93 km) to its confluence with the Middle and South Forks to form the main Flathead River in Montana. For centuries the Kootenai Indians traveled this course and called it "Wolf Trail." Today, like all rivers making up the Flathead, it is part of the Wild and Scenic Rivers system. Black and grizzly bears, mountain lions, gray wolves, martens, wolverines, lynx, bald and golden eagles, ptarmigan, grouse, pileated woodpeckers, mountain goats, sheep, moose, elk and mule deer live all along this rugged, heavily timbered drainage which defines the entire western slope of Glacier National Park.

The British Columbia section has the best fishing. Clear and clean, it is the permanent residence of westslopes and whitefish, and summer home to the last stand of jumbo bull trout that are said to migrate nearly 150 miles (240 km) from Montana's Flathead Lake to spawn in British Columbia tributaries during the fall. As it courses down through the granitic geography of Montana, the North Fork loses its biological richness to the point that any aquatic food produced can support only a minimal density of fish. Numbers of trout and their sizes are moderate at best, and resident fish over 15" (38 cm) are almost unheard of. No doubt this also explains why predacious bull trout don't spend much time in this river.

With North Fork bull trout, finding them is the most difficult part of the program. Although constantly on the move, their numbers decrease each season owing to their propensity to eat almost anything—and to anglers who feel international laws against killing this threatened species do not include them.

Prior to 1950, tributaries high up the South Fork of the Flathead were the premier spawning arteries for spectacular runs of bulls and big westslopes coming out of Flathead Lake. The completion of Hungry Horse Dam in 1952 ended that, wiping out an estimated half of the bull-trout population in the entire Flathead system. There is a small population of bulls in Hungry Horse Reservoir that continue spawning up the South Fork drainage, but this leaves the North Fork as the most important spawning river for Montana bull trout.

In addition to anglers illegally intercepting bulls in the main river as they leave Flathead Lake on their way to the North Fork to spawn, lake trout lie in wait at the river mouth for returning fry. Along the way there is unrelenting destruction of streams by bottom-line-mentality lumber companies. Logging plans on both sides of the U.S.–Canada border include clear-cut harvesting on all but a few crucial streams that provide spawning for both bull trout and west-slope cutts.

But the ramifications don't end there. The first trees to go will be the few remaining, highly valued stands of old-growth timber that form ancient travel corridors for imperiled animals like gray wolves, grizzlies and bald eagles. There is also the very real threat of oil and gas drilling on the northern boundary of Glacier National Park in the North Fork basin, and a proposed open-pit coal mine just over the border in British Columbia that would rival the one near Sparwood. If these projects materialize, silt and sludge will inevitably find their way into the river system and spell an end to the already decimated Flathead bull-trout population.

Westslope cutthroats are much easier to find in the North Fork than bull trout, but only because they are more adapted to small-stream environments. Until they reach 14" (34 cm) or so, their diet is almost exclusively aquatic insects, scuds, leeches and terrestrials that hit the water. Westslopes come readily to any dry fly or nymph. Even a large hopper pattern presented during sometimes smothering hatches of pale morning duns, blue-winged olives, gray drakes or caddis will usually elicit strikes. Using a dozen different patterns, fly fishers have reported 100-trout days on upper stretches of this river. Fortunately, the more productive sections can only be reached by a strenuous hike that discourages all but the most dedicated anglers, and with some lower parts of the river being nearly sterile, intrusion by other species of fish will take a while. Logging, mining and drilling notwithstanding, the upper portion of the river appears safe for the time being.

Elk River

ANOTHER EXCELLENT RIVER, THE ELK, starts its journey at the southern tip of Banff National Park high in the Rockies, then slides down the west slope along British Columbia Highways 43 and 3 through Elkford, Sparwood, Fernie and Elko before emptying into Lake Koocanusa (the impounded Kootenay River) near Highway 93. As roadside rivers go, the Elk is in a truly beautiful setting—Rocky Mountain ridges so high you almost hurt yourself trying to see the tops, wide, green meadows framed by aspens and cottonwoods with endless folds of dark pines beyond, and long, jagged rock ledges and gravel bars that hold the river to its course. It is home to westslope cutts over 20" (50 cm) long and bull trout that can eat them. It also has mountain whitefish that are very impressive on light gear—and don't snicker—these are great fighters that have saved the day for more than one fly fisher when the trout weren't active.

The Elk was nearly written off as recently as 1995. Trout fishing had been declining the previous few years due to overfishing ("overkilling" it is now admitted) when a serious flood of meltwater and heavy ice occurred in the spring of '95. Fishing that summer was the poorest on record, and it was feared cutthroat and bull-trout populations had been devastated. To allow them to rebuild, a two-year no-kill moratorium was imposed on the entire river throughout the 1996 and 1997 seasons; and during 1998, several sections remained no-kill and will into the future. Many local residents didn't even bother to fish, some because they realized the fish needed a chance to recover, others because, "If I can't take home fish to eat, what's the sense?"

The good news is the cutthroat trout population rebounded dramatically and remains high even after an article published in *Fly Fisherman* magazine in 1997 mentioned the Elk. Fishing pressure—primarily by American fly fishers—during the following two summers was excessive, and the number of river guides increased from three to a dozen. With this arose the usual controversy between local anglers who considered the river "theirs," and those who provided guide services to "outsiders."

Three sections of the river are notable. From the bridge north of Highway 43 above Sparwood to the bridge on Highway 3 below Sparwood, the river is more like a strong stream with brush-lined banks, braids and bars. There are also more deadfalls and log jams up here than lower down, so drifting this section can be dicey. Westslopes hold in the classic runs, and bull trout like deeper water. There are few sustained hatches in the upper end, but as elsewhere on the river, dry attractor patterns like Hoppers, Irresistibles, Stimulators and

Humpies will pull cutts to the top, while nymphs, marabou streamers, Zonkers and Muddlers will take them deep, and sometimes large bulls as well.

Where British Columbia Highway 3 (the Crowsnest Highway) crosses, the river reaches flatter country and slows. From there, down past Fernie to Morrisey Provincial Park, the fishing is usually very good and sometimes borders on outstanding. Much of this middle section can be fished on foot, but the best method is to drift. Cartoppers and inflatables can be used in low-water months, and with caution during spring runoff. However, hiring a local guide is recommended, at least on the first trip.

There are miles of classic cutthroat lies and typical hatches of western may flies and caddis flies from June through September. Westslopes might reach 21" (53 cm) in this section—about as long as they get—and 12–16" (30–40 cm) are common. Feisty whitefish will take small nymphs and dries (again, don't pooh-pooh these—most whitefish actually fight better than westslopes or bulls). Here in the deep runs, too, there are big bull trout, which come up from Lake Koocanusa to spend the summer harassing smaller resident fish. Hook a white-fish or cutt over a deep hole and it will sometimes disappear in the maw of a monster bull, just like a perch in the jaws of a large pike, or a rockfish in the gaping maw of a lingcod. It's spooky how big the bulls can be in this river.

The third section of the Elk begins at Morrisey Provincial Park. From the highway, it appears that the river drops down through a steep canyon, but this is an illusion. It actually winds high up along the hillside, then drops down to meet the river at Morrisey, while the river gradient stays fairly constant. The illusion is further enhanced because the river leaves picturesque farm country and is compacted between steep canyon walls for several miles to the take-out at Elko Provincial Park. The bottom structure of the river does change, however, from sand and gravel to become more rocky.

There are good hatches of may flies, caddis and some golden stones here, and in the spring large stone flies emerge. This is also where the largest west-slopes hang out. For dry-fly enthusiasts, Adams, Elk Hair Caddis, Irresistibles and low-water patterns like Stimulators and Parachute Hoppers are excellent throughout summer and early fall. While 100-fish days have been recorded along this stretch, a more typical day would be 25–30 cutthroat with a couple of them over 18" (46 cm).

Although fishing pressure on the Elk has recently increased dramatically, it still isn't anything close to the crowds found on premium fisheries in Montana or elsewhere in the States. Plan to start here any time after July 4th, when the spring runoff recedes, and fish right through mid-October when bulls of monumental proportion become extremely aggressive just prior to spawning.

St. Mary River

PROBABLY THE MOST PRODUCTIVE westslope cutthroat river in British Columbia is the St. Mary below Kimberley in the Purcell Mountains. It is characteristic of rivers on the eastern slope of the Columbia Trench: classic, clear, freestone water with excellent hatches of may flies, caddis and stone flies. Like the Elk it can be divided into three different zones.

The upper river above St. Mary Lake is more like a tumbling mountain stream: small, steep, swift, confined and crystalline. There is limited road access and it's brushy, so even if you make it to the water, casting is very difficult. Big cutts up here get to be about 9" (23 cm), but they are eager and act more like little rainbows than the usually deliberate cutthroats.

The middle section begins at the lake outlet. From there for the next 16 miles (26 km) or so to Wycliffe, the river takes on more archetypal western river attributes, with dozens of braided channels containing great pools and runs, and most of it designated fly fishing only. From Mark Creek below Marysville power station to the McPhee Bridge on Highway 95A, all trout and char must be released. As with everywhere on the St. Mary, only one single hook can be used per line. Again, dry patterns that match the hatches—attractors, Prince Nymphs, Pheasant Tail Nymphs, Hare's Ears and a variety of Bead-head Nymphs—will consistently take westslopes.

Below Wycliffe, the river enters a canyon with limited access until it reaches the bridge at St. Eugene Mission. Fishing in the canyon can be excellent, but once you've entered, you are locked into going several miles down the river unless a half-mile hike straight up turns your crank.

Mission Bridge to the confluence with Kootenay River at the top end of

Lake Koocanusa makes up the third zone of this river. This is fairly flat country, similar to the farmland middle section of the Elk. Several kilometers of gravel dropped over countless high-water seasons form long, wonderful bars and drop-offs, steep banks, pools, and runs that change every spring. Down here, so close to the huge Kootenay River that drains much of southeastern British Columbia, the mix of trout includes Blackwater and Kamloops rainbows, westslopes, bull trout, brook trout, mountain and lake whitefish, and probably several other species. All come to the fly, and the strike will often indicate the model of fish you've hooked. Everything from tiny Pale Morning Duns to big Hopper patterns elicit the slow roll and deliberate take of a cutthroat, which then hammers it out below the surface. Kamloops rainbows sip or slash, then rip line and do cartwheels, while Blackwaters grab fiercely and run. Whitefish nearly always take small patterns softly, but give a good accounting of themselves. Big Muddlers, Buggers, and minnow patterns bring no-nonsense takes from bulls that whip their heads and writhe.

After the St. Mary joins the Kootenay, the tiny take-out area is about 1 mile (1.6 km) on down the Kootenay across from Fort Steele—and it's tricky. If you miss it, there isn't much you can do except drag your boat up a steep, rocky bank and through trees. Also, most of the land along the lower stretch is private, so wade fishing is not a practical option. If you decide to drift this section of the river, you are strongly advised to use a local guide.

Other Waters

AGAIN, WE'VE TOUCHED ON only a fraction of the waters available in this British Columbia–Alberta–Montana region. There are many other excellent places, and one of the best methods of "discovering" good fishing water is to get a topographical map, then trace the tributaries of major rivers and lakes known to contain the species you want to go after. You won't find truly virginal water, but the fishing just might be better than you ever dreamed. And remember, because native westslopes and bulls are so predictable, what works on them in one piece of water will generally work elsewhere with minor pattern and presentation adjustments.

One final word: because bull trout are too close to becoming threatened or endangered over such a wide range, of the two game fish discussed here, probably only westslopes should be actively pursued.

Jim Crawford's Must-Have Patterns for Westslope Cutthroats and Bull Trout

- Dry: Adams
- Elk Hair Caddis
- Hopper
- Humpy
- Irresistible
- Parachute Hopper
- Stimulator
- Nymph: Bead-Head Nymph
- Hare's Ear
- Pheasant Tail Nymph
- Prince Nymph
- Streamer: Muddler
- Woolly Bugger
- Zonker

CHAPTER 43

STILLWATER TECHNIQUES FOR RAINBOWS AND BROOK TROUT

Brian Chan

C ANADA IS CERTAINLY WELL ENDOWED WITH FRESHWATER fishing opportunities. One of our most abundant fishing resources in this country is the virtually hundreds of thousands of lakes that support a multitude of fish species. This chapter will focus on those smaller lakes frequented by rainbow and brook trout, one or both of which species are found in some lakes and streams in every province.

The natural distribution of rainbow trout was originally confined to the Pacific slopes of North America, while that of brook trout was east of the Great Lakes. The popularity of both of these salmonids as sport fish resulted in widespread introductions across the country, beginning as far back as the late 1800s.

Although both are called trout, rainbows and brookies are taxonomically quite different. Rainbows have recently been reclassified into the *Onchorynchus* or Pacific salmon genus because of their more common ancestral lines to that family rather than with brown trout and Atlantic salmon. Brook trout are members of the char family, *Salvelinus,* which also includes lake trout, bull trout, Dolly Varden and arctic char. The major physiological difference is that rainbows spawn during the spring months and brook trout in the fall. Both are considered opportunistic feeders, with aquatic and terrestrial invertebrates (including insects) making up a large portion of their respective diets. In multi-species lakes, larger, more aggressive rainbows and brookies will feed on forage fish such as members of the minnow (shiners, chubs, suckers), alewife and smelt families.

I consider a small lake to be one with less than 500 acres (202 hectares), or those waters small enough to still get around easily in a cartop boat with a small outboard motor. The lake may have permanent inlet and outlet streams, which provide natural spawning areas as well as ensuring adequate circulation of the lake water. Other small lakes are landlocked or have only intermittent creek systems. These are typically much more productive than lakes with permanent creek systems as there is little or no flushing of water, thus dissolved nutrients are recycled and accumulate over time. Lakes with higher levels of basic elements like calcium, phosphorus and nitrogen, have the ability to grow more invertebrates or fish food, thus the opportunity for larger fish sizes.

In my mind the ideal rainbow or brook-trout lake has a surface area of about 150 acres (60 hectares), a maximum depth of 70' (21 m) and an average depth of 20' (6 m) or less. This lake would also have a small seasonal inlet and outlet creek, and there would be extensive areas of shallow water known as the littoral or shoal zone. Shoals are extremely important to the overall productivity of a lake because light can penetrate to the lake bottom and allow photosynthesis to occur. This results in rooted and floating plant growth such as pondweed, milfoil and lily pads, the sort of lush vegetation that provides habitat for much of the food sources of trout and char.

Food Sources

KNOWING THE FOOD BASE in a lake is the first step toward becoming successful at catching fish. Freshwater shrimp, midges or chironomids, may flies, damsel flies, dragonflies, caddis flies and leeches are staple food items of both rainbow and brook trout. Some or all of these invertebrates are found in small lakes across the country. Becoming familiar with the various aquatic insect and crustacean life cycles and their habitat preferences in a lake tells an angler where the trout and char will be feeding. Similarly, understanding the life histories of forage fish, including their feeding and schooling habits, will help determine when and where to use baitfish imitations.

Freshwater Shrimp

FRESHWATER SHRIMP are a major food source in many of the most productive lakes of the western provinces. They inhabit lakes with neutral to alkaline waters and high concentrations of dissolved calcium, which is critical to maintaining the chitinous exoskeleton of these freshwater crustaceans. Shrimp live amongst the submerged aquatic vegetation, woody debris and bottom substrate of the shoal areas in a lake. They mate many times during the year and are always available as a food source. Adult gammarus shrimp can reach over ⅝" (16 mm) in length, and the most common colors encountered are olive to dark green. Shrimp propel themselves through the water using a series of swimmerets on the underside of their body, so their movement is best imitated by using 2–4" (5–10-cm) long, slow, strip retrieves. As imitations should be fished close to the bottom of a shoal, intermediate- and slow-sinking fly lines are perfect for a proper presentation.

Midges or Chironomids

MIDGES OR CHIRONOMIDS are the first major aquatic insect hatch of the year in lakes, and emergences continue throughout the open-water period. Adult chironomids, ⅛–¾" (3–20 mm) in body length, are similar in appearance to mosquitoes, the major difference being a female midge does not bite. Stillwater populations are often very abundant with numerous species found in the same body of water.

Trout and char really focus their feeding attention on the larval and pupal stages of this insect. Chironomid larvae, which look like thin, segmented worms, live in tubes situated in the bottom substrate. The most abundant populations are found at the bottom of the shoal zone, so fish cruise just off the bottom and hunt out the larvae as they peer from their tubes. Common larval colors are maroon and green, or a combination of these two colors. Chironomid larvae transform into the pupal stage within the larval tube. Fully developed pupae then leave their tubes and rise to the surface to emerge into the adult stage. Common pupal colors are various shades of green, brown, maroon and black.

A good chironomid hatch would see hundreds of thousands of pupa rising helplessly through the water column as ravenous trout gorge on them. Because so much chironomid habitat is in the shoal zone, or in water that is 25' (7.5 m) deep or less, a floating line is perfect for fishing both larval and pupal imitations. It may be used with various leader lengths, with weighted or unweighted flies, to fish any depth range on the shoal. Fish will feed on the rising pupae at very precise or narrow depth zones within the water column. Anglers should start out by fishing a pupa close to the bottom, then gradually fish it shallower.

The chironomid retrieve is extremely slow, or the fly is "dead-drifted"— fished with no retrieve. When the fish are very selective in depth, a strike indicator can be used with great success. The indicator acts as a small bobber, one that keeps your fly suspended at the exact depth the fish want to eat the real chironomid pupae. The other key to being successful at chironomid pupal fishing is matching, as closely as possible, the size and color of the particular species emerging that day. Observant anglers use small aquarium nets to scoop pupae and adults from the water to most accurately identify the hatch.

May Flies

MAY FLIES ARE COMMON INSECTS to small stillwaters, lakes and slow-moving waters, where anglers should expect to see nymphs ⅛–½" (5–12 mm) long. *Callibaetis* (speckle-winged) may flies are probably the most prevalent species found across Canada, but are most abundant in nutrient-rich lakes of the western provinces, where nymphs and adults are ¼–½" (6–12 mm) in length. Ideal habitat includes the lush vegetation growing on shoal areas of a lake and the silty, sandy or gravel-covered bottoms of shoals. Fully developed nymphs typically swim toward the surface in 2–4" (5–10-cm) bursts and emerge into the dun phase of an adult.

Migrating nymphs make very easy meals for cruising rainbows and brookies, and newly emerged adults sitting in the surface film are also easy targets. A floating fly line works well for both nymphal and adult may-fly imitations. Weighted nymph patterns and longer leaders will help you effectively fish the deeper parts of a shoal. Imitating a newly emerged dun requires a full-floating fly and often some pinpoint casting accuracy as you anticipate the next rise of an actively feeding fish.

Caddis Flies

CADDIS FLIES are those aquatic insects whose larval stage build and live in portable houses or cases made of bits of vegetation or sand particles. A caddis fly hatch provides some of the best dry-fly action of the fishing season. Several species of lake-dwelling caddis flies have adult stages with bodies exceeding 1" (25 mm) in length. These large, newly emerged adults virtually run across the water in their attempts to get airborne, and this scampering action drives trout and char crazy as anglers have witnessed during their very aggressive feeding rises.

Fish also feed on the larval and pupal stages of caddis flies, so it is important to understand their complete life cycle. Caddis fly larvae crawl along the bottom of the shoal zone, leaving distinctive trails as they seek food in the form of detritus and the carcasses of fish or other animals that may have succumbed in the water. Rainbows and brookies search out caddis fly larvae and ingest the complete larval case. Fishing a larva imitation means using either a slow-sinking line that gets your fly down, or a floating line with a weighted pattern on a long leader. Whichever technique is used, the fly must be presented as close to the bottom as possible.

The larvae eventually mature and transform into the pupal stage while still in their larval house or case. A fully developed pupa works its way out of the larval case, then using a pair of oar-shaped legs, propels itself upward to the surface. Fish feed aggressively on these swimming pupae because they are easy to catch and also because feeding can be done sub-surface, which reduces their exposure to predators.

The caddis pupa swim to the surface is best duplicated with intermediate- or slow-sinking lines. Allow your fly to sink to the bottom of a shoal, then initiate a fast-strip retrieve of 2–4" (5–10-cm) pulls. Once a pupa reaches the surface film, the adult caddis fly crawls out of its old pupal husk, dries its wings, then attempts to get airborne.

Imitating the adult caddis requires a floating line and dry flies. You will know adult caddis are being eaten by the slashing, swirling rises seen all along a shoal. Watch for individual fish rising and feeding in a particular direction, then cast ahead of it and begin a fast 2–4" (5–10-cm) -long hand-strip to imitate that scampering motion of the real insect. Sometimes rainbows and brookies will swirl over the real fly to drown it, then pick it up just subsurface. If you appear to get continual strikes but don't hook a fish, try letting the fly sit after the initial rise—and be prepared for the return strike.

Damsel Flies and Dragonflies

DAMSEL FLIES AND DRAGONFLIES are also very common inhabitants of the shoal zone of nutrient-rich lakes. Both of these aquatic insects are long-lived, spending as many as four years in the nymphal stage before emerging. As adults they may survive well into the fall months of the year they hatch before succumbing to cold air temperatures. Several damsel fly species inhabit lakes within Canada, and anglers should expect to see nymphs of up to 1" (25 mm) long.

Their most common colors are light olive to dark green and various shades of brown. Damsel fly nymphs seek lush, submerged vegetation where they can prey on shrimp and nymphs. When mature, a nymph swims up to within 2–3' (60–90 cm) of the surface, then swims horizontally until reaching a stem of bulrush, cattail or some other plant that is growing out of the water. It then crawls up the plant stem and out of the water, after which its nymphal skin splits and the adult form emerges.

Rainbows and brookies feed heavily on may fly nymphs as they migrate en masse to emerge. Floating and intermediate-sinking are the fly lines of choice to fish the emergence swim of these slender nymphs. The observant angler will see damsel fly nymphs swimming slowly in a sinusoidal motion just under the surface and realize what is happening.

Dragonfly nymphs also hunt their prey within vegetation-covered shoal areas. These robust nymphs reach over 1 ¾" (45 mm) in length and prey on anything smaller than themselves. Their preferred diet items are shrimp and may fly nymphs. When fully developed, the nymphs will crawl or swim along the bottom of a shoal to the lake's edge. There they crawl out of the water onto some shoreline vegetation where the adult form emerges from the old nymphal skin. Anglers will see these cast nymphal cases strewn about the shoreline vegetation. Typical emergences result in large numbers of nymphs, during which trout and char typically have major feeding frenzies. Dragonflies emerge all summer long, but the most intense hatches occur during about a two-week period in early summer. Slow- and fast-sinking fly lines will get your dragonfly nymph down to the bottom. Combine this retrieve with slow, 1 ½–3" (38–75 mm) hand-strips to imitate their real movement pattern.

Leeches

MANY SPECIES OF FRESHWATER FISH love eating leeches, and rainbow and brook trout are no exception. Leeches are present in most lakes and very abundant in small, nutrient-rich stillwaters. They can be found swimming almost anywhere in a lake, but prefer spending most of their time hiding under rocks, logs or clumps of vegetation, and are usually more active at night.

Leeches swim in an up-down sinusoidal motion and when fully extended can reach over 4" (10 cm) in length. Common colors are mottled brown and green, black, and maroon. It's a good rule to fish leech patterns whenever you see them swimming as there are probably many more moving around than the one or two you may observe. The best place to fish leech patterns is on a shoal or close to the bottom along the deeper edges of a shoal. Try using slow- to fast-sinking lines and wait long enough for your fly to reach bottom before initiating a retrieve. A fairly slow hand-twist or hand-strip retrieve of 2 ½–5" (6–12 cm), along with occasional twitches of the rod tip, will provide the right action to your fly.

Baitfish

MINNOWS OR BAITFISH are present in many lakes inhabited by rainbows and brookies and become important food items when trout and char become large enough to eat them. Many minnow species show schooling tendencies, which makes them easier targets for foraging predators. Minnow-feeding fish reveal to an angler several tips about what is occurring, or what their feeding strategy is at that particular time. Typically, one sees baitfish fleeing in all directions, even jumping clear of the water as they are being chased, while at other times, although unseen, they will be just ahead of a swirling, slashing fish.

Depth sounders or fish finders can be valuable for finding baitfish and those predators following close behind. Floating and various density sinking lines used with appropriately sized and colored baitfish imitations offer some very exciting fly-fishing opportunities. The key is either to place a fly ahead of a surface-feeding fish, then entice a strike by quickly stripping it past the fish, or to cast a sinking line beneath located schools of baitfish, then strip your fly up through the school. Either method means being quick on the cast and maintaining a fast-paced retrieve.

Equipment Selection

A GOOD ALL-ROUND FLY ROD for rainbow and brook trout in small lakes is 9–9 ½' long, matched to a 6–7-weight line. You may want to consider a graphite rod as they are light and load a fly line easily, making them much more enjoyable to cast. Shop around and find the best deal you can on a good quality graphite rod with a reasonable warranty. It's usually a case of "you get what you pay for."

Select a reel that will hold the weight class of fly line chosen, plus at least 75 yards (70 m) of 20-lb test backing. Basic fly lines required to match the various insect hatches and other food that trout and char eat include floating, intermediate- or slow-sinking, and fast- or extra-fast-sinking. Carry your extra lines on spare reel spools so quick line changes can be made as feeding patterns shift.

Most lake fly-fishing situations mean fishing out of a boat, canoe or float tube. Whichever you choose, there is some basic equipment that should be in your fishing craft to make you more efficient on the water. Being well anchored is very important to ensure the proper presentation of the various insect life stages that have been discussed, for a boat that does not move means you have the best control over your retrieves and detection of strikes. Cartop boats or canoes should be double-anchored (bow and stern), so the craft does not move around whenever the wind direction shifts. Float tubes and pontoon boats require only one anchor as you can compensate for wind changes by using your flippers.

Place some outdoor carpeting on the floor of your boat or canoe. This protects your fly lines and reduces or muffles any sounds you make. Remember that sound travels faster and louder in water than in air and that fish have excellent hearing abilities. Carry a landing net to make it easier to land your fish and to handle them for quick, efficient releases. Select a net with small-diameter mesh fashioned from soft cotton or soft, knotless nylon. These materials limit the abrasion on a fish's skin, reducing the loss of their protective layer of slime. Finally, use barbless hooks to make the release of your catch easier—on you and the fish.

BRIAN CHAN'S MUST-HAVE PATTERNS FOR INTERIOR TROUT

- Dry: Lady McConnell
- Parachute Adams
- Tom Thumb
- Wet: Baggy Shrimp
- Bead Head Leech, Maroon
- Blood Worm
- Chironomid Pupa, Black
- Halfback
- Kamloops Caddis Pupa

CHAPTER 44

WIND BLOWING? START TROLLING!

Robert H. Jones

C ASTING FLIES WITH A WELL-BALANCED OUTFIT IS ONE OF life's joys, especially when the fish are cooperating. However, when the wind starts blowing, pleasure decreases in direct proportion to its speed and intensity. You have two choices: give up or troll.

If you opt for the latter, select patterns with bulk, like leeches or dragonfly nymphs. Two standby patterns are the Woolly Worm in black, "muddy" maroon, olive-green and olive-gold, plus the Carey Special in various color combinations. I favor a peacock herl body with a hackle of blue-phase pheasant rump feather. Simple, easy to tie and effective.

If the lake contains Blackwater or Tzenzaicut strain rainbows, cutthroat trout, Dolly Varden or bull trout, bear in mind that all are meat eaters, preferring small fish to aquatic insects or invertebrates. Use streamer patterns that represent shiners, sticklebacks, sculpins, or juvenile suckers, squawfish or salmonids—whichever are most common. Dependable patterns usually incorporate a silver body with a light-colored hair underwing, darker-colored top wing, and a few strands of Krystal Flash or Flashabou. An exception is the Muddler Minnow and its many offspring—sculpin imitations that use natural-colored turkey wing and deer hair.

As all of these critters are found close to the bottom, a full-sink line is a better choice than a sink-tip. In most cases, a 9' leader is sufficient.

Seek areas offering protection from the wind's direct force—behind an island or in the lee of a peninsula or irregular shoreline.

Trolling without a motor may pose problems while fishing alone and lacking a rod holder because you need both hands free to row or paddle (I like the Scotty 265 Fly Rod Holder). Place the rod handle on the deck between your feet, with the reel handles facing upward and the rod tip hanging straight back over the stern. Set the reel's drag lightly and depend on the ratchet to prevent overruns. This allows you to row slowly or control the drift as required. Don't worry about setting the hook if a fish hits—in most cases the boat's momentum will do the job.

No, it isn't fly fishing in the true sense, but it beats not fishing at all.

Robert H. Jones' Must-Have Trolling Patterns For Rainbows and Brookies

- Carey Special
- Muddler Minnow
- Woolly Worm (black, maroon, olive)

Poached Rainbow Trout

Brings out the natural flavor
(Makes four servings)

1 large or 4 small pan-sized trout
2 tbsp—olive oil—30 mL
½–1 cup—each chopped onion, carrot and celery—125–250 mL
1–2 cups—liquid (white wine, fish stock, water)—250–500 mL
(or 50/50 wine and water)
Salt and pepper to taste
2 sprigs—fresh herbs (thyme, dill or tarragon)
1 lemon, thinly sliced

1. Clean fish, wash and pat dry.

2. Heat olive oil in poacher. Sauté vegetables in oil for 5 minutes, add liquid and bring to a slow simmer.

2. Season inside of trout with salt and pepper to taste; then place on rack. With a slotted spoon, remove some vegetables from the stock and place in the cavity, adding some thyme and lemon slices. Place a few lemon slices on top of the trout, and add remainder to the stock. Lower rack into the stock and cover poacher. Bring to a simmer (never boil) and poach until fish is opaque. This method takes somewhat longer to cook fish, so check often by probing at the thickest part.

3. Remove rack and carefully transfer trout to a large plate. While fish is still hot, remove skin from the top side only. Remove and discard vegetable stuffing from the cavity. Place trout on a platter and garnish with herbs and fresh lemon slices.

4. Serve with a simple mayonnaise sauce made from fresh minced dill (tarragon, or chives) with lemon juice and mayonnaise. Thin with white wine if required. A dash of hot sauce helps heighten flavors.

If lacking a fish poacher, use a roasting pan with a rack.

–Wayne Phillips

CHAPTER 45

KOKANEE!

Brian Chan

KOKANEE ARE LANDLOCKED DESCENDANTS OF SOCKEYE salmon and even share the Latin designation *Oncorhynchus nerka.* They are generally found in large, relatively unproductive lakes or reservoirs where their food base is a range of zooplankton that occurs at varying depths. Zooplankton are those tiny, red, green or translucent organisms often seen suspended or twitching through the water.

Typically, these fish are ½–1 ½ lb (225–675 g), and the most popular fishing tactic consists of trolling a small, fluorescent green or pink spoon or plug, trailing it behind a small willow-leaf troll or similar attractor. The lures may also be baited with worms or maggots. Definitely not much there of interest to fly fishers, but bear with me—it gets better. . . .

Fisheries' managers have worked with the Provincial Fish Culture Program toward developing a small-lakes kokanee stocking program in the southern and central British Columbia Interior. Individual lakes are assessed to determine their ability to support kokanee and maintain a sport fishery. All of these waters are nutrient rich and support high densities of zooplankton, plus an abundance of major aquatic invertebrates that form the diet of rainbow trout and other salmonids present in the system. Kokanee have flourished in these waters and with no detrimental effects to existing rainbow or char fisheries.

A major surprise to anglers was the switch in diet made by introduced kokanee. Once large enough, they began moving from zooplankton to larger invertebrates like chironomid larvae and pupae and the nymphs of may flies and damsel flies. This came to light when fly fishers targeting rainbow trout began catching kokanee. To make things even more interesting, these fish were attaining weights in excess of 3 lb (1.4 kg). Their acrobatic fighting abilities and excellent taste as table fare caught the attention of even the most diehard rainbow anglers. Word spread quickly, and many devoted kokanee fly fishers now frequent these waters.

In large lakes, kokanee are usually found in deep water as they follow the daily vertical migration patterns of zooplankton. They have, however, adapted amazingly well to small lakes. Feeding on chironomids, may flies and damsel flies means spending time in the shallow shoal zones of a lake, which is why fly fishers are successful at intercepting them.

Kokanee are a schooling species, so angling success depends on finding a school and staying with it. On small lakes this means paying particular attention to the location of insect emergences. Keeping a sharp lookout for chironomid or may fly adults, then fishing directly over these hatches provides the best chances of finding kokanee (and rainbows). As swallows, nighthawks and gulls are very adapted at locating recent insect hatches, binoculars are an essential tool for searching out potential action spots.

Fly-fishing tactics are similar to those used for rainbow trout, but a major consideration is that the soft mouths of kokanee require more care while playing them. This poses a problem as they basically go crazy once hooked. Kokanee jump, make long runs and always seem to know where the anchor ropes are hanging. To increase the percentage of fish landed, tie in a 6" (15 cm) length of Shock Gum about halfway down the leader. This "shock absorber" really comes into play when a kokanee is close enough to see the boat and starts a series of twisting roll-overs in a final attempt to get free.

The same chironomid, may fly and damsel fly patterns used for trout will work for kokanee, but always ensure the hooks are extra sharp. Their takes are often very soft or subtle, so it is essential that a straight-line connection between fly line and leader be maintained at all times during a retrieve. This means taking a few minutes before starting to fish to stretch out any coils or memory in your line or leader. Also, during retrieves, remember to point your rod tip right at the water to maintain that straight-line connection.

When fishing from a boat, always use the double-anchoring system—one from the bow and one from the stern—so your boat remains in the same position despite changes in wind direction. Floating, intermediate-sinking and fast-sinking lines all work at various times. By midsummer, when water temperatures on the shoals become too warm for kokanee, they concentrate in deeper areas just off the drop-off zones. In these cases, fish finders become an important tool in locating them.

Some kokanee lakes to consider include Bridge, Horse and Deka in the vicinity of 100 Mile House in the Cariboo, and Stump Lake located south of the city of Kamloops. These lakes are large enough that a cartopper with a small outboard are required to move quickly from shoal to shoal.

A final tip: Kokanee are ultra-cautious in shallow water, so if they are feeding on chironomid pupa in water less than about 16' (5 m) deep, consider using a strike indicator. You must pay close attention the indicator as a soft take may register as only a slight sideways movement. When a bright-silver fish rockets 5' (1.5 m) into the air to confirm the strike, get ready for a truly memorable scrap.

CHAPTER 46

JACK SHAW:
THE FATHER OF CHIRONOMID FISHING

Robert H. Jones

T HE INVENTOR'S NAME APPEARING MOST OFTEN IN THE FLY
patterns chapter is Jack Shaw; however, nine patterns represent but a
few of those developed by the man many consider to be the "father of
chironomid fishing."

Born in 1916 in Montreal, Quebec, Jack was 9 years old when his parents
moved to Burnaby, British Columbia, where his lifelong passion for fishing
began in the local creeks. He left school at age 11 and entered the work force,
but continued fishing whenever possible.

After moving to Kamloops in 1940, Jack met Dorothy Lawrence and they
married in 1942. He also discovered fly fishing, which led to tying flies. He
quickly determined that imitative patterns produced more consistent results
than attractor patterns, so in order to learn more about the insects he wanted to
duplicate, he acquired the first of several aquariums. For years thereafter, hatches of may flies, damsels, dragonflies, caddis and chironomids flitting throughout their house became common occurrences, even in midwinter. In the meantime, by studying aquatic insects in their environment, Jack learned to imitate
their movements through manipulation of his line and rod tip.

Although several productive new patterns evolved from his observations, his
dissatisfaction with their colors led to photographing the insects. He eventual-

ly elevated this to an art form by capturing amazingly detailed close-ups of swimming insects, then enlarging them to large Cibachrome prints. By 1962 Jack was using a series of chironomid patterns he had developed, but it wasn't until 1966 while working at Burfield's Ski and Sport Shop in Kamloops that he introduced them to anglers. He taught night school fly-tying classes for 15 years, and three of his students are contributors to this book: Brian Chan, Jim Crawford and Ralph Shaw. (Although not related, Jack and Ralph were the closest of friends and fishing companions.)

He was the author of two popular best sellers: *Fly-Fish the Trout Lakes with Jack Shaw* and *Tying Flies for Trophy Trout,* both of which are still in print. As well, he was a frequent contributor to *BC Outdoors* magazine. Author, photographer, teacher, conservationist and a highly respected amateur entomologist, Jack Shaw spent a lifetime sharing his knowledge with others. With his passing on February 2, 2000, an important page in British Columbia's fly-fishing history was turned, but his written words and fly patterns have left a legacy that will last forever.

CHAPTER 47

VANCOUVER'S URBAN TROUT FISHING . . . AND BEYOND

George Will

O NE OF THE THINGS I REALLY LOVED ABOUT LIVING IN Vancouver was that whenever I was overtaken by urban angst, no matter what time of year—weather notwithstanding—within minutes I could be flicking flies over the surface of some bit of water. The places I am about to describe only hint at the variety of fishing opportunities in the region and are simply some of my personal favorites. Some of the stillwaters can be fished from shore, but a float tube, canoe or small cartopper will make the world of difference.

There are about a dozen shallow, low-elevation lakes in the Fraser Valley. Mill Lake in Abbotsford is typical. It's hidden in a little municipal park behind the Seven Oaks shopping mall, just off the Fraser Highway. The lake is surrounded on three sides by housing, but there is a parking lot and boat launching ramp (motors prohibited).

It's very weedy along the edges, which makes casting from shore difficult. Wind is seldom a problem, so this is a good candidate for tubing. About 50 acres (20 hectares) in area, less than 350 yards (320 m) across and 700 yards (640 m) long, Mill Lake is shallow—about 30' (9 m), tops—and its long axis is southwest–northeast. The bottom is fairly dark and the water tea-colored. There are good insect hatches, especially chironomids. Rainbow trout predominate but there are also crappie, which readily take flies, plus goldfish and catfish. Sorry, I have no productive patterns for the latter to offer.

This little lake has afforded me some of the biggest surprises of my angling career. There are a few trout in there that would have even the most ardent Interior-lake devotee salivating. Each spring, some brood stock from the Inch Creek hatchery are included with the tens of thousands of 10" (25-cm) stock used to replenish the lake. Local anglers have photos of trout in the 8-lb (3.6-kg) -plus range which, alas, most often fell to worm-drowners—but I know of several whales that were hooked on flies. A few hints about Mill Lake: You must have a boat or float tube; you should fish close to the weed beds; and finally, you should know how to fish chironomids just under the surface.

The trout are very active in the early spring. By early summer the fishing gets lousy due to weeds and warm water, but it picks up again in late fall. Insect hatches are irregular, and when the trout feed it's usually voraciously and in quick bursts. You must observe these feeding patterns closely and be ready to change flies in an instant. Carry a range of chironomid patterns in No. 14–10, ranging from orange through brown shades to black. Don't drop a dry fly on every rising fish, for more often than not they are slurping midge larvae just below the surface. A good technique is to observe the direction a particular fish is moving, then cast a chironomid just ahead of it and carefully watch your leader for the slightest twitch. Another hint—grease your very long (12–20' / 3.6–6 m) leader right up to the fly so it hangs just under the surface film.

The same comments apply to most other shallow lakes in the region, including Deer Lake and Burnaby Lake (right inside Greater Vancouver). Traveling east on Highway 7 along the south shore of the Fraser River and hanging a left at Whonnock leads you to Whonnock Lake, which is full of black crappie and good numbers of cutthroat and rainbow trout. Dark flies tend to do the trick for the trout—a Black Gnat fished dry or a Doc Spratley will cover most situations. The crappies—some of which would qualify as "slabs" in southern climes—eagerly take small yellow and white bucktails.

There are several other lakes off Highway 7, but one worthy of mention is Sayers (Cedar) Lake, north of Mission. This is in a restricted area that is open only from 6:00 A.M. to 6:00 P.M. except weekends and holidays. To get there you must sign in at the Stave Falls Prison Camp, during which procedure your vehicle might be searched. Why put up with this hassle? Because this small lake offers cutthroat, Dolly Varden and a few brook trout, plus rainbows—not just any rainbows, but dropouts from the Fraser Valley Trout Hatchery net pens that are positioned in the lake. They are obviously well fed, for trout to 17 lb (8 kg) have been reported.

There are also quite a few small, higher-elevation lakes located in the eastern portion of the Fraser Valley. Lindeman Lake, one of the most accessible, is typical of many of the region's mountain lakes. To get there, turn right off the Trans-Canada at Sardis, proceed south to Vedder Crossing, then turn left along the Chilliwack Lake road. After about 24 miles (39 km), keep your eyes peeled for a small road leading off to the left (sometimes there is a sign, sometimes not). Park in the Post Creek Campground and hike the trail. It's a steep trek in places, but only 1 mile (1.6 km), so you should make it in a half hour if you aren't a tobacco freak. If you didn't lug in your float tube, the best fishing is from the rocks at the north end.

The first time I visited Lindeman Lake was on a hot July day in the mid-1970s. Upon arriving, I was deeply impressed by the water's turquoise brilliance, the vista marred only by a half-submerged sleeping bag (there must have been a story there). The trail, such as it was, continued around the left side of the lake to an area of freshly fallen boulders (some nervous looks upward at this point). As I made my way along the rocks, I could see a few fathoms down into the depths and immediately noticed the cruising shapes of innumerable trout.

With the sense of immediacy and panic that only anglers can appreciate, I set up my gear, cursing as I missed guides and fumbled with flies and knots. I began with a dark-colored dry fly (a Black Bivisible, I think), and those poor starving trout. . . . You would think they had never seen food before! Once I switched to a small, dark, caddis imitation, they swarmed it, several trying to grab it at the same time. To cut a short story even shorter, I had a field day.

On other occasions, a green caddis nymph retrieved slowly worked well. Tips: Pack out your garbage, watch your back-cast, and take a camera. About 2 miles (3.2 km) farther along the trail that takes you to Lindeman, and maybe 600' (180 m) higher in elevation, is Greendrop Lake, which offers more of the same type of fishing for rainbows to 1' (30 cm) long or better.

For those who love to fish moving water, the Lower Mainland offers almost endless opportunities from the mighty Fraser to classic mountain streams. A few of the better waters are found within the Vancouver city limits. Two of my favorites, the Capilano and Seymour, are located on the north shore. As it was near my home, I fished the Capilano a lot.

Once a classic salmon and steelhead stream, the Cap is now truncated by the Cleveland Dam. Fortunately, Fisheries and Oceans Canada established a huge hatchery just below the dam, about 4 miles (6.5 km) from the saltchuck. Access is difficult from Keith Road to Capilano Canyon Park because of private residences. Most of the river is boulder-strewn with plentiful rapids and pools in the upper section, and the water level is controlled by the dam. It is generally fishable except during heavy runoff periods, but high water often means looking out for kayakers and other crazies in rubber rafts.

I fish the Capilano in two areas only—the mouth and the canyon. The mouth contains cutthroat and, in season, staging salmon and a few steelhead. There I anchor my boat out of range of the snaggers and cast flies to the milling salmon, which arrive in late summer and fall. The phenomenal success of the salmon-enhancement program has meant that thousands of adult coho return to the Capilano every few years to spawn and die (they don't really get to spawn, just die). I have found fishing at the mouth best around high tide. Often, there are dozens of leaping fish in the air at the same time, and lustful males will attack anything they suspect is interfering with their chances with the females. Both males and females lash out at anything they believe may endanger their eggs (usually cutthroat trout). Color is the key to making a coho bite: Silver, orange, red and yellow seem to do the trick, particularly the fluorescent versions.

So, there I am anchored at the river mouth, flinging bucktails at passing coho. Every so often there is a mighty tug at the end of my line, and around 10 lb (4.5 kg) of streamlined silver launches into the air. While I play the fish, I shift my gaze upward to a seemingly endless stream of cars whizzing back and forth over the Lions Gate Bridge. Talk about surreal experiences.

Fishing Capilano Canyon is another story—there are deep pools and precipitous rapids (watch your footing here). When fish are in the river, space is at a premium. Favored spots like the Cable and Dog Leg pools are lined with anglers. I prefer some of the downstream pools, which are less crowded and offer better opportunities for fly fishing (a fast-sinking line is essential). They require a bit of a hike, but as the trails in the park are in great shape and are very scenic, who complains about a little exercise? Anyway, the canyon section is normally closed to salmon fishing in the fall (only when there are strong fish returns do they open it up). There are always plenty of cutthroat, though, and a few steelhead in the winter and early spring.

P.S. It is absolutely mandatory to take all out-of-town visitors to the hatchery. It blows their minds.

The Seymour River is much the same as the Cap, but a little wilder and with more hiking required. The winter steelhead run is much stronger, and there is a huge run of pink salmon on each odd year. A small pink bucktail is very effective when they are milling around in the estuary.

There are several classic trout streams farther out in the Valley. Some contain salmon and steelhead as well as trout. The Skagit River has native rainbows, Dolly Varden, a few bull trout, and even some leftover brook trout from a long-ago introduction. A real gem—in fact, it is still my favorite trout stream on this planet.

Located just west of Hope at the extreme eastern end of the Valley, the Skagit is about a two-hour drive from Vancouver. You can access the upper river from the Hope–Princeton Highway or from the Skagit Valley Road. To reach the 26 Mile Bridge, where I normally park, requires about a 25 mile (40 km) drive on gravel. The bridge is just east of the confluence of the Klesilkwa and the Skagit. From there, downstream, the river almost doubles in size. It can be floated but with extreme caution as there are numerous log jams.

There are access points all the way downstream to Ross Lake. The Skagit features clear, cold water and a freestone bottom. It twists and turns for over 30 miles (48 km) through pristine first-growth forest, providing an endless series of rapids and pools. To say it is beautiful would be a gross understatement.

Water level is the real determining factor for fishing the Skagit. The spring freshet often continues well into summer, but one can usually begin to wade safely by mid-July, and from then on until freeze-up.

There are excellent insect hatches, including may flies, stone flies and caddis. During rises the flies of choice are a No. 18–16 Adams or a No. 12 Deer Hair Sedge. When there is no visible action, stone fly or sedge nymphs can be drifted in the deeper runs and pocket water. But this is a truly classic dry-fly stream, so between the rises I usually just sit and look around me. The scenery is spectacular and the wildlife very approachable. I once shared the same run with a black bear and a small herd of black-tailed deer, as well as a kingfisher and a bald eagle.

There are really no other rivers to compare to the Skagit, but a few others in the Valley have their own particular charms. The Vedder offers huge runs of enhanced coho and steelhead. The lower, easily accessible stretches are often crowded, but there are places upstream where you can have beautiful runs all to yourself. They take a bit of legwork to hike into and some clambering down and back up steep cliffs, but it can be rewarding.

The Harrison offers a tremendous cutthroat fishery in its lower reaches, the Alouette has good returns of winter steelhead, and so it goes. Ponds, lakes, creeks and rivers—a little bit of everything to tempt anglers. Some are right in the city itself, others a bit farther out, but all within reasonable traveling distance. It may seem hard to believe that there are so many angling opportunities available to one of Canada's largest cities, but it's a fact. And that's no fish story.

GEORGE WILL'S MUST-HAVE PATTERNS FOR THE FRASER VALLEY

- Black Gnat
- Chironomid (orange, browns, black)
- Doc Spratley

CHAPTER 48

THE FRASER VALLEY'S LONESOME CRAPPIE

George Will

IT HAS ALWAYS SEEMED STRANGE TO ME THAT BLACK CRAPPIE, a game fish held in high esteem throughout most of North America, is looked upon with such disfavor by British Columbian anglers. If it isn't a trout or salmon, it's obviously a trash fish. Oh well.

Crappies are aliens. After their introduction into Washington state waters back in the 1930s, they swam north and discovered the lower Fraser River's shallow backwaters and tributaries were much to their liking. They have since found their way into virtually every shallow lake in the region.

My first encounter occurred when I started fishing Whonnock Lake. I was casting a Mickey Finn into small holes in the shoreline vegetation, hoping to entice one of the hog cutthroat I'd been told inhabited the lake. At one point my fly was suddenly engulfed, but by a very untroutlike fish. At first I thought it was a decent-sized smallmouth bass (of which there aren't any in Whonnock), but quickly realized it was a huge crappie. I measured it at 15" (38 cm) against my net. To hell with the cutts! Before that day ended my arms were like wet dishrags from catching similar-sized fish, but rest assured that enough were retained to provide a meal. They are delicious eating, and most eastern anglers rank them over walleye for flavor and texture.

I kept returning to Whonnock and started fishing seriously for crappies.

Yellow was the main color that attracted them, and I eventually developed a killer bucktail pattern I called the Crappie Basher. On the shank of a No. 10, 3x long hook, wrap medium silver Mylar. For the wing, tie on a small clump of yellow hair, a small clump of white, then another of yellow. I prefer polar bear but anything seems to work. Build up a fairly large head of red thread.

Crappie are schooling fish, so if you find one you find them all. They really like the weedy margins of lakes, but I have also found them suspended midwater, especially during their spring-spawning period. At that time a fast sinking line and a yellow or chartreuse jig-fly works well.

Because anglers rarely bother them, there are some truly enormous crappie populations in many Fraser Valley lakes. I recall days when I hooked one on every cast for hours on end, and some reached mind-boggling sizes. One day while my Dad and I were fishing a Pitt River backwater, we got into a pod of monsters. Several were over 15" (38 cm), and one nudging 20" (50 cm) went at least 4 lb (1.8 kg), maybe more. That's right—close to the International Game Fish Association world record of 4 lb 8 oz (2.1 kg)!

Here's another twist. Until recently, there wasn't even a limit on crappie—they didn't even rate a mention in the fishing regs. The limit is still quite liberal (20 per day), but they remain virtually ignored. Hey! I don't mind. Whenever I return to the Vancouver area for a visit, I think it's great having a fishery like that almost exclusively to myself. But I'd appreciate it if you'd keep it under your hat.

GEORGE WILL'S MUST-HAVE PATTERN FOR BLACK CRAPPIE

- Crappie Basher

HAZELNUT-CRUSTED CRAPPIE

Turns crappie fillets into something wonderful
(Makes four servings)

8—crappie fillets, skinned
1 cup—hazelnuts—250 mL
Salt and freshly ground black pepper
1—egg, beaten
Butter or oil for frying

1. Toast hazelnuts in 350°F (180°C) oven for 10-20 minutes. While still warm, rub in a towel to remove as much brown skin as possible. Chop coarsely and spread on a plate.

2. Lightly season fillets on both sides with salt and pepper to taste. Dip in egg wash and coat one side with hazelnuts.

3. Heat a heavy, nonstick pan, add a tsp of butter or oil, and fry fillets nut-crusted side down. When nuts are golden brown, turn fillets and finish cooking. Be careful when turning so the nut coating stays on. A nonstick, flexible spatula works best.

–Wayne Phillips

CHAPTER 49

WINTER AND SUMMER STEELHEAD
IN BRITISH COLUMBIA

Barry Thornton

B RITISH COLUMBIA'S STEELHEAD OFFER AMAZING ANGLING sport, often when most of the country has entered the seasonal deep-freeze. Thanks to the "Pineapple Express"—the warm Hawaiian high-pressure zone that draws warm air over the region from the Pacific Ocean—rivers rarely freeze. This is when winter steelhead *(Oncorhynchus mykiss)* ascend coastal streams, driven by that ultimate biological urge to perpetuate their race.

British Columbia has over 11,000 rivers and streams. Many support steelhead but are so inaccessible that they rarely ever see an angler. For example, during the 1995–96 steelhead season, 231 streams reported steelhead-angling activity. This number will vary each year, usually between 200 and 400 streams. (Note: British Columbia steelhead licenses are valid from April 1st until March 31st of the following year.)

British Columbia is divided into five primary steelheading regions, with Vancouver Island, Skeena and the Lower Mainland regions leading in the total number of steelhead caught. But Vancouver Island and the Lower Mainland have the largest number of anglers, followed by Skeena. The other two, Thompson–Okanagan and Cariboo, are primarily summer steelhead regions.

A hatchery production program started in the late 1970s has increased the numbers of winter steelhead returning to where anglers now beach three times as many as they did in the early 1970s, yet angler numbers have increased only marginally. For some communities this "controlled" hatchery introduction has provided a tremendous tourism and economic boon. In fact, during the 1995–96 season, half of all steelhead caught on Vancouver Island were from streams in the Alberni Valley: the Somass, Stamp, and Sproat rivers.

In the summer of 1996, the Fisheries Branch of the Ministry of Environment, Lands and Parks, issued the British Columbia Fisheries Program Strategic Plan for 1996–2000. Titled *Conserving Our Fish Resources,* it highlighted four strategic priorities to fulfill their mandate:

1. To conserve wild fish populations and their habitat.
2. To manage for sustainable use of fish.
3. To build support for resource stewardship.
4. To support cooperative arrangements with First Nations.

All were admirable and had the full support of British Columbia anglers. The number-one priority—to conserve wild fish populations—is a goal organized steelheaders have lobbied for since the late 1960s. There is the belief that each stream has evolved a special, very individual race of steelhead which is site-specific to that particular watershed. All enhancement programs must accommodate those individual races of fish if we are to protect their wild gene pools.

To preserve wild steelhead stocks actively, many rivers are managed for wild fish only. One, Gold River on Vancouver Island, has shown the wisdom of this management strategy as it continues to remain in the British Columbia "Top 10" list year after year, despite repeated pressure from small vested interest groups to introduce hatchery augmentation.

Based upon the tackle they use, British Columbia steelheaders can be divided into three principle angling groups: float fishers, drift fishers and fly fishers. They can be found on virtually every steelhead stream, and except for fly fishing, their angling method is determined by in-stream structure and bottom conditions. Where a stream has a sandy bottom, you will usually find steelheaders using the drift-fishing technique. They cast out a lure tied to the mainline, with a sinker attached to take the lure down to the bottom where the vast majority of steelhead lie. The lure is drifted downstream, bouncing along the bottom, then swung in a crescent along the tailout where the pool rises.

Steelheaders using the float method often have a similar terminal hook-up to drift fishers, but they attach an adjustable float on the mainline so their bottom-bouncing lure will ride over in-stream boulders without hanging up. Both methods can be as simple to use as described, or a highly sophisticated art practiced by those few top steelheaders—the "Fish Hawks"—who annually beach large numbers of fish.

I have often said that winter steelhead fly fishers are masochistic, and for most of the winter I include myself in this category. Winter steelhead fly fishers know their odds of hooking fish are greatly reduced. Unlike summer steelhead, which will often actively rise or chase a fly, winter steelhead rarely move from their river bottom lie. They seem to completely enter an inappetent state which inhibits any feeding.

My experiences have been that there is active food-ingesting that can be associated with feeding behavior only when steelhead first enter a river, when the waters warm in April, or when they are in the spawned-out kelt stage returning to the ocean. But fly fishing for winter steelhead is a very appealing sport, and it provides another dimension for active steelheaders.

Although British Columbia offers many winter steelheading choices for a traveling angler, bear in mind that rivers are managed specifically for their special needs. Before venturing on any river bank, make certain you are familiar with the regulations and restrictions relating to that specific stream.

Fly Fishing for Winter Steelhead

THE SINK-TIP FLY LINE appeared to drag slightly as it drifted with the main current. One minute the floating portion was on the surface, the next it had stopped and disappeared. I leaned back with the rod, reacting as quickly as I could to set the barbless hook. I felt solid resistance, followed by a slight give as it came toward me, then saw the silver flash as a steelhead turned in the current and shot upstream. This was a good fish, chrome bright, obviously fresh in from the ocean.

The fish broke the surface once, twice, then in a spectacular leap shot high above the main pool, a good 6' (1.8 m) into the air. Fortunately, his earlier leaps had forewarned me and I bowed to this Herculean effort of a classic West Coast steelhead. This was the second strike in that same location, and surprisingly I found myself wanting to cast once again and dead-drift my fly rather than play this prime 12-lb (5.5-kg) steelhead. But that emotion quickly passed as the hooked fish began a rapid, steady swim upstream past fallen logs and large boulders which were characteristics of this pool.

With Churchillian determination, it entered the shallows at the pool's head and continued swimming upstream in the fast water. His power was admirable. On reaching the shallow rapids of this smaller stream, his dorsal fin surfaced, and I saw the tremendous power of his tail as he shot through, striving for the next pool upstream.

I cinched up on my Hardy fly reel, palming the spool as hard as I could without snapping the 12-lb test leader. He paused, spurted forward again, paused once more, then turned and drifted downstream with the current. He was expended and came swiftly to the beach where I was standing. I waded out, and with my needlenose pliers quickly removed the fly.

Checking the leader and retying the Pink Campbell fly, I cast again to that most productive slot at the pool's tailout. In smaller West Coast streams, it has been my experience that steelhead will take your fly on the first drift through a pool or run. For that reason it is important to guesstimate the correct drift for that first cast. Do not overestimate! There is nothing more frustrating than hanging up and having to break off, often spooking fish in the pool with your line. First, cast to the pool's head and drift past the white water of the shallows. This is the drop-off into the main pool. One of the primary holding areas for steelhead, it should be fished so your fly drifts down the fast water at the head, then drops down over the lip of the drop-off into the slower current below.

During my talks on steelhead fly fishing, I always emphasize that when you first reach a steelhead pool, plan your casts in such a manner that you are virtually dissecting the entire pool. Consider the three main areas: the head, pool and tailout. Begin at the head and start your cast so you are mathematically and methodically drifting your fly from the closest water to the water farthest from you. These drifts should be parallel to each other, so that you are certain not to have missed any holding water. It is amazing how a single rock will alter the underwater current in such a manner to provide a specific "holt"—a spot, often unseen on the surface slicks, where steelhead will lie.

Move downstream and start again to dissect the pool mathematically. Begin with a drift close in, then methodically drift your fly farther and farther out, right to the other side. Interestingly, steelhead will often lie in the shallows near each side at this deeper part of the pool, although they may just as often lie in the deepest water available.

When you have finished drifting the main pool, move downstream and dead-drift the tailout. Watch it, for this is where 80 percent of all steelhead are hooked. Why steelhead prefer this particular part of every pool is difficult to determine, but we do know it is the result of the light factor in the shallower water and the specific flow of the current.

Every pool has one major holding slot where fish will lie. Locating this slot involves the "hunting" aspect of steelheading. Once located, it is fair to say that this will be the holding slot for the remainder of that year. Often, providing there are no major floods, this holt may remain for years. It is for these holts that the steelheader searches each season. Once found, he will likely use the 20/80 rule, that is he will spend 20 percent of his time to catch 80 percent of his fish by concentrating on these holts. The remaining 80 percent of his time will be used to hunt for further holts for future fishing.

Rarely does a winter steelhead dash out, grab your fly, then streak back to its holding area. It does happen with kelts on occasion and with a few summer-run fish, but these are the exception. Most strikes are simply a mouthing of your fly, which happens to be passing where the fish is holding. At a tailout, any trick you can use to slow your fly, making it easy for a fish to take, will produce more strikes.

Fly Fishing for Summer Steelhead

SUMMER STEELHEAD BEHAVE DIFFERENTLY than winter steelhead. One summer I had the opportunity to watch three experienced river fly fishers hook and release summer steelhead by employing a very effective technique I had never seen before. Their tactics seemed to trigger summer steelhead to strike as the fly was stripped back upstream past them, and on several occasions fish darted from areas where they were holding and grabbed the flies in exciting, smashing strikes.

They were using a deepwater system referred to as "dredging" or "scooping" a pool. We were on a 12-day rafting–camping–fly-fishing jaunt on a West Coast mainland river. It was three-to-one in terms of fly-fishing techniques, for I am a "dead-drifter" with my flies and was loath to switch. Fortunately, I didn't have to except to experience this method, for the steelhead came to my technique and flies almost equally as well as they did to my companions' effective tactic.

The scooping technique is quite simple: A 12–20' lead-core fly line is attached to either a floating fly line or a sinking line by using loops, or by attaching them with a short length of 30-lb test monofilament line.

The loop system was the easiest, for various lead-core line weights could be easily changed as the pool depths changed. We were fishing a glacial river, which did not require long leaders in the milky-colored water. Attached to the end of the lead-core was a short butt of 20-lb test monofilament, then a shorter section of 15-lb test as a tippet. The total leader length was no longer than 20" (50 cm).

To fish with this tackle, an angler waded out as far as possible at the top of a pool. Naturally, a dogleg pool (right angle) was the easiest to fish. Once positioned, the angler cast across the river at about a 45° angle downstream. Time was allowed to let the lead core and fly sink to the bottom, or as near as possible. If necessary, the line might be mended to keep it as straight as possible for the strip retrieve. The angler then began a slow-strip, fast-strip, varied-strip retrieve, keeping a firm grip on the fly line as it came back through the guides.

Because the angler was out in the river, possibly standing in chest- or waist-deep water, the retrieve continued until the lead-core line reached the rod tip, for there could be fish holding close by. After a few casts and retrieves, the angler stepped downstream a few feet, then repeated the process until he felt the pool was fully covered. Strikes rarely occurred as the fly line sank, rather, while it was being stripped back through the pool.

The dead-drift retrieve requires a much different technique, utilizing a sinking or sink-tip fly line. Using this system, an angler stays close to shore and casts upstream, mends the line, then allows the fly to dead-drift through the pool or run. Strikes occur as the fly drifts downstream and rarely when it swings after the drift.

Summer steelhead are deepwater fish on return to their natal streams, much like coho and chinook, hugging low down in locations where they have a steady current in which to rest. However, unlike spawning salmon, summer steelhead often feed while in a river. It is this active feeding desire that allows fly fishers to target them with bait imitations and dry flies.

In both the scooping and dead-drift systems there are exceptions. One for me occurred on the second day of our trip, while I was dead-drifting the upper section of a pool close to a rock ledge. My fly had completed its drift and I was fast-stripping in the loose fly line to prepare for another cast. A 20-lb (9-kg) summer steelhead buck came out from under a rock ledge, grabbed my swinging fly, then shot back for the ledge. The bite of my barbless hook sent him a good 6' (1.8 m) into the air, then he shot downstream. I had no chance to set the hook or gain control of the flipping fly line before it started peeling from my reel.

This was one of those real knuckle-dusters, for my fingers received a number of sharp raps before I could turn my hand to palm the spinning spool. Fortunately, the fish dashed downstream in a straight line, and I was able to gain a modicum of control before he began the characteristic rainbow trout leaps and powerful head shakes. By this time he was directly in front of my partners, all of whom offered sage words of advice and, eventually, a helping hand on my shoulders to steady me as I waded back to shore. We finally brought to beach a beautiful, chrome-bright summer steelhead which we quickly measured as 39" (1 m) before releasing him. This one highlighted the many we were all so fortunate to beach on this trip.

Would I recommend the scooping fly-fishing method for river fishing? You bet! However, I also recommend just as strongly dead-drifting for steelhead and salmon in rivers. The lessons I learned when I did experiment with scooping gave me one more tool in my arsenal to fly fish effectively in our West Coast rivers.

British Columbia provides vast opportunities for steelheaders to pursue this supreme trophy trout. In addition, new fly-tying materials offer a kaleidoscope of effective patterns, and new fly lines and the methods developing to fish with them provide almost unlimited possibilities with which to experiment.

Barry Thornton's Must-Have Pattern for Steelhead

- Girdle Bug
- Pink Campbell
- Silver Skunk

CHAPTER 50

MATCHING THE WORM HATCH

Robert H. Jones

THE PUNTLEDGE WORM WAS ORIGINATED BY DAVE LORNIE, who lives beside the Puntledge River near Courtenay, British Columbia. An inventive and accomplished tier, Dave freely admits the idea came while winter steelheading with a friend who consistently outfished him with pink worms of soft plastic.

"Worm hatches" are common on West Coast streams. When heavy rains wash earthworms into the water, it is common to see them drifting freely in the current or to find clusters of a dozen or more trapped in potholes.

Variegated pale pink and white chenille was his material of choice, for the color was right and chenille is soft and flexible while floating through the current. Unfortunately, that particular shade was discontinued but other shades of whitish pink will do.

As a worm is fished close to the bottom, it requires heavy weighting. Dave uses Partridge low-water singles in No. 2, 1, 1/0 and 2/0. Up to 7" (18 cm) of .035" lead-fuse wire can be wound onto the shank of the larger sizes. Flak jackets and steel helmets are optional.

To tie, start the thread behind the hook eye and spiral it rearward to the bend. Bind lead wire in just ahead of the bend, then wind it tightly forward to ⅜" (10 mm) of the eye and break it off.

Tie in end of chenille at the bend. Untwist about 4" (10 cm) to the left until the core is straight; then untwist 15–20 more turns. Pinch twisted portion in the center, then fold it forward to the bend. Pinch chenille to the bend and release the trailing end, which will twist tightly into a tail.

Make three wraps of thread around the chenille, then spiral the thread forward. Wind chenille forward in tight wraps, tie off ⅛" (3 mm) behind the eye and trim. Tie in four strands of pearlescent white Flashabou, then form a neat head.

For an Improved Puntledge Worm—Dave's favorite—don't cut the chenille after tying it off. After tying in the Flashabou, untwist 3" (8 cm) of chenille, double it back to the shoulder, tie off and trim. Wind thread forward and tie off behind the hook eye.

Dave uses an 8-weight rod with a weight-forward floating line. The leader should be roughly twice as long as the average depth being fished, with tippets 6–8-lb test.

For a dead-drift on runs or pools, cast upstream, keep your rod tip high and strip line in as it comes back toward you. If it stops, raise the tip and wait. If there is no movement, it's probably a rock, so shake it loose. If you detect movement, continue waiting until you feel the fish turn sideways, then set the hook—which will usually be in the hinge of the fish's jaw.

The overall size, length and weight of the worms can be adjusted by varying the hook sizes, diameter of the chenille, and the length of material back-twisted then doubled back on itself. Please note that Dave's back-twisting method also works well on other extended-body flies.

CHAPTER 51

OPEN-OCEAN SALMON

Barry M. Thornton

It has been over a quarter of a century since I first waded the Pacific Ocean waters at the estuary of a small creek. I was there to explore a new sport fishery—saltwater fly fishing for salmon. I had read about pioneer fly fishers attempting to catch salmon on a cast fly, but rarely did those earlier British Columbia authors express much enthusiasm. In fact they often stated in their writing that Pacific salmon seldom showed any interest in cast flies, like their Atlantic salmon cousins.

There were a few, however, like Bryan Williams, British Columbia's first game warden, and Roderick Haig-Brown, surely the most famous and respected fly fisherman of our province. Both gentlemen wrote of powerful experiences with salmon hooked on a cast fly in salt water. In fact, it was Haig-Brown who had advised me to try this special estuary, having described "northern" coho that frequented it in late September and October as weighing in the teens.

My acquaintance with Rod was the result of our common efforts for steelhead. He had agreed to sit on a steelhead advisory board which I had established when I was president of the Steelhead Society of British Columbia. Rod told me that Pacific salmon would take a cast fly under certain conditions in the autumn when they were marshaling to ascend their home rivers. This was the situation which took me to that particular estuary.

I was fortunate that first autumn. There was a good run of hook-nosed northerns schooling along the beaches of that estuary. For reasons I was to become aware of in later years, they were difficult to entice to a fly, but the incredible power of those fish that I did manage to strike—some weighing over 15 lb (7 kg)—hooked me like no other lure could. It sent me on a decades-long search to master the skills of fly fishing for Pacific salmon.

I was convinced in those early years that it stood to reason if Pacific salmon would take a fly when they were in the estuary or on the beaches near their home river, they would also take a fly in the open ocean. It did not take long to prove this theory. As I became more experienced, I realized there are three distinct periods in the ocean phase of the life cycle of Pacific salmon when they can be caught consistently on a cast fly. It was also a time to differentiate between the Pacific salmon species, for I found each is available at different times and in different circumstances.

When fly fishing in the shallows, I discovered coho and chinook salmon could be hooked on a regular basis, providing I was near an actively feeding school of salmon, and there was an obvious concentration of baitfish in the immediate area. Chinook and coho are the sport salmon of the Pacific coast. Without a doubt the chinook is "King" of the Pacific salmon due to its size and deep, dogged struggles when hooked. The coho, on the other hand, is "Prince" of the Pacific salmon because of its flashy, surface-battling struggles. Both are powerful fish that require patience and skill for an angler to boat. Pinks are the delicate species of salmon, much smaller than coho and chinook, but what they lack in size they make up for in power. The pink is "Princess" of the sporting Pacific salmon.

On their summer migration, pinks become accessible to anglers along coastal shorelines near their home rivers. Fly fishers look for "locator" pinks— leaping salmon that herald the appearance of schools of these feisty salmon. The other two species, sockeye and chum salmon, are not common targets of fly fishers except at precise locations and times. However, it is exciting to know that a few anglers in recent years have begun perfecting patterns that appear to interest some of these fish to strike.

Political interference has done much to disrupt the evolution of Pacific salmon as sport fish. Regulations, in effect since it seems "forever," prohibit sport fishers from targeting most salmon in fresh water. Some very limited, site-specific regulations have allowed fishing for coho and chinook in freshwater streams, but pinks, sockeye and chums are rarely opened for anglers. This is tragic and a travesty of the use of a common resource. There is a vast surplus of these three species in many British Columbia watersheds, fish that could be the core of a salmon freshwater sport fishery, which would ensure many stream guardians and a rich, evolving, recreational resource.

Pacific salmon fly fishing in salt water is best divided into three life-cycle stages. The first stage is open saltwater fly fishing for juvenile salmon that are in their first or second year in the ocean. These young fish are often called "blue-backs," a regional term used for salmon under 5 lb (2.3 kg). Bluebacks can be either coho or pink salmon. Small chinooks in their early ocean years are called "jacks."

Vast rafts of bluebacks are often available to fly fishers in open-water situations many miles from shore. There, salmon feed on euphausiids—more commonly known as "pink feed"—near the surface. Tide lines and flotsam often concentrate salmon during these April, May and June periods, providing fly fishers a focus in what is otherwise a very large ocean. I have found it interesting to discover pink and coho salmon schooling in the same areas at this time of the year.

The second stage is open saltwater fishing for migrating, maturing salmon. For the fly fisher, angling is done on shallow shoals, near kelp beds or close to inshore structures. This is likely the most exciting time, for along the Pacific coast there are thousands and thousands of islands, fjords, bays and shorelines where salmon will concentrate for indefinite periods before continuing their homeward journeys. This is the time for the "hunter"—the fly fisher who will travel and search, expecting no two days to ever be the same, but knowing that just beyond the next point of land there could be an incredible concentration of salmon just waiting for his cast fly.

The third stage is best termed as "full adult" estuary fishing. This is when salmon have completed their oceanic odyssey and reached their home estuary. They are fully grown and their body chemistry is beginning to alter their shape, color, and inner organs in preparation for the final journey up their home river to spawn.

Fly-fishing equipment has changed dramatically in the past two decades. Graphite fly rods have made what were once heavy-rated rods like 8- and 9-weight, quite light—many under 4 oz. The result is that fly fishers can cast for several hours every day and for many days in succession. For Pacific salmon, the most common American Sportfishing Association (ASA)–rated fly rod is the 8-weight. This is what I recommend for all salmon except the smaller pinks, which can be effectively handled with a 6-weight outfit.

Fly reels have also improved, with many being resistant to saltwater corrosion. Salmon are large, powerful fish that must be played from the reel at all times. Without a doubt, the fly reel is the most important tool of the salmon fly fisher and should be your prime investment for this fishery. Do not skimp!

Fly lines have likely seen the most dramatic changes in the past two decades. There are an almost unlimited variety on the market, with a vast number of unique features from special saltwater floaters to deepwater sinkers. I recommend three basic fly lines for the Pacific salmon fly fisher, which will cover the three seasonal situations where these fish are caught.

First is a floating line matching the rod's ASA rating (a No. 8 line for an 8-weight rod). This line is best used with weighted and unweighted flies while beach fishing or while pursuing bluebacks early in the spring. It is also effective when baitfish are seen skittering across the surface while being chased by actively feeding coho.

Second is a sink-tip line, again matching the ASA rod rating. As an interesting aside, I have found that a fly line one number higher or lower than the rod's ASA rating can be used effectively. A sink-tip line is used in situations similar to a floating line; however, it has the decided advantage of being more effective in shallow areas when the water is clear and not clouded with summer algae bloom.

Third is the "work horse"—a weighted line—usually in the IV- or V-sinking class. This is the line you will use the majority of the time to counter fast-moving tidal currents while getting your fly down to depths where the salmon are feeding.

To these standard 90' (20 m) fly lines I usually attach 100' (30 m) of running sinking line, then 200 yards (180 m) of Dacron backing as a base upon which these lines can sit in the fly reel. Remember, you can never have too much backing. A large chinook will have you through your fly line and into the wet line before you have effective control of your unit. Then it is a matter of bringing the fish back to the boat, or if it continues its locomotive run, even chasing the fish with your boat.

Fly patterns for Pacific salmon have seen the most dramatic change in recent years. At one time large bucktail patterns were usually cast for salmon, but they were rarely effective unless fast-trolled as a lure. It was not until fly fishers began to simplify their patterns that consistent success occurred. Experimenting tiers used smaller and smaller hooks, switched to stainless steel, and used silver and simplicity in their fly construction. Successful patterns began emerging, like the Pink Eve, Red Glennis, Clouser Minnow, Weigh Wester, and the Thorn series. These have become highly effective Pacific salmon patterns, and with these as a basic core, fly anglers have created many effective variations. An experience I had one summer with the Silver Thorn demonstrates this very effective pattern.

Our boat was tied to a kelp bed surrounding a small islet in Clayoquot Sound, on the west coast of Vancouver Island. It was cloudy, in fact an ideal summer day for being on the water. The previous day we had found salmon in this same location at high noon, one hour into the flood. It was now one o'clock, and as was often the case, baitfish were beginning to school alongside the kelp bed in a long, compact group. It was obvious the salmon were forcing this behavior, for we saw several of them leaping and breaking water in the near vicinity.

Casting to the outside of the baitfish school, my partner quickly hooked a water-walking Prince. Soon, I too had one of these beauties to my reel and we boated a double. We were both using a standard Silver Thorn pattern, and we decided to see if variety would also work. We quickly boated coho with a pink Hakai Thorn, a chartreuse Tonquin Thorn, and a Silver Thorn Flashtail. At this time I also began experimenting with various stripping techniques, close to the boat where we could see the salmon strike. A slow strip brought fish to the fly, then a stop-strip triggered a strike. We dappled the fly on the surface, swept it back and forth, even jigged it. All were effective, but when we switched to other heavily dressed patterns, it was rare to have a fish strike. There was no doubt that this pattern worked in these waters, and they have since proven themselves many times in similar circumstances.

As well as the basics of casting and retrieving, there are several skills which a saltwater fly fisher needs. In my book *Saltwater Fly-Fishing for Pacific Salmon* (1995, Hancock House), I detailed many of these skills and outlined several tips aimed at helping the novice and experienced fly fisher. I include only a few here, as follows:

- Fly fishers pursuing Pacific salmon in ocean conditions need to become familiar with tides and the effects of currents.
- Weather is a major factor in a day's activity, and fly fishers need to be prepared for extremes with protective sunglasses, hats, rain gear and warm clothes. I have found that I wear the same woolen clothes in August that I do while duck hunting in December. The ocean has a constant temperature, varying only by a few degrees between seasons.
- The saltwater salmon fly fisher must be a hunter, one who can learn to interpret the wildlife signs that tell where there are feeding salmon. This requires an intimate knowledge of gulls and other seabirds—when they are at a loafing bar, or when they are following the activity of surface-feeding salmon.
- Finger protection is a must for saltwater retrieves. I always use Lycra "Stripping Guards," produced by Petersons, and I have a pocket of Band-Aids should they be required. Surface grit running over your finger acts like tearing sandpaper, and there are times when a powerful fish yanks fly line through your hand like a burning rope.
- Anchoring is a necessary technique to counter tide flows and currents in order that you can get your fly line down to the depths where salmon are feeding.

Even though Pacific salmon fly fishing was tried by fly fishers many decades ago, it is still in a pioneering stage. It is the West Coast fishery of the future that is available to all—from the beach or from a boat, at some wild coastal inlet or in the center of urban activity. It is a fly fishery of the future, with no specific traditions and no definitive tackle restraints. Good luck as you, too, become "hooked" by what is a unique and action-filled fly fisher's utopia. Like the journey of the Pacific salmon, it will be an odyssey filled with new equipment, new journeys, and new fly-fishing opportunities.

BARRY THORNTON'S MUST-HAVE PATTERNS FOR PACIFIC SALMON

- Hakai Thorn
- Pink Eve
- Pink Eve Redeye
- Silver Thorn
- Silver Thorn Flashtail
- Tonquin Thorn
- Weigh Wester

CHAPTER 52

LORNIE'S FIRECRACKER

Robert H. Jones

W HEN DAVE LORNIE STARTED FISHING FOR COHO IN SALT water, he noticed that most of his friends' catches were made with small herring trolled or mooched as cut plug. To make a cut plug, the head is severed from the body at a beveled angle; then the hook is inserted through the shoulder area. This causes the bait to spin when drawn through the water, its speed of rotation depending on the bevel and the arc of roll on the angle.

Being a dedicated fly fisherman who avoids bait, Dave created a "flure" (fly-weight lure) that spins in a similar fashion. Dubbed the "Firecracker," its light weight is easy to cast, and it catches coho and chinook salmon quite well, thank you. See 461 for photo.

To tie Firecrackers you require large (⅜") diameter braided Mylar tubing (silver or pearlescent white), No. 1 Eagle Claw L67C Billy Pate hooks, some 4" (10-cm) lengths of fine copper wire (from an old electrical cord), 3/0 white Uni-thread, invisible sewing thread, 3 mm diameter adhesive eyes (chartreuse or green), red marking pen (fine), 5-minute clear epoxy, a few 2 ½ x 2 ½" (63 x 63 mm) squares of waxed paper, some round toothpicks, and locking forceps.

Cut a 2 ½" (63 mm) length of tubing. Against the front end of the tubing, gauge the distance back from the hook eye to the bend, and at the latter point push the hook eye through the braided Mylar and out the end.

Place hook in the vise and lock four or five wraps of thread behind the eye. Slide a length of wire through the tube and bind the front end with three wraps. Slide the tubing forward and bind the ends down, trim any exposed ends, then form a small, neat head. Tie off and cut thread.

Remove hook from vise. Smooth tubing rearward, pinch material and wire together, and then ¼" (6 mm) from the end, form the tail by making three wraps of invisible thread and three half-hitches. Trim thread and exposed wire.

Use the marker to draw on gills, then apply an eye to each side of the head. Bend body into desired curve—like a banana—then grip the hook eye with locking forceps. Mix a small amount of epoxy on a square of waxed paper, stirring it with a toothpick. Then coat the entire body. Rotate the fly until the epoxy sets.

When casting or trolling a Firecracker, use about 2' (60 cm) of fairly stiff 10-lb test tippet and attach it to the leader with a small swivel.

Whether you choose to call this a fly, lure or flure, don't be surprised by the fact that even when larger baits are present, salmon are attracted by this flashy, tightly rotating Firecracker.

CHAPTER 53

SALTWATER BUCKTAILING FOR SALMON

Robert H. Jones

WARNING! THIS CHAPTER IS NOT ABOUT FLY CASTING; IT is, however, about fishing with flies and with fly rods and reels. Although some fly fishers look down their collective noses at anything that smacks of trolling, this facet of sport fishing has flourished on the West Coast saltwater scene for about a century. And if the truth be known, a great many saltwater fly-flingers intentionally trail their flies over the stern while hunting for bait schools or other signs of feeding salmon. Referred to as "skip-fly fishing," the rod is handheld with the tip pointing rearward. If a salmon appears and follows without taking, the angler can either jerk the fly ahead or strip line from the reel to drop it back, often enticing a strike. When this happens—and it often does—there is no need to set the hook, believe me.

"Bucktailing" is a totally different technique that requires some preparation and rerigging of tackle, and might even—gasp!—involve using a spinner, or—horrors!—a sinker. It refers to high-speed trolling for coho and chinook salmon with streamer flies. The technique originated at Cowichan Bay, British Columbia, during the early 1900s; however, it has been adopted and modified for use throughout much of our coastal waters.

To indicate the effects bucktailing can have on anglers, I like to relate the comment Ralph Shaw made during the mid-1980s, while we were rigging our tackle prior to heading out on the water. "You know," he said, "for their own safety and well-being, folks who plan on bucktailing for coho should be required to take a physical examination." He finished tying on his fly and tugged on the leader to test its strength. "Then, anyone not medically certified as having a strong heart and good bladder control would know they should stick to less hectic forms of fishing."

Ralph's tongue-in-cheek comment related to the explosive strike a coho makes on the surface, often within 15–20' (4.5–6 m) of a boat. Picture a fly skittering across the surface at 8 miles (13 km) per hour. Now add a coho hitting it while traveling in the opposite direction at about the same speed. Imagine the sound a reel spool makes going from completely inert to instant, sustained rotation at bearing-burn-out speed. Scary stuff.

Anticipation plays a big part in the bucktailing game, for coho are often seen pacing a fly for several seconds before suddenly racing ahead, then swapping ends to charge back and engulf it on the run. The strength and violence of what follows must be experienced to be appreciated. Unhindered by heavy sinkers, dodgers or flashers, coho are the swiftest and most aerobatic of all Pacific salmon, notorious for making long runs directly away from a boat, then racing back toward it while the angler tries frantically to retrieve slack line.

Some anglers also target "feeder chinooks" during the winter months. These are immature fish which are not ready to spawn and may range in size from "shakers" weighing 2–3 lb (900 g–1.4 kg), to bruisers of 30 lb (14 kg) or more. The average, however, is about 8–12 lb (3.6–5.5 kg). A point upon which all anglers agree is that feeder chinooks, pound for pound, are stronger and much more active than larger salmon on their spawning migrations.

The preferred fly rods for salmon or steelhead are 9–10 ½' in length, usually 7–8-weight if targeting coho, and 9–10-weight for chinooks. Whichever, the rod handle should have a fighting butt. On the rod is mounted a large, single-action fly reel. Depending on a reel's capacity, with the fly line and backing removed, up to 500 yards (460 m) of 15–20-lb test monofilament can be spooled. While this might appear to be overkill, it is better to err on the side of abundance. At any rate, 300 yards (275 m) should be the minimum.

A cassette-style reel allows for quick changes from casting to trolling mode, but a standard fly reel with a spare spool will do. The reel should have an easily adjustable, butter-smooth drag. It should be set lightly; otherwise, snapped leaders occur with heartbreaking regularity. Many anglers simply engage the ratchet.

Leaders are about 6' long. For small flies they may be as light as 8-lb test, but 10–15 is more the norm. Pacific salmon are not leader-shy. Some anglers join a leader to the main line with a small barrel swivel, while others claim large swivels make a fly swim better.

Flies are 1–8" (2.5–20 cm) long, and average 4–6" (10–15 cm). Dressings contain every color in the spectrum, but some combinations are more popular than others. The general rule is to match a fly as closely as possible to the size and color of the predominant bait.

Polar bear hair is favored for tying bucktails, but long hair from a deer tail is an acceptable substitute. Although lacking the flexibility, translucency and light-reflecting qualities of polar bear hair, it can be enhanced by blending in long strands of Flashabou, Krystal Flash or Angel Hair. Don't shy away from using synthetics for the entire fly—some of the newer materials have won over legions of converts (self included).

While fairly basic hair-wing patterns dominate the scene, some incorporating feather wings may outperform them at times. An Olive or Green Lefty's Deceiver is one with a good track record, as is a Catface Streamer in similar colors (a pattern designed by Shawn Bennett of Moonlight Flies in Sidney, British Columbia).

The smallest patterns are tied to represent shrimp. Although thoughts of a shrimp skimming speedily along the surface might seem absolutely ludicrous, small flies of red, pink and orange can be quite productive during May and early June, a period when coho and feeder chinooks target primarily on "red feed"—a term which encompasses euphausiids and other slightly larger shrimp. Later in the season when baitfish become their main food source, patterns imitating herring, anchovies, pilchard or needlefish take over, and their lengths are increased accordingly.

Most of the popular baitfish patterns consist of simple two- or three-color hair dressings over a body of silver tinsel or Mylar. A typical two-color pattern has a back of green, blue, purple or gray, with belly colors of white, pink, red, orange or yellow. Three-color patterns are similar, but belly dressings are usually white.

Color combinations vary from one area to another. Around the Comox

Valley, where I live, purple backs ranging from light mauve to dark royal purple are popular, but 20 miles (32 km) north of us, the Campbell River bucktailers favor green backs, and 20 miles (32 km) south, gray is preferred around Deep Bay and Qualicum Beach. Whatever is chosen, the accepted rule is light colors for dark days, and vice versa.

Many anglers prefer "tube flies" because they are versatile and last longer. The body material is tied to a short length of hollow plastic or metal tubing, and then the fly is threaded onto the leader ahead of the hooks. One advantage is that flies can be stored without hooks, and another is that a damaged hook can be instantly replaced—an important consideration if that particular pattern is what seems to be working.

Rigging a tube fly is simply a matter of tying a single hook onto a length of leader, or two hooks in tandem for longer patterns. A straight-ringed eye is fine for a single hook, but turned-up eyes are preferred for tandems. The hooks should have straight rather than offset points to prevent the fly from rolling. If you're using a single hook, the point should ride downward. With tandems, some prefer the tail hook to ride point up and the front hook point down, but others claim fewer fish are lost if both hook points are on the bottom. I use only one hook, but position it well back in the body material. After threading the leader through the tube and positioning the hook, I push a toothpick firmly into the front end of the tube and break it off flush with the head. This ensures the hook stays properly positioned, but the distance to the hook can be adjusted by simply pulling the leader through the tube.

Many anglers use a spinner directly ahead of the fly, claiming its vibration and flash attract more strikes. The most popular models are Indiana and Colorado blades of polished abalone shell, but metal blades of silver, fluorescent red and chartreuse are also productive. Some use spinners mounted on wire shafts, but others simply thread a blade and clevis onto the leader. If going this route, use a folded metal clevis rather than a drilled clevis, as they cause less abrasion on the line. However, check the line occasionally for signs of wear from the rotating clevis.

While there are no absolutes regarding trolling speeds, low and high extremes are about 5 and 10 miles (8 and 16 km) per hour, and the average about 6–8 miles (10–13 km) per hour. Early in the season, slower speeds will attract the most action, but by late fall coho usually want their bucktails served at high speed. Ralph Shaw's rule of thumb is, "Keep increasing the speed until you're dead certain that you're going much too fast, then double it." Perhaps I should point out that Ralph catches a lot of salmon this way. I should also mention that, over the years, many anglers have left their lines trailing as they put their boats up to planing speeds while moving from one place to another, and they've had coho smack their speeding flies. What instantly happens may involve a full range of misfortunes—complete outfits torn from the angler's hand, rods broken, reels seizing up, leaders popping, loss of control of basic bodily functions. One thing is certain—there are seldom any fish landed.

Although rods can be handheld while bucktailing, it works best if they are positioned almost parallel to the water in stern-mounted rod holders. Cock the rod shaft about 20–30° from horizontal to dampen its whipping action. There is a reason for this—if the fly skips free of the water, the rod tip is suddenly free of tension so it flexes forward, then back again. This happens very quickly, but when the tip starts rearward, there is suddenly a bit of slack in the line—and it's amazing how often it is just enough to throw a loop of line around the rod tip. Now this, too, makes for some excitement if a fish hits about then.

If using side-mounted holders, position the rod so it angles back, its tip parallel to the water. Trolling distances behind the boat vary according to conditions. The average is 20–60' (6–18 m), but in mirror-calm water the lines may be extended up to 200' (60 m). With a light chop on the surface—which most consider optimum bucktailing conditions—lines are often shortened until flies are in the trailing edge of the prop wash, barely 15–20' (4.5–6 m) from the stern.

Ideally, a bucktail—with or without a spinner—should swim just under the surface without breaking through. Although coho often take them this way with abandon, there are times when a sinker is called for. Under most circumstances, ½–2 oz is sufficient. If a clip-on, sliding sinker is used, position it 15–20' (4.5–6 m) ahead of the fly. If using a fixed sinker, tie a keel-shaped model no more than a rod length ahead of the fly. If the leader is longer than the rod, landing a fish can range from difficult to impossible.

When coho are surface feeding, good eyesight and attention to detail usually provide the clues necessary to find potential action: diving or circling gulls indicate bait being pushed to the surface by feeding fish, as do sudden flashes as sunlight reflects from leaping baitfish. If small diving birds like murrelets and guillemots (sea pigeons) indicate deep-swimming bait, concede to modern technology and switch on the depth recorder. If the bait is deep, a sinker of up to 4 oz might make the difference between catching coho or simply taking a boat ride. The maximum weight you can hang on your line will, of course, depend on your rod.

Never troll in a straight line. Weaving back and forth in lazy, irregular patterns causes flies on the outside of a turn to increase in speed, while those inside slow down. If the outside fly garners the first strike, a slight increase in trolling speed might prove more productive overall.

Never run your boat directly through schooling baitfish. Determine their direction of travel, then swing wide and make an angled approach so your flies intersect them. Executing a series of wide figure-8 turns ahead of the school permits continuous presentation of your flies as long as the bait remains in sight.

Erratic trolling also allows flies trailing on a long line to pass back and forth through the boat's wake. Whether coho are attracted to the motor's sound or the stream of bubbles created by its whirling propeller is debatable. Whatever the reason, coho will approach the wake, often close enough behind a boat to be clearly visible.

Bucktailing usually starts in April with "bluebacks"—immature coho of about 3 lb (1.4 kg). While they can be sporty on light tackle, serious bucktailers wait until the fish have increased in size. The ultimate sport arrives when big, hook-nosed "northern coho" appear on the scene during the fall, usually around mid-September to October, during the latter half of the spawning season. Some are hefty bruisers that weigh well into the teens and occasionally peak at 25 lb (11 kg) or more.

Northerns account for a lot of snapped leaders, broken rods, seized reel bearings, rapped knuckles and frazzled nerves during their relatively short appearance, which simply bolsters the belief of many anglers that they are the ultimate trophy salmon.

Bucktail Tube Flies

THE FOLLOWING PATTERNS will meet virtually every situation you might encounter along the British Columbia coast. The wing material can be polar bear hair, bucktail, combed acrylic yarn, or one of the many synthetics now available. Dressing lengths may vary from 2–8" (5–20 cm). The body is braided, silver Mylar tubing. and wing colors are listed in the order they are applied to the body, with the topping last.

A good source of plastic tubes are Q-Tip cotton swabs, which are 2 ⅞" (7 cm) long. You require only an inch or so for each body. If using fairly large-diameter, braided Mylar, build up the tube's diameter with thread or yarn.

If desired, cut the braid longer than the tube—no more than ⅔ of the wing length—then unravel the trailing strands after the fly is tied. Slide braid over the tube, bind the front end with white 3/0 Uni-Thread—three wraps and a half-hitch—then trim thread. Smooth braid toward the tail and use invisible sewing thread to secure with three wraps and three half-hitches. Coat the body with clear nail polish and set aside to dry.

If desired, a small clump of red hair, combed yarn or hackle fibers can be tied in at the throat. Tie on the wing by stacking one color atop the other, then build up a fairly large head. The head can be colored with a felt-tip marker and cemented, but I lock the thread with Krazy Glue. After it dries I stick an adhesive eye to each side, then coat the head with 5-minute clear epoxy.

A short sleeve of rubber or soft plastic tubing can be forced over the rear end of the body to hold the hook eye in position, but I much prefer securing the body and leader together with the point of a round toothpick.

Pattern Colors

1.	Autumn Leaf	Yellow, red
2.	Bill's Beau	Yellow, fluorescent green
3.	Blue Baron	White, dark blue
4.	Dependable	White, pale pink, pale gray
5.	Devil Tail	White, red
6.	Green Hornet	White, dark green
7.	Green Ghost	White, fluorescent green
8.	Green Orange	White, orange, midgreen
9.	Gray Ghost	White, gray

10.	Ginger Jake	White, orange
11.	Lady Laura	White, red, dark gray, pale pink, mauve
12.	Lady Norma	White, fluorescent blue
13.	Lady Vera	White, pink,
14.	Shrimp	Pink, yellow, pink
15.	Mickey Finn	Yellow, red, yellow
16.	Moby Dick	White
17.	Pink Shrimp	White, fluorescent pink
18.	Polar Mist	White, light blue
19.	Saratoga	White, midgreen
20.	Soldiers Rip	White, purple
21.	Witch Doctor	White, black
22.	Zulu	White, black, peacock herl

CHAPTER 54

COASTAL CUTTHROAT TROUT

Bill Luscombe

"SEE-FOOD" DIET—THAT'S THE TERM USED MOST OFTEN BY anglers in British Columbia to describe the feeding habits of coastal cutthroat trout. If they see food, they eat it. Yet this isn't always as true as it claims to be.

Many years ago when cutthroats were abundant from Alaska to California, west of the Cascade Mountains, anglers took those trout in huge quantities, often catching them by using just about anything they tied on their lines. This feeding habit, unfortunately, turned out to be the cutthroats' demise. They were so easy to catch that the populations plummeted due, primarily, to overfishing, which was compounded later on by loss of habitat.

Today, coastal cutthroat have been recognized as needing a helping hand, and restocking programs are meeting with some success. Lucky for us that they are—for it would be a shame to lose this beautiful native British Columbian because of our stupidity and ignorance.

Coastal cutthroat still inhabit much of their original territory, although in lower numbers. They are highly adaptable, frequenting various waters from pristine lakes and streams to tea-colored backwaters and bogs, as well as running to the ocean where they cruise the shorelines of brackish estuaries and beaches near the river mouths.

They are beautiful trout, easily distinguishable from their Interior westslope cousins and from rainbow trout. Coastal cutts are very silver, whereas westslopes show much more of a yellow hue to their body. All cutthroat have a large mouth and a maxillary that extends past the back of the eye; rainbows have a smaller mouth and their maxillary does not extend that far. A cutt is heavily spotted with small black spots covering the majority of its flanks, often right to the belly, but the spots of a rainbow seldom extend past midpoint of its flanks. The most easily recognizable characteristic of the cutthroat, however, is the red-orange slashes beneath each side of the lower jaw—rainbows show no such markings.

Rainbows and cutthroats are true trout and very close relatives. Both spawn in the spring, and where they occupy the same waters they often hybridize to produce a cuttbow, which shows characteristics of both species. It has a slightly smaller mouth than a normal cutthroat, fewer spots, and still shows a faint red slash under the lower jaw. It also shows the usual light pink stripe down the sides so characteristic of the rainbow trout.

As a rule, cutthroats like big meals and their preferred diet consists of salmon fry, sculpins, sticklebacks and smaller trout. In waters that don't contain these big morsels, they survive on the usual trout fare of chironomids, leeches, and various nymphs and adult insects. They are true opportunists and will often take a big offering, even during a hatch of other insects; yet they can sometimes be as selective a quarry as any other fish.

Cutthroats in coastal lakes most closely deserve the label of "see-food" diet. With the variety of food available in lakes, they are the least selective of the species. Spring brings with it the midge hatches and these trout key in on them. Chironomid fishing for cutts can be exceptional at this time.

If a lake has feeder streams which are used by spawning salmon, cutthroats will school near the creek mouths in the spring and wait for fry to migrate into the lake. Fishing a fry pattern across the drop-off at a creek mouth during the fry migration is deadly—one of the most productive ways of angling for these trout. Throughout the season, lake-dwelling cutthroats find a leech or stickleback pattern hard to resist, and a black Woolly Bugger fished deep and slow has been the demise of more cutts than I care to mention.

Cutts have a habit of finding their way into some very unusual spots and once there tend to grow quite large if left unmolested. A perfect example is a small sphagnum bog near my home on southern Vancouver Island. The open-water portion of this little spot is maybe 90 yards (80 m) across in all directions, a remnant left over from days when the Cowichan River used to flow through the area. The river has long since moved to another course, but the bog developed in its stead.

Private lots surround the spot and access is severely restricted. The trout, however, pay that no mind. In my younger days I used to wander down there in gum boots, my spinning rod in hand, and cast a small yellow and red Panther Martin spinner into the bog's brown waters. Every second or third cast produced a cutthroat that was bright silver, full of scrap, and best of all, about 2 lb (900 g) in weight. I must have tangled every second or third fish in the roots and moss that floated along the shore of that little lake, but a long pole with my net tied to it usually solved the problem.

Beaver ponds and bogs often support populations of coastal cutthroats, so it is certainly worth your while to check them out. Most anglers pass them by without a second thought, so the trout are left alone to feed and grow. Without being exposed to lures or flies, these fish are suckers for the first imitation to be offered to them. Stickleback patterns are deadly in tea-colored waters such as these.

Stream-dwelling cutthroats are another story. These trout can be so selective it drives even the most patient of anglers crazy. Smaller cutts will feed much like a rainbow, selectively taking nymphs and adult insects as hatches present themselves throughout the season. However, larger trout often ignore the hatches, preferring sculpins, fry and minnows that inhabit most streams and rivers of the coast. Patterns like the Muddler Minnow, Rolled Muddler and Mickey Finn are the bane of these fish.

During the autumn when salmon move into the rivers and streams to spawn, cutthroats lie a few feet behind them, waiting for the occasional errant egg to drift by. These trout can sometimes be seen actually banging into the sides of salmon, trying to jar eggs from the pregnant hens. Simple, single-egg patterns tied from chenille or small craft pompons, bounced right along the bottom through holding water, work extremely well during the salmon spawn, and cutthroats will often take them with wild abandon.

Sea-run cutthroats are the most mysterious—and most admired—of this species. Early spring will find sea-runs in the very lower reaches of the rivers and streams, feeding actively on outward migrating salmon fry. Any minnow pattern tied to imitate the species of migrating fry will take these fish. The trout are aggressive at these times and hit hard. As the fry move out into the estuaries and ocean, the cutts follow.

Beach fishing is a great way to try for these trout. While catching them can be difficult, finding them is the greatest challenge. Oceangoing cutthroats prefer shorelines of cobble and barnacles as sandy shores seldom provide enough of the right forage to support them. Beaches near creek mouths that have rocky bottoms are the best, especially if structures like old pilings or docks are nearby. There they find needlefish and fry in amongst the rocks and floating debris, and the trout utilize these structures for protection as well. Patterns like the Mickey Finn, Rolled Muddler and Professor are especially effective for sea-runs.

To effectively fish sea-runs, a fly fisher needs nothing more than a 5–6-weight system with a floating or intermediate-sinking line, and a few of the previously mentioned patterns. Long casts and quick retrieves are the norm. The quick-strip retrieve is important to remember. Since these trout prey on minnows and fry, they expect them to be moving quickly while trying to escape their fate. Strip your fly quickly and maintain that speed. Sometimes a trout will follow your fly a good distance, often creating a slight wake behind it. It's hard to maintain your composure when this occurs, but if you alter your retrieve, almost invariably the fish will refuse the fly and turn away. A steady quick-strip will often convince the cutt that this is as fast as the fly can go, or that it hasn't yet "seen" the predator, and the trout will gobble it up before the fly makes good its escape.

Yes, this cutthroat trout is a true coastal British Columbian. From the crystal clear waters of high alpine lakes to the murky depths of sphagnum bogs, it lives and—given the chance—thrives. Its adaptability and see-food diet have enabled it to survive the by-products of human progress such as urban sprawl, pollution, and overfishing. To continue its survival, all it needs is a chance. The future of coastal cutthroat is still in doubt, but at least there appears to be some light at the end of the proverbial tunnel. Provincial fisheries management programs have recognized the cutthroats' plight and are working to ensure their survival through a combination of restocking programs and barbless hook, catch-and-release regulations.

In the meantime, cutthroats provide coastal anglers with a wide array of year-round fishing opportunities. To continue doing so they require our help. Do them—and yourself—a favor by releasing the cutthroats you catch. Of all the game fish on the coast, they are the most vulnerable. Their numbers have been severely depleted over the past half century, yet they continue providing us with immense enjoyment. If ever a species deserves our full support in being allowed to survive, it is British Columbia's coastal cutthroat trout.

BILL LUSCOMBE'S MUST-HAVE PATTERNS FOR COASTAL CUTTHROAT TROUT

- Mickey Finn
- Muddler Minnow
- Professor
- Single egg
- Rolled Muddler
- Woolly Bugger

CHAPTER 55

THREE FOR THE BEACH

Robert H. Jones

SWAPPING FLIES IS A TIME-HONORED PASTIME AMONG ANGLERS, and I have been the recipient of some outstanding patterns over the years. One that works well for sea-run cutthroat along the saltwater beaches is the American Coachman bucktail. The original was given to me by the late Dave Martin of Courtenay, British Columbia, in the late 1950s, but I now tie it much sparser and tart up the wing with a bit of Krystal Flash. See page 430 for photo.

SPARKLE AMERICAN COACHMAN

Hook: Eagle Claw L067 No. 6
Thread: red
Tail: red calf tail or hackle fibers
Body: yellow floss
Wing: stacked white polar bear, bucktail or calf tail, and pearlescent white Krystal Flash
Hackle: brown

1. Tie in tail so tips extend ½" (12 mm).

2. Tie in body, wrap forward and trim.
3. Tie in wing so tips extend halfway back along the tail; top with six strands of pearlescent white Krystal Flash; then tie in hackle and wrap twice.

GLENNIE'S PINK 'N' SILVER

PROFESSIONAL FLY-FISHING GUIDE Rory Glennie is an inventive tier who produced two very productive saltwater patterns during the 1990s. The first Pink 'n' Silver he gave me was about 1 ½" (38 mm) long, had a wing and tail of medium pink polar bear hair, a darker pink thorax and head, and a silver body. When asked why he had used a gold hook, Rory replied, "Something about that combination produces better results than flies tied on nickel or bronze, so I don't fight it." See page 433 for photo.

Hook: Eagle Claw L1197G No. 8
Thread: Dark pink or red
Body: Silver tinsel
Wing/Tail: Medium pink polar bear, calf tail or hackle fibers

1. Tie on tail so tips extend ¾" (18 mm).
2. Tie in tinsel and wrap forward to ⅛" (3 mm) behind eye.
3. Tie off tinsel and trim; then wrap thread back ⅛" (3 mm), building thorax to twice the body diameter.
4. Tie in wing so tips are even with those of the tail; then build up head until slightly smaller than thorax.

GLENNIE'S PEARL MICKEY

ANOTHER GLENNIE PATTERN that proved productive on coho is the Pearl Mickey. A version of the venerable Mickey Finn, it is tied quite sparse and topped with pearlescent white Flashabou (Rory is adamant about using Flashabou for this pattern). See page 432 for photo.

Hook: Mustad 3123 No. 6
Thread: red
Body: silver tinsel
Wing: stacked yellow and red polar bear, bucktail or calf tail, and pearlescent
         white Flashabou

1. Tie in tinsel even with hook point, wrap forward and trim.
2. Tie in 15–20 yellow hairs so tips extend ¼" (6 mm). Follow with 6 to 10 red
   hairs, then six strands of Flashabou.

CHAPTER 56

A PASSION FOR PINKS

Bill Luscombe

A UGUST BRINGS FISHING DOLDRUMS TO MOST FRESHWATER areas of British Columbia save for bass and pike waters. It is a time when most fly fishers put away their rods, pack up the family and hit the beach. On the West Coast, fly fishers still pack up their rods, but only to throw them into their vehicles and head for the river estuaries in pursuit of pink salmon.

At this time of year every fly fisher and spin-caster capable of raising a rod heads for the river mouths. Wading off the beaches, sometimes up to their waists in the clear ocean, they cast to singles and pairs of jumping pink salmon. Pinks tend to school, and the appearance of only a few jumping fish belies the fact that there are many more just below the surface, possibly hundreds.

Pink salmon *(Oncorhynchus gorbuscha)* inhabit the cold waters of the north Pacific Ocean, ranging from central Washington state north to Alaska and across to northeast Asia. They have the shortest life span of any Pacific salmon and spawn in two-year cycles. Every second summer they return to the streams and rivers that bore them to make their contribution to the survival of their species. On the mainland coast of British Columbia, pinks return every odd year, while on the eastern coast of Vancouver Island, they run in even years. A few rivers are unique in this regard because of very successful hatchery programs. As a result there are smaller runs even in the "off" years. What a bonus for anglers! Every year you can fish some estuaries with a reasonable chance of success.

As salmon go, pinks are the smallest. While their maximum weight is estimated at 12 lb (5.5 kg), they average 4–5 lb (1.8–2.3 kg) when fully mature. They are nicknamed "humpies" because of the characteristic humped back the males develop during their spawning migration. Identification of these fish is quite easy as they have large, oblong, blotchy spots on their tails rather than the small round spots found on coho and chinooks. They also lack the characteristic black mouths of chinooks or the black tongues of coho.

One of the favorite methods of fly fishing for pinks is to wade from shore, and there is a definite technique to this. Slow retrieves are the key, and when combined with the soft takes of these fish, it makes the strikes almost undetectable. It feels much like hooking into floating weed, and knowledgeable anglers always set the hook at the first sign of resistance. They end up setting the hook into a lot of weeds, but they also hook a lot of salmon.

Pinks are very soft mouthed, so you must take care not to pressure them too much once hooked. If you are overaggressive when playing them, the hook will pull out. Although they love to run, they seldom go long distances like coho, so you have little need to pressure a fish too much unless you plan to release it.

During a pink salmon spawning run, anglers catch many more fish than the law allows them to keep, thus catch-and-release is practiced unless they quit after killing their limit. This isn't too difficult with pinks, since their short runs allows anglers to bring fish quickly to hand. Barbless hooks combined with their soft mouths, allow for quick, easy releases (barbless hooks are now mandatory when fishing for salmon in salt water). It is a documented fact that approximately 80–90 percent of all salmon properly released, survive to spawn or be caught again.

Pinks that are killed make excellent table fare if cooked fresh. They don't freeze well; however, and many people, myself included, like to bake up a fresh salmon as dinner the same evening as it was caught and smoke the rest (they are outstanding!).

When fishing the beaches near river mouths, it is best to take up a position and allow the pinks to come to you. If you spend the day moving from spot to spot, you'll not be as successful since the schools slowly cruise along the shoreline. The exception to this is at low tide. When the tide drops, move near the river mouth. The pinks often funnel in and are "fish in a barrel" until the tide rises again.

When casting into tidal flows or the current of a river mouth, remember to mend your line to present the fly to a fish as its natural prey would appear. Casting crosscurrent and dragging the fly back is a common mistake most anglers make when beach fishing. The drag makes the fly move in the wrong direction, just as in a river, and you get significantly fewer strikes because of it.

Fly patterns are simple ties that imitate the food of pink salmon, which feed mostly on small shrimp and other tiny crustaceans, plus squid and baitfish. Small streamer patterns of blue, pink or green over silver bodies, tied on stainless steel hooks in No. 8–2 work well and are most common. Pink appears to be their favorite color, which is probably due to the fact that they feed significantly on krill.

If you plan to fish the estuaries, it is wise to remember that you are dealing with salt water. Maintain your gear diligently or the salt will ruin it in short order. Anodized reels are the rule of the day to help prevent rust and corrosion.

Chest waders are a necessity since you will be wading deep. Make sure your wading boots have sturdy soles and that the legs have sewn-in knee patches to protect areas that may come in contact with barnacles. If you wear a full length vest, remove fly boxes and other gear from the lower pockets. If you don't and end up wading deeper than the bottom of the vest, whatever is in your bottom pockets will be soaked in salt water. Once you get home, hose down your boots and waders, then disassemble your reels and flush the parts with warm water to get rid of any residual salt. I cannot stress good maintenance enough when dealing with ocean water. I've seen many instances of good gear ruined due to lack of proper maintenance.

The opportunities that the pink salmon sport fishery offers along British Columbia's coast are just beginning to be recognized by anglers. With the decline in some site-specific coho and chinook salmon populations, pinks are being hailed as a great alternative. With their numbers holding steady, even on the increase in some areas, this newfound sport fishery should see a significant increase over the next few years. Check out this new angling opportunity. You'll find yourself having a whole lot of fun, and it's nice to know that pink salmon make a tasty alternative to the regular summer fare of hamburgers and hot dogs.

CHAPTER 57

PINKS AND SOCKEYE ABOVE TIDEWATER

Robert H. Jones

B OTH PINK AND SOCKEYE SALMON ARE FAIR GAME ABOVE THE high-tide mark in some rivers, but one must always check the freshwater fishing regulations to make sure. Oddly enough, salmon running long distances upstream are often in better physical condition than those entering short coastal rivers. Sockeye over 200 miles (320 km) from salt water in the Fraser River may be mint bright, while those only 2 miles (3.2 km) upstream on a Vancouver Island stream might already show signs of spawning colors.

Both pink and sockeye are schooling fish, so find one and you find many. It is usually just a matter of searching the pools and tail-outs for signs of movement—polarized glasses are *de rigueur*—but caution is advised as they are easily spooked by looming shapes, clattering rocks and sloppy casts.

These are seldom big fish, so an 8-weight that is suitable for large rivers might be considered overkill on smaller streams. Be warned, however, that the similarity in general size and appearance parts dramatically when a fish is hooked. Pinks will put up a grand battle on light tackle, but sockeye are somewhat faster, stronger and have more stamina.

In shallow flows, stick with a floating line and weighted flies, adjusting the leader length to suit the average water depth. This reduces the number of hang-ups, provides better line control, and skittish salmon seem less intimidated by a line floating on the surface compared to one drifting through their midst.

Simple fly patterns incorporating marabou or combed acrylic in pink, red, chartreuse, blue, green or mauve are good prospects. Others are Glennie's Pink 'n' Silver, Polar Shrimp, and Pink Frammus in No. 8–2, depending on water clarity.

SEARED PINK SALMON STEAKS WITH TOMATO SALSA

A perfect summer dish
(Makes four servings)

4—pink salmon steaks
Olive oil
Salt and pepper to taste

SALSA

3—tomatoes, seeded and diced
1–2—jalapeno peppers, seeded and diced
½ cup—red onion, diced—125 mL
2 tbsp—cilantro, chopped—30 mL
1 tbsp—balsamic vinegar—15 mL
2 tbsp—olive oil—30 mL
Salt and pepper to taste

1. Mix salsa ingredients and let stand at room temperature for 30 minutes for flavors to develop. (Fresh pineapple or other acidic fruit may be substituted for the tomatoes.)

2. Sear salmon steaks in a hot skillet until golden brown. Turn down heat and cook through. Serve steaks on a bed of salsa or mound salsa on top of the salmon.

–Wayne Phillips

CHAPTER 58

TEMPTING TACKLE-BUSTING CHUMS

Dr. Martin Lamont

O F THE PACIFIC SALMON, CHUMS *(Oncorhynchus keta)* WERE of little interest to saltwater anglers until the 1990s. With El Niño–related disruptions in coho and chinook stocks during that period, more attention was directed at these late-running salmon and a popular fishery—mostly involving trolling with lures or mooching with cut plug herring—began to evolve. Those anglers quickly learned what fly fishers in rivers have known all along: chums are strong, brutal brawlers. In fact, many anglers feel that pound-for-pound they are the strongest of all Pacific salmon.

Large numbers of chums enter the rivers when low-pressure weather systems of late fall sweep in from the ocean, drenching the West Coast with heavy rains. Chums seldom migrate far upstream, especially in short rivers like those found on Vancouver Island, and are often found in lower reaches close to the estuary. A good starting point is from the first tidal pool to 1 mile (1.6 km) upstream. For this reason it pays to check local tide tables for the flood tide, which usually brings fresh, new fish into the lower reaches.

By the time chums enter a river, their ocean mantle of bright silver is taking on a distinctive pattern of mottled red-purple and green-olive hues. The males, their hooked kypes armed with fierce-looking teeth, are aggressive and spoiling to fight with each other over the redds. It is this attack mode a fly fisher stimulates by presenting a fly, which is basically an attractor pattern.

Some basic patterns are simple yarn flies in fluorescent green or red. In the often muddied spate waters of fall, green offers greater visibility to the fish. However, there is no exact formula for chums, so experiment occasionally with blue or yellow-orange yarn. My favorite pattern is the Green and Pink Frammus originated by Vic Stevens of Courtenay, British Columbia. Although intended for winter steelhead, it works well for chums. It is simply a body of green chenille and a wing of pink acrylic yarn, or reversed with a pink body and green wing. I use No. 6–2 hooks, with the larger size for colored water.

Those new to chum fishing often underestimate these heavyweights and use tackle that is too light for the task. While the average weight of male chums is about 10 lb (4.5 kg), they have been recorded at well over three times this size. Even 10-lb chums can be unbelievably strong tackle-busters, so a 9–10-weight outfit is suggested. My favorite is a 12', 10-weight fiberglass rod, treasured for its ability to take the pounding and abuse of chum fishing.

A sink-tip line with a shortened head is useful for mending a dead-drift through pods of schooling chum. Alternatively, try a floating line in shallower flows. Tippets should be heavy—nothing less than 10-lb test—4' (1.25 m) long for colored water, 9' (2.75 m) in clear conditions. Flies can also be presented with a classic down-and-across swing. At the end of each drift, let your fly hang downstream in the current for a short while, then retrieve upstream with steady, slow-to-medium pulls of 2' (60 cm) or so (reel to knee), and be prepared for an often subtle take.

Take care when approaching chums holding in thin water as they spook easily. In colored water they prefer slower flows close to the bank or in back eddies, and they often hold right at an angler's feet. If you can see fish but they refuse to bite, remember that they are not feeding—you must trigger that attack mode. Present your fly repeatedly over the same area and at the same depth before covering new water. Fish fresh from the ocean are ready takers, but shortly after settling over the redds, they lose interest in biting flies.

The window of opportunity to tangle with these exceptionally strong, challenging opponents is admittedly short, but we who are addicted to chum salmon feel they are well worth the effort.

CHAPTER 59

SMALLMOUTHS ON AN ISLAND IN THE PACIFIC

Robert H. Jones

PICTURE THOUSANDS OF DEDICATED ANGLERS LIVING IN THE midst of an abundant population of large, healthy smallmouth bass, yet relatively few bothering to fish for them. Hard to believe? Perhaps, but this unusual situation exists in British Columbia, on southern Vancouver Island. Perhaps the reason why can be explained, in part, by the fact that "Islanders" have good saltwater fishing for five species of Pacific salmon, sea-run steelhead in many rivers, plus rainbow and cutthroat trout in most streams and lakes. With such a bounty of native fish available, introduced smallmouth bass are not only ignored by most anglers, some consider them little more than coarse fish.

This obvious bias by salmon and trout snobs is fine and dandy with Vancouver Island's relatively small band of bass anglers, for they enjoy uncrowded fishing. However, change is occurring as the Island's population expands. Many new residents arriving from eastern Canada and the U.S. have fished for smallmouth bass on their home turf, and it doesn't take long to determine that their tackle and tactics work just as well on the Island variety. As a result of this slowly increasing interest, native-born West Coasters are also becoming aware of the sporting qualities smallmouths offer.

Smallmouths can hardly be classed as newcomers on the British Columbia scene. They were introduced to Canada's westernmost province in 1901, originally in Christina Lake, in the southeastern corner of the province known as the Kootenays; and in Langford and Florence lakes near Victoria, on the southern tip of Vancouver Island. In 1920, a few Langford Lake smallmouths were transported about 20 miles (32 km) north to Saltspring Island and released in St. Mary Lake. Three years later, Florence Lake bass were transferred to Spider Lake, near Qualicum Beach. This is still the northernmost limit of their range on Vancouver Island. Over the years, other transplants were made—mostly by bass enthusiasts rather than the provincial fishery branch—and at present 17 lakes accessible to the public contain smallmouth bass.

Reports of trophy-sized smallmouths have cropped up over the years, but authenticating them has proved futile. Included in these unconfirmed reports was an 11-lb 2-oz (5-kg) bass mentioned in a 1958 tourism promotion booklet produced by the provincial government. Despite its source, the provincial fisheries branch has no record of such a behemoth. More recently, the *Victoria Times Colonist* newspaper reported a 9-lb 8-oz (4.3-kg) bass from Langford Lake in June, 1988, and one of 9 lb 2 oz (4.1 kg) from Spider Lake in April, 1989. Unfortunately, neither of these word-of-mouth fish was ever confirmed, nor has photographic evidence ever been made available.

Nevertheless, big bass do exist on the Island. The *Victoria Times Colonist* once ran an annual "King Fisherman" contest, in which all entries had to be officially weighed and witnessed. From 1957 until 1984, the heaviest smallmouth entries were usually over 6 lb (2.7 kg). The two heaviest ever entered were 7 lb 4 oz (3.3 kg), one each from Elk and Matheson lakes in the Victoria area.

While Vancouver Island smallmouths grow to respectable sizes, many enthusiasts feel that if they had the abundance and variety of high-protein food available to their eastern and southern counterparts, the world record would stand an excellent chance of falling to an Island fish. However, other than three-spined sticklebacks and sculpins, Vancouver Island lakes are devoid of forage fish. Fortunately, there are good populations of aquatic insects and leeches in most lakes, plus crayfish in some. Studies of stomach contents have disclosed that juvenile trout and bass also account for part of their diet, as do terrestrial insects.

That Island smallmouths attain such respectable proportions on meager rations can probably be attributed to their long growing season. The southwestern coast of British Columbia enjoys a fairly moderate year-round climate.

Winters are usually of short duration, snow is infrequent, and freezing temperatures seldom last long enough to form ice on the lakes containing bass, all of which are at low elevations. While this used to mean year-round bass fishing to those willing to put in the time and effort, there is now a closed season from April 15 to June 15 to protect smallmouths during their spawning period.

All of the bass lakes contain rainbows, and several also offer cutthroat trout. In fact, anglers concentrating on smallmouths in some lakes are often forced to endure interruptions by pesky trout weighing 4–5 lb (1.8–2.3 kg), but few ever seem to complain too loudly. The following lakes in the Victoria region contain all three species (area in acres is shown in parentheses): Beaver and Elk (combined total 554), Durrance (20), Langford (148), Matheson (62), Prospect (178) and Thetis (88). Glen Lake (42) has only smallmouths and rainbows. A few miles north of Victoria, Shawnigan Lake (1,327) has all three, plus kokanee salmon.

Saltspring Island is reached by ferry from Sidney to Fulford Harbour, or from Crofton to Vesuvius. Cusheon Lake (67) has cutthroat trout and smallmouths, both of which appear to peak at about 3 lb (1.4 kg). St. Mary Lake (482) offers both species of trout, plus smallmouths that have been recorded locally at 8 lb (3.6 kg). Among Island bass anglers, St. Mary is considered most dependable for large fish.

Farther north on Vancouver Island are six lakes offering both species of trout, plus smallmouth bass of sizes guaranteed to increase one's heart rate. They are Diver (38), Green (33), Holden (93), Long (84), Quennell (297) and Spider (141) lakes. Of these, Long and Spider are good bets for large bass.

Fly rodders make up a high percentage of serious bass anglers, and those with experience elsewhere have no problem adapting to the Island variety. Some lakes have exceptionally clear water, others are fairly dark, and nutrient-rich lakes like Quennell have dense algae blooms during the late summer and fall (and usually offer the best fishing). This being the case, a fly selection that covers a good range of sizes and colors will be to your advantage.

Small poppers with heads about the size of pencil erasers can be deadly during early morning and late-evening hours. The secret is to learn how much popping is enough, and how loud it should be. Too large or too loud will usually send smallmouths scurrying for parts unknown.

If weed growth is heavy, try a small Deer Hair Bug. Being relatively weed-proof, they can often be skipped over obstructions and dragged through vegetation without fouling the hook.

Whichever surface approach you are using, never be in a hurry to start your retrieve. Allowing a popper, bug or fly simply to sit quietly on the surface for up to a half minute or more often goads a bass into striking. If it doesn't, before starting your retrieve, simply jiggle your rod tip enough to impart the slightest bit of movement to your offering. It's suspenseful, but exciting when a smallmouth inhales it with a loud slurp, or better yet, leaps into the air beside it, arches over, then grabs it on the way down—assuming, of course, that you haven't panicked and jerked the fly away.

Large dry flies (No. 10–4) like a bushy Tom Thumb, Mikulak Sedge and Madam X are often productive during the day until the midsummer sun reaches its apex and bass seek deeper water; then these tactics are best relegated to early morning and late evening hours.

During the bright, warm days of summer, use a depth recorder to locate underwater structure and a temperature probe to determine the comfort zone in which bass are suspended. The preferred temperature range in most lakes appears to be about 62–64°F (16.5–17.5°C), perhaps a bit cooler than elsewhere.

As with many other freshwater species, when in doubt as to which fly to start with, think "leech." When fished on slow-sinking lines, the Blood Leech, Mohair Leech and Acrylic Leech are all fairly dependable patterns for taking bass (and trout) during warm weather. If sticking with a floating line, try large, buggy-looking nymphs and Woolly Buggers with bead heads, or Clouser Minnows.

During the summer months, urban lakes are subjected to heavy daytime use by boaters, water-skiers and swimmers. For this reason, some anglers in the Victoria and Nanaimo areas confine their summer bass fishing strictly to nighttime—often from midnight until dawn. Most use float tubes or small inflatable boats to surface fish with small poppers and bugs. One fly rodder confided that he considered it a poor night on Langford or Glen if at least one 4-lb (1.8-kg) bass was not landed and released, and that bass of over 6 lb (2.7 kg) had been occasionally recycled at both lakes.

Anglers planning a visit to Vancouver Island to sample this fishery are advised that several lakes containing bass have restrictions concerning the use of motors. Depending on their location, these include no motors of any kind, motors of no more than 10 h.p., or electric motors only. Some lakes also have maximum speed limits in specific areas.

Some urban lakes in the Victoria and Nanaimo areas are almost totally surrounded by houses and private property; therefore, vehicle parking near launch sites is limited. It pays to check out small lakes beforehand, not only to determine where to launch, but also where to park.

Accommodations poses no problem as lakes in the Victoria, Nanaimo and Qualicum Beach areas are readily accessible to every class of hotel and motel imaginable, plenty of bed and breakfast operations, plus a multitude of private and public campgrounds. On Saltspring Island, Cusheon Lake has two resorts; St. Mary Lake, seven. Bed and breakfast accommodation and campgrounds are also available.

For those wishing to combine smallmouth bass with chinook or coho salmon fishing, plan on mid-June or July for the Victoria area. June weather can be undependable, so take rain gear. Figure on August to mid-October for combined fishing in the Nanaimo and Saltspring Island areas. Early October insect hatches in all lakes can result in outstanding dry-fly action for mixed bags of bass and trout. October can be a fine month, weatherwise, but tote rain gear just in case.

Some dedicated Vancouver Island bass anglers are certain the world record can be broken by a smallmouth from one of the Island lakes. Whether this is fact or fancy remains to be seen, but in the meantime we have fun trying, more often than not on lakes almost devoid of competition.

BOB JONES' MUST-HAVE PATTERNS FOR WEST COAST SMALLMOUTH BASS

- Dry: Madam X
- Mikulak Sedge
- Tom Thumb
- Leech
- Blood Leech
- Mohair Leech
- Streamer: Clouser Deep Minnow
- Woolly Bugger

CHAPTER 60

THE BOTTOM FISH BONANZA
OF BRITISH COLUMBIA

Robert H. Jones

FROM A RECREATIONAL SALTWATER ANGLER'S PERSPECTIVE, THE term "bottom fish" encompasses pretty well all species lacking silver scales and adipose fins. Some, like kelp greenling and Pacific mackerel, are sleek and streamlined with beautiful markings and coloration; others, like flounders and cabezon, are downright homely—oddly shaped with mottled brown colors. No matter what they look like, most are worthy opponents on tackle that matches their particular sizes, and the speed and strength of some may surprise you. In addition, just about all are excellent table fare.

Fishing for Pacific salmon and bottom fish is symbiotic. Few anglers would spend the time, effort and money to plan a trip aimed specifically at catching bottom fish. Most encounter them accidentally while fishing for coho or chinook salmon, and in so doing discover they provide an interesting diversion whenever salmon are scarce or off the bite. Nevertheless, a few of us will actually pass up a few hours of prime-time salmon fishing to concentrate on prospecting the bottom. To quote a fishing companion who is equally enamored: "I love the suspense. When you're out there after coho, you know that's probably what you're going to catch. But when you put that fly down on the bottom, you haven't got a clue about what's going to bite. It could be a 6" (15-cm) sculpin, a 10-lb (4.5-kg) cabezon, a 40-lb (18-kg) lingcod—you just never know. . . ."

The Fish

The Peterson Field Guide to Pacific Coast Fishes lists nearly 300 species of bottom fish in the coastal waters of British Columbia, but there are so many variables involved it is impossible to state with any degree of accuracy where a particular species may be found, their abundance, or the maximum sizes they might attain.

The species of greatest interest to fly fishers are those which can be reached with standard tackle without resorting to ridiculous means. I write here of fly "casting," not mooching or strip-casting with monofilament and a heavy sinker, which, when all is said and done, is a very sensible way to present a fly—or anything else—at great depths. But then you might just as well go one step further and use a sturdy rod and multiplying reel, which are far more suitable for the task. My best halibut to date weighed 85 lb (39 kg). It was hooked in 250' (75 m) of water while I was using a Shakespeare Ugly Stik rod, somewhat similar in action to a pool cue, a multiplying Penn GTi 310 reel and 80-lb test braided Spectra line. After the half-hour struggle it took getting that brute up to the boat, all I wanted to do was sit in a corner of the cabin and whimper quietly until my shoulders and arms stopped aching. Thoughts of attempting that task with a 10–12-weight fly rod still causes bouts of uncontrollable shuddering.

There are no "absolutes" concerning bottom fish, but generally those of smaller sizes—under 5 lb (2.3 kg)—are found in shallow water ranging from the shoreline to depths of 50' (15 m) or so. Examples are flounder, greenling, immature lingcod, and several of the 24 species of rockfish found off the British Columbia coast. At middepths, 50–150' (15–45 m), basically the same species are encountered, but they tend to be larger, and you will probably run into more spiny dogfish (small sharks) and mackerel. Deep water, 150–600' (45–180 m), is where the largest fish are "usually" found, like brilliant orange-colored yelloweye rockfish to 25 lb (11.4 kg), potbellied lingcod to 50 lb (22.7 kg) or more, and Pacific halibut that might well weigh over 400 lb (182 kg). "Usually" is stressed because big lingcod and huge halibut are occasionally caught in 15' (4.5 m) of water or less, and dinky little rockfish can be found at 600' (180 m). However, these are exceptions, not the rule.

The Tackle

WATER DEPTHS BEYOND 30' (9 m) are often difficult to fish efficiently with fly-casting tackle, especially when strong tidal currents, brisk winds and wave action are factored into the equation. However, with decent conditions and a fast-sinking line, depths to 60' (18 m) or more can be covered fairly well. Much will depend on precisely how hard you are willing to work at it. At any given time you might be casting over rocky shoals, shallow bays with sandy bottoms, fast-flowing tidal narrows, or steep drop-offs into deep water.

Tackle constraints reduce the number of target species to those families which include bullheads, flatfish, greenling, rockfish, dogfish and mackerel. Basically, whatever you use for salmon fishing will work well for bottom fish. Having two or three outfits suited for specific tasks makes it easier to meet changing conditions and allows you to match your tackle to the fish being sought. The most popular rod lengths are 9–12' and have a fighting butt to reduce arm and wrist fatigue.

Shooting heads are preferred over full-length lines, and the reels storing them should have enough capacity for the running line and at least 200 yards (180 m) of backing. Even though you may not intentionally be fishing for chinook or coho salmon, it is not unheard of for one to inhale your offering as it plunges toward bottom. For this reason, the reel should also have a butter-smooth, easily adjustable drag.

A 6-weight outfit with a sink-tip or intermediate sinking line is fine around docks, jetties or kelp beds for mackerel, greenling, and rockfish, all of which swim or suspend at varying depths. If fishing for flounders from a boat, a fast-sinking line is a better choice as this species is usually at depths of 25' (7.5 m) or more and almost always right on the bottom.

If larger fish are sought at greater depths, go to an 8-weight with a 500–800 grain sinking line. While some anglers advocate a 10-weight for large cabezon, lingcod and halibut, the truth is that all but the very largest can probably be handled on 8-weight gear. It just takes a little longer.

Short heads created from lengths of lead-core trolling line can also be useful at times. These are easily fashioned by cutting a piece of line to the desired length, then forming a loop at each end. Peel back the braided nylon outer line to expose 4" (10 cm) of lead wire and break it off. Smooth out the braided line and fold the tag end back to form an open loop about 1" (25 mm) long. Bind the tag end and running line together with nylon thread, whip finish and coat with flexible head cement or Pliobond. Lead-core heads of 1–6' in length come in handy when you need that little bit of extra weight to get down where the action is. Simply loop one between the fly line and leader butt.

Bottom fish aren't the least bit leader-shy, so a 4' butt section with 2' of 10–15-lb test tippet will suffice. If intentionally targeting large lingcod or halibut, a tippet testing 20 lb is a better choice. This is more to provide abrasion resistance rather than strength. With the exception of spiny dogfish, wire leaders aren't required.

While fly fishers love to fuss and fret over fly patterns, bottom fish usually bite whatever is dangled in front of them. The only pattern you really need is Bob Clouser's Deep Minnow in various sizes and colors—period. I use Super Hair or Ultra Hair, tying them up to 6" (15 cm) long with white bellies and a single complimentary color on top. My three favorite back colors are medium green, bright pink, and chartreuse. If you feel you simply must tart it up with a few strands of Flashabou or Krystal Flash for added visibility, be my guest—but it isn't really necessary.

The efficiency of a Clouser Minnow is in its design: tied on a single hook with heavy barbell-shaped lead eyes, the point rides up just like a leadhead jig, which deflects obstructions and helps hook fish solidly in the upper jaw. The largest hook size I use is No. 2, usually Eagle Claw Billy Pate Tarpon models, or if a longer shank is desired, Tiemco 9394. As the lead eyes are positioned about ½" (13 mm) behind the hook eye, the slender, slinky-looking fly has an undulating motion as it is retrieved. To get maximum action, use a loop knot to tie on the fly. I find the Non-slip Mono Knot easy to tie and very dependable at nearly 100 percent strength.

If thoughts of having only one fly pattern in your box gives you near-terminal heebie-jeebies, add some large Woolly Worms in whichever gaudy color combinations strike your fancy. These patterns offer an excellent chance to rid your tying bench of assorted hideous materials that might otherwise never be used. One suggestion, though—tie a set of lead eyes right behind the hook eye so the fly will ride point up with that enticing up-down-up swimming action.

The Tactics

THE TWO MOST CRITICAL FACTORS affecting saltwater angling—whether salmon or bottom fish—are wind and tide. Worst-case scenarios are tidal currents running one way, a stiff breeze blowing the other way, large swells rolling in off the open Pacific, and a cross chop. The only anglers who can fish in such conditions—if they are really that desperate—are trollers using heavy sinkers or downriggers to take down their offerings. Possessing all the right tackle and a boxful of perfect flies is of no use if you can't reach the fish, but fly fishers might be able to save the day by getting in the lee of an island or peninsula.

Best-case scenarios are high or low slack tides with no wave action, current or wind—mighty rare occurrences on the West Coast, believe me. Thankfully, there are many occasions when conditions do come close enough to permit hours of enjoyable fishing.

Most salmon anglers agree that the prime fishing periods are high and low slack tides, plus a half hour or so on each side when tidal currents are fairly slow. This also sums up the best periods for bottom fishing, especially at depths greater than 15–20' (4.5–6 m). Thus, an angler must decide whether to fish for salmon or try for whatever is down there on the bottom.

The most efficient way to present your fly is from a stationary boat. Anchor from the bow, then fish one person from the bow and one from the stern. Depths of up to 20' (6 m) seldom pose a problem at getting down, but beyond that use the "slack-line-drop" method. First, cast out as far as you can comfortably, then strip another 30–40' (9–12 m) of line from your reel and let it lie in loose coils on the deck or, better yet, in a plastic tub or box to prevent it from hanging up or getting stepped on. Strip in the line, then cast your fly "upstream" into the current and quickly shake the remainder of the slack line through the guides. This allows it to sink in a more level configuration rather than swing down like a pendulum. Your casts should be made in such a way that the anchor rope will be avoided, and if possible, so your line won't drift under the boat.

A good way to judge how deep you are getting is to compare the depth indicated on the depth sounder to the length of your cast. If the black box reads 60' (18 m) and you are casting 60' (18 m), your fly won't reach bottom. If you are reaching out 80' (24 m) or more, your fly still won't cover much of the bottom. However, shaking loose line through the guides after each cast allows you to stay close to the bottom over a reasonable distance, with the length of time down and the distance covered depending on such variables as line density, water depth and current speed.

Strip in line just fast enough to stay in touch with the fly, giving it occasional erratic twitches, until it hangs perpendicular from the rod tip. Once more shake out a few feet of line, then wait until it straightens before paying out more. This increases the time your fly is down there fishing for you. When the drift is finished, don't be in too great a hurry to strip it in for the next cast, for fish will often swim up off bottom to follow a fly, sometimes for surprising distances.

Once the tide starts running too fast to continue fishing the bottom efficiently, pull anchor and cruise around to look for schools of black rockfish feeding on the surface. A real favorite with many anglers, these fish appear to have been stamped from the same mold as smallmouth bass. Although their average size is about 2–4 lb (900 g–1.8 kg), they have been recorded to 10 lb (4.5 kg). What makes them unique among the rockfish family is that large schools are often found feeding right on the surface. This can be disappointing for anglers who think they have hit a salmon-feeding bonanza, but great sport for those who appreciate the fighting qualities of these strong, determined battlers. Aside from mackerel, they are one of the few bottom fish that can be caught right on the surface, and they will actually take floating or barely submerged flies.

When the tide is running, black rockfish favor the downstream side of kelp beds, especially those located around sheer bluffs, rock piles, small islets and points of rugged shoreline. As tidal currents build up speed, baitfish move into the protective lee of the kelp beds, making them attractive targets for the voracious blacks. Their presence can usually be detected by baitfish skittering across the surface as they are pursued by porpoising rockfish.

Although you can take fish right on top while using a floating line, your best choice for surface-feeding blacks is a sink-tip or intermediate sinking line. They are herding the baitfish from below, so you can also hit them down deeper. Finding a large school of black rockfish on top can provide some of the fastest-paced fishing you will ever encounter in salt water—or anywhere else for that matter.

While commercially caught lingcod have been recorded at over 100 lb (45 kg), those found throughout most coastal inshore regions average less then 10 lb (4.5 kg). However, some remote areas along the western and northeastern coast of Vancouver Island offer ample opportunities for fish weighing 20 lb (9 kg) or more, as do the central and northern mainland coast, and the Queen Charlotte Islands. The strength and stamina of these toothy critters makes landing a large one on fly tackle an accomplishment worth bragging about.

Other shallow-water bottom fish of interest are brown and copper rockfish which average up to 5 lb (2.3 kg), kelp and rock greenling to 3 lb (1.4 kg), and cabezon—largest members of the sculpin family. Sculpin? As in bullhead? If you think it strange that a fly fisher would knowingly hope to catch a bullhead, odds are that you have never encountered a cabezon, also known as giant marbled sculpin. Recorded to weights of 30 lb (13.6 kg), the average encountered around coastal British Columbia waters is in the 8–20-lb (3.6–9-kg) range. They possess the size and strength to guarantee memorable encounters, especially the first time one looms up from the murky depths with its dinner-plate-sized pectoral fins spread outward, then opens its huge, rubbery-lipped mouth to reveal a pale blue-green interior. Spooky.

If targeting flounder, look for flat, sandy bottoms at depths of 20–40' (6–12 m). And I'll tell you what—be prepared for a surprisingly tough scrap. Matched against a 6-weight outfit, a 12" (30-cm) fish will outfight most freshwater fish of equal weight. Get into a flounder bed with fish of 18" (45 cm)—a real bonanza—and you might even consider switching to 8-weight tackle.

For greenling, various species of rockfish, juvenile lingcod and cabezon, fish around kelp beds in depths to 50' (15 m), but often much shallower. If the kelp is growing around a rock pile or small islet, all the better, for larger fish will also be attracted. If there is a sharp drop-off nearby, this is where to prospect for larger lingcod and rockfish.

Although salmon trollers throw real hissy fits whenever a Pacific mackerel chomps on their herring- or anchovy-baited hooks, fly fishers usually enjoy the tussle these amazingly strong, swift-swimming fish put up. Pound for pound, mackerel will pull harder than a salmon and do it a heck of a lot faster. They have been recorded to weights of 6 lb (2.7 kg) but seldom top 3 lb (1.4 kg)—which is maybe a good thing as we might never land them. When schools are present in an area, you may find them at almost any depth.

Another scourge of salmon anglers are spiny dogfish. Although these small sharks peak at 20 lb (9 kg), one of half that weight will give a good account of itself on a fly rod. These fish often school close to the surface in unbelievably large numbers, and should you hook one, be prepared for a dogged, determined fight. Be warned that these toothy critters have two dorsal fins, and each has a long, sharp spine of solid bone in front of it. Also to be avoided are the teeth—they aren't large, but there are hundreds of them, all sharp as razors. For this reason, a 6" wire leader is recommended.

It is doubtful that bottom fish will ever replace salmon in the hearts of anglers, but I have found that those who take time to indulge in this interesting and often exciting facet of saltwater fly fishing are seldom disappointed.

ROBERT H. JONES' MUST-HAVE PATTERNS FOR BOTTOM FISH

- Clouser Deep Minnow
- Woolly Worm

OVEN-ROASTED HALIBUT

A sweet and succulent feast
(Makes four servings)

4 pieces—halibut—allow 6–8 oz (170–250 g) per person
2—garlic cloves, thinly sliced
Drizzle of olive oil
2 tbsp—oil, or butter—30 mL
Salt and pepper to taste

1. Heat a heavy skillet or roasting pan in 350°F (180°C) oven for 5 minutes, then

remove. Add 2 tbsp oil and garlic to skillet and place fish on top. Roast fish until flesh is no longer opaque, about 10 minutes per inch (4 minutes per cm) of thickness. Do not overcook or the halibut will dry out.

Oven-roasted halibut comes out a lovely ivory color. Alternatively, roast it with your favorite toppings, but mound them toward the middle so the natural ivory color shows. To highlight the color, garnish with thin strips of roasted sweet red pepper.

–Wayne Phillips

CHAPTER 61

IF KEEPING A FISH TO EAT, DO IT PROPERLY!

Vera Jones

IT'S A FACT THAT MOST FLY FISHERS PRACTICE CATCH-AND-release, but many keep part of their catch for consumption. After all, shocking as it may seem to those who advocate strict catch-and-release for all fish at all times, the original intent of fishing was not for enjoyment, but to put food on the table. And for some anglers in some situations, this is still the case; however, those who choose to fly fish enjoy the best of both worlds.

Compliance with fishing regulations and moral values aside, some anglers release everything they catch simply because they don't like the taste of fish. I can't help but wonder if the reason for their dislike might be related to having never tasted fresh, properly cared-for and prepared fish. Unfortunately, a lot of fish is wasted because anglers don't follow a few simple steps to ensure it stays in prime condition.

Although it's impossible to cover field care and storage for all fishing situations, there is one practice that should always be avoided: Never, ever, place live fish on stringers. The stress of being caught then dragged around in the warmer surface water is often enough to do them in, and once a fish dies the flesh starts absorbing water through osmosis. Immediately! For this same reason, dead fish—uncleaned or cleaned—should never be stored in water.

Anglers who traditionally keep fish for consumption know the value of being well prepared ahead of time. If wading or fishing from shore, a woven wicker creel or canvas bag serves to carry their catch. A creel provides ventilation, and can be lined with greenery like ferns or willow branches, which keeps the fish separated so the air moves freely between them. An alternative is to carry a few sheets of coarse, clean burlap, which can be dampened, squeezed fairly dry, then crumpled up and placed between the fish. A canvas creel should also contain greenery or burlap, but has an added advantage—it can be occasionally dipped into the water to wet down the exterior. Evaporation of the water then provides a cooling effect to the interior.

Never place dead fish in direct sunlight to dry out, in a plastic bag to cook in its own rapidly decaying juices, or in the rubberized pouch of a fishing vest for the same reason.

Anglers fishing from boats generally have aboard an insulated cooler or box containing ice, either crushed, blocks, or cubes in plastic bags. Crushed ice is best as the fish can be completely covered and layered, chilling them thoroughly. Frozen gel packs are also suitable, and can be reused as often as necessary after washing them off and refreezing the contents.

The ideal cooler has a plastic, wood or metal grid that fits in the bottom, which allows ice water and fluids from the cleaned fish to trickle out through a drain tap. A cooler should be long enough to allow large fish to be laid straight, as *rigor mortis* (stiffening of muscle tissue) occurs after death. Cleaning or filleting a bent or curved fish is difficult, and straightening it out tears the flesh apart.

Once a decision is made to keep a fish, it should be killed as quickly and humanely as possible. In most cases, a sharp blow to the top of the head will suffice, but some saltwater species like rockfish, flounder and halibut seem almost indestructible. They are best stunned, then their gills cut to bleed them.

Carry a sharp knife to bleed and clean your catch. If you can't clean a fish right away, the following quick method of bleeding it offers a temporary solution. Hold a fish by its head so the tail hangs down. Insert a knife blade crossways through the top of the gills, then cut downward to the throat by following the curve of the gill. Grasp the wrist of the tail and quickly turn the fish upside-down. The amount of blood that gushes out is surprising, and it takes only a few seconds to drain almost completely. If in a boat, this last step should be done while holding the fish over the water—and don't worry, the blood is biodegradable. This simple procedure takes only a few seconds, but removing blood from the flesh enhances its quality and is also of benefit for long-term frozen storage.

A fish should be cleaned or filleted as soon as possible, but this isn't always possible. My only advice here is that while cleaning a fish, take care not to puncture the innards, for the contents will taint the flesh. Also, ensure that you remove all of the gills and kidney—that dark, congealed bloodlike strip along the backbone—for these are the first organs to start decaying.

Rather than immersing a fish in water to wash it off, rinse it quickly with sprayed water, then wipe it clean with a damp cloth or paper toweling. If there is no spray available, simply wipe it clean and package it for storage.

At home, fish stores well for a day or two in the refrigerator. Place smaller fish in a resealable plastic bag nestled in a container of ice. Drain the container and replace the ice as necessary. Alternatively, line a container with a dampened towel or paper towels, place the fish on top, then cover the container with plastic wrap.

Freezing fish at home requires proper packaging materials that provide good barriers against oxygen and water vapor. Polyethylene plastic bags (like bread bags) and wax paper don't work because they are too porous. "Cling wraps" like Saran Wrap provide the required barrier, plus they cling tightly to the fish thus discouraging air pockets. Aluminum foil is also nonporous, but as it punctures easily it should be used only as an initial wrap.

There are several ways to freeze fish successfully. For short-term storage, press cling wrap or foil over the fish to squeeze out the air. A secondary outer wrap is necessary—I recommend heavy freezer paper that is waxed on the inside and allows writing the contents and date on the outside. Alternatively, the fish can be placed in a polyester "freezer" bag (others are not suitable). Then submerge the bag in a sink or container of cold water so as to squeeze out the air. Seal the bag and use a secondary wrap over it.

Glazing fish with a coating of ice isn't practical for home use because it takes time and an extremely low freezer temperature, but a similar method uses Tupperware or similar plastic containers and allows for long-term storage. Put fish and a bit of water in the container, then place it in the freezer. When frozen, add enough water to cover the fish. The previous bit of water will anchor it so it won't float. Refreeze. Top up with water if any part of the fish protrudes from the ice. Another long-term storage procedure is to place fish in a polyester "freezer" bag. Squeeze out air, seal and place in the freezer. When the fish is frozen, place the package inside another slightly larger freezer bag, add a bit of water in between the two bags, then seal the outer bag. Freeze again to anchor the inner bag; then open the outer bag to add more water. Replace in the freezer, water-filled side down, and refreeze.

There are several ways of defrosting fish. If you have ample time, thaw fish in the refrigerator, but expect it to take 24 hours for a 1-lb (500-g) package. For faster thawing, submerge the fish in a bowl of cold water, adjusting the faucet so a steady stream circulates and spills out of the bowl. Be sure to keep the fish in its vapor-proof wrapping while it's thawing. A 1-lb package will take from 30 to 60 minutes to thaw.

Microwaving will thaw frozen fish at defrost power (about 30 percent), with a 1-lb portion will taking about five minutes. Follow the manufacturers' instructions.

Never keep thawed fish for cooking later. Prepare it immediately. On the other hand, a single portion or a few portions of fish frozen in a small block can be baked, poached, and broiled without thawing—just double the cooking time. This is an excellent way to preserve flavor, moisture and nutrients.

Deep frying in hot oil or pan frying is the most common way of serving fish. Chill the fish pieces to lessen the amount of oil they will absorb during cooking.

Overcooking fish is a common abuse. The general rule, applicable to all fish, is 10 minutes for each inch (4 minutes for each cm) of thickness measured at its thickest point. Thus, cooking a fish or fillet that is 1" thick requires five minutes on one side, then five on the other.

Despite what people who don't like eating fish maintain, most fish is safe to eat. The largest risk of illness comes from consuming raw oysters, clams and mussels. Reports and epidemiological studies by the U.S. Center for Disease Control, which compiled data on illnesses caused by food, indicate that by excluding raw mollusks and shellfish, the risk of illness drops to one in a million—much below beef and poultry.

The second largest risk is from fish taken in recreational and subsistence fisheries, when contamination occurs during handling, storage or cooking. In other words—bacterial or viral infection can be eliminated by proper handling, storage and cooking. It's that easy. Putting the risk into perspective, you're 10 times more likely to be struck by lightning than to become ill from eating fish.

CHAPTER 62

SELECTED FLY PATTERNS

Where known, the name of the pattern inventor is shown in brackets. The tier's name appears in italics.

Dry Flies

Adams (Leonard Halladay)
Jim Crawford
Hook: standard light wire No. 18–10
Thread: fine diameter blue-gray or blue dun
Tail: hackle fibers
Body: Adams gray Poly Dubbing, very fine
Wings: grizzly hackle tips
Hackle: grizzly neck
(Vary hackle colors to match local may fly hatches.)

Adams, Bastard
Bob Scammell
Hook: Mustad 94840 or Tiemco 101
Thread: gray monocord
Tail: elk body hair
Body: Orvis Beaver Adams dubbing
Wing: white polypropylene yarn
Hackle: one brown, one grizzly

Adams, Parachute
Brian Chan
Hook: dry fly No. 14–10
Tail: black moose hair
Body: dubbed gray Antron
Wing: white goat or Antron
Hackle: 2 grizzly feathers

Ant, Black Fur
Kevin Fancy
Hook: Mustad 94840 No. 20–10
Thread: black nymph thread
Body: black spun fur
Hackle: dyed black

Ant, Poly (Bob Scammell)
Bob Scammell
Hook: Mustad 94831 No. 22–14
Thread: black monocord
Body: two "blobs" Orvis Black Beaver dubbing
Wing: white polypropylene yarn
Hackle: black

Black Gnat
Kevin Fancy
Hook: Mustad 94840 No. 12–10
Body: black chenille
Hackle: black cock or hen
Wing: gray duck quill

Blue-Winged Olive
Martin Lamont
Hook: Mustad 3913B, 94833 No. 20–10, 1x fine
Tail: cock-hackle fibers, olive, same length as
   shank
Body: dubbing—olive, olive-gray or olive-yellow
   (alternative: stripped peacock eye quill, natural
   or dyed to match hackle)
Hackle: Two blue dun/olive dry-fly hackles

Caddis, Elk Hair (Al Troth)
Martin Lamont
Hook: Mustad 94840, 9671 or 9757B No. 18–10
Body: hare's ear fur
Hackle: furnace cock, palmered
Rib: gold wire, fine
Wing: elk hair, tan
Head: butt ends, extended over eye and trimmed

CDC Waterhen Bloa (Chris Marshall)
Chris Marshall
Hook: Partridge GRS7MMB
Thread: yellow silk
Body: yellow silk, dubbed over lightly with mole
   fur
Wing: dense CDC oiler feather, natural gray
Hackle: coot (waterhen) undercovert, maximum
   of two turns

Deer Hair Bug (Bill Carter)
Paul Marriner
Hook: Mustad 3399A No. 8–4
Tail: calf tail (color of choice)
Body: spun deer hair, clipped to a cigar shape
Hackle: orange, palmered

Foam Spider (Bill Black)
Steve Galea
Hook: Tiemco 100 or Mustad 94845 No. 12–10
Thread: yellow 6/0 prewaxed
Body: yellow foam, preformed bug body
Legs: yellow rubber hackle, three strands; use
   black waterproof marker to mark with bars
Antennae: yellow Krystal Flash

Griffith's Gnat (George Griffith)
Steve Galea
Hook: Tiemco 101 or Mustad 94589 No. 28–18
Thread: olive 6/0, prewaxed
Rib: gold wire, fine
Body: peacock herl
Hackle: grizzly, palmered

Hopper (Art Winnie)
Jim Crawford
Hook: Mustad 9671 No. 12–6
Thread: brown, yellow, red—strong
Body: floss—yellow, white, insect-green or brown
Extended body: yellow or white high-density foam
Tail: red hackle fibers
Rib: brown hackle, palmered, clipped
Wing: turkey with deer-hair overlay
Head: deer hair, clipped Muddler style (leave
    some long for overwing); tie in last
*(Yellow works best in Montana and British
Columbia)*

Hopper, Letort (Ernie Schwiebert & Ross
    Trimmer)
Bob Scammell
Hook: Mustad 94831 or 9672 2XL, or 3XL No. 16–6
Thread: fluorescent orange
Body: Phentex yarn scored, slashed and frayed
Rib: buttonhole twist counterwound to catch and
    hold frayed Phentex
Underwing: one section mottled turkey quill tied
    flat over body
Wing and Head: deer hair spun, built up, clipped
    to shape

Hopper, Parachute (John Hill)
Jim Crawford
Hook: Mustad 9671 No. 12–8
Thread: match body color—strong
Tail: optional
Body: any bright color—yellow, white, orange,
    green—tapered
Head: same as body, built up slightly
Wing: turkey extended along top of body; gray or
    brown grizzly hackle tied parachute style
    around white post of fur or hackle
Legs: pheasant tail with knot to simulate leg joint

Humpy, Olive (Jack Horner)
Martin Lamont
Hook: Mustad 7957B, 94840, Tiemco 101 or 1XF
    wide gap No. 16–6
Thread: olive, 6/0
Tail: deer
Body: olive thread
Back: deer
Wing: white calf
Hackle: medium to dark dun

Irresistible (Joe Messinger)
Kevin Fancy
Hook: dry fly No. 16–10
Tail: guard hairs of white-tail deer or woodchuck
Body: natural gray/brown deer hair trimmed to
    shape
Wings: guard hairs of white-tail deer or wood-
    chuck
Hackle: medium blue dun

Lady McConnell (Brian Chan)
Brian Chan
Hook: dry fly No. 16–10
Tail: grizzly hackle tip with white Z-Lon
Body: black, green or brown tying thread
Shellback: deer hair
Hackle: 2 grizzly feathers

Madam X (Doug Swisher)
Bob Jones
Hook: Mustad 94840 No. 6
Thread: yellow
Tail: brown deer hair
Body: yellow thread
Wing: brown deer hair
Legs: white rubber, small

March Brown, American (Preston Jennings)
Kevin Fancy
Hook: Mustad 94840 No. 14–10
Thread: orange
Tail: dark brown hackle fibers
Body: brown, dubbed rabbit or fox
Wing: lemon wood duck flank, upright and
   divided
Hackle: grizzly and dark brown

Mikulak Sedge (Art Mikulak)
Bob Jones
Hook: Mustad 9672 No. 12–8
Thread: brown or tan
Tail: natural elk or deer
Body: dubbed seal and poly or blended Phentex
Wing: natural elk or deer
Hackle: brown or dun
Head: butt ends of wing

Mosquito
Kevin Fancy
Hook: Mustad 94840 No. 18–12
Thread: black
Tail: grizzly hackle fibbers
Body: one light and one dark moose mane
   wound together
Wing: grizzly hackle tips, upright and divided
Hackle: grizzly

Clive's Slider (Clive Schaupmeyer)
Clive Schaupmeyer
Hook: 1/0–4/0 steelhead short or long
Thread: size A orange Danville's Plus or equivalent
Body: chartreuse artificial hair with gold and pink
    pearl flash strands
Head: yellow foam plug
*(Various combinations of body and flash colors may
be used)*

Stimulator (Randall Kaufman)
Bob Scammell
Hook: Mustad 94831 or Tiemco 200R No. 16–4
Tail: elk hair, natural or bleached
Abdomen: orange or yellow Fly Rite or Antron
    dubbing
Rear Hackle: grizzly or brown, palmered through
    abdomen
Rib: gold or copper wire, fine, reverse-wrapped
    over rear hackle
Thorax: orange or yellow Fly Rite or Antron dub-
    bing to contrast abdomen
Wing: elk hair, natural or bleached
Front Hackle: grizzly or brown dry-fly hackle to
    contrast rear hackle, palmered through thorax
Head: fluorescent orange tying thread

Tom Thumb
Ralph Shaw
Hook: Mustad 9671 No. 16–8
Thread: black, waxed 6/0 Uni-Thread
Tail: deer hair
Body/wing: deer hair
(Late-season deer hair is always the best choice)

Tying a Tom Thumb
Ralph Shaw

1. Wrap thread rearward around shank until even with hook point, then back to the center.

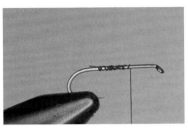

2. Select small clump of hair for tail. Position on top of shank so tips extend one hook-gap length beyond bend. Trim butts slightly beyond center. Wrap tightly back to the hook point. Cement hair on shank.

3. Cut clump of hair about three times the diameter of tail. Position so tips extend about 1 ½–2 shank lengths beyond bend (this determines the length of the wings). Hold hair firmly in place as you wrap forward. The butts should spiral down around the shank, creating a ragged, uneven body that aids in flotation. Make well-spaced wraps back to hook point, then forward to about ⅛" (3 mm) behind the eye.

4. Gather long hair together and fold forward to form back. Make two loose wraps around hair and shank, slowly draw tight and make two more tight wraps.

5. Lift hair tips up and back to form wing and then wrap thread under front base of wing to hold it upright. Form head, tie off, trim and cement. Trim any overly long hairs from underbody, but leave it fuzzy and ragged—an important characteristic of the body.

Wulff, Gray (Lee Wulff)
Kevin Fancy
Hook: Mustad 7957B No. 14–8
Thread: gray
Tail: natural brown bucktail
Body: blue-grey wool or dubbing
Wing: natural brown bucktail, upright and divided
Hackle: blue dun

Wulff, Royal (Lee Wulff)
Bob Jones
Hook: Mustad 7957B No. 14–8
Thread: black
Tail: elk
Body: peacock herl, red floss, peacock herl
Rib: gold wire, fine
Wing: white calf tail, bucktail, polar bear hair
Hackle: brown

Wulff, White (Lee Wulff)
Kevin Fancy
Hook: Mustad 7957B No. 14–8
Thread: black
Tail: white bucktail
Body: white dubbing or yarn
Wing: white calf tail, bucktail, polar bear hair
Hackle: badger

Streamers

Aztec, Black (Dick Nelson)
Bob Jones
Hook: Mustad 94841 No. 6
Thread: black
Tail: black acrylic yarn, three strands
Body: black acrylic yarn, single strand
Rear wing: black acrylic yarn, three strands
Back: black acrylic yarn, seven single strands
Head: black (eyes optional)
1. Tie in tail so it extends 2" (5 cm) from bend.

2. Cut off two strands ahead of thread, leave remaining strand for body.
3. Tie in rear wing to same length as tail.
4. Tie in short, single strand so it stands upright (the wing will be a series of comblike teeth).
5. Wind body forward one turn, tie in second strand. Repeat up to ⅟16" (1.6 mm) of eye.
6. Form small head, trim and cement.
7. Comb out tail and then comb the back. Trim at a slight angle from front to rear—¼–⅜" (6–9 mm) high.

Clive's Baitfish (Clive Schaupmeyer)

Clive Schaupmeyer

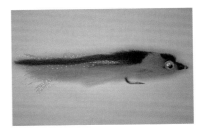

Hook: 1/0–4/0 steelhead long shank
Thread: black Danville's Plus or equivalent size A
Body: layered black or dark blue, gray and white Phentex with flash strands
Head: gray and black or dark blue Phentex tied pompon style and trimmed
Eyes: dumbbell brass or colored pearlescent
(Imitates baitfish like lake whitefish. Layer shades of body material to simulate dark to light shading on natural baitfish.)

1. Tie head with loops of Phentex, then cut, comb out and trim.
2. Dress as lightly as possible and trim head tightly to minimize casting weight.

Black-Nosed Dace (Art Flick)

Kevin Fancy

Hook: Mustad 38941 No. 12–10
Tail: short tuft bright red yarn
Body: silver tinsel, flat
Rib: silver tinsel, oval
Wing: stacked white, black (black bear), natural brown bucktail (black, about ¾ length of white and brown)

Bucktail (Charlie Guiguet)
Bob Jones
Tube: plastic tube from Q-Tip cotton swab
OR
Hook: straight eye, standard length to 3XL No.
2–2/0
Thread: white 3/0 Uni-Thread, colored with felt-
tip pen
Body: braided silver Mylar tubing
Wing: polar bear hair, bucktail, combed acrylic
yarn, synthetics, colors of choice (Green/Orange
is shown)
Throat: (optional) red hair, combed yarn or hackle
fibers
Eyes: (optional) adhesive
Head: coat with 5-minute clear epoxy
Hook holder: ⅜" (9 mm) sleeve of rubber or soft
plastic tubing forced over rear end of body

Bunny Fly (Scott Sanchez)
Martin Lamont
Hook: Mustad 9672 3XL No. 4–2
Thread: same color as body
Tail/Body: black, pink, blue, orange, fluorescent
green rabbit fur strip; tie in at bend, then wind
forward to create body

Canary
Paul Marriner
Hook: Mustad 38941 No. 2
Underwing: orange Krystal Flash
Collar/Wing: marabou plumes wound on collar
style—½ pink, ¼ orange, ¼ yellow

Candied Whitefish (Dave Smallwood)

Dave Smallwood

Hook: Tiemco 811S No. 1/0–4/0

Thread: clear monofilament (fine)

Body: Ultra Hair stacked 20 strands black over 30 strands white over 30 strands purple over white clump about half the diameter of a pencil

Eyes: adhesive

Head: 5-minute epoxy

1. Tie white hair behind eye to encircle shank.
2. Stack on purple, white and black hair. Form a tapered head, tie off and trim.
3. Mix and apply epoxy to head and shoulder of fly; use only enough to coat the fibers without running or sagging.
4. Allow epoxy to start hardening (almost set but still malleable). Use Kodak Photo-Flo Solution or liquid detergent as a wetting agent on thumb and forefinger to prevent sticking.
5. Remove fly from vise, liberally wet thumb and forefinger with wetting agent, and then squeeze epoxy from side to side as you spread the fibers to obtain the desired silhouette. Ensure the hook point and gap are not obstructed by the epoxy.
6. After head dries, apply eyes, draw in gills with red marker and apply a second coat of epoxy

Catface Streamer (Shawn Bennett)

Bob Jones

Hook: Mustad 34011 No. 1

Thread: .004 clear Uni-mono

Body: pearl Diamond Braid

Belly: white polar bear

Beard: red polar bear

Wing: stacked white polar bear, chartreuse Polar Flash, chartreuse polar bear, peacock herl

Sides: green-dyed grizzly saddle hackle

Eyes: adhesive—chartreuse

Head: 5-minute epoxy

Cathy's Coat (Barry Thornton)
Barry Thornton
Hook: Mustad 34011ss No. 6–4
Thread: red
Body: fluorescent red plastic strips
Wing: strands of polar bear hair, white and pink,
    with Krystal Flash, pink and red
Tail: pink polar bear hair

Chartreuse Caboose (Bill Chunik)
Bill Chunik
Hook: Daiichi 2055 No. 10–8
Thread: black
Tail: chartreuse marabou feather, long webby
    fibers
Body: chartreuse marabou dubbed on thread and
    wound on
Thorax: red wool or dubbing
Wing Case: stiffer tips of a chartreuse marabou
    feather

Clouser Deep Minnow (Bob Clouser)
Bob Jones
Hook: Tiemco 9394 No. 8–2
Eyes: dumbbells or Bead Chain, color of choice
Belly: white bucktail, polar bear hair or synthetic,
    about 20 strands; should extend 2–3" (50–75
    mm) from bend for saltwater, pike or muskie
Back: Krystal Flash, 20 strands, pink or chartreuse
    hair or synthetic, 20 strands, stacked, same
    length as belly

1. Tie eyes ¼" (6 mm) from hook eye.
2. Tie in belly behind hook eye, bring thread back
    under dumbbells, wrap twice around material
    and shank, then forward and half hitch.
3. Reverse hook in vise, stack Krystal Flash and
    hair. Do not tie behind the dumbbells.

Clouser Deep Minnow, Simplified
(Bob Clouser)
Paul Marriner
Hook: Mustad 9671 No. 6
Eyes: dumbbells—gold, silver or painted a bright
color, mounted so hook point rides up
Body: not required on nickel-plated hooks, silver
Belly: white bucktail, very sparse, tips extend ½
shank length behind hook bend
Back: red or chartreuse bucktail with a few
strands of Krystal Flash, very sparse, same
length as belly

Coachman, Sparkle American (Bob Jones)
Bob Jones
*(See "Three for the Beach," page 388 for tying
instructions.)*

Cosseboom, Fluorescent Green
(John C. Cosseboom)
Paul Marriner
Hook: Mustad 80500BL No. 8–2
Tag: flat silver tinsel and Chinese red Uni-stretch
Rib: silver tinsel, oval
Body: fluorescent green or chartreuse floss or
Uni-stretch
Wing: gray squirrel tail
Hackle: yellow, tied in as a collar slanted rearward
Head: red

Edson Tiger, Dark (William R. Edson)
Bob Jones
Hook: Mustad 38941 No. 10–4
Thread: yellow
Tag: gold tinsel, flat
Tail: two small yellow neck-hackle tips back to back
Body: yellow chenille, fine
Throat: tips of two small, red neck hackles

Wing: natural brown bucktail, dyed yellow

Cheeks: jungle cock or gold Mylar

(The wing-ends of an Edson Tiger should be fairly even and extend just beyond the hook bend to prevent fouling while casting.)

Edson Tiger, Light (William R. Edson)

Bob Jones

Hook: Mustad 38941 No. 10–4

Thread: black

Tag: gold tinsel, flat

Tail: lemon wood duck showing two black bars

Body: peacock herl counterwound with fine gold wire

Wing: yellow bucktail

Topping: two crimson hackle tips, maximum ⅓ of wing length

Cheeks: jungle cock or gold Mylar

Fancy's Orange Sunrise (Kevin Fancy)

Kevin Fancy

Hook: Mustad 9672 No. 10–2

Thread: black

Tail: orange cock-hackle fibers

Body: orange dubbing (angora goat or seal)

Rib: oval gold tinsel or none

Wing: three orange cock-hackles on each side (or orange hair)

Beard: red hackle

Ghost, Black (Herbert L. Welch)

Bob Jones

Hook: Tiemco 300 No. 10–6

Thread: black 6/0

Tail: yellow hackle fibers, sparse

Rib: silver tinsel, flat medium

Body: black floss

Throat: yellow hackle fibers

Wing: four white saddle hackles

Cheeks: jungle cock

Ghost, Gray (Carrie G. Stevens)

Kevin Fancy

Hook: Mustad 9575 No. 4–1/0

Body: orange floss

Rib: medium flat silver tinsel

Throat: white bucktail covered by golden pheasant crest

Wing: golden pheasant crest feather, followed by four bronze dun saddle hackles over which are tied five or six strands of peacock herl

Shoulder: silver pheasant body feather or mallard flank

Cheek: jungle cock or substitute

Head: lacquered black

Glennie's Green 'n' Silver (Rory Glennie)

Martin Lamont

Hook: Mustad 34007 or Tiemco 9394 2x–3x No. 8

Thread: white

Tail: polar bear hair or FisHair, sparse

Body: silver tinsel overwrapped with a few turns of silver wire or silver Krystal Flash coated with head cement. With nickel-plated hook, no dressing required.

Wing: white polar bear hair or FisHair, sparse. Pull out guard hairs and use only under fur.

Head: fluorescent green

Glennie's Pearl Mickey (Rory Glennie)

Bob Jones

(See "Three for the Beach," page 389 for tying instructions.)

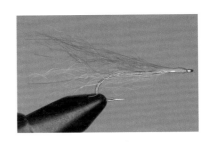

Glennie's Pink 'n' Silver (Rory Glennie)
Bob Jones
*(See "Three for the Beach," page 389 for tying
instructions.)*

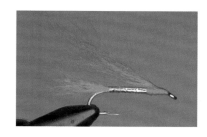

Great Pumpkin (Brooks Fly Fishing Club)
Clive Schaupmeyer
Hook: 1/0–4/0 steelhead, short or long
Thread: orange Danville's Plus or equivalent size A
Body: orange artificial hair or Icelandic sheep
  wool with gold flash strands
Head: orange body fur (can also use spun deer
  hair or Phentex)
Eyes: dumbbell brass or pearlescent

Lefty's Deceiver (Lefty Kreh)
Bob Jones
Hook: Eagle Claw 34007 No. 4–1/0
Thread: red
Tail: six white saddle hackles, tips curving in
Body: flat silver or Mylar tinsel
Wing: white bucktail in two sections, one on top,
  one under hook shank, one olive-green barred
  hackle on each side

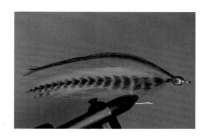

Magog Smelt (Frier Gulline)
Bob Jones
Hook: Mustad 94720 8xL No. 4–2
Thread: black
Tail: teal body feather fibers, sparse
Body: silver tinsel, flat medium
Throat: red hackle fibers, sparse
Wing: bucktail, sparsely stacked white, yellow,
  then violet
Topping: peacock herl, five or six strands
Shoulders: two teal body feathers, ⅓ of wing
  length
Cheek: jungle cock

Malherbè Special (Dave Smallwood)

Dave Smallwood

Hook: 34007 No. 1/0–5/0

Thread: Kevlar or Bernoulli's Strong, to match body

Tail: FisHair, chartreuse

Topping: Flashabou, pearlescent green

Rear collar: bucktail, fluorescent pink

Front collar: bucktail, fluorescent chartreuse

Both bucktail clumps about the diameter of a pencil.

1. Attach FisHair and Flashabou to rear ⅓ of hook.
2. Position butts of pink bucktail in center of hook shank, make three loose wraps about ⅛" (3 mm) behind ends, tighten slowly to flare into encircling collar; tie off and cement.
3. Position chartreuse bucktail ahead of pink and repeat steps as above. (weed guards optional)

Mickey Finn

Bill Luscombe

Hook: Tiemco 300 No. 10–4

Thread: black

Body: silver tinsel, flat

Rib: silver tinsel, oval, fine

Wing: stacked yellow, red, yellow

Muddler, Marabou (Dan Bailey)

Kevin Fancy

Hook: Mustad 9671 No. 10–2

Thread: black

Tail: red wool

Body: flat gold tinsel

Wing: yellow marabou over small bunch of gray squirrel tail

Head: spun deer hair

Muddler Minnow (Don Gapen)
Martin Lamont
Hook: Mustad 9671 No. 12–2
Thread: brown
Tail: natural turkey wing quill, slightly longer
than hook gap
Body: gold tinsel, flat
Wing: gray squirrel tail, then mottled brown
turkey wing on each side with tips flaring up
Head: natural deer hair, spun and clipped to shape

Muddler, Rolled (Tom Murray)
Bill Luscombe
Hook: Mustad 9671, 9672 No. 12–10
Thread: red
Tail: mallard flank, ½ hook length, ¼" (6 mm)
wide and folded lengthwise twice
Body: silver tinsel
Rib: silver wire, counterwound
Wing: mallard flank, ½" (13 mm) wide, folded
lengthwise twice and tied in so ends are even
with tail ends
Head: small clump of light brown deer hair, spun
and clipped to an arrow shape, flat on the bot-
tom; leave a few hairs laying back to form part
of wing

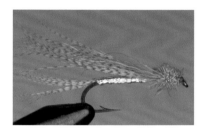

Nine-Three (Dr. J. Hubert Sanborn)
Kevin Fancy
Stinger: Mustad 9671 No. 10
Thread: black
Body: Palmer on green-olive and one black saddle
hackle from bend to head of hook; join with
loop of 8–10-lb test monofilament, ½" behind
hook bend
Hook: Mustad 9671 No. 6–4
Thread: black
Body: gold tinsel, flat
Wing: three black saddles tied on top, three green
or olive saddles on each side; tips should reach
just beyond stinger head

O'Keefe Special (Brian O'Keefe)
Brian O'Keefe
Hook: Mustad 9672 No. 12–6
Thread: black or dark brown
Tail: brown hackle fibers
Body: reddish brown mohair
Wing: sparse black bear hair tied to reach end of
   tail
Beard: dark brown, hackled

Perch Special (Bob Jones)
Bob Jones
Tube: plastic or metal
OR
Hook: Tiemco No. 2, 4XL 9394
Body: braided gold Mylar slid over tubing and
   Krazy Glued
Hook holder: ⅜" (9 mm) sleeve of rubber or soft
   plastic tubing forced over rear end of tube
Thread: white 3/0 Uni-Thread, colored with felt
   tippen
Wing: Ultra Hair or substitute, stacked dark
   green over olive green
Belly: white Ultra Hair
Throat: orange Ultra Hair
Sides: yellow Ultra Hair
Eyes: adhesive, red
Head: coat with 5-minute clear epoxy
(Using synthetics makes this much more durable.)

1. To provide a good silhouette, mount the belly
   in two staggered clumps, followed by the
   throat.
2. Rotate the body and mount the wing in three
   staggered clumps of olive green, then one of
   dark green.
3. Tie in each side, build the head to a tapered
   shape and Krazy Glue.
4. Use a dark brown felt-tip marker to make vertical bars down each side of the wing.
5. Apply adhesive eyes, then coat the head with
   5-minute epoxy.

Pink Campbell (Barry Thornton)
Barry Thornton
Hook: Mustad 3401ss No. 4–2
Thread: fluorescent red
Body: white and pink polar bear hair with pink
    and red Krystal Flash
Tail: pink polar bear hair

Pink Eve (Barry Thornton)
Barry Thornton
Hook: Mustad 3401ss No. 6–2
Thread: pink
Body: silver oval tinsel
Wing: (optional) pink hair or synthetic
Eyes: (optional) Bead Chain

Pink Eve Redeye (Barry Thornton)
Barry Thornton
Same as above with addition of a red or pink glass
bead on each side of the head.

Pink Smelt
Bob Jones
Hook: Mustad 94720 8XL No. 4–2
Thread: gray
Body: silver tinsel, flat medium
Rib: silver oval, small
Belly: bucktail, white
Wing: bucktail, stacked yellow, then pink
Cheek: jungle cock

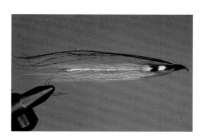

Polar Aztec (Dr. Martin Lamont)
Martin Lamont
Hook: 3XL–4XL streamer hooks with a straight eye
Body: if using black or bronzed hook, silver tinsel
Wings: polar bear under fur or FisHair
Tie first wing halfway along shank, move forward
and tie another; up to six wings create a transpar-
ent, flexible fly with a large silhouette.

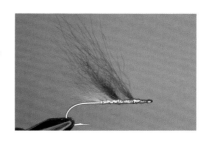

Polar Ice (George Taylor)
Bob Jones
Hook: Mustad 39841 No. 2
Tail: stacked polar bear hair, pearl Krystal Flash
  and light blue bucktail, extending a shank
  length beyond bend
Body: braided craft tinsel
Wing: stacked polar bear hair, pearl Krystal Flash,
  light blue bucktail and dark blue bucktail
Head: three turns oval silver tinsel followed by
  black thread

Polar Shrimp
Martin Lamont
Hook: Mustad 36890, Eagle Claw 1197B or Orvis
  1645 No. 6–2, weighted or unweighted
Tail: red hen saddle hackle fibers or polar bear
  hair
Body: chenille, hot orange
Wing: white polar bear hair or calf tail, sparse
Hackle: (optional) hen, orange

Pop-Lips (Bob Popovics)
Dave Smallwood
Hook: Tiemco 811s No. 1/0–4/0
Thread: 3/0, to match body
Tail: white bucktail ½ pencil diameter, 2–3 times
  longer than hook shank, 6–8 white saddle
  hackles, pearl Flashabou
Head: white lamb fleece, clear GE Silicone II
Eyes: adhesive prism
*(Fly's swimming action can be adjusted by trimming
the lip.)*

1. Tie in bucktail near hook bend.
2. Tie in hackles one at a time to encircle shank,
   add Flashabou.
3. Comb fleece with a wire dog brush; tie in
   small amount, tips rearward, forming a veil
   encircling wing.

4. Add clumps of fleece, tips forward, packing tightly rearward as you fill the shank; use bodkin to pick out any fleece tips that become tied down.

5. Trim bottom of body flat to clear hook point and gap. Trim remaining fleece into a bullet shape.

6. Add another clump of fleece at bottom of head for lip, and trim any excess fleece from above and behind the lip. Use Kodak Photo-Flo Solution or liquid detergent as a wetting agent on thumb and forefinger to prevent sticking.

7. Fan the lip, then apply silicone, working it well into the fibers.

8. Apply silicone over the head in a smooth layer

9. Wait 5–10 minutes, then trim lip to shape and add eyes.

10. Add second coat of silicone over entire head and lip.

Professor (Christopher North)
Bill Luscombe
Hook: Eagle Claw L1197N No. 8–4
Thread: black
Tail: red hackle fibers
Body: yellow dubbing or yarn
Rib: gold tinsel, embossed
Wing: gray squirrel tail
Beard: dark ginger

Purpetraitor (Bob Scammell)
Bob Scammell
Hook: Mustad 9672 3XL No. 10–4
Head: Conehead, copper
Tail: purple marabou blended with a few strands of purple Krystal Flash
Body: purple and silver chenille
Hackle: black saddle, palmered from tail to head

Roberts' Woolly Boolly (Marty Roberts)
Marty Roberts
Hook: Mustad 79580 or Eagle Claw 281 No. 8–6
Thread: black
Tail: bright blue marabou
Hackle: blue saddle that fans out ½–¾" (13–19 cm)
Body: black or olive chenille

Royal Letort (Bob Scammell)
Bob Scammell
Hook: Mustad 9672 3XL No. 10–4
Weight: lead wire
Body: peacock herl
Waist: red floss
Rib: gold wire, fine, counterwound
Underwing: white marabou topped with 10–12
    strands pearlescent white Krystal Flash
Wing: white deer hair
Head: white deer hair, spun and clipped

Silver & Red Flash Fly
Martin Lamont
Hook: Mustad 34007 or 3407 No. 4–2/0, weight-
    ed or unweighted
Thread: red
Tail: silver Flashabou
Body: silver Flashabou, wrapped and coated with
    cement or epoxy
Wing: silver Flashabou blended with a few
    strands of red
Hackle: red saddle
Head: red

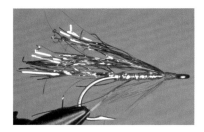

Silver Skunk (Wes Drain)
Barry Thornton
Hook: Mustad 34011SS No. 4–2
Thread: black or silver
Ribbing: silver tinsel
Body: black chenille, weighted or unweighted
Wing: white polar bear hair
Tail: white polar bear hair

Slim Pickin's (Jim Leith)
Bob Jones
Hook: Mustad 33956 or Eagle Claw L058 3xl No. 6
Thread: black
Tail: pheasant tail fibers (about 20)
Body: pheasant tail fibers (about 20)
Beard: butt ends folded down behind head and
    trimmed short

Supervisor (Joseph S. Stickney)
Bob Jones
Hook: Mustad 9575 No. 4–1/0
Thread: black
Tail: red wool, short
Rib: silver tinsel, oval narrow
Body: silver tinsel, flat medium
Wing: white bucktail, very sparse, then four
    slightly longer, light blue saddle hackles
Topping: peacock herl, six strands
Shoulders: two pale green, short, stubby shoulder
    hackles
Cheeks: jungle cock

Thor (Jim Pray)
Bob Jones
Hook: Eagle Claw L058 No. 12–10
Thread: black
Tail: orange hackle fibers
Body: red chenille
Hackle: brown tied on as collar, tied back and
    down
Wing: white calf tail

Thorn, Silver (Barry Thornton)
Barry Thornton
Hook: Mustad 34011ss or 34007ss No. 6–2/0
Thread: silver
Body: silver tinsel chenille
Throat: bright red wool or red FisHair
Wing: peacock sword
Tail: peacock sword, 6–8 strands silver Krystal
    Flash

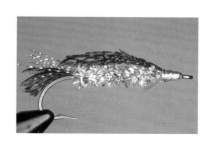

Thorn, Silver Variations: Same as Silver Thorn except for parts listed

Thorn Flashtail, Silver (Barry Thornton)
Tail: silver Mylar, frayed

Thorn, Hakai (Barry Thornton)
Wing: pink bucktail or polar bear hair
Tail: pearlescent Mylar braid

Thorn, Tonquin (Barry Thornton)
Wing: 4–6 strands of chartreuse Krystal Flash
    covered with chartreuse-colored polar bear hair
Tail: pearlescent Mylar braid, unraveled

Tweety Bird (Clive Schaupmeyer)
Clive Schaupmeyer
Hook: 1/0–4/0 steelhead long shank
Thread: orange Danville's Plus or equivalent size A
Body: chartreuse and yellow artificial hair with
    flash strands
Head: yellow Phentex tied pompon style and
    trimmed
Eyes: dumbbell brass or colored pearlescent
Head is tied using loops of Phentex, then cut,
combed and trimmed. Head can also be formed
with body fur.

Weigh Wester (Bob Jones)

Bob Jones

Hook: Tiemco 9394 No. 6–4

Thread: monocord 3/0, light gray

Tail: white bucktail, polar bear hair or synthetic

Body: 3" (76 mm) braided white pearlescent
Mylar—small, (⅛") diameter

Eyes: red, 2 mm adhesive

Cement: Krazy Glue

Epoxy: clear, 5-minute

Miscellaneous: toothpicks, 3 x 3" (76 x 76 mm)
squares of waxed paper, locking forceps

1. Make several wraps of thread around shank
   just ahead of bend.
2. Bind tail on top of shank so tips extend about
   1 ½" (4 cm).
3. Spiral thread forward to within ⅛" (3 mm) of
   hook eye.
4. Slide end of tubing over hook eye for ¼" (6
   mm), make one loose wrap of thread, tighten
   and wrap tightly forward to hook eye; half
   hitch twice and trim thread.
5. Stroke tubing rearward over the shank, turning it inside out (watch out for the hook
   point!).
6. Smooth tubing from head to tail, then use a
   dubbing needle to arrange trailing strands
   evenly around the hook bend.
7. Grip trailing strands between thumb and forefinger, and pull gently rearward. Don't let go.
8. Pinch tag end of thread between nail of forefinger and tip of second finger. Make three
   tight wraps around body ahead of the bend;
   half hitch three times and trim.
9. Apply drop of Krazy Glue to thread collar,
   another at the nose.
10. After Krazy Glue dries, apply adhesive eyes to
    each side of body about ⅛" (3 mm) ahead of
    thread collar.
11. Squeeze epoxy onto waxed paper, using tooth-
    pick to mix it.

12. Grip front of hook eye with tip of locking forceps jaws. With fly body at a 45° angle, start applying epoxy at the collar and work toward the nose while rotating it.

14. Continue rotating fly, tilting it up or down so epoxy coats the body evenly.

15. Once epoxy sets, set fly aside and let the body cure.

(For a slimmer fly, pluck off several strands of the trailing Mylar..)

Wire Worm

Martin Lamont

Hook: Mustad 3906, 9672 or Tiemco 2457 2x wide, 2xs No. 20–10

Head: brass bead

Body: colored wire (yellow, green, red, black, brass, copper) of diameter to suit fly size

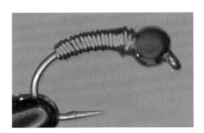

Zonker (Dan Byford)

Jim Crawford

Hook: Heavy wire 4xl No. 10–2/0

Thread: to match overbody

Body: pearlescent Mylar tubing

Overbody: rabbit fur strips twice as long as hook, any color

Hackle: long, any color (helps keep fly from spinning)

Options: weighted with lead wire under Mylar, bead head, dumbbells, adhesive eyes, double fur strip

Zonker, Simplified (Dan Byford)

Paul Marriner

Hook: Mustad 79580 No. 4

Thread: red Uni-thread 6/0

Body: silver or gold braided Mylar tubing

Tail & Wing: rabbit strip (color of choice)

CHIRONOMIDS AND NYMPHS

Al's Peacock Nymph (Al Unger)
Al Unger
Hook: Tiemco T200R No. 14–6
Thread: black
Tail: badger hackle fibers
Underbody: dark wool; spread Flexament on
   underbody just before wrapping peacock herl
Body: peacock herl strands twisted and wound
   on; leave thread at rear and wrap it over the
   herl
Wing Case: black raffia
Beard: badger hackle fibers

Baggy Shrimp (Richard Anderson)
Brian Chan
Hook: Tiemco 2457 or Mustad 80200BR No. 16–10
Tail: synthetic dubbing mix in olive to dark green
Body: synthetic dubbing mix in olive to dark
   green
Shell back: clear scud back
Rib: copper or gold wire, fine

Bead Head Nymph (Jim Crawford)
Jim Crawford
Hook: heavy wire No. 16–10
Thread: match color of body
Head: brass bead—gold, copper, black
Body: hare's ear or fine-fiber synthetic dubbing
Rib: fine gold or copper wire, or very fine flat
   tinsel
Wing case: pheasant tail or hackle fibers
Tail: fur or hackle fibers to match wing case

Blood Worm (Jack Shaw)
Brian Chan
Hook: 2XL nymph hook in sizes No. 12–8
Tail: black bear hair
Body: fine maroon chenille
Rib: fine copper tinsel or copper wire
Hackle: several strands of cock pheasant rump
    fibers

Brook's Stone (Charlie Brooks)
Bob Scammell
Hook: Mustad 9672 No. 10–4
Thread: black monocord
Underbody: lead wire, heavy
Body: black fuzzy yarn, heavy
Rib: flat nylon monofilament, brown or copper
    wire
Gills: white or light gray ostrich herl
Legs: one grizzly and one brown-dyed grizzly
    hackle
Tail: two goose biots or black rubber strands

Canadian Nymph (Kevin Fancy)
Kevin Fancy
Hook: Mustad 94840 No. 12–6
Thread: black
Tail: black bear hair
Rib: oval gold tinsel
Body: dyed black seal
Wing case: woven gold tinsel

Chironomid, Black & Gold (Jack Shaw)
Ralph Shaw
Hook: Mustad 9671 or Tiemco 2487 No. 14–12
Thread: black
Body: Phentex, black
Rib: gold wrap
Tail: grouse, sparse
Shellback: turkey or grouse
Thorax: peacock herl
Bubble: white wool

Chironomid, Black & Silver (Jack Shaw)
Ralph Shaw
Hook: Mustad 9671 or Tiemco 2487 No. 14–12
Thread: black
Body: Phentex, black
Rib: silver wrap
Tail: grouse, sparse
Shellback: turkey or grouse
Thorax: peacock herl
Bubble: white wool

Chironomid, Brown Pheasant (Jack Shaw)
Ralph Shaw
Hook: Mustad 9671 or Tiemco 2487 No. 14–12
Thread: black
Body: cock pheasant tail fiber
Tail: grouse, sparse
Shellback: copper cock pheasant side feathers
Thorax: peacock herl
Bubble: white wool

Chironomid Pupa, Black (Jack Shaw)
Brian Chan
Hook: curved shrimp/pupae No. 16–10
Body: black Frostbite or Super Floss
Rib: copper, gold or silver wire, fine
Thorax: peacock herl
Shell back: cock pheasant tail fibers
Gills: white ostrich herl

Chironomid, Turkey & Gold (Jack Shaw)
Ralph Shaw
Hook: Mustad 9671 or Tiemco 2487 No. 14–12
Thread: black
Body: turkey feather fiber
Rib: gold
Tail: grouse, sparse
Shellback: turkey
Thorax: peacock herl
Bubble: white wool

Chironomid, Turkey & Silver Butt (Jack Shaw)
Ralph Shaw
Hook: Mustad 9671 or Tiemco 2487 No. 14–12
Thread: black
Body: brown turkey fiber
Tail: maroon
Butt: silver tinsel
Shellback: magpie
Thorax: peacock herl
Bubble: white wool

Dynamite Boatman (Wayne Phillips)
Wayne Phillips
Hook: Tiemco T3761 No. 14–10
Thread: dark olive
Body: peacock herl
Shellback: at the back, tie in strip of black plastic
    bag or cassette tape and pull it forward
Belly: tie in pearl Antron Sparkle Yarn at back
    and draw forward, covering bottom of body
    (this imitates the air bubble)
Legs: black or white rubber legs, perpendicular to
    body

Early Brown Stonefly Nymph
Kevin Fancy
Hook: Mustad 3960B IXL No. 18–14
Thread: 6/0 brown
Tails: rusty-brown feather fibers
Body: flat monofilament over rusty-brown rayon
    floss
Wing case: dark gray-brown feathers set in vinyl,
    trim to shape
Legs: rusty dun hen hackle

Fabulous Filo Nymph (Wayne Phillips)

Wayne Phillips

Hook: Tiemco T5263 No. 10–6

Thread: dark olive

Tail: olive fibers from pheasant rump feather, root beer Krystal Flash

Body: olive filoplumes, wound as hackle or spun into a dubbing loop and wound on, a few root beer Krystal Flash strands tied in before wing case

Wing case: wide pearlescent tinsel

Beard: olive fibers from pheasant rump feather

Flashback Stone (Andrew Somerset)

Andrew Somerset

Hook: curved nymph model 3xL No. 14–12

Tail: black hackle fibers

Abdomen: black dubbing

Rib: pearl Krystal Flash or Flashabou

Thorax: black dubbing

Legs: black hackle fibers

Wing case: pearl Flashabou

Flash in the Pan (Eric Schrader)

Eric Schrader

Hook: Mustad 9672 No. 8–4

Thread: dark olive

Tail: olive marabou and black Krystal Flash

Body: olive Crystal Chenille

Wing case: black Krystal Flash

Beard: reddish pheasant tail fibers

Gold-Ribbed Hare's Ear

Martin Lamont

Hook: Mustad 3906, 3906B 1xL–3xL No. 20–8

Thread: black, 6/0

Tail: hare's guard hair from cheek or over eye

Body: dubbed hare's ear fur

Rib: gold wire, fine

Wing case: mottled turkey

Thorax: dubbed hare's ear fur, picked out

Halfback (John Dexheimer)

Brian Chan

Hook: nymph 2XL No. 14–8

Tail: cock pheasant tail fibers

Body: peacock herl

Shell back: cock pheasant tail

Throat: cock pheasant tail fibers

Hare's Ear Nymph

Kevin Fancy

Hook: Mustad 3960B No. 18–8

Thread: brown

Tail: brown partridge fibers

Body: dubbed hare's ear fur (pick out to make shaggy)

Legs: brown partridge fibers tied in at throat

(There are many variations; it can also be tied with a fine oval gold tinsel rib or with a wing case of pheasant tail fibers.)

Hellgrammite (Doug Prince)

Martin Lamont

Hook: 4XL No. 8, 6, 4, straight eye, bronze or black

Tail: black, hen hackle, a few short, stubby fibers, or goose biots tied V-shape

Body: black chenille, fine

Antennae: black goose biots or hen hackle fibers

Thorax: black chenille, single wrap

1. After tying in tail, tie in body and wrap forward two turns.

2. Tie in hackle, make single wrap and cover hackle with two wraps of chenille.

3. Repeat all the way up, creating a segmented effect.

4. Crop hackle fibers close to body to create the appearance of short legs.

Horsehair Nymph (Charley Moore)

Bob Jones

Hook: Mustad 3134 or Eagle Claw L281 4XL No. 4

Thread: black

Tail: black goose biot or folded black rubber
legging

Body: black thread (for a slim body) or chenille

Back: black bear hair or synthetic

Hackle: tan hen, webby

*(The trick to tying this fussy pattern is folding the
back forward and winding ahead for a half dozen
wraps, then folding the material rearward and
wrapping back to hold it in position. Tie in a clump
of hackle, wind the body forward ahead of it, then
fold the back forward again. Sheridan Lake Resort
owner Bob Leith said the best way to tie this pattern
is to pay someone else to do it for you.)*

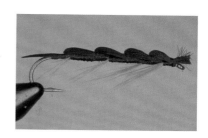

Hot-Wired Whole Squirrel Hide

(Bob Scammell)

Bob Scammell

Hook: Mustad 94831, 9671 or Tiemco 5262 2XL
No. 12–8

Thread: Danville monocord, gray

Tail: hair from back ridge of a red squirrel

Body: dubbed blue-gray hair from red squirrel
belly

Rib: copper wire, medium

Thorax: dark hair with guard hairs from red
squirrel flank, dubbed over a medium lead wire
base

Kamloops Caddis Pupa

Brian Chan

Hook: 2XL nymph hook No. 12–8

Body: olive to dark green synthetic seal fur

Rib: bright green Super Floss

Shell back: cock pheasant tail fibers

Thorax: peacock herl

Throat: cock pheasant rump fibers mixed with
peacock Angel Hair

Collar: peacock herl
*(May be tied in various colors with or without a
beard of red saddle fibers.)*

Pheasant Tail Nymph (Frank Sawyer)
Jim Crawford
Hook: Fine wire, extended No. 16–10
Thread: black or dark brown
Body: rooster pheasant tail
Ribbing: gold or copper wire, fine
Thorax: peacock herl
Wings: pheasant tail tippets
Wing Case: pheasant tail
Tail: several pheasant tail tippets

Prince Nymph (Doug Prince)
Jim Crawford
Hook: heavy wire No. 16–8
Thread: black
Tail: dark gray goose biot
Body: peacock over underbody of lead wire or
    yarn
Rib: gold or silver wire or flat tinsel
Hackle: furnace (may also use CDC fibers)
Wings: white goose biot

Prince Nymph, Bead Head (Doug Prince)
Steve Galea
Hook: Tiemco 3761 No. 16–8
Thread: red 6/0
Head: brass bead
Tail: brown goose biots
Rib: gold Mylar
Body: peacock Herl
Wing: white goose biots
Hackle: brown hen

Prince of Darkness (Bob Morenski)
Bob Jones
Hook: Tiemco 3671 or Mustad 3906, No. 10–8
Thread: black 6/0
Tail: goose biots, black
Body: weighted, dark olive Crystal Chenille, medium
Rib: gold wire, fine
Shell: peacock herl, 6 strands
Wing: goose biots, white
Hackle: natural black saddle

1. Wrap hook shank, tie black biot on each side of shank to form tail, weight with copper wire.
2. Tie in following materials in this order: rib, peacock herl, Crystal Chenille.
3. Wrap Crystal Chenille forward to form body.
4. Pull peacock herl forward to form shell, secure with rib.
5. Tie in hackle and make two to three wraps.
6. Tie in white biots to form wing and finish head.

Short Black Booger (Mike Burrington)
Bob Scammell
Hook: Mustad 94831, 9671 or Tiemco 5262 2xl No. 12–6
Thread: fire-orange Uni-thread
Weight: medium lead wire
Body: black and silver tinsel chenille, medium
Hackle: natural black saddle

Sydenham Peacock (Jim Weir)
Andrew Somerset
Hook: 3xl nymph No. 14–12
Thread: black or red
Tail: goose wing fibers
Abdomen: peacock herl
Rib: copper wire
Thorax: peacock herl
Wingcase/legs: goose wing fibers

WET FLIES

Bead-Head (Syd Brock)
Paul Marriner
Hook: Mustad 9671 No. 6
Bead: gold or silver
Tail: Krystal Flash, three or four strands
Body: chenille
Throat: sparse clump of bucktail or calf tail, color
  to contrast chenille

Bugger, Martin's Nasty (Marty Roberts)
Marty Roberts
Hook: Mustad 79580 or Eagle Claw 281 No. 8–4
Thread: black or match body
Tail: 50/50 black and olive marabou, plus thin
  strip of black rabbit fur 50 percent longer than
  marabou
Hackle: olive saddle
Body: olive chenille

Bugger, Moira River (Chris Marshall)
Chris Marshall
Hook: No. 2–1/0 3XL or 4XL streamer
Thread: red fluorescent
Tail: white marabou
Hackle: black or dark dun webby saddle hackle,
  palmered
Body: fluorescent white medium chenille
Stripe: 4–5 strands pearlescent Krystal Flash on
  each side, extending to end of tail, bound to
  the body with the palmered hackle

Bugger, Woolly (Russell Blessing)
Marty Roberts
Hook: Mustad 79580 or Eagle Claw 281 No. 8–4
Thread: black or matching body
Tail: black marabou
Hackle: black saddle
Body: chenille, black or olive
Ribbing: (optional) silver or gold wire

Carey Special
(Dr. Lloyd Day and Col. Thomas Carey)
Bob Jones
Hook: Mustad 9671 No. 8–2
Thread: red or black
Body: peacock herl or small chenille (color of
    choice)
Rib: (optional) gold or silver wire, fine
Hackle: cock ring-necked pheasant rump, blue
    phase

Crappie Basher (George Will)
Bob Jones
Hook: Mustad 9672 3XL No. 10
Thread: red
Body: silver tinsel
Wing: stacked yellow, white, yellow
Head: red

Despickable (Bob Scammell)
Bob Scammell
Hook: Mustad 3906 No. 10–8
Thread: black
Body: black chenille, medium
Hackle: natural black saddle
Back: eight strands strung peacock herl

Doc Spratley (Dick Prankard)
Martin Lamont
Hook: Mustad 9672 No. 14–4
Tail: speckled galena hackle fibers
Body: black wool, seal fur or floss
Rib: silver wire on small patterns, oval tinsel for
    larger ones
Beard: galena hackle fibers
Wing: ring-necked cock pheasant tail fibers
Head: green or bronze peacock herl, small

Doc Spratley's Intern (Kevin Fancy)

Kevin Fancy

Hook: Mustad 9671 No. 8–4

Thread: black

Tail: gray squirrel tail fibers

Body: grizzly hackle palmered over black ostrich
   herl

Rib: oval silver tinsel

Wing: golden pheasant tail fibers, rolled

Head: ball of peacock herl

Flash Fly

Andrew Somerset

Hook: heavy-wire scud model No. 16–12

Thread: flame orange

Tail: cerise hackle fibers

Body: orange crystal chenille

Wing: chartreuse wool, trimmed short

(Colors may be varied to match water conditions.)

Frammus, Green & Pink (Vic Stevens)

Martin Lamont

Hook: Mustad 7958 No. 6–2

Thread: as for wing

Body: chartreuse chenille

Wing: pink acrylic yarn, combed

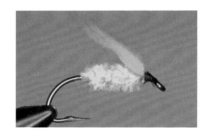

Fry or Alevin (Tony Route)

Martin Lamont

Hook: Mustad 9671 or Tiemco 5262 2XL No. 10, 8
   or 6, nickel or bronzed

Yolk sack: pale pink/yellow

Body: if nickel hook is used, no body or tail
   required

Wing: white polar bear hair or FisHair, sparse,
   extended to hook bend; add a few strands of
   silver Flashabou

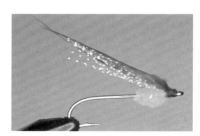

Alternative Fry or Alevin Pattern:
Body: silver Krystal Flash, wrapped
Wing: sparse white hair with sparse wing of green
    Krystal Flash extending beyond hook bend
Head: adhesive eyes on each side of egg sack;
    cover with 5-minute clear epoxy

Girdle Bug
Barry Thornton
Hook: Mustad 34007 No. 4–2
Thread: red
Body: fluorescent pink chenille, two pairs of
    white rubber legs, weighted or unweighted
Tail: four strands of white rubber legs

Jig-Fly
Paul Marriner
Hook: Eagle Claw 640 No. 6 (1/16 oz. jig head)
Head: red, pink, white, yellow or chartreuse
Tail: Krystal Flash, three or four strands extend-
    ing about a shank's length behind bend
Body: chenille, color to contrast head

Leech, Acrylic (Bob Jones)
Bob Jones
Hook: Eagle Claw L058 3XL No. 10–4
Thread: maroon
Head: (optional) small Bead Head or Cone Head
Body: maroon, combed acrylic yarn
Side: (optional) brown or copper Flashabou, one
    strand each side

Leech, Bead Head Maroon (Brian Chan)
Brian Chan
Hook: 2x long streamer No. 12–6
Bead: gold, copper or black metal
Tail: synthetic dubbing, e.g. Simi-Seal or Mohair
    Plus, in maroon
Body: dubbed Simi-Seal or Mohair Plus, combed
    out

Leech, Blood (Jack Shaw)
Bob Jones
Hook: Mustad 9672 or Eagle Claw L058 3XL No.
10–4
Thread: black
Tail: dark reddish-brown mohair
Body: dark reddish-brown mohair

1. Tie in a small clump of loose mohair for the tail.
2. Tie in a strand of mohair at the top of the bend and wrap it forward to the hook eye while stroking the mohair rearward. Tie off and cement; then brush the hair to loosen it. Stroke the hair so it is fairly flat along both sides and forms a top and bottom wing that flows smoothly back over the tail.
3. Grip the hook eye with a hemostat, dip the fly in boiling water for a few seconds and then smooth the wings rearward.
4. After wings dry, trim them so they curve to meet the tail about ½" (12 mm) behind the bend.

Leech, Bug-eyed Crystal (Bob Morenski)
Bob Jones
Hook: Mustad AC9672 No. 8–4
Thread: 3/0 monocord, color matching shell
Eyes: silver Bead Chain
Tail: marabou, two strands Krystal Flash on each side
Body: Crystal Chenille, color of choice
Shell: marabou
Hackle: saddle

Leech, Purple Egg-sucking
Martin Lamont
Hook: Mustad 9672 3XL-4XL No. 8–2, weighted
   or unweighted
Tail: purple marabou, same length as shank
Body: purple chenille, diameter to suit fly size
Hackle: purple saddle, palmered
Rib: silver wire, fine
Head: pink chenille, small or medium

Leech, Jack Shaw's Mohair (Jack Shaw)
Bob Jones
Hook: Mustad 9672 or Eagle Claw L058 3XL No.
   10–4
Thread: black
Butt: seal fur or polar bear underhair
Midbody: black mohair
Front body: black angora wool
Rib: gold, silver or copper, fine

Leech, Mohair
Paul Marriner
Hook: Tiemco 400T No. 10–6, bent up to shape
Weight: lead wire (or substitute) wrapped over
   front portion
Body: mohair yarn (color of choice), wrapped
   around hook and combed out

Leech, Shepherd (Jeff Shepherd)
Jeff Shepherd
Hook:Mustad 3665A No. 12–8
Tail: black marabou, very sparse, a few strands of
black Krystal Flash
Body: purple or purple-gray mohair (carefully
pull fibers back as you wind them on)

Leech, String

Martin Lamont

Front hook: any 3XL streamer hook No. 2–2/0

Rear hook: same size, standard shank length, straight eye

Thread: to match wing

Eyes: dumbbell

Loop: braided Spectra, 15–25-lb test

Body: Crystal Chenille to match strip

Wing: rabbit strip

In Step 7, the hooks are held apart while binding the strip to the rear hook. Cut a heavy rubber band and bind to each end a small hook fashioned from piano wire. Fasten one end of the "snubber" at an anchor point level with the vise jaws (e.g. a screw eye in the wall), the other to the front hook eye.

1. The rear hook is attached by a loop extending behind the front hook. This loop must be long enough to thread through the eye of the rear hook, then pass over the bend.
2. Bind on dumbbells ¼" (6 mm) behind front hook eye.
3. Starting behind hook eye, bind front ends of loop on tightly. Lay loop over top of dumbbells, wrap thread under, then bind tightly down to the bend and cement.
4. Wrap chenille on both hooks, then attach rear hook to loop. Threading the loop from under the eye will make the hook ride point down and vice versa.
5. Place front hook upside down in vise and tie in strip. Extend rear hook straight back, measure length of strip and cut.
6. Hold eye of rear hook between thumb and forefinger and reverse wrap six turns of thread behind eye. Place hook in vise.
7. Attach "snubber" between hook eye and anchor.
8. Hold strip to the rear, spread hair over the thread. Bind strip behind hook eye, half hitch three times and trim.

9. Use sidecutters to cut front hook at the bend. Smooth exposed edge with a Carborundum stone.

10. If desired, the loop can be colored to match the strip with a waterproof marker.

(My favorite body and Flashabou combinations are black/blue and pink, pink/purple, white/green, green/silver, blue/pink, purple/pink and blue.)

Lornie's Firecracker (Dave Lornie)

Bob Jones

Hook: No. 1 Eagle Claw L67C

Thread: 3/0 white Uni-Thread, invisible sewing thread

Body: braided Mylar, ⅜" diameter, silver or pearlescent white

Eyes: adhesive 3 mm diameter, chartreuse or green

Also required: fine copper or brass wire, red marking pen (fine), 5-minute clear epoxy, round toothpicks, waxed paper, 3 x 3" (76 x 76 mm) squares, locking forceps

(See "Lornie's Firecracker," page 373 for tying instructions.)

Lester the Lobster (Joe Kambietz)

Bob Jones

Hook: Mustad 9672 No. 8–2

Thread: fluorescent red

Eyes: black 15-lb monofilament melted at ends; tie in directly above hook point and wrap body material around the eyes so they extend from head

Beak: fluorescent red thread or copper tinsel

Feelers: two to four strands of orange Krystal Flash and orange bucktail

Rib 1: 4-lb test clear monofilament (wound after all other steps complete)

Back: ⅛–¼" (3–6 mm) wide orange surveyor's tape or scud back (body size determines width), pulled over body after hackle and rib

Rib 2: oval copper tinsel

Body: orange wool, tapered down toward eye

Hackle: orange, palmered over body

Tag: fluorescent red thread with a V-shaped tail
extending over hook eye

Montreal (Peter Cowan)

Kevin Fancy

Hook: Eagle Claw L063 No. 12–10

Tail: narrow strip from dyed red duck quill

Body: claret silk floss

Rib: gold tinsel, flat

Hackle: claret cock or hen

Wing: speckled hen or turkey quill

Partridge Series (Partridge Yellow Shown)

Martin Lamont

Hook: Mustad 3906, Partridge K12ST, TMC 3761
2x heavy No. 18–10 1XS or 2XS

Thread: silk—use as body and head—yellow,
green, olive, orange, tan

Hackle: brown or gray speckled partridge hackle,
tied to extend slightly longer than shank

Pheasant Tail Crayfish (Bob Morenski)

Bob Jones

Hook: Eagle Claw L063 2XL No. 16–8

Thread: 6/0 tobacco brown

Eyes: 20–40-lb test monofilament melted on ends

Claws: fibers from ring-necked pheasant center
sword (claws, backshell and tail are all one piece)

Legs: brown saddle hackle

Body: 50/50 bobcat fur blended with cream
Antron yarn or tan rabbit fur

Rib: 28-gauge varnished copper wire

1. Wrap hook shank back toward bend. Tie in
enough fibers to form two full claws no longer
than hook shank. Don't trim.

2. Position eyes on top of shank slightly past
bend, secure with figure-8 wraps.

3. Use stem of eyes to help separate and form

claws. Pull remaining pheasant tail back over eyes and secure. Add a little dubbing between the claws and eyes.

4. Weight with double layer of copper wire extending half way down shank.
5. Tie in saddle hackle stem first, concave side facing hook point.
6. Dub half of hook shank, wrap hackle over dubbing, secure and trim.
7. Tie in ribbing and dub remainder of hook shank.
8. Pull pheasant tail forward and secure just behind hook eye. Don't trim.
9. Wind rib to front, secure and whip finish.
10. Trim pheasant tail to form tail and lacquer. Pick out dubbing along ribbed section to simulate gills.

Psychedelic P-Quad (Bob Sheedy)
Bob Jones
Hook: Eagle Claw L063 2XL No. 10
Thread: flame orange monocord 3/0
Weight: lead or copper wire
Tail: medium olive marabou tuft
Body: medium brown Crystal Dub
Ribbing: gold wire, fine
Hackle: partridge
Wing: teal
Head: orange

Puntledge Worm (Dave Lornie)
Bob Jones
Hook: Partridge Low Water No. 2–2/0
Thread: Red
Weight: .035 lead fuse wire, length to cover shank
Body: pink/white variegated chenille, medium
Flash: pearlescent white Flashabou, 4 strands
(See "Matching the Worm Hatch", page 332 for tying instructions.)

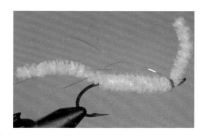

Single Egg

Bill Luscombe

Hook: Tiemco 2457 No. 10–6

Thread: white 3/0

Body: egg yarn, red, orange, pink, chartreuse, pink

Tokaruk's Special (Bob Sheedy)

Bob Jones

Hook: Mustad 3906 No. 10–1/0

Thread: black

Weight: lead or copper wire

Tail: black marabou

Body: dark olive Crystal Chenille

Ribbing: gold wire, counterwound

Hackle: black saddle

Whiskers (Louis M. Butterfield)

Bob Jones

Hook: Mustad 9671 No. 6

Thread: red

Tail: red hackle fibers

Body: green Crystal Chenille

Hackle: orange, palmered

CHAPTER 63

BEG, BORROW, SCROUNGE AND RECYCLE

Jack Davis

THE FIRST FISH CAUGHT ON A FLY TIED BY THE ANGLER WHO created it is never forgotten. In my case it was a bragging-sized brown trout coaxed from the waters at the Forks Pool of Ontario's Credit River. It happened on a Father's Day after a 45 minute trip from my home in Mississauga. I can remember clearly everything about that event—except the name of the fly that I used. All I can dredge from memory is that the trout took a streamer I had tied using fur from a road-killed rabbit.

Arthritic shoulders now hamper my mediocre casting efforts, and as my eyes aren't as good as they were in my younger days, I no longer tie what were often weird and wonderful creations of fur and feather. Nevertheless, I still retain memories of the thrill and satisfaction of those fish fooled by the flies I tied.

These days, I look with amazement at the proliferation of synthetic materials available for tying flies, for with the exceptions of threads and tinsels, my creations were tied primarily with natural materials. Most utilized something taken from birds or game harvested by either my own hunting efforts or those of friends, and in many cases it was salvaged from road kills or other "found" birds and beasts. Nevertheless, I note that some fly-tiers still look beyond the tempting, colorful, plastic-wrapped offerings decorating those tackle shop displays, and many continue collecting as much of their own natural material as possible.

Looking back at how I went about building up a stock of fur, hair and feathers, it doesn't appear that much has changed over the years. For the most part little effort is required, but it pays to be prepared. Carry the following items in your vehicle so you can take advantage of what might be found along the roadside: side-cutter pliers, a sharp knife with a sturdy blade, scissors (kitchen shears are better), a pound of borax laundry powder in a self-sealing plastic bag (to keep it dry), more of the same bags in which to store your treasures, a couple of larger-sized garbage bags, and a pair of rubber gloves or disposable plastic gloves.

Depending on where one lives, squirrels, woodchucks and gophers are frequent victims of road traffic, and their tails provide material for hair-wing flies and streamers. Use side-cutters to snip the tail from the body. It's much faster than using a knife, and in many cases you don't even have to handle the carcass. A point here, though—if the carcass is actually on the road or the shoulder, throw it well off to the side so the carnage isn't perpetuated when other creatures try to feed on it.

The entire hides from these critters also provide some great material, so if the kill is fairly recent and not too badly damaged, taking the time to skin it out and borax it is to your advantage. Once at home, stretch the hide and tack it around the edges to a piece of plywood, scrape off any excess fat, slap some more borax on it, and set it aside in a cool, dry spot to cure.

Porcupines are another animal that is often killed on the nation's highways and byways. They, too, are a source of many useful items. The body hair has many applications, and the small quills create excellent extended bodies for some patterns. The larger quills have long been used as floats for still fishing, which leads me to wonder if some of the medium-sized ones could be used as strike indicators on floating lines.

Also, depending on your location, you might encounter creatures like red or gray foxes, cottontail rabbits, varying hares, muskrats, marten and mink that have been clipped by vehicles. Mind you, there may well be something in your particular game regulations that prohibits the possession of fur-bearing animal parts, so I urge you to check this out before you start collecting.

If you hunt, virtually everything you shoot is a source of material. Fly tiers have known for many years the value of deer hair. The long white hair from the tail creates a lifelike "breathing" action in the water, and it can be easily dyed to any color desired. It is an excellent choice for dressing streamer patterns. The body hair is hollow, making it the first choice for hair-winged dry flies. It can be used in its natural color or dyed. The white hair around the belly and rump is best for dying, but some interesting combinations can be arrived at by dyeing brown hair in colors like orange, red, yellow and green, especially if using fluorescent dyes.

Deer body hair also sculpts beautifully. After spinning it onto a hook shank and packing it tightly, it can be cut and trimmed to create buoyant, high-floating patterns for Atlantic salmon and steelhead, and multicolored bass bugs.

Elk, caribou, antelope and moose also offer a wealth of tying material. Elk hair is longer and coarser than deer hair, but much more durable. Caribou is even more buoyant than deer hair, but much more fragile. It does, however, make excellent spun and clipped bodies. Antelope hair is quite coarse and is also useful for spun and clipped bodies. Moose hair is long and lends itself to ribbing material and various body parts like tails, legs and antenna. Being durable, it can even be used for tying long-winged streamers for pike and muskie.

Hair from black, brown and grizzly bears is always a welcome addition to a tier's collection, and lucky, indeed, is one who lays hands on a supply of polar bear hair. It is translucent and dyes beautifully, losing none of its translucency in the process. No other natural material matches its sinuous, eel-like swimming action in the water.

Mountain sheep and mountain goats are both good sources of winging material for streamer patterns, and the soft body hair of bighorn sheep makes great dubbing.

Other sources of material are trappers, taxidermists and furriers. Trappers, for example, could be a source of fur from aquatic animals, especially muskrat, otter and beaver, all of which have soft underfur that makes excellent dubbing and stiff guard hairs that can be incorporated in many buggy-fly patterns. Taxidermists and furriers can be approached to see if they will sell trimmings, or better yet, barter in exchange for finished flies.

Don't overlook waterfowl. In their natural colors or dyed, they provide "must have" feathers for many patterns. Coots are not especially sought after by waterfowlers, but are of interest to tiers. High-grade, dun-colored hackles come from the body, and the wing feathers are perfect for making upright, divided wings for dry flies.

Many consider the wood duck North America's most beautiful waterfowl. Its feathers are a valuable addition to any tier's bench because, as with most ducks, nearly all can be used. Scaup, canvasbacks and redheads furnish dry-fly wings, and the white breast and barred, brown flank feathers of hooded mergansers are always in demand, as are those from the pintail, and the blue-wing and green-wing teal (the throat feathers make fine fan wings).

Mallards are a fly-tier's dream as virtually every feather is valuable when creating many of the old, established Atlantic salmon patterns. Splendid fan wings can be made from its delicate, barred breast feathers, and the green head feathers are often used for tails. The barred, brown feathers go into the wings and tails of trout flies while the barred flank feathers can be used for minnow imitations.

Matched Canada goose wing quills are used in many Atlantic salmon patterns, and also for nymph wing cases, bodies and legs. Don't overlook those of white domestic geese, which can be dyed every color of the rainbow.

Pretty well all of the plumage of cock ring-necked pheasants can be utilized. Fibers from the long tail feathers are used for nymph bodies, shell backs, legs, antenna, tails and cheeks. Rump feathers, especially those with a blue tinge, are what makes the Carey Special in its many guises such a productive pattern. And don't overlook feathers from a hen pheasant. They are softer and less colorful, but useful in many wet-fly and nymph applications.

A wild turkey is also covered with useful feathers. One can only wonder at how many Muddler Minnow and Hopper patterns have been tied using the paired, mottled wing feathers of these birds. The biot quills (short side of the first flight feather on each wing) make great legs, tails and bodies for nymphs and dry flies. The tail consists of primary and secondary feathers. Primaries make great wing cases on nymphs, but should be strengthened with a coat of Pliobond or Flexament prior to use. Secondaries are softer feathers and are useful for bodies, legs, tails and wing cases. Shoulder feathers from the body can be used to create parachute or upright thorax wings. Simply trim out the quill tip and bunch the fibers together. Domestic white turkeys are also a great source of feathers, for they can be used as is or dyed.

Birds of many species may be found as road kills and can provide a fly tier with a wide variety of material. However, there is another caveat here as some provinces may have laws against possessing songbirds or parts thereof—so check the regulations.

An adult crow yields some interesting neck and rump hackles, and the pesky starling contributes fine breast feathers which can be used to make cheeks and eyes in many patterns.

And so the list goes. Almost any dead creature you might encounter is a potential source of fur or feathers. Keep a sharp eye on the sides of roads while driving, and when something is spotted, carefully pull off the road and amble back to check it out. If it looks promising, simply retrace your steps, retrieve your "road kill kit," then get to work. I can't think of a cheaper way to bolster your supply of fly-tying material. Happy harvesting!

CHAPTER 64

CANADA'S CROSS-COUNTRY FLY-TYING MATERIAL

Ralph Shaw

"OH NO," ELAINE GROANED. "I'VE HOOKED THE BEAVER!" We were casting flies over the shoals of Hyas Lake, near Kamloops, targeting large rainbows that were patrolling the shallows in search of traveler sedges. My wife's assumption seemed reasonable, for a large beaver had appeared right around sunset and had frequently crossed our path as the evening progressed. However, as the "beaver" swam under the stern of our boat, I saw it was, in fact, a large trout—large enough that I doubted the No. 12 Tom Thumb it had taken would stay lodged in its jaw.

What followed was a terrific fight between an experienced, well-equipped angler and a strong, heavy fish. It ran, it jumped, it bulldogged, then did it all over again and again. But its determination to escape was more than matched by Elaine's determination to land it. After what seemed an eternity in the rapidly fading light, the monster finally wallowed on its side and Elaine led it toward the waiting net. This happened on August 29, 1980, and at 8 lb 9 oz (3.9 kg), I believe it still stands as the largest trout taken from that lake over the last 40 or more years.

This story, however, is not about big fish, but the material used to tie patterns which catch them—deer hair. The Tom Thumb is but one example of a pattern that is tied using nothing but deer hair, thread and a hook—very simple and effective. The point not to be missed is that flies tied of deer hair catch a great many fish.

Of all the natural fly-tying materials available to North American tiers, none is more easily accessible than deer hair. Each hunting season, from the Atlantic to the Pacific, from Florida to the northern parts of our continent, Canadians harvest tens of thousands of deer, and American hunters take millions. This surely makes deer hair the most abundant and easily obtained of all natural materials.

The two primary species in Canada are white-tailed and mule deer (black-tailed deer are a subspecies of mule deer). White-tails are found from coast to coast, while mulies live in the western part of our country. The only province with no deer is Newfoundland, but it does have moose and caribou. Elk and caribou hair are basic materials for many patterns in their own right and can be used as substitutes if deer hair is unavailable. Moose hair is of limited use because it is coarse and brittle; however, it is an important ingredient in several fly patterns.

I am often asked, "Which deer hair is best?" For most purposes my answer is an early November white-tail, followed by a late-October mule deer, and in third place, a late fall coastal black-tail. Having said this, it is important to realize that all winter-coat deer hair makes suitable material for tying. In areas with a cold climate, a September deer hide just out of its summer coat has very even hair, which I like for some patterns. Prime late-season hair is about 1 ½–2" (4–5 cm) long and is very versatile. Good early season hair is about 1" (25 mm) long, very even in length, and best for small patterns. The best hair for streamer patterns, in order of preference, comes from the tails of white-tailed, black-tailed and mule deer.

Over the years I have prepared many deer hides for fly-tying materials. The process is very simple. Cut and scrape all the excess fat or meat from the hide. While trimming the hide, be sure to save the white hair at the rear and underside. Place the skin hair-side down on a 4' x 4' sheet of ¾" plywood, then stretch it outward and nail it around the edges. Give it a generous coating of pickling salt—at least ⅛" (3 mm) thick—and rub it well into the hide. Place the stretcher board level in a shed, carport or other dry place and allow the hide to cure until spring. The skin will be hard, dry and odorless.

After removing the nails, use a sharp knife to cut the hide into suitable-sized pieces for storage. First, cut it into long strips about 6" (15 cm) wide, then cut across the strips every 4" (10 cm). One deer hide will provide a lifetime supply and ample to share with friends. For safe storage from moths, use self-sealing plastic bags or plastic food containers with tight lids.

When curing deer tails it is important to take care while skinning them out. Carefully split the skin down the center of the white underside, then skin around the tail bone with a sharp knife. If there is dried blood in the hair, it is easily removed by washing the skin in cold water. The skin can now be stretched and nailed onto a board in a similar manner to a hide, rubbed with salt and left to dry. Tails from white-tailed deer have long white hair that is second only to polar bear hair for tying bucktail or streamer flies. Black-tail hair is also good, but I consider mule deer tails to be of limited use.

Virtually all fly-tying shops carry supplies of this important material, but being a good scrounger is part of the fun of fly-tying—and very important for those with limited funds. Good sources of deer hides and tails are hunters, cold storage lockers, game processing facilities, trimmings from local taxidermists or tanneries, even highway kills. However, in the latter case it may be prudent to check with local conservation authorities about the legal implications.

When dealing with fresh deer hides or tails in mild weather, it is important to process them quickly. If unable to do this right away, place them in plastic bags and store them in a freezer until you can spend the time necessary to do the job properly.

An important quality of deer hair is that it is hollow, thereby making it an ideal material for dry-flies (although it is also used in many wet patterns). Across Canada, deer-hair patterns that suggest insects indigenous to the northern hemisphere will catch fish. Sedges, may flies, mosquitoes, chironomids and white moths are common examples. These insects are important food for trout, char, grayling and whitefish, and can easily be imitated in their terrestrial state by the selective tying of Tom Thumbs, which are among the simplest and most effective of all deer-hair patterns. At the end of this chapter, the variations of the Tom Thumb used to create imitations of specific insects underscores the great adaptability of deer hair—and reveals why this particular pattern has national applications. It can be used to match the hatch, or in generic situations to look like many types of floating insects. The Humpy is quite similar to a Tom Thumb, but incorporates a colored body and has a hackle in front of the wings.

Deer hair can be used exclusively to tie such seasonal, terrestrial patterns as beetles, crickets and black ants. My first experience with a Black Ant was on Peterhope Lake, again near Kamloops, and that fish weighed in at 6 lb 7 oz (2.9 kg). Needless to say, a few Black Ants can always be found in my fly box.

Other patterns which qualify on the grounds of purity are the many variations of dragonfly nymphs designed for fishing in deep water, freshwater shrimp and water boatman—all created with this versatile material.

There are deer-hair flies tied to attract every major freshwater game fish in Canada, plus a number of saltwater species. For Atlantic Salmon on the East Coast, popular patterns like the Bomber, Buck Bug and Rat-Faced MacDougal use deer hair as the primary material, with some hackle or feathers to complete the pattern.

Deer hair has long dominated many bass bug patterns. Most have tails of hackle or rubber strands, but the main fly body is deer hair which is spun onto the hook shank, packed tightly, then trimmed to shape. Some are shaped to slide quietly through water, others to create a disturbance by popping or gurgling. Patterns are achieved by spinning the hair on the hook shank in bands of complementary colors—usually yellow and black, yellow and red, yellow and green, or red and white. Popular deer-hair bass bugs are the generic Hair Frog and Hair Mouse, plus the Whithair Bug and Gerbubble Bug. There are a host of others too numerous to list, but most are simply variations of these four basic patterns.

There is a growing popularity for fairly large patterns designed to attract pike and muskie. One which employs spun and clipped deer hair is the Krazy Kicker Frog, while the Clouser Minnow uses long hair, preferably from a white-tail. There is no question that new patterns will emerge, and as they do you can bet that interest in good sources of late-season white-tail and mule-deer hides and tails will increase.

Many hair-wing bucktail patterns, popular for saltwater species like coho and chinook salmon, have undergone significant changes with regard to the amount of synthetic materials used. Ultra Hair, FisHair, Super Hair, Angel Hair—an ever-increasing range of new materials are available—and they certainly have their place. However, many of us still prefer traditional patterns like the Mickey Finn tied with dyed red and yellow hair from the tail of white-tailed deer, and even newer patterns like the ubiquitous Clouser Minnow and Muddler Minnow, both of which are used in fresh and salt water.

There is a band of West Coast anglers who are addicted to taking steelhead on dry flies whenever possible. A number of patterns incorporating deer hair have been developed with this specific goal in mind, again, with some also employing hackle or other materials. The late Andy Anderson, a well-known pioneer among British Columbia fly fishers, tied a series of deer-hair dry flies for fishing on the Thompson River. Although this river is world famous for large, brawny steelhead that rise readily to surface presentations, Anderson fished primarily for resident rainbow trout which often weighed 5 lb (2.3 kg) or more. Anderson's patterns were designed to imitate grasshoppers, stone flies and other large insects, and his success with them was legendary. Other examples of pure deer-hair patterns are the Riffle Dancer and Bulkley Mouse. An interesting variation of the latter uses moose hair to create the Bulkley Moose. Variations on the Atlantic salmon Bomber pattern are also popular in northern British Columbia—Purple Bomber, Cigar Butt, Air British Columbia, and the Disco Mouse, to name a few.

The list of game fish taken on flies is growing, and along with it the recognition of this important natural material that is so much a part of our renewable resources. Each year thousands of deer hides are wasted, so if you are not utilizing this gift in your fly-tying and fishing, you are missing out on a very important and useful material. Another important aspect is that by nonhunters relying on hunters for their sources of material, their outdoor interests find a common bond.

In an age that sees the increasing use of synthetics, this is one natural material deserving of a higher place in the tying of flies. The only barrier is one's experience and imagination. If you are looking for a material to create your own unique pattern, deer hair offers great potential. In fact, the further I go in researching the use of deer hair in tying flies, the more I am convinced enough material can easily be amassed to write an entire book on the subject.

CHAPTER 65

BUNNY STRIPS

Ralph Shaw

AFTER DEER HAIR, RABBITS AND HARES ARE PROBABLY NEXT on the list for providing a source of useful material that is available pretty well throughout North America. In one form or another, wild bunnies range from the Pacific to the Atlantic, and from Florida to the High Arctic. They provide exciting sport for hunters, excellent meat for the table, and for fly fishers in particular, a source of fur that is excellent for making natural dubbing and narrow fur strips which are used in numerous fly patterns.

Across Canada there are two races of cottontail rabbits and three of native hares, as well as introduced European hares. By far the most prolific are snowshoe hares, followed by eastern cottontails. There are also many populations of feral rabbits spread throughout the country. In fact, my own rabbit hunting on the central east coast of Vancouver Island is limited to feral populations.

Hares turn white in the winter while rabbits retain their gray color all year. Domestic and feral rabbits range from jet black to pure white, with various shades of gray in between, and some with varying shades of browns. White and light-colored hair can easily be dyed. A note here that if you wish to dye a hide, do so before drying it. This eliminates drying it twice. However, a dried hide or even strips can be dyed at any time.

Skinning one of these critters is about as easy as it gets. Cut around the hind paws, slice the hide from each hind foot to the anus, cut the tail off, then simply peel the hide down toward the head. It's something like taking off a rubber glove. To store fresh hides awaiting processing, simply put them in a plastic bag and keep them in a freezer.

After removing the skin, I split it down the middle of the belly, then tack it hair-side down on a suitable-sized piece of plywood. The hides are quite thin and can be easily dried. I use powdered borax to speed the curing process. Place the stretched hide in any cool, dry place until it has dried. I find it easiest to cut a hide into strips about ³⁄₁₆" (5 mm) wide while it is still on the board. Cut across the hide, not lengthwise, using a sharp knife and a ruler or straightedge as a guide.

When wet, this fur takes on many qualities associated with marabou feathers. Being soft and very mobile in a current, it is ideal for leeches and long worm- or eel-like patterns in purple, black and maroon. Snowshoe hares in their white winter coat are ideal for dying, as are white domestic or feral rabbits.

Many pike flies utilize long strips of rabbit fur: popular patterns like Dave Whitlock's Hare Waterpup, Hare Grub and Hare Worm series, the Bouface series, Woolhead Sculpins, and the venerable Zonker. All in all, rabbit and hare strips are a welcome addition to any fly tier's assortment of material.

CONTRIBUTORS' BIOGRAPHIES

Brian Chan

BRIAN CHAN combines a career with a subject that is his passion. An ardent fly fisher since the late 1960s, he is a professional fisheries biologist who has been managing small lake-trout fisheries for the Province of British Columbia since the mid-1970s. He is active in conservation efforts at the local and provincial level and a regular speaker at Fly Fishing Conclaves, sportsman's expositions and fly-fishing clubs. Brian writes for several outdoor magazines, including *Fly-Fishing and Tying Journal, The Canadian Fly Fisher* and *BC Outdoors.* He has contributed to several books on fly fishing and tying, wrote the best seller *Flyfishing Strategies for Stillwaters* (1991), co-authored *"Morris and Chan" on Fly-Fishing Trout Lakes* (1999), produced two volumes of instructional videos on lake fly fishing, and is a regular guest on regional and national sport fishing TV shows. Brian and his wife, Janine, live in Kamloops, British Columbia.

Ken Coupland

BORN IN ENGLAND, Ken moved to Port Hope, Ontario, with his father after the First World War. He grew up near the Ganaraska River and started fly fishing in the late 1930s with a U.S. Simple fly reel (25 cents) and a Horrocks-

Ibbotson rod ($3.25), both of which he still has. A Queen's University graduate, his career as a mechanical engineer included the chemical industry and military and management consulting. He has pursued his interests in fly fishing and photography in British Columbia, Alberta, Ontario, Quebec, Labrador, the Maritimes and the UK. He has fished for most species Canada has to offer, including Atlantic and Pacific salmon, arctic char, brook and rainbow trout, and bass. A member of a camp on the Upper Eagle River in Labrador, he spends a week there each year with a few friends, and he has only missed spending a week in Algonquin Park three times in 40 years.

Jim Crawford

BORN AND RAISED at north Lake Tahoe, Jim has a B.A. from Menlo College (1965), and he did his MBA at the University of Santa Clara and Stanford University. He moved to Canada in 1969 with Jostens Inc. and has lived in British Columbia, Alberta, Saskatchewan, Manitoba and Ontario. He retired from Jostens as Senior VP in 1993, and he is now president and CFO of Campus Images, a division of Castle Operating Enterprises with over 500 photographers dedicated exclusively to digital electronic imaging. Jim has written over 200 feature articles for North American magazines, plus two fly-fishing books, and another is under way. He is the Alaska and Western Canada field editor for Mike Fong's *The Inside Angler* newsletter. A specialist in saltwater fly fishing, he has fished in nearly every state and province and in much of Mexico. Jim and wife Linda presently have homes on Flathead Lake in Montana, and in Courtenay, British Columbia.

Jack Davis

BORN IN TORONTO, Ontario, in 1920, Jack's first trout on a fly came from the Credit River. He served in the Canadian Armed Forces from 1939 to 1945. Although wounded in action, he managed to arrive home with his war bride, Doris. He started freelancing in the 1950s and joined the Outdoor Writers of

Canada (OWC) in 1959. He held various editorial positions with *The Port Credit Weekly, The Moncton Free Press, The Peterborough Examiner, The Mobile Traveller* and finally, *Ontario Angler & Hunter.* He retired in 1985, then served as OWC's executive director until December, 1999. In recognition for his conservation ethic, he won the Canadian Imperial Bank of Canada Silver Tray Award (1964), Carling Conservation Award (1965), OWC's Pete McGillen Award (1976 and 1978), Greg Clark Award (1980), *Fishing News* Lifetime Achievement Award (1999), and an Ontario Ministry of Natural Resources Award for Professionalism and Integrity (1999). His books include *Tall Tales* (1979), *Canadian Boating's Family Fishing Handbook* (1991), and *Tall Tales and Blatant Lies* (1999). Jack lives in Peterborough, Ontario.

Gord Ellis

Gord is a full-time writer, journalist and broadcaster, who specializes in the outdoor pursuits of fishing, hunting and camping. He is the fishing editor for *Ontario Out of Doors* magazine, the outdoor writer and columnist for the *Thunder Bay Chronicle Journal Times News,* and he covers the outdoors beat for CBC radio in Northwestern and North Central Ontario. He also writes a regular column for the *Minnesota Outdoor News,* and his writing has appeared in publications ranging from *Outdoor Life* to *Reader's Digest.* He has fly fished since childhood and has had the chance to fish a fly for just about very freshwater species from coast to coast. Gord lives in Thunder Bay, Ontario, with his wife, Cheryl, and sons Devin and Austin.

Kevin Fancy

KEVIN DISCOVERED his calling in life on the shores of Ontario's Lake Nippissing in the mid-1960s at the age of six. A deep-seated love of the outdoors and a passion to teach steered him into a career as a self-taught journalist in the early 1980s. As an award-winning writer, he considers himself a teacher, activist, promoter and storyteller. His favorite subjects are those outdoor pursuits he loves most—fishing, tying flies, camping—virtually any outdoor experience that provides excitement, adventure and a sense of accomplishment. Since the 1980s, the works of "Chuckwagon"—as he is known to his friends for he's also an excellent camp cook—have been published in *Canadian Sport Fishing, Outdoor Canada, Canadian Camper, Ontario Fisherman, Provincial Angler*, the *Ottawa Citizen*, plus dozens of newspapers and magazines across Canada and in the U.S. Kevin and his wife, Lynne Marie, live in Nepean, Ontario.

Steve Galea

STEVE'S FASCINATION with fly fishing was inspired by the outdoor magazines of his youth. A kindly neighborhood tackle junkie and his garage-sale prices conspired to allow the 12-year-old boy a bona fide fly-fishing rig. That formative summer was spent harassing any cat that crossed his driveway-casting-lane, and catching smallmouth and rock bass on the nearby Rouge River. From there things grew out of control. An avid fly fisherman and tier, he spends at least 75 days a year on local streams chasing panfish, bass, pike or trout. As the news editor and humorist for *Ontario Out of Doors* magazine and a contributor to several other publications, Steve often puts his misadventures to print. And, occasionally, he gets things right. He lives in Ontario's Haliburton Highlands, just minutes from fine smallmouth bass, trout, and panfish water and a short drive from famous Algonquin Park.

George Gruenefeld

WELL KNOWN ON CANADA'S OUTDOOR SCENE, since the late 1960s George has written about fishing and hunting as a newspaper columnist, feature writer, and regional correspondent for many major North American magazines and as editor of several Canadian publications. He has also produced and published a book on Atlantic salmon fishing. An avid angler and hunter, he has traveled extensively across North America and around the world, seeking the best angling and hunting. George grew up in Quebec, where he spent much of his time fishing eastern streams and hunting on hardwood ridges and windswept barrens. As the editor of *Western Sportsman,* he spent several years on the Prairies, where he chased big Saskatchewan white-tails and gunned for ducks, geese and upland birds. Also the editor of *BC Outdoors* and *BC Sport Fishing,* he resides in North Vancouver, British Columbia, where Pacific salmon, trout and high-country game fill his daydreams.

Glen Hales

BORN AND RAISED in Belleville, Ontario, Glen has fished since he was old enough to hold a willow pole. He grew up prowling the Bay of Quinte shoreline and wading the Moira River and other streams; he took up fly fishing in the late 1980s. A fly-fishing guide since 1993, Glen is noted for putting his clients into steelhead, brown trout, brookies, bass, muskie, garpike and carp on eastern Ontario rivers and the Bay of Quinte. He holds the Ontario record for carp on a fly—38 lb (17.3 kg)—and several of his fly patterns have won awards. He is an instructor at annual fly-fishing workshops with Quinte Flyfishing and the *Ontario Out of Doors* Spring Fishing Shows. Glen's photographs of fishing and hunting scenes, wildlife, and landscapes have been published in magazines across Canada, and he is the associate photo editor of *The Canadian Fly Fisher* magazine.

Robert H. Jones

A WRITER SINCE 1975, full-time since 1980, Bob is the fishing editor at *BC Outdoors,* associate editor of *BC Sport Fishing,* and a contributor to several regional, national and international publications. Born in Vancouver, British Columbia, in 1935, he left school at age 14 to become a logger—the same year he started fly fishing. A military career spanning 27 years allowed him to travel and fish throughout much of Canada and Central Europe. He is a past president, life member and Pete McGillen-Award recipient of the Outdoor Writers of Canada; a member of the Outdoor Writers Association of America; and a member of The Writers' Union of Canada. The author of *Make Your Own*

Fishing Tackle (1984), *Tangled Lines and Patched Waders* (1996), *Warped Rods and Squeaky Reels* (1997), and co-author of eight other books, he has won 16 writing awards. Bob and Vera, his wife and business partner who frequently outfishes him, reside in Courtenay, British Columbia.

Vera Jones

VERA (NÉE FEDOROWICH) was born and raised in Manitoba, where in 1955 she met and later married Bob Jones. Their British Columbia honeymoon involved fly fishing on the Shuswap River, where she caught a bullfrog. During Bob's career in the RCAF, they lived in Comox, British Columbia; Germany; Ontario; Germany again; Ontario again; then back to Courtenay, British Columbia, when Bob retired in 1980. Vera wrote a popular cooking column in a local newspaper for seven years, and her articles appear in *BC Outdoors* and *BC Sport Fishing*. Quite comfortable jigging for halibut, Buzz-Bombing for salmon, or bobber-tossing for winter-run steelhead, Vera didn't take up fly fishing until 2000, when Bob forgot to put away his favorite 5-weight graphite fly rod.

Martin Lamont

AS A CHILD IN SCOTLAND, Martin was encouraged by his parents to explore freely. He quickly discovered angling and recalls the assistance given by neighbors, friends, and renowned professionals during his formative years. A dentist by profession, an avid outdoorsman, conservationist and fly fisher by avocation, his introduction to competition fly fishing was in 1987. He was a Fly Fishing Canada team member when it entered its first World Championship in England, preceding eight wonderful years of overseas competition and learning which culminated in Kamloops, British Columbia, in 1993. He embraces the diverse, thoughtful and imaginative dimensions of interest and creativity, as well as natural history, science, technology and the artistry of fly fishing. As the pursuit of fish—one of mankind's oldest activities—has been documented throughout the history of literature, Martin is proud of his associations with the

Outdoor Writers of Canada and Fly Fishing Canada. He and his wife, Helen, live in Comox, British Columbia.

Bill Luscombe

BORN IN BRITISH COLUMBIA in 1957, Bill grew up right beside the Fraser River delta. A hunter and angler for most of his life, he took up fly fishing in the late 1970s. He started teaching fly-fishing courses in the late 1980s, and he is a Canadian Firearms Safety Education Course instructor. A full-time Registered Professional Forester for the provincial government, Bill and his wife, Susan, live in Duncan on Vancouver Island. An award-winning freelance outdoor writer and photographer, he is the fly fishing columnist for *BC Sport Fishing,* and has also been published in *The Outdoor Edge, BC Outdoors, Western Sportsman, Island Fish Finder, Reel Angler, BC Freshwater Fishing Guide,* and *BC Hunting Guide.* Bill is on the Internet at www.flyfishingworld.com and www.sportfishingbc.com. He is an active member of the Outdoor Writers of Canada and a former director of the Northwest Outdoor Writers Association.

Mark Krupa

A FREELANCE PHOTOGRAPHER and writer since 1990, Mark's travels in search of exotic, ineffable moments in angling have taken him across North America, and abroad to India, the Amazon and Russia. He is photo editor at *The Canadian Fly Fisher,* and his work has appeared in numerous books and calendars, plus a broad range of magazines including the *Atlantic Salmon Journal, Real Fishing, In-Fisherman, BC Outdoors, Sentier Chasse-Peche* and *American Angler.* The photo-library of his company, Horizons Unlimited, contains over 7,000 slides, featuring a vast selection of freshwater fish species, landscapes and waterscapes. A member of the Outdoor Writers of Canada and the Outdoor Writers Association of America, Mark supports his angling addiction by working as an actor and stunt man in television and film. When not fishing or practicing karate, he meanders the streets of Montreal, convinced that one day "all roads will become rivers."

Chris Marshall

CHRIS WAS BORN in Yorkshire, England, where he misspent his youth in pursuit of wild, native brown trout in the moorland streams. In 1960, at the age of 21, he immigrated to Canada to seek his fortune. A writing teacher until his retirement in 1997, he has also written professionally for over twenty years. His work, both fiction and nonfiction, has been published in Canada, the U.S., England, and Australia. He has also written a weekly fishing column for the *Belleville Intelligencer* for the past twelve years. Between 1989 and 1995, he was fly-fishing editor for *Canadian Sportfishing*. He has had two books published: *Criteria Internalised by Impression Markers in Assessing Written Composition* (1979) and *Fly-Fishing Across Canada* (1991). Chris and his wife, Liz, live in Belleville, Ontario, where he's currently avoiding retirement stagnation by editing and publishing Canada's first fly-fishing magazine, *The Canadian Fly Fisher*.

Paul Marriner

PAUL STARTED FLY FISHING in the 1960s and has since visited a dozen countries seeking Atlantic and Pacific salmon, trout, bass and . . . whatever. He has represented Canada at eight World Fly-Fishing Championships (Team Captain, 1994–1996) and is a member of the Outdoor Writers of Canada and Outdoor Writers Association of America. A guest lecturer at numerous fly-fishing symposiums, he won the 1991 Gregory Clark Award for outstanding contributions to the arts of fly fishing. His masthead credits include *FlyLife (Australia), Fly Fish America, The Fishing News, Outdoor Canada, Fly Fisherman's Virtual Fly Shop, The Canadian Fly Fisher* and *The Angling Report*. In addition, several hundred articles have appeared in other national and international magazines. His books include the 1994 OWC award-winning *Atlantic Salmon: A Fly Fishing Primer, The Ausable River Journal, The Miramichi River Journal,* and *Modern Atlantic Salmon Flies*. Paul and his wife, Nancy, live in Mahone Bay, Nova Scotia.

Drew Myers

A FREELANCE OUTDOOR WRITER and photographer from the Toronto area, Drew has been involved with the outdoors since childhood. A member of the Outdoor Writers of Canada, he started writing for publication while still in his teens. He is a field editor with *Ontario Out of Doors,* a contributor to *Ducks Unlimited* magazine, and his work has appeared in various American publications. Drew has worked for Trout Unlimited in stream-rehabilitation projects and as a fly-tying instructor for Fly Fishing Canada. He presents fishing seminars at the Spring Fishing Show and radio programs about angling. When not working toward an anthropology/geography degree at Carleton University, he guides for lake trout, pike and grayling in the Northwest Territories, plus steelhead and brown trout in southern Ontario. When Drew isn't slaving over his latest outdoor writing project, he can usually be found working a fly rod on some local waterway.

Burton J. Myers

BURT MYERS is the editor/associate publisher of *Ontario Out of Doors.* During his writing career he has received numerous awards, including the prestigious Greg Clarke Editorial Writing Award. In 1985 he was honored with the Pete McGillen Award, presented to Outdoor Writers of Canada members who have reflected the highest standards of professionalism. Other recognition includes awards for public service as a Cub Scout leader, volunteer firefighter and in 1992 an award by the Province of Ontario for long-standing community service. Burt has served on scores of advisory committees. He is a founding member of Muskies Canada, the founding chairman of the Ducks Unlimited (DU) Canada Toronto Chapter, and currently serves on DU Canada's national board of directors. He has served on the OWC board of directors, three times as president. Burt and his wife, Jennifer (the associate editor of *Profit* magazine), live in Scarborough, Ontario, with their twin children, Cameron and Victoria.

Wayne Phillips

ON HIS FIRST FISHING TRIP in 1951 when he was five, pike stole Wayne's heart, and a lifelong passion for fishing began. Fly fishing entered his life in the late 1970s and has become, not just a sport, but a way of life. After exploring Montana rivers and streams, he and his wife, Janelle, purchased a home in Ennis, in the heart of Montana's fabled blue-ribbon trout streams. Angling highlights include steelhead on the Dean River, lake trout in Great Slave Lake, brown trout on Montana's Madison River, rainbows on Idaho's Henry's Fork, pike and grayling in Saskatchewan, and tarpon and bonefish in the Florida Keys. He began writing professionally in 1984 and has written over 800 newspaper columns and articles for many magazines in Canada and the U.S. Other interests include good food, fine wine, collecting fly reels and fishing books, and developing recipes for game and fish.

Bob Rife

NEWSPAPER JOURNALIST Bob Rife became outdoors editor of the *Globe and Mail* in 1968, developing a weekly section of five to eight pages that radio/TV personality Gordon Sinclair praised on air as the "best outdoors pages in the country." His articles on conservation and humor won four national Kortright Awards. He has written one book and contributed to three others. In 1983 he was presented with the Greg Clark Award for "outstanding contributions to fly fishing." Elected president of the Outdoor Writers of Canada in 1970, he also served on its board for more than 20 years. After retiring from *The Globe* in 1993 at age 65, he was asked to join *Ontario Out of Doors* magazine as news editor. Despite debilitating strokes in 1997, he continued writing, typing with, as he puts it, "one finger on the wrong hand." His subsequent articles have appeared in regional newspapers and *The Canadian Fly Fisher* magazine.

Marty Roberts

MARTY HAS BEEN CHASING smallmouth bass along the eastern shores of Lake Erie since the mid-1960s and with a fly rod since 1985. A freelance outdoor writer since the mid-1980s, he has written a popular newspaper column for several years, had feature articles published in numerous Canadian and American magazines, and has contributed to several outdoor books and video projects. Along the way his writing and photography have garnered four national awards. Since joining the Outdoor Writers of Canada in 1986, he has served as a director, vice-president, president and chairman of the board. He was awarded a Life Membership in 1997. Marty and his wife, Dawn, presently reside in Fort Erie, Ontario.

Ken Robins

KEN HAS HAD A LIFELONG PASSION for trout fishing. He has fly fished with his family and friends for the various species of salmonids from the Atlantic coast to the Pacific coast. He has published many articles and photographs on the topic of fly fishing, and together with his wife, Sue, has taught fly casting to many beginners. But mostly Ken enjoys giving slide shows, dealing with all aspects of fly fishing, to clubs and fly-fishing forums. He is a longtime member of the Outdoor Writers of Canada, the Ontario Federation of Anglers and Hunters, the Kitchener–Waterloo Flyfishers, Trout Unlimited, and the Federation of Fly-Fishers. Ken and his family live in Stratford, Ontario.

Bob Scammell

BOB HAS BEEN FISHING—mostly in Alberta—for more than 50 years, 35 of them as a fly fisherman. In 1987 he was a member of Canada's first-ever team in the World Fly Fishing Championships in England. His outdoor columns have been appearing weekly in various Alberta newspapers since the mid-1960s. Over the years, those columns, along with his freelance magazine articles and columns, have won several Outdoor Writers of Canada awards and a few

Outdoor Writers Association of America awards. Two of Bob's books have won the OWC Award of Excellence for Books: *The Outside Story* (1983), a collection from the first 10 years of his newspaper columns, and *Good Old Guys, Alibis and Outright Lies* (1997), a collection of his outdoor humor. His book *The Phenological Fly*, still in print, deals with Alberta's best fly hatches and the patterns to imitate them.

Clive Schaupmeyer

A NATIVE ALBERTAN, Clive began fishing as a youth in the mid-1950s and took up fly fishing in the early 1970s. An avid trout-stream fly fisherman, he has been pursuing pike with flies since 1990. He started freelance writing in 1983, and his feature articles have since appeared in regional and national magazines including *Outdoor Canada, Western Living, Western Sportsman, The Outdoor Edge, Alberta Fishing Guide*, and *Conservator.* A part-time commercial agricultural photographer, his photograph of a boy fishing was judged by the Outdoor Writers of Canada as the best outdoor photograph published in Canada in 1996. His first book, *The Essential Guide to Fly-Fishing*, was published in 1997. It proved extremely popular with anglers and quickly made the Canadian bestseller list. In his "spare time," he makes presentations on fly fishing, tying and photography at workshops throughout Alberta. Clive and his wife, Willie, live in Coaldale, Alberta.

Ralph Shaw

BORN AT COLD LAKE, Alberta, in 1926, Ralph started fishing six years later— catching shiners with a piece of string and a bent pin. This progressed to catching trout when he and his brother began dangling flies from willow poles. Since that early beginning Ralph has specialized in fishing trout with artificial flies and, more recently, in taking salmon and bottom fish in salt water. A lifelong crusader for sane fish and wildlife conservation practices, he retired as a school principal in 1983 after 35 years in education, but continues his conservation activities. He received the Order of Canada in 1984 for his work in these endeavors and the

Canada 125 Medal. His popular weekly outdoors column in the *Comox Valley Record* has won several writing awards, and he contributes regularly to *The Outdoor Edge, BC Outdoors, Outdoor Canada, Fish Finder* and *Island Angler.* His first book, *Ralph Shaw's Vancouver Island Adventures,* was published in 2000. Ralph and Elaine, his wife and partner, live in Courtenay, British Columbia.

Jack Simpson

BORN IN HASTINGS, Ontario, right beside Rice Lake, Jack started fishing during his childhood in the 1930s. A University of Toronto graduate with a degree in electrical engineering, he formerly owned and operated UMG Cable Telecommunications Inc. and presently owns and operates Argord Corporation, manufacturer of electric motors. Jack has served on the board of the Izaak Walton Fly Fishers, and as secretary-treasurer of the Outdoor Writers of Canada, of which he is a life member and a Pete McGillen-Award recipient. He is a founding member and executive director of Fly Fishing Canada, and he served as president of FIPS-Mouche (International Federation of Fly Fishing) from 1991 to 1997. Jack organized the first Fly Fishing Team Canada in 1987 and served as team captain for the first four years. He has fished extensively throughout North and South America, Cuba, Australia, New Zealand and Europe, often accompanied by his wife, Anne, also an ardent fly fisher.

Dave Smallwood

BORN IN ALBERTA in 1956, Dave started fly fishing 13 years later, initiating a search for the perfect excuse to avoid school and work. After 20 years of fishing around eastern Canada and the U.S., he was asked to leave Quebec for failure to remember the French words for Gray Ghost. He settled in Saskatchewan in 1988, where six years later he developed, and continues to offer, Northern Fly-Fishing Seminars throughout northern Saskatchewan and Manitoba. Participants are taught the techniques required to fly fish for lake trout, pike, walleye, whitefish, suckers and grayling. Dave turned to writing and photography in 1995, and his work has since appeared in *Field & Stream, Angler, Warmwater Fly-Fishing,* and *American Angler.* He is the fly fishing editor for *Western Sportsman* and a feature presenter at the Canadian National Sportsmen's Shows. Dave resides in Air Ronge, Saskatchewan, with his wife, Susan, and two children, Owen and Emma.

Andrew Somerset

ANDREW HAS BEEN FISHING longer than he can remember. He became convinced at a tender age that the only proper way to fish moving water is with fly tackle, not because of any sense of moral superiority, but because spinners are expensive and flies are cheap. By the time he learned the error of his ways, he had sunk too much money into fly tackle to ever give it up. He writes a regular column for *Fly Tyer* magazine, and has written on fly fishing, fly-tying, and conservation issues for a variety of outdoor magazines including *American Angler, The Canadian Fly Fisher, Flyfishing & Tying Journal, Ontario Out of Doors,* and *Outdoor Canada.* Andrew is a past president of the Forest City Fly Fishing Club in London, Ontario, where he lives with his family.

Russ Swerdlyk

BORN AT THUNDER BAY in 1949, Russ started fishing and hunting around his northern Ontario home early in life. He still lives there and still hunts and fishes whenever time from his real job as a school principal permits. An avid fly fisherman and tier, he lectures frequently on both topics. His "life list" of fish taken on flies includes brook, rainbow, brown, lake and coastal cutthroat trout, Dolly Varden, pike, walleye, whitefish and smallmouth bass. An outdoor writer since the late 1960s, Russ is an active member of the Outdoor Writers of Canada and the Outdoor Writers Association of America. He wrote a fly-fishing column for the now discontinued *Ontario Fisherman* magazine, and presently writes a column for *Northern Ontario Angler and Hunter.* His feature articles also appear in *Ontario Out of Doors, Field and Stream, Sports Afield, Outdoor Canada* and *Real Fishing.*

Barry M. Thornton

ONE OF BRITISH COLUMBIA's best-known outdoor writers, Barry has been involved with fishing, hunting and the outdoors for most of his life. He was founding chairman of the Steelhead Society of British Columbia and elected its president three times. After a successful 35-year career in education, he hung up his school principal's hat in 1993 and has since been writing and photographing full time. He has written five books: *Steelhead: the Supreme Trophy Trout* (1978), *Saltwater Fly Fishing for Pacific Salmon* (1995), *Steelhead* (1995), *Salgair: A Steelhead Odyssey* (1997), and *Fly Fishing: The Thornton Anthology.* He has also co-authored four books, published over 1,000 articles and 1,200 photographs, and presented over 100 lectures. His articles have received awards from the Outdoor Writers of Canada and the Northwest Outdoor Writer's Association. The American Fisheries Northwest Chapter presented him with their Roderick Haig-Brown Memorial Award in recognition of his writing. Barry and his wife, Frances, live in Comox, British Columbia.

Mark White

AS A CHILD, Mark lived near West Vancouver's Ambleside Beach, where tidal pools were his playground and salmon fishing was at the family's doorstep. Mark was 13 when his father moved to Kelsey Bay on the east coast of Vancouver Island. The Sayward Valley was a wilderness setting, where black bears, black-tail deer, cougars and grouse were abundant, and the Salmon and White rivers teemed with cutthroat trout and steelhead. Mark chose a career in advertising sales and has been the advertising sales manager at *BC Outdoors* magazine since the early 1980s. He took up outdoor photography in the mid-1980s (mostly through trial-and-error) and has since had hundreds of pictures published in magazines, periodicals and promotional material, garnering several photography awards along the way. A member of the Outdoor Writers of Canada and the Outdoor Writers Association of America, Mark lives in Vancouver with his wife, Eva.

George Will

GEORGE STARTED FISHING the lakes and rivers around his home town, Winnipeg, Manitoba, in the 1950s. He left the Flatlands in the 1970s and moved to the West Coast to continue graduate school. He later taught anthropology and archaeology at Simon Fraser University and the University of British Columbia. Even then he managed to fish up to 150 days a year. He started free-lance writing during this same period, and in 1986 he became the editor of *BC Outdoors* magazine, where he remained until 1994. He has since written a novel and presently lives in Anchorage, Alaska, where he works in the digital photography field. George has flung flies in Costa Rica, Mexico and Cuba, in every province and territory throughout Canada, plus many of the American states. He is still looking for that elusive woman who fly fishes, ties flies, hunts, appreciates good single malt scotch, and owns the distillery.

Frederick H. Wooding

FRED SERVED FOR NEARLY 10 YEARS as director of information and educational services of what is now the Department of Fisheries and Oceans Canada, as well as the former Fisheries Research Board of Canada. He is the author of two internationally acclaimed best sellers: *Wild Mammals of Canada,* a specially bound copy of which was presented to HRH the Duke of Edinburgh, head of the World Wildlife Fund; and *The Angler's Book of Canadian Fishes* (1959), a specially bound copy of which was presented to Prime Minister John Diefenbaker. This book proved so popular that it was reprinted in 1972 as *The Book of Canadian Fishes,* then again in 1994 as *Lake, River and Sea-Run Fishes of Canada.* A member of the Outdoor Writers of Canada and the College of Fellows of the Royal Canadian Geographical Society, Fred now lives—and continues writing—in Saanichton, British Columbia.

FISHING SHOP DIRECTORY

While every effort has been made to provide a complete and current list of shops, inevitably some may have been missed. If a shop has inadvertently been missed, please contact the publisher at info@jgbooks.com. A current, up-to-date directory of shops is maintained at the publisher's website at flyfishingsource.com.

Alberta

Barrhead Sports
5029 – 50 St.
Barrhead, AB T7N IAI
780-674-2929

Battle River Sports & Tackle
4912 – 50 Ave.
Stettler, AB TOC 2LO
403-742-0673

Bow River Troutfitters
2122 Crowchild Tr. N.W.
Calgary, AB T2M 3Y7
403-282-8868
www.bowrivertroutfitters.com

Canterra Sports Inc.
2 – 1104, 20 Ave. N.W.
Calgary, AB T2M IE8
403-210-0118
Toll-Free: 1-800-441-2669

Caroline Supplies
5116 – 50 Ave. (BOX 340)
Caroline, AB TOM 9MO
403-722-3922

Cast Away Sports
15 – 5030, 50 St.
Sylvan Lake, AB T4S IR5
403-887-3292

Country Pleasures
570, 10816 Macleod Tr. S.W.
Calgary, AB T2J 5N8
403-271-1016
www.countrypleasures.com

Crowsnest Angler, The
22614 – 27 Ave. (BOX 400)
Bellevue, AB TOK OCO
800-267-1778
www.telusplanet.net/
public/cnangler/html

Denny's Fly Tying Specialties
10804 – 129 Ave. N.
Edmonton, AB T5E OL6
780-472-1257
www.telusplanet.net/public/
flytying

Fish Tales Fly Shop
420, 9737 Macleod Tr. S.W.
Calgary, AB T2J OP6
403-640-1273
www.fishtales-flyshop.com

Fishin' Hole, The
1035 West Edmonton Mall
Edmonton, AB T5T 3J7
780-444-1220
www.thefishinhole.com

Fishin' Hole, The
9078 – 51 Ave. N.W.
Edmonton, AB T6E 5X4
780-465-0877
www.thefishinhole.com

Fishin' Hole, The
12719 – 97 St.
Edmonton, AB T5E 4C1
780-469-6630
www.thefishinhole.com

Fishing Center, The
101, 12725 – 82 St. N.W.
Edmonton, AB T5E 2S9
780-473-4498
www.thefishingcenter.com

Hanson's Fishing Outfitters
813 First St. S.W.
Calgary, AB T2P 1N3
403-269-9371
www.hansons-outfitters.com

Hoyt's Wholesale Sports
410 – 6 St. S.
Lethbridge, AB T1J 2C9
403-327-5760

Jasper Source for Sports
406 Patricia St. (BOX 487)
Jasper, AB T0E 1E0
780-852-3654
www.jaspersports.com

Jerry's Sport Shop
21508 – 27 Ave.
Bellevue, AB T0K 0C0
403-564-4696

Jigs Rigs & Tales
7 – 142 Dickins Dr.
Fort McMurray, AB T9K 1X4
780-790-3555

Lac La Biche Sporting Goods
13337 – 101 Ave.
Lac La Biche, AB T0A 2C0
780-623-4145

Lodgepole General Store
BOX 119
Lodgepole, AB T0E 1K0
780-894-3520

Marksman Guns and Sports
312 – 13 St. N.
Lethbridge, AB T1H 2R8
403-327-7595

Monod Sports
129 Banff Ave. (BOX 310)
Banff, AB T0L 0C0
403-762-4571

On-Line Sport & Tackle
600 Patricia St. (BOX 730)
Jasper, AB T0E 1E0
780-852-3630
www.visit-jasper.com/
online.html

Outdoorsman, The
4, 1023 Allowance Ave.
Medicine Hat, AB T1A 8A9
403-529-9248

Performance Sports
208 Bear St. (BOX 2440)
Banff, AB T0L 0C0
403-762-8222
www.alpineanglers.com

Ram River Sports
5027 – 45 St.
Rocky Mountain House, AB
T4T 1B6
403-845-4160

Ribtor Sporting Goods
318 – 11 Ave. S.E.
Calgary, AB T2G 0Y2
403-262-6994
www.ribtor.com

Roberts Fly Shop
104, 2 Ave. W. (BOX 1183)
Cochrane, AB T4C 1B2
403-932-5855
www.robertsflyshop.com

Ron's Outdoor Source for
Sports
5014 – 4 Ave. (BOX 6540)
Edson, AB T7E 1T9
780-723-4284

Russell Sporting Goods
128, 8228 Macleod Tr. S.E.
Calgary, AB T2H 2B8
403-258-0545
www.russellsports.com

Sportsmen's Choice
103B, 3292 Dunmore Rd.
Medicine Hat, AB T1B 2R4
403-504-1990

Sportsmen's Den, The
2 – 7619 Gaetz Ave.
Red Deer, AB T4P 1M6
403-347-7678

Sylvestre's Source for Sports
4808 – 50 Ave. (BOX 5097)
Bonnyville, AB T9N 2G3
780-826-4458

Timberline Source for Sports
5024 – 49 St.
Innisfail, AB T4H 1M6
403-227-4444

Timberline Source for Sports
6308 – 46 St.
Olds, AB T4H 1M6
403-556-8472

Wapiti Sports
1506 Railway Ave.
Canmore, AB T1W 1P6
403-678-5550

West Winds Fly Shop Ltd.
109 – 9919 Fairmount Dr. S.E
Calgary, AB T2J 0S3
403-278-6331

Westgate Gunsports
10116 – 175 St. N.W.
Edmonton, AB T5S 1A1
780-489-9638

Wholesale Sports
225 – 58 Ave. S.E.
Calgary, AB T2H 0N8
403-253-5566
www.wholesalesports.com

Wholesale Sports Outfitters
12505 – 97 St.
Edmonton, AB T5G 1Z8
780-477-3737
www.wholesalesports.com

Wilson Mountain Sports
Bldg. A, Samson Mall
Lake Louise, AB T0L 1E0
403-522-3636
www.lakelouisewilsons.com

British Columbia

70 Mile General Store
Hwy. 97 N. & Greenlake Rd.
(BOX 129)
70 Mile House, BC V0K 2K0
250-456-7744

A & C Sports
337 Banks Rd.
Kelowna, BC V1X 6A1
250-763-8033

Alberni Seafood & Tackle
5104 River Rd.
Port Alberni, BC V9Y 6Z1
250-723-9333
www.diehardangler.com

All-Star Sports Trail
1241 Cedar Ave.
Trail, BC V1R 4B9
250-368-5556

Babcock Fly & Tackle
110, 1140 Austin Ave.
Coquitlam, BC V3K 3P5
604-931-5044
www.babcockflytackle.com

Backcountry
10040 – 100 St.
Fort St. John, BC V1J 3Y4
250-785-1461

Barren Fly & Tackle
510 – 4 St.
Kaslo, BC V0G 1M0
250-353-2617

Bear Creek Sports
2012 Springfield Rd.
Kelowna, BC V1Y 5V8
250-861-4838

Belle's Sporting Goods
7285 James St.
Mission, BC V2V 4N4
604-826-8050

Benshona Custom Rods &
Tackle
1 – 2070 Harvey Ave.
Kelowna, BC V1Y 8P8
250-860-4244

Berry's Bait & Tackle
14651 Westminster Hwy.
Richmond, BC V6V 1A4
604-273-5901
www.berrysbait.com

Bob's Sporting Goods
4150 Hastings St.
Burnaby, BC V5C 2J4
604-298-8551

Boundary Bay Water Sports
1 – 15531 24 Ave.
White Rock, BC V4A 2J4
604-541-9191
www.boundarybay.com

Bucky's Sport Shop
171 Craig St.
Duncan, BC V9K 1V8
250-746-4923
www.buckys-sports.com

Cariboo Fly & Tackle
1196 Chew Ave.
Dragon Lake, BC V2J 4E1
250-747-3273

Castlegar Sports Centre &
Fly Shop
1951 Columbia Ave.
Castlegar, BC V1N 2W8
250-365-8288

Cheyenne Sporting Goods
267 Wallace St. (BOX 1963)
Hope, BC VOX ILO
604-869-5062

Chilliwack Dart & Tackle
Shop
2 – 9120 Young Rd.
Chilliwack, BC V2P 4R5
604-793-9922

City Centre Hardware &
Sport
380 City Centre
Kitimat, BC V8C IT6
250-632-3522

Colwood Food & Tackle
(PetroCanada)
1736 Island Hwy.
Colwood, BC V9B IH8
250-478-7222
www.pacificcoast.net/~
tackleman/

Corlane Sporting Goods Ltd.
1140 – 102 Ave.
Dawson Creek, BC VIG 2CI
250-782-2111
www.pris.bc.ca/corlane/

Cougar Mountain
Adventures
36 – 4314 Main St.
Whistler, BC VON IB4
604-932-3474
www.cougarmountainat
whistler.com

Cycle 'N' Sports
9 – 2720 Mill Bay Rd.
Mill Bay, BC VOR 2PO
250-743-7433

Exeter Sporting Goods
320 Birch Ave. s. (BOX 1738)
100 Mile House, BC VOK 2EO
250-395-4626
www.exetersportinggoods.
com

Fine Flies for Fishermen
295 w. Victoria St.
Kamloops, BC V2C IA5
250-828-6149

First Cast Trout Shop &
Guide Service
Beaver Lake Resort
3571 Lansbury Court,
Westbank
Kelowna, BC V4T IC5
250-878-4225

Fish Tales Tackle Shop
4640 Keith Ave.
Terrace, BC V8G 4KI
250-635-5667

Fraser's Tackle
33365 – I Ave.
Mission, BC V2V IG9
604-826-9899

Fred's Custom Tackle
I – 5580 Vedder Rd.
Chilliwack, BC V2R 3M7
604-858-7344

French Creek Marina Store
Unit 5, 1025 Lee Rd.
Parksville, BC V9P 2EI
250-248-8912

Gibsons Family Sports
900 Gibsons Way (BOX 857)
Gibsons, BC VON IVO
604-886-4635

Gill's Fishing Tackle
Warehouse
Unit 4 – 19300, Hwy. 10
Surrey, BC V3S 6K2
604-530-6266
Toll-Free: 1-866-530-6266
www.gills-fishing.com

Gone Fish'n Tackle Co.
13756 – 104 Ave.
Surrey, BC V3T IW6
604-582-2771

Gone Fishin'
5069 Johnston Road
Port Alberni, BC V9Y 5L6
250-723-1172
www.gonefishinshop.com

Gord's Tackle Box
7300 Vedder Rd.
(BOX 2083 Sardis Main,
Sardis)
Chilliwack, BC V2R IA5
604-858-5306

H & H Guns & Sporting
Supplies
19B South Shore (BOX 781)
Lake Cowichan, BC VOR 2GO
250-749-4102

Hanson's Fishing Outfitters
102, 580 Hornby St.
Vancouver, BC V6C 3B6
604-684-8988
www.hansons-outfitters.com

Happy's Source for Sports
256 – 6 St.
Courtenay, BC V9N IMI
250-334-4143

Harry's Sporting Supplies
615A Oliver St.
Williams Lake, BC V2G 3W1
250-398-5959

Harvey's Sporting Goods
9781 – 2 St.
Sidney, BC V8L 4P8
250-656-4393

HB Pro Tackle
184 S. Kimberly Ave.
(BOX 113)
Greenwood, BC V0H 1J0
250-445-6646

Herby's Fly and Tackle
3325 – 31 Ave.
Vernon, BC V1T 2H5
250-545-9820
www.herbyfly.com

Highwater Tackle
113 Lonsdale Ave.
North Vancouver, BC
V7M 2E7
604-986-3239

Hillcrest General Store
5012 – 50 Ave.
Pouce Coupe, BC V0C 2C0
250-786-5352

Home Hardware
Main St. (BOX 1360)
Fort Nelson, BC V0C 1R0
250-774-6303

Home Hardware
1410 Winnipeg St. (BOX 980)
Squamish, BC V0N 3G0
604-892-3711

Home Store
4690 Cumberland Rd.
Cumberland, BC V0R 1S0
250-336-8711

Hometown Sports
321 Highway 16
Burns Lake, BC V0J 1E0
250-692-7205

Hub Sports Ltd.
33719 Essendene Ave.
Abbotsford, BC V2S 2G7
604-859-8316

Hunter's Sporting Goods
14904 – 104 Ave.
Surrey, BC V3R 1M7
604-584-3006

Island Outfitters
3319 Douglas St.
Victoria, BC V8Z 3L2
250-475-4969
www.fishingvictoria.com

Jaymer's Fly & Tackle
2847 Shaughnessy St.
Port Coquitlam, BC V3C 3H1
604-944-2479

Jin Mee Fishing Tackle &
Video
7709 Royal Oak Ave.
Burnaby, BC V5J 4K2
604-438-7749

Kamloops Fly Shop, The
104 – 1366 Hugh Allan Dr.
Kamloops, BC V1S 1L8
250-377-8461
www.kamfly.com

Kent Outdoor Sports
7046 Pioneer Ave.
Agassiz, BC V0M 1A0
604-796-0006

Kootenay Fly Shop
A21 – 7 Ave., Hwy. 3
(BOX 2140)
Fernie, BC V0B 1M0
250-423-4483
www.kootenayflyshop.ca

Kootenay Wild Hunting &
  Sporting Supplies
1317 R. Cranbrook St. N.
Cranbrook, BC V1C 3S7
250-489-1289

Lakestream Flies & Supplies
107 – 1505 Main St.
Penticton, BC V2A 5G7
250-770-1696
www.members.home.net/
  lakestreamflyshop

Little Fort Fly & Tackle
Hwy. 5, and Hwy. 24
(BOX 75)
Little Fort, BC V0E 2C0
250-677-4366
www.littlefort.com

Logan Lake Fly Shop
Lower Mall (BOX 629)
Logan Lake, BC V0K 1W0
250-523-9711

Lonestar Sporting Goods
5028 – 50 Ave. (BOX 385)
Chetwynd, BC V0C 1J0
250-788-1850

Marine Traders Ltd.
6791 Wharf St.
Powell River, BC V8A 1T9
604-485-4624
www.marinetraders.com

Meegan's Store
3126 Wharf St. (BOX 790)
Queen Charlotte, BC V0T 1S0
250-559-4428

Michael & Young Fly Shop
10484 – 137 St.
Surrey, BC V3T 4H5
604-588-2833
www.myflyshop.com

Misty River Tackle &
   Hunting
5008 Agar Ave.
Terrace, BC V8G 1J1
250-638-1369
Toll-Free: 1-800-314-1369

Mountain Man Outdoors
   Ltd.
901 Baker St.
Cranbrook, BC V1C 1A4
800-796-4666

My Tackle Box
133 – 1835 Gordon Dr.
Kelowna, BC V1Y 3H4
250-860-1298
www.can-info.net/
   cyberman/tackle/

Newman's Great Outdoors
104 – 149 Fulford Ganges Rd.
Salt Spring Island, BC
V8K 2T9
250-537-5860

Northcoast Anglers
3217 Kalum St.
Terrace, BC V8G 2M8
250-635-6496

Northern Trout Fitters Fly
   & Tackle Shop
770 Central E. St.
Prince George, BC V2M 3B7
250-562-3597
Toll-Free: 1-800-665-3597
www.troutfitters.bc.ca

Oscar's Source for Sports
1214 Main St. (BOX 550)
Smithers, BC V0J 2N0
250-847-2136
www.hiway16.com/oscar

Outdoor Explorers
5880 York Rd.
Duncan, BC V9L 3S4
250-715-0900
www.outdoorexplorers.com

Outfitter Sports
801 Baker St.
Cranbrook, BC V1C 1A3
250-426-6688

Peter's Sports Shop
505 Duncan Ave.
Courtenay, BC V9N 2M6
250-334-2942

Powderkeg Outdoor Supply
2052 Nicola Ave. (BOX 767)
Merritt, BC V1K 1B8
250-378-9211

Revelstoke Outdoor Sports
709 W. Victoria Rd.
(BOX 2387)
Revelstoke, BC V0E 2S0
250-837-2525

River Sportsman Ltd.
2115 Island Hwy.
Campbell River, BC V9W 2G6
250-286-1017
www.riversportsman.com

Robinson's Outdoor Store
1307 Broad St.
Victoria, BC V8W 2A8
250-385-3429
www.robinsonsoutdoors.com

Ruddick's Fly Shop
1654 Duranleau St.
Vancouver, BC V6H 3S4
604-681-3747
www.ruddicksflyshop.com

Rutland Sports Centre
156 Asher Rd.
Kelowna, BC V1X 3H6
250-765-6956
www.trout-flies.com

Saddleback Sport & Marine
82, Nelson Ave. S. (BOX 27)
Nakusp, BC V0G 1R0
250-265-3111

Sealand Tackle
1840 Stewart Ave.
Nanaimo, BC V9S 4E6
250-754-1432
www.sealandtackle.com

Seymour Tackle
Unit 102, 223 Mountain
   Hwy.
North Vancouver, BC V7J 3V3
604-986-7595

Sidney Sporting Goods
1C – 9764, 5 St.
Sidney, BC V8L 2X2
250-656-9255
www.sportfishingbc.com/ssg

Spinners Sports
164 – 1436 Island Hwy.
Campbell River, BC V9W 8C9
250-286-6166

Spirit Pond Sports
401 Finlayson St. (BOX 676)
Sicamous, BC V0E 2V0
250-836-4782
www.spiritpond.bc.ca

Split-Shot Fly & Tackle
701 Glendale Ave. (BOX 169)
Salmo, BC V0G 1Z0
250-368-3474

Sports Centre, The
639 Baker St.
Nelson, BC V1L 4J3
250-352-2015

Spud Valley Sporting Goods
1380 Birch St.
Pemberton, BC V0N 2L0
604-894-6630

St. Mary Angler Fly Shop
1 – 340 Mark St.
Kimberley, BC V1A 3A1
250-427-1744
www.stmaryangler.com

Steveston Marine &
    Hardware
3560 Moncton St.
Richmond, BC V7E 3A2
604-277-7031
www.stevestonmarine.com

Steveston Marine &
    Hardware
201 – 19700 Langley By-Pass
Langley, BC V3A 7B1
604-530-7031
www.stevestonmarine.com

Steveston Marine &
    Hardware
1603 W. 3 St.
Vancouver, BC V6J 1K1
604-733-7031
www.stevestonmarine.com

Stillwater Sports
4849 Delta St.
Delta, BC V4K 2T9
604-946-9933

Surplus Herby's
248 Tranquille St.
Kamloops, BC V2V 3G3
250-376-2714
www.surplusherbys.com

Surplus Herby's
527 S. Mackenzie Ave.
Williams Lake, BC V2G 1C8
250-392-5362
www.surplusherbys.com

Taws Cycle & Sports
4597 Marine Ave.
Powell River, BC V8A 2K7
604-485-2555

Taylor-Wilton Trail Ltd.
1235 Bay Ave.
Trail, BC V1R 4A5
250-368-9177

Teddy's Tackle
10125 View St. (BOX 1129)
Chemainus, BC V0R 1K0
250-246-9704
www.members.home.net/
    teddystackle

Timberland Sports
2 – 1705 Campbell Way
(BOX 163)
Port McNeill, BC V0N 2R0
250-956-3544

Trail Bay Sports
5504 Trail Ave. (BOX 678)
Sechelt, BC V0N 3A0
604-885-2512

Trayling's Tackle Shop
635 – 2 Ave. w.
Prince Rupert, BC V8J 1H1
250-624-9874

Trout Water Supplies
4 – 1515 Westgate Rd.
Kelowna, BC V1Z 3X4
250-769-6642
Toll-Free: 1-888-823-6633

Turner's Fly Shop
3519 Kingsway
Vancouver, BC V5R 5L8
604-434-7716

Tyee Marine & Fishing
    Supplies
880 Island Hwy.
Campbell River, BC V9W 2C3
250-287-2641

Vernon's Outdoor Store Ltd.
2709A – 43 Ave.
Vernon, BC V1T 3L2
250-558-1523

West Coast Fishing Tackle
2147 E. Hastings St.
Vancouver, BC V5L 1V2
604-254-0004

Westside Stores Ltd.
450 – 360 Trans-Canada
Hwy. S.W.
Salmon Arm, BC V1E 1B7
250-832-8141

Whistler Hardware & Gift
101 – 4305 Skiers Approach
Whistler, BC V0N 1B4
604-932-3863

Manitoba

B J Sales & Service
Hwy. 10 N. (BOX 16)
Wanless, MB R0B 1T0
204-682-7415

Black's Cycle & Sporting
Goods Ltd.
211 Main St. S.
Dauphin, MB R7N 1K5
204-638-4751

Fishin' Hole, The
1522 Regent Ave.
Winnipeg, MB R2C 3B4
204-586-8021
www.thefishinhole.com

Ginnie's Pro Tackle Stop
109 – 2nd St. W.
The Pas, MB R9A 1L3
204-623-4774

Jig 'N' Rig Bait & Tackle
701 – 4 St.
Brandon, MB R7A 3H6
204-727-1927

L & M Sports Excellence
226 Fischer Ave.
The Pas, MB R9A 1L2
204-623-3000

MacDonald's Sporting
Goods
246 Saskatchewan Ave. E.
Portage, MB R1N 0K9
204-857-3496

Mike's Bait & Tackle
350 Main St. N.
Russell, MB R0J 1W0
204-773-3983

Northern Angler Fly & Tackle
17 – 7 Ave. N.W.
Dauphin, MB R7N 1K1
204-638-7740
www.northernangler.mb.ca

South Shore Marina
South Shore Rd.
Falcon Lake, MB R0E 0N0
204-349-2234

New Brunswick

Angler's Fly Shop
1199 Bridge St.
Bathurst, NB E2A 1X4
506-548-3001

Dunc's Fly Shop
1595 Hickey Rd.
Saint John, NB E2J 3V3
506-696-2565

George's Fly Shop
33 Renous River Rd.
Renous, NB E9E 2C9
506-622-8226

Losier Chasse et Peche
3093 Brideau
Tracadie, NB E1X 1A5
506-395-2917

Nepisiguit River Company
96 Main St.
Bathurst, NB E2A 1A3
506-548-5575
www.rivercompany.com

W.W. Doak
331 Main St.
Doaktown, NB E9C 1E1
506-365-7828
www.wwdoak.com

Wayne's Rod & Gun
870 Hanwell Rd.
Fredericton, NB E3B 6A3
506-459-5038

Newfoundland

Fisherman's Hardware Ltd.
Placentia Bay
Little Harbour East, NF
A0B 2H0
709-465-3102

Northern Lights Ltd.
170 Hamilton River Rd.
(BOX 2168, Station B)
Goose Bay, NF A0P 1E0
709-896-5939

Schwartz Source for Sports
BOX 910
Deer Lake, NF A0K 2E0
709-635-2947

Source for Sports
230 Airport Blvd., Fraser
  Mall
Gander, NF A1V 1L7
709-256-4848

Sports Shop, The
256 Water St. (BOX 1375)
St. John's, NF A1C 5N5
709-722-3344

Nova Scotia

Brad's Outdoor Adventures
40 Kings Rd.
Sidney, NS B1P 5E7
902-564-4573

Ferguson's Sport Shop
2136 Maple St. (BOX 586)
Westville, NS B0K 2A0
902-396-5409

Fishin' Fever Tackle Shop
2858 Agricola St.
Halifax, NS B3K 4E7
902-454-2244
www.fishinfevertackle.com

Green Highlander Fly Shop
99 Woodlawn Rd.
Dartmouth, NS B2W 2S6
902-435-9446
www.greenhighlander.com

Hi-Liner Fishing Gear and
  Tackle
9 – 155 Chainlake Dr.
Halifax, NS B3S 1B3
902-457-4968
www.hiliner.com

Strathdee's Fly Shop
31 East Big Intervale Rd.
  (BOX 88)
Northeast Margaree, NS
  B0E 2H0
902-248-2076

Veinotte's Hearth Home &
  Leisure
969 King St.
Bridgewater, NS B4V 1B9
902-543-1460
www.veinottestoves.zip411.net

**Northwest
Territories**

Wolverine Sports Shop
50 St. & 51 Ave. (BOX 367)
Yellowknife, NWT X1A 2N3
867-873-4350
www.wolverinesportsshop.
  com

Yellowknife Hardware
5024 – 51 St.
Yellowknife, NWT X1A 2N6
867-873-4537

Ontario

Al Flaherty's Outdoor Store
2066 Dufferin St.
Toronto, ON M6E 3R6
416-651-6436
www.alflahertys.com

Albert's Sports & Workwear
822 Riverside Dr.
Timmins, ON T4N 3W1
705-264-8189
www.sportsandworkwear.com

Angler's City
65 Unionville Gate, Unit 3
Unionville, ON L3R 9S6
905-305-6622

Angler's Edge, The
9 Municipal St.
Guelph, ON N1G 1G8
519-763-3231

Angler's In
105 Main St.
Ignace, ON P0T 1T0
807-934-2227

Angler's Pro Shop
Hwy. 71 (BOX 279)
Nestor Falls, ON P0X 1K0
807-484-2525

Angling Outfitters
577 Dundas St.
Woodstock, ON N4S 1C9
519-539-5494

Angling Specialties
2104 Hwy. 7 w., Unit 15
Concord, ON L4K 2S9
905-660-9707

Angling Specialties
325 Parkway West
Mississauga, ON L5B 3X9
905-275-4972

Angling Specialties
3251 Kennedy Rd., Unit 4
Scarborough, ON M1V 2J9
416-609-0804

Angling Sports Inc.
317 Adelaide s.
London, ON N5Z 3L3
519-649-7429

Archie's Stop 'N' Go Live
    Bait & Tackle
169 Adelaide N.
London, ON N6B 3G9
519-432-0880

B & D Bicycle & Sports
3478 Petawawa Blvd.
Petawawa, ON K8H 1X3
613-687-4624

B & R Tackle
3310 King St. E.
Kitchener, ON N2A 1B3
519-748-6313

Backwater Tackle & Line
171 King St.
Midland, ON L4R 4K6
705-527-7351

Barklay's Sports
423 Bloor St. W.
Oshawa, ON L1J 5Y5
905-436-0644
www.barklays.com

Baron Outdoor Products
1 Stafford Rd.
Nepean, ON K2H 9N5
613-596-4415
www.lebaron.ca

Bennett's Bait 'N' Tackle
158 Hwy. 15
Smiths Falls, ON K7A 5B8
613-283-0683

Brightwater Fly Fishing
336 Cumberland St.
Ottawa, ON K1N 7J2
613-241-6798
www.brightwaterflyfishing.
    com

Brushey's
518B Main St.
Powassan, ON P0H 1W0
705-724-5493

Burns Fishing & Outdoor
    Supplies
Unit 1 – 685 Plains Rd. E.
Burlington, ON L7T 2E8
905-681-8803

Caledonia Bait & Tackle
192 Caithness W.
Caledonia, ON N3W 1B2
905-765-3215

Callander Bait & Tackle
    Variety Store
6 Main St.
Callander, ON P0H 1H0
705-752-5968

Central Sports
610 Yonge St.
Toronto, ON N4Y 1Z3
416-964-8226

Coby Outdoors Bait & Tackle
R.R. 1
Coboconk, ON K0M 1K0
705-454-3866

Complete Bait & Tackle
15 Chaffey St.
Huntsville, ON P1H 1H4
705-789-4123

D & R Sporting Goods
485 Memorial Ave.
Thunder Bay, ON T7B 3Y6
807-345-3323

Discount Bait & Tackle
10 Queen St.
Lindsay, ON K9V 1E9
705-878-5844

Discount Bait Tackle &
    Variety
2150 Trout Lake Rd.
North Bay, ON P1B 7S2
705-474-6991

Ed's Eau Buoy
Gas Bar (BOX 99)
Erieau, ON N0P 1N0
519-676-8266

Eli's Guns & Tackle
75 Norfolk St.
Simcoe, ON N3Y 2W1
519-426-9042

Emm's Sports Outdoor
    Outfitters
103 Queen St.
Lindsay, ON K9V 1G7
705-324-5563

First Choice Fishing Tackle
    Ltd.
833 Woolwich St. N.
Guelph, ON N1H 6J2
519-837-8333

Fish-On Tackle
535 Church St. E.
Delhi, ON N4B 1V5
519-582-8758

Fishing Hut, The
410-A Cumberland St.
Cornwall, ON K6J 4C8
613-933-4636

Fishing Plus
16 Lansdowne w.
Peterborough, ON K9J IYI
705-740-2303

Fishing World Outdoor
  Centre
247 Centennial Parkway N.
Hamilton, ON L8E 2X3
905-573-2288
www.fishingworld.on.ca

Fletcher Sports
Hwy. 6 N. at Ledgerock Rd.
(R.R. 5)
Owen Sound, ON N4K 5N7
519-371-8587

Fly Box, The
6 Bayfield St., Suite 502
(BOX 357)
Barrie, ON L4M 3A4
705-734-1090
Toll-Free: 1-888-745-1671
www.flybox.ca

Forks Fly Shop, The
74 McKenzie St.
Inglewood, ON LON IKO
905-838-3332

Gagnon Sports
385 Bloor St. w.
Oshawa, ON LIJ 5Y5
905-725-5798
www.gagnonsports.com

Goble's Gun & Tackle
334 Sovereign Rd.
London, ON N6M IA8
519-455-4277
www.goblesgunandtackle.com

Goble's Gun & Tackle
107A Concession St. E.
Tillsonburg, ON N4G 4W4
519-842-7442
www.goblesgunandtackle.com

Goderich Bait and Tackle
201 Huron Rd.
Goderich, ON N7A 2Z8
519-524-7910
www.goderichbait.com

Gone Fishin'
25 Munroe St.
Cobourg, ON K9A IB8
905-372-1714

Grand River Troutfitters
790 Tower St. S. (Hwy. 6)
Fergus, ON NIM 2R3
519-787-4359
www.grandrivertroutfitters.
  com

Great Lake Outfitters
Hwy. 26 (R.R. 2)
Collingwood, ON L9Y 3ZI
705-445-1622
Grimsby Tackle
515 Main St. w.
Grimsby, ON L3M IT6
905-945-0399

Grindstone Angling &
  Outfitters
24 Mill St. N.
Waterdown, ON LOR 2HO
905-689-0880

H & H Tackle
1053 Colborne St. E.
Brantford, ON N3T 5MI
519-753-4226

Hook & Bow
660 Atherley Rd.
Orillia, ON L3V 6P2
705-325-5873

Hooked & Tackled
2956 Eglington Ave. E.
Scarborough, ON MIJ 2E7
416-438-2310

Huron Sports Outfitters
Hwy. 4
Kippen, ON NOM 2EO
519-263-2141

J & S Tackle
137 Goderich St.
Port Elgin, ON NOH 2CI
519-832-2827

Jack's Live Bait
No. 2 Hwy. (BOX 94)
Delaware, ON NOL IEO
519-652-9237

Jaye's Bait & Tackle
90 Pulley Rd.
Wheatley, ON NOP 2PO
519-825-9908

Kingsway Sports
765 Woolrich St. N.
Guelph, ON NIH 3Z2
519-824-7223

Le Baron Outdoor Products
8365 Woodbine Ave.
Markham, ON L3R 2P4
905-944-0682
www.lebaron.ca

Lefebvre's Outdoor Sports
122 Main St. w.
North Bay, ON P1B 2T5
705-474-5920
www.losgear.com

Lucky Catch Bait & Tackle
331 Midland Ave.
Midland, ON L4R 3K8
705-526-0102

Lucky Fishing Tackle
1267 Gerrard St. E.
Toronto, ON M4L 1Y5
416-466-3567

Lucky Fishing Tackle
4227 Sheppard Ave. E.
Unit D3
Toronto, ON M1S 5H5
416-609-8838

Magnetawan Bait & Tackle
Hwy. 520 & Hwy. 124 (R.R. 2)
Magnetawan, ON P2A 1P0
705-387-3361

Manotick Bait & Sporting
   Supplies
1019 River Rd.
Manotick, ON K4M 1B4
613-692-4142

Mike's Trail & Tackle
Hwy. 29, R.R. 4 (BOX 1418)
Brockville, ON K6V 5Y6
613-498-2277

Minden Live Bait and
   Tackle
Sugarbush Trail (R.R. 1)
Minden, ON K0M 2K0
705-286-4826

Minnow Man
157 Manitoba St.
Bracebridge, ON P1L 2B7
705-645-4385

Moxy's Bait & Tackle
905 Regional Rd. 55
Lively, ON P3Y 1E7
705-692-1810

Natural Sports
1572 Victoria St. N.
Kitchener, ON N2B 3E5
519-749-1620
www.naturalsports.on.ca

Nelson's Great Outdoors
1539 Dundas St. w.
Toronto, ON M6K 1T6
416-538-6278

Norm's Bait & Tackle
820 Front St.
Hearst, ON P0L 1N0
705-362-5775

Norris's Live Bait & Tackle
8877-A, Hwy. 42 (R.R. 2)
Westport, ON K0G 1X0
613-273-6462

Northern Tackle Co.
505, Hwy. 118
Bracebridge, ON P1L 1T8
705-646-0326

Northport General Store
   Bait & Tackle
R.R. 2
Picton, ON K0K 2T0
613-476-4066

Orvis Green Drake Outfitters
342 Richmond Rd.
Ottawa, ON K2A 0E8
613-828-1915
www.greendrake.com

Outback Tackle
877 Berford St. (BOX 873)
Wiarton, ON N0H 2T0
519-534-2803

Outdoors Plus
Maple St. & York St.
(R.R. 2, BOX 4 Woods Rd.)
Haliburton, ON K0M 1S0
705-457-3113

Paul's Outfitting
66 Greer Rd., Bldg. 1
(Site LA 0 R.R. 1)
Port Sydney, ON P0B 1L0
705-385-1260
Toll-Free: 1-877-212-2697
www.msk-biz.com/pauls
   outfitting

Penny's Motel & Tackle
   Shop
Hwy. 26 E.
Thornbury, ON N0H 2P0
519-599-3909

Peter's Tackle & Bait
22 Secord Dr.
St. Catharines, ON L2N 1K8
905-934-2512

Pickard's Fishing Pro Shop
151 Main St. (BOX 421)
Wellington, ON K0K 3L0
613-399-3649

Pollack's Fly Fishing
337 Queen St. E.
Toronto, ON M5A 1S9
416-363-1095
www.starpages.com/pollacks
flyfishing

Pro Bait & Tackle
469 Kingsway Blvd.
Sudbury, ON P3B 2E1
705-674-6113

Pro Gear Outdoor Specialists
1575 Upper Ottawa St.
Hamilton, ON L8W 3E2
905-575-1338
www.progearoutdoors.com

Pro Tackle Co.
19 First Ave. (BOX 861)
Timmins/Schumacher, ON
P0N 1G0
705-268-8069

Proline Taxidermy Live Bait
& Tackle
1906 Jane St.
Toronto, ON M9N 2T3
416-244-0315

Quinte Outdoor Sports
Hwy. 62, Northlands Centre
(R.R. 5)
Belleville, ON K8N 4Z5
613-967-6600

Rainbow Sports
10 Wyman Rd., Unit 4
Waterloo, ON N2V 1K7
519-746-2650

Ramakko's Tackle World
125 Loachs Rd.
Sudbury, ON P3E 2P8
705-522-8889
www.ramakkos.com

Re-Run Sports
124 Bishop St. N.
Preston, ON N3H 2K1
519-653-2579

Red's Little Hooker Bait &
Tackle
14 Oakland Blvd.
Elliot Lake, ON P5A 2T1
705-848-8401

Reel To Reel Plus
1065 Carp Rd.
Stittsville, ON K2S 1B9
613-831-1521
www.reelplus.com

Rerrie's Bait
4659 Kingston Rd.
West Hill, ON M1E 2P8
416-282-5876

Richard's Rod & Reel Service
Hwy. 613 N. (BOX 126)
Devlin, ON T0W 1C0
807-486-0514
www.rodreel.com

Rick's Happi Hooka
Custom Tackle
2 St. Paul
Collingwood, ON L9Y 3N9
705-444-1373

Skinners Sports Ltd.
50 Kings St. E.
Toronto, ON M5C 1E5
416-863-9701

Smart Bait & Tackle
130 Bell Farm Rd., Unit 5A
Barrie, ON L4N 6J4
705-728-7927

Sports Action
1555 St. Laurent Blvd.
Ottawa, ON K1G 1A1
613-741-0999

Stephen's Sporting Goods
80 King St. W.
Bowmanville, ON L1C 1R4
905-697-2546

T & T Sports
166 Grand River Ave.
Brantford, ON N3T 4X6
519-751-2671

Tackle & Target Sporting
Goods
209 – 2 St. S.
Kenora, ON P9N 1G1
807-468-3145

Tackle Box, The
119 Main St.
Iroquois Falls, ON P0K 1G0
705-232-4456

Tall Tales Live Bait & Tackle
310 King St. E.
Cambridge, ON N3H 3M8
519-650-3465
www.talltales.on.ca

Tightline Fisherman's
Warehouse
1050 Brock Rd.
South Pickering, ON L1W 3X4
905-837-0544

Trading Post, The
1332 Great Northern Rd.
Sault Ste Marie, ON T6A 5K7
705-759-4518

Trombly's Tackle Box
595 West St. S.
Orillia, ON L3V 5H7
705-327-3474
www.tromblystacklebox.com

Trout Lake Bait & Canoe Co.
3791 Trout Lake Rd.
North Bay, ON P1B 8G4
705-497-3511

Turner's Tackle
22051 Loyalist Parkway
(R.R. 2)
Carrying Place, ON K0K 1L0
613-394-2705

Twin River Tackle
1852 – 3 Ave. E.
Owen Sound, ON N4K 2M6
519-371-6099

U Bait & Tackle
250 Woodward Ave.
Blind River, ON P0R 1B0
705-356-2767

Wally's Baits
3195 Sandwich St.
Windsor, ON N9C 1A7
519-256-2841

Wilson's Sporting Tradition,
Inc.
26 Wellington St. E.
Toronto, ON M5E 1S2
416-869-3474
www.wilsonorvis.com

Wortner Gun Works
433 Queen St.
Chatham, ON N7M 2J1
519-352-0924

Prince Edward Island

Island Rods & Flies
18 Birch Hill Dr.
Charlottetown, PEI C1A 6W5
902-566-4157
www.islandrodsandflies.com

Ritchie's Army-Navy Surplus
51 Allen St.
Charlottetown, PEI C1A 2V6
902-368-3939

Quebec

A D Sport Enr
7 des Bouleaux
Port-Cartier, PQ G5V 1Z4
418-766-8018

A La Maison du Moucheur
Enr
1515 Bd Wilfrid Hamel
Quebec City, PQ G1N 3Y7
418-681-6100

A Techniques Chasse &
Peche
3395 Blvd. Taschereau
Greenfield Park, PQ G4T 2G1
450-656-6446

Accomodagie du Pecheur Inc.
309 Rte. 138
Escoumins, PQ G0T 1K0
418-233-2757

Angler's Roost
285 St. Jean Blvd.
Pointe Claire, PQ H9R 3J1
514-426-0440

Appats Beaux Vers Enr
120 Ave. Grande Decharge
Delisle, PQ G0W 1L0
418-668-3419

Atelier du Moucheur
382 Boulevard Jessop
Ribouski, PQ G5L 1M8
418-722-6993
Toll-Free: 1-800-707-3528

Au Bon Marche (Bernard)
Inc.
12535 1E Ave.
St-Georges, PQ G5Y 2E4
418-228-2463

B & L Sport Inc
3146 Ste. Cathering E.
Montreal, PQ H1W 2C2
514-525-5354

B C Sports Enrg
124 1E Ave. O
Amos, PQ J9T 1V2
819-732-3279

B & R Patterson
12 Sunny Bank
Gaspe, PQ G4X 2M8
418-368-2361

Baron Centre de Sport Ltee
932 Notre Dame O
Montreal, PQ H3C 1J9
514-866-8848

Boucher Germain Sports
980 Bd d'Iberville
St. Jean sur Richelieu, PQ
J2X 4A7
450-347-3457

Boutique Chasse et Peche
101–B Cousineau
Salaberry-De-Valleyfield, PQ
J6S 1P3
450-371-6334

Boutique Classique Angler
414 McGill
Montreal, PQ H2Y 2G1
514-878-3474

Boutique La Fine Mouche
Enr
304 Rte. 132
St-Godefroi, PQ G0C 3C0
418-752-3632

Bow Lieu Chasse & Peche
35-B Pelletier
St. Antonin, PQ G0L 2J0
418-867-3552

Brabant & Philips Ltd.
310 Notre-Dame
Gatineau, PQ J8P 1L1
819-663-5352

Chasse Et Peche Chicoutimi
1120 Bd. Talbot
Chicoutimi, PQ G7H 7R2
418-690-9620

Claude Turcotte Sport Ltee
7001 St. Michel
Montreal, PQ H2A 2Z3
514-721-1862

Coureur Des Bois Enr
1935 Blvd. de Comporté
Riv Malbaie, PQ G5A 1N9
418-665-6087

Dagenais Sport Inc
108 Bd. Ste. Rose
Ste. Rse., PQ H7L 1K4
450-625-2322

Depanneur Du Boutte
1 Ambroise E.
Bearn, PQ J0Z 1G0
819-726-2674

Dorion Sports Enr
2075 Bd. du Jardin
Chsbrg, PQ G1G 3Y2
418-626-5262

Excellence Sports
149 Bd. St. Jean Baptiste
Chtgy, PQ J6K 3B1
450-692-6888

Fabrimouche Enr
4270 Bd. de la Rive Sud
Levis, PQ G6W 6N1
418-833-7907

Fauchon Sport
99 Begin
Ste-Claire, PQ G0R 2V0
418-883-3055

Ferland Sport
259 Notre-Dame
Rxton Falls, PQ G0H 1I0
450-548-5777

Fern Sports Chasse & Peche
73 Ch de Montreal E.
Masson Angers, PQ J8N 1K3
819-986-1473

Ferronnerie Martineau Enrg
102 Angus N.
E Ang, PQ J0B 1R0
819-832-2390

Flibotte Gilles Sports
2780 Nichols
St. Hyacinthe, PQ J2S 2X1
450-773-2462

Intersports Dolbeau-
  Mistassini
1375 Bd. Wallberg
Dolb Mistsn, PQ G8L 1H3
418-276-3010

L A Chasse-Peche
4901 Ste. Catherine E.
Montreal, PQ H1V 1Z9
514-899-8653

L M Sports
2554 Ave. Ste. Anne
St. Hya, PQ J2S 5J3
450-773-0735

L'Ami du Moucher
7390 rue Notre Dame
Trois-Rivieres Ouest, PQ
  G9B 1L8
819-377-4367

L'Atelier du Moucheur Enr
382 Jessop
Rimouski, PQ G5L 1M8
418-722-6993

L'Aviron Chasse Et Peche Inc.
2887 Bd. du Cure Labelle
Prevost, PQ J0R 1T0
450-224-7909

La Boite a Mouche
1120 Blvd. Talbot
Chicoutini, PQ G7H 7R2
418-543-4721

Lachance Chasse & Peche
    Enr
1435 King E.
Fleurmont, PQ J1G 118
819-563-9676

Lafreniere & Ethier Enrg
31 Principale
Gracefield, PQ J0X 1W0
819-463-2192

Le Coin du Moucheur
843-1 Rue L'Ere
Limoilou, PQ G1J 2X8
418-524-4000

Londero D Sport
349 Blvd. du Seminaire N
St-Jn-Sur-Rich, PQ J3B 8C5
450-349-2332

Magasin Latulippe Inc.
637 St. Vallier O
Quebec, PQ G1K 6W8
418-529-0024

Mailloux Remi
1042 Rg Notre-Dame
Girardville, PQ G0W 1R0
418-258-3343

Marche C Huard Ltee
117 Rte. 132 O
Gascons, PQ G0C 1T0
418-396-2741

Morency S & L Enr
123 de la Belle Rive
Beauport, PQ G1E 5S8
418-667-0311

Morin Sports
117 St. Charles, Borromee
Joliette, PQ J6E 4R3
450-759-3312

Nature Action
4318 Chateauguay
Jonq, PQ G7X 7V5
418-542-1991

Nature Chasse & Peche
10435 1e Ave.
St-Georges, PQ G5Y 6X8
418-227-0270

P.A.S. Sports
43 Ave. Du Roi
Montmagny, PQ G5V 4B5
418-248-9327

Paquin Ludger & Fils Inc.
891 Ouimet
St. Jov, PQ J0T 2H0
819-425-3451

Paradis Du Pecheur Enr
507 Bd. Des Ruisseaux
Ds Ruiss, PQ J9L 3G6
819-623-6858

Peche Plus
1428 des Hauts-Bois
Val d'Or, PQ J9P 6T7
819-824-3673

Performance Chasse-Peche
303-B Notre Dame
Repentigny, PQ J6A 2R9
450-582-9302

Pro Peche
405 – 9 Ave.
Iberville, PQ J2X 1K4
450-358-4446

Relais Plein Air Enr
5647 Rte. 117
Ste Aga N., PQ J8C 2Z8
819-326-8295

Rive Sud Chasse & Peche
2794 Bd. de la Rive Sud
St. Romuelle, PQ G6W 7N2
418-839-4038

Sexton & Sexton
1 Mackay Rd.
Cascapedia St.-Joules, PQ
G0C 1T0
418-392-5628

Sport C R
2 Ave. William
Vaud Dreuil, PQ J7V 2G3
450-424-4171

Sport Marcel Langlois Inc.
1159 Galt O
Sherbrooke, PQ J1H 2A3
819-566-8424

Sport Plus
144 Principale
St-Apollinaire, PQ G0S 2E0
418-881-2024

Sporteque Enrg
760 Bd. St-Joseph
Drummondville, PQ J2C 2C3
819-477-7144

Sports Jean Roch Charest Inc.
774 Cushing
Acton Vale, PQ J0H 1A0
450-546-2669

St-Germain Sport
25-C Rte. 201
Coteau du Lac, PQ J0P 1B0
450-763-0179

Ste Helene Bicycle &
  Sports
1283 Ste-Helene
Longueuil, PQ J4K 3S4
450-674-4898

Varietes A Gadoury Inc.
204 Ave. Louis Cyr
St. Jean de Matha, PQ
J0K 2S0
450-886-2700

Villemure Chasse & Peche
  Inc.
1591 – 9 Ave.
Grand'mere, PQ G9T IX5
819-538-8205

Saskatchewan

Bender's Guns & Archery
414 North Railway St. E.
Swift Current, SK S9H IC7
306-773-8683

Fishin' Hole, The
805 Circle Dr. East, 8
Saskatoon, SK S7K 3S4
306-665-7223
www.thefishinhole.com

Gene's Sports
719 La Ronge Ave.
La Ronge, SK S0J IL0
306-425-3040

Great Northern Rod &
  Reel
1755 Park St.
Regina, SK S4N 2G3
306-359-7378

Northern Fly Fisherman
1 Stephenson Cr.
Saskatoon, SK S7H 3L6
306-665-0076

Pokey's Tackle Shop
1001 Osler St.
Regina, SK S4R 8N5
306-359-1910

Reel Marine Service
Fishing Lake (BOX 1060)
Foam Lake, SK S0A IA0
306-272-3859

Wholesale Sports Outdoor
  Outfitters
3 – 401, 46 St. E.
Saskatoon, SK S7K 0W8
306-931-4475
www.wholesalesports.com

Yorkton Rod & Rifle
11 – 3 Ave. N.
Yorkton, SK S3N ICI
306-782-2923

Yukon

Sports North
408 Baxter St.
Whitehorse, YK YIA 2T5
867-667-7492

Sportslodge Source for
  Sports
305 Main St.
Whitehorse, YK YIA 2B4
867-668-6848

INDEX